THE FASCIST PARTY AND POPULAR OPINION IN MUSSOLINI'S ITALY

The Fascist Party and Popular Opinion in Mussolini's Italy

PAUL CORNER

OXFORD
UNIVERSITY PRESS

Great Clarendon Street, Oxford, OX2 6DP,
United Kingdom

Oxford University Press is a department of the University of Oxford.
It furthers the University's objective of excellence in research, scholarship,
and education by publishing worldwide. Oxford is a registered trade mark of
Oxford University Press in the UK and in certain other countries

© Paul Corner 2012

The moral rights of the author have been asserted

First published 2012

Impression: 1

British Library Cataloguing in Publication Data
Data available

Library of Congress Cataloging in Publication Data
Data available

ISBN 978–0–19–873069–9

Printed in Great Britain by
MPG Books Group, Bodmin and King's Lynn

Acknowledgements

Writing a book is a fairly lonely occupation, fortunately enlivened every now and then by the help and encouragement of friends and colleagues. Not all of those who helped me in the production of this volume can be mentioned here, but some must not be left out. I wish to thank my colleague at the University of Siena, Massimo Borgogni, who generously 'covered' for me in Siena during a sabbatical in 2007–8 that permitted me to continue researching the book. During that year I was fortunate in being awarded the annual *Fondazione Monte dei Paschi di Siena* Fellowship at St. Antony's College, Oxford, and I have a debt of gratitude, therefore, not only to the *Fondazione*, but also to the Warden and Fellows of St. Antony's, and in particular to colleagues at the European Studies Centre, for their hospitality and friendship. David Nasaw of the Graduate Center of the City University of New York was kind enough to help me during a brief stay in the city in 2008, as did Marta Petrusewicz of Hunter College. My appreciation is offered to both for their time and their unfailing generosity. Since I can no longer thank him in person, I should also like to record—with much sorrow—my debt to the late Tony Judt, who welcomed me for a period to the Remarque Institute of New York University shortly before his tragic illness. A final word of thanks goes to my wife, Giovanna Procacci, for her unrelenting understanding of the problems of researching and writing a history book. A poor reward for her patience is that she now knows more about provincial Fascism than anyone knows or, indeed, would ever want to know.

Siena, September 2011

Contents

II. THE PARTY AND THE PEOPLE IN THE 1930s

List of Abbreviations and Glossary of Terms

affarismo	shady business dealing
beghismo	infighting, factionalism
confino	domestic exile
fascio	local fascist organisation
federale	provincial fascist leader
FGC	*fasci giovanili di combattimento*, federation of young fascists
fiduciario	police or party informer, spy
GDR	German Democratic Republic (East Germany)
gerarca, gerarchi	fascist leaders, local and national
GIL	*Gioventù italiana del Littorio*, fascist youth organisation
GUF	*Gruppi universitari fascisti*, fascist university groups
INA	*Istituto Nazionale Assicurazione*, fascist insurance company
INFPS	*Istituto Nazionale Fascista per la Previdenza Sociale*, fascist national welfare organisation
MVSN	*Milizia Volontaria di Sicurezza Nazionale*, fascist militia
ONB	*Opera Nazionale Balilla,* fascist schoolchildren's organisation
OND (*Dopolavoro*)	*Opera Nazionale Dopolavoro*, fascist leisure organisation
ONMI	*Opera Nazionale Maternità e Infanzia*, fascist organisation for maternity and infants
OVRA	[not an abbreviation] fascist secret police
PNF	*Partito Nazionale Fascista*, National Fascist Party
podestà	fascist mayor of a *comune*
PPI	*Partito Popolare Italiano*, Italian Popular Party
PSI	*Partito Socialista Italiano*, Italian Socialist Party
Questura, Questore	police station, chief of police
ras	powerful local fascist leaders
RR.CC.	*Carabinieri* (police)
SED	Socialist Unity Party (East Germany)
squadristi	violent blackshirt activists, organised in squads
squadrismo	violent actions of the above
UPI	*Uffici Provinciali Investigativi*, fascist police detective bureaux
ventennio	synonymous with 'fascist regime' (twenty years)

Archival Abbreviations

ACS	Archivio Centrale dello Stato
ADN	Archivio Diaristico Nazionale
AGR	Affari Generali e Riservati
b.	busta
CR	Carteggio Riservato
DGPS	Direzione Generale Pubblica Sicurezza
MDRF	Mostra della Rivoluzione Fascista

Introduction

On 12 August 1924, in the rural hinterland of Rome, a railway worker, clearing out a conduit beside the rails, found a blood-stained jacket. His discovery prompted further investigation and, four days later, a shallow grave was identified nearby, evidently hastily prepared and rapidly covered. Immediately investigated by the local police, it proved to contain the decomposing body of Giacomo Matteotti, a socialist member of the Italian parliament who had disappeared after being seized and bundled into a car in the centre of Rome some two months previously. The discovery of the corpse made fascist denials of involvement in the disappearance of the deputy no longer credible, although precisely who was to blame was far from clear. Public outrage at the murder was immediate and directed against the fascist government, which vacillated in the face of repeated calls for its resignation. Thus was precipitated the already simmering 'Matteotti crisis'—undoubtedly the most serious challenge to Mussolini's domination after the 1922 March on Rome and destined to remain the most serious until the fateful meeting of the fascist Grand Council in July of 1943 which would finally unseat the *duce*.[1]

The Matteotti crisis has a particular significance in the history of Fascism because it was a moment—or rather a period of months—during which the facade of unity within the movement fell away to reveal fundamental differences among fascists about both methods and objectives. The crisis was, therefore, not just a crisis in the relationship between the fascists and the rest of the country, much of which had been prepared to concede to a Fascism of dubious respectability the benefit of the doubt up to that point, but also an internal crisis within the movement itself. Prior to the March on Rome the quest for power had concentrated fascist minds and permitted unity in pursuit of a common objective but, with Mussolini installed as head of the government and the battle against the socialists apparently won, the many different interpretations of what Fascism might mean began to make themselves heard. Certainly, the blackshirts had much in common with each other when it was a question of defeating the 'enemy' but, equally certainly, there were profound differences between them when it came to deciding how the victory should be used. The threat which the Matteotti murder represented to the survival of Fascism made clarification of where Fascism was directed and how it was to get there imperative, therefore. Hesitation was seen by many as likely to lead to the downfall of the movement to which they had dedicated their lives in the previous three or four years. Radical intransigents and moderate fascists traded arguments, and, at times, blows, and even Mussolini's place as leader was brought into question.

[1] See Mauro Canali, *Il delitto Matteotti*, Bologna, Il Mulino, 2004.

The Matteotti murder is not exactly the starting point of this study, but it is the point at which many of the issues that are its underlying themes become very apparent. The relationship between Mussolini's government in Rome and the provincial fascist movements was severely tested during the months of the crisis, revealing differences between provincial interests and those of the national government which would continue to exist, and at times make themselves very evident, during the course of the entire *ventennio*. What was at stake in the Matteotti crisis was not only public power—the survival of the fascist government—but also private and personal careers, as local fascist leaders felt the carpet being pulled from under their feet. Who controls, and for what purpose, were questions with very wide-reaching implications in late 1924.

The tension between centre and periphery, between the national and the local, is, of course, a familiar theme of Italian studies—inevitably so, given the enormous differences between regions and the very strong local allegiances that continued to exist within the country after Unification. Initially bent on a centralization of authority, the first Italian governments soon found that, in the interests of legitimation and consensus, local autonomies had to be respected and the 'municipal' face of Italy was reinforced in important ways in the decades following Unification, generating political and administrative problems between national and local government which remained in part unresolved.[2] In addition, in a predominantly agricultural country, mobility between regions was low, with strong kinship networks remaining local and making little reference to the centre. Tensions persisted and it is the theme of continuing tensions between the claims of the centre and the resistance of the periphery that constitutes one of the guiding lines of this study.

Certainly, the history of a newly united Italy is not be read exclusively in terms of local resistance to national impositions, but, as readers here will quickly appreciate, an underlying assumption of this study is that, in Italy, the local is in many ways more antithetical than complementary to the national. The history of other nations suggests there is nothing unusual in this. Traditional lines of enquiry often find a national culture gradually transforming local cultures, with elites moulding nations, generally starting from the centre and spreading outwards.[3] In most studies of the fascist period the nationalizing thrust is approached in this way. The analysis starts from the centre and then works outwards towards the provinces, usually beginning with Mussolini and eventually ending up in Monza or (perhaps) Messina. Here, and rather differently, my intention has been to look at the progress of the fascist movement from the perspective of the provinces, and of the provincial fascists, rather than from that of the centre. What the fascist movement represented in the provincial context and how the movement was lived by both fascists and non-fascists are the main issues examined in the following pages. The competing and often contradictory impulses represented by the workings of local and national politics are central to this study, therefore. The theme, already complex, is further complicated by regional

---

[2] Raffaele Romanelli (ed.), *Storia dello stato italiano dall'Unità ad oggi*, Rome, Donzelli, 1995; also Ibid., *Il commando impossibile*, Bologna, Il Mulino, 1995.

[3] A classic study, presented in these terms, is Eugen Weber, *Peasants into Frenchmen. The Modernization of Rural France 1870–1914,* Stanford, California: Stanford University Press, 1976.

difference within Italy, the Fascism of Reggio Emilia being very different from that of Cosenza or Palermo. Inevitably, given the characteristics of the fascist movement, the North and the Centre tend to dominate the picture but, as far as possible, I have attempted to draw examples from each of the different regions, although the attempt has been necessarily conditioned to some extent by the availability of materials.

Centre/periphery relationships stand at the heart of almost any analysis of the difficult history of united Italy. They assume a particular importance, however, for the study of a movement that proclaimed the all-inclusive nature of the state ('everything within the State, nothing outside the State, nothing against the State' was Mussolini's well-known centralizing dictum) and aimed above all at the creation of a strong and coherent sense of nation among the population. This was the principal objective of the fascist programme. A new sense of the nation which, on the evidence of 1919 and 1920, the experience of the First World War had patently failed to realize among Italians, was to be achieved under Fascism. Many fascists appreciated only too well that nations are essentially 'social and cultural constructs', and that, therefore, they need constructing.[4] The task assigned to the fascist party—the *Partito Nazionale Fascista* (PNF)—was precisely this, the construction of a sense of common, collective, purpose among Italians: the generation of a 'community of believers' who had internalized the concept of nation and were prepared to work towards the realization of national palingenesis. In this process of social and cultural engineering, the party was to be the guiding element, leading the people in the creation of a unified fascist nation and performing the essential pedagogic function of explaining the meaning of Fascism to the Italian masses. But one problem the movement faced was that this 'meaning' was not always immediately clear. Much of the struggle over what Fascism stood for and over the direction the movement should take was played out at the local level within the provincial fascist party organizations, where people fought about what the local party should be doing (in particular, who should be doing it) and how this could be related to Mussolini's grand design.

The success or failure of the PNF in carrying out its task is a central theme of this study. A great deal is now known about the workings of the PNF, in part because of the number of local studies of the fascist movement produced over the last thirty years,[5] and we are not short of political biographies of

---

[4] On this question in relation to modern Germany, an interesting parallel example, see Alon Confino, *The Nation as Local Metaphor. Württemberg, Imperial Germany, and National Memory, 1871–1918*, Chapel Hill, University of North Carolina Press, 1997.

[5] A major contribution, which, unfortunately, ends with 1922, is Emilio Gentile, *Storia del Partito Fascista 1919–1922. Movimento e Milizia*, Rome & Bari, Laterza, 1989. For the first 'wave' of local studies, see in particular Simona Colarizi, *Dopoguerra e fascismo in Puglia*, Bari, Laterza, 1971; Paul Corner, *Fascism in Ferrara 1915–1925*, London, Oxford University Press, 1975; Antony L. Cardoza, *Agrarian Elites and Italian Fascism. The Province of Bologna 1901–1926*, Princeton, Princeton University Press, 1982; Alice Kelikian, *Town and Country under Fascism*, Oxford, Clarendon Press, 1986; Frank Snowden, *Violence and Great Estates in the South of Italy: Apulia 1900–1922*, Cambridge, Cambridge University Press, 1986. Regional studies are provided by Salvatore Sechi, *Dopoguerra e fascismo in Sardegna*, Turin, Fondazione Luigi Einaudi, 1971, and Frank Snowden, *The Fascist Revolution in Tuscany 1919–1922*, London, Cambridge University Press, 1989. Among more recent studies are those of Giulia Albanese, *Alle origini del fascismo. La violenza politica a Venezia 1919–1922*, Padua, Il Poligrafo, 2001; Tommaso Baris, *Il fascismo in provincia. Politica e realtà a Frosinone (1919–1940)*, Rome & Bari, Laterza, 2001; Matteo Mazzoni, *Livorno all'ombra del fascio*, Florence, Olschki, 2009; Francesca Alberico, *Le origini e lo sviluppo del Fascismo a Genova*, Milan, Unicopli, 2009.

Mussolini.[6] Where we are weaker, perhaps, is in studies that relate the periphery to the operations of the central state in a satisfactory manner. As anyone who has lived in provincial Italy for any time will appreciate, this relationship has been and remains one of the constant problems of the Italian state. What Rome commands and what the province does are often very different things. This difference is not just a question of competition between local and national identities; identities, as we all now know, can be multiple and overlapping and are not necessarily exclusive (although in the Italian case the neat Matroyska model seems hardly to fit the bill). It is much more a question of the instinctive, historically determined, attitude of the individual and the local to the Italian *State*—so often resented, opposed, and, when possible, thwarted by its citizens.[7] My own experience of more than twenty years in Siena—a city with an extremely strong (and very exclusive) local identity—suggests to me that the relationship between the traditions of Siena going back hundreds of years, civic identity, and a centralizing, fascist, dictatorial regime was unlikely to be easy. The crucial question in Siena was whether the people of the *Palio* would adapt to Fascism or whether Fascism would be adapted to them. The tensions between the forces in play were all too obvious, and no doubt the tensions which were evident in Siena were reproduced in many other areas of Italy, to a greater or lesser degree.

The central argument of what follows is that, in key respects and despite considerable efforts at mediation between the national and the local, the fascist movement foundered on its inability to penetrate many local situations in an efficient, attractive, and above all 'nationalizing' way. This failure frustrated the overarching national objectives of the movement. From the first, the fascist movement had seen itself as a response to division; dictatorship was justified as a necessary unifying factor in a deeply divided country. But Italy proved stronger than Fascism. The characteristics of the country, the methods of political transaction, the idea of how power should be used—all combined to defeat the original centralizing impulse of the fascist movement. Put in a different way, my thesis is that the much-proclaimed fascist 'national rebirth' of Italy faltered at the medieval gates of a hundred towns and cities as local traditions—and local interests— met up with the novelty, but also the threat, of the national movement.

In many places these tensions between local and national were reflected in the functioning of the provincial fascist party. The first half of this book looks at the evolution of the party in the provincial context and aims to assess the degree to

---

[6] The major study is Renzo De Felice, *Mussolini*, seven vols, Turin, Einaudi, 1966–97; also Richard Bosworth, *Mussolini*, Oxford, Oxford University Press, 2002; Martin Clark, *Mussolini: A Study in Power*, London, Pearson Longman 2005; Antony L. Cardoza, *Benito Mussolini: The First Fascist*, London, Longman 2005.

[7] An almost classic description of this attitude appears in the personal diary of a fascist militiaman in 1940. 'In Italy it is assumed that the individual is dishonest. There is a competition in cunning between the State and the individual. The State seems to be saying: "Try to make a fool of me if you are really the dishonest person I take you for." The individual replies: "If that's the way things stand, then I'll try." This is the reason there is such a tendency in Italy to cheat the State—something which (if the truth were told) gives a certain pleasure.' Diary of Paolino Ferrari, Archivio Diaristico Nazionale (ADN), DG/89, entry for 30 May 1940.

which the local PNF succeeded in becoming or failed to become that well-oiled machine for the production of good fascists that it was meant to be. This section also attempts to understand how the local party fitted into local politics and local society. If the authority of the party was not always what it might have been, who was really pulling the strings? Moreover, if, as is suggested here, national fascist objectives may have been defeated by the persistence of local, provincial, and regional imperatives among the fascists themselves and also by the ways in which the fascists exercised their power at a local level, then it is necessary to ask the question: did it really matter, or was the Italian fascist state able to assert itself within the country in ways which side-stepped the local party organizations? Was there a central 'technocratic/bureaucratic' side to the fascist regime capable of rectifying the defects of the local party organizations?

The centre/periphery question is complicated by a further factor. Local tensions and local loyalties were overshadowed by the figure of the charismatic leader. Fascism and what became known as 'Mussolinism' were widely recognized at the time to be different phenomena; sometimes, as we shall see, they were even thought to be in conflict. The role of the party has to be evaluated in this context. Comparisons with Nazi Germany are useful here. As several studies have shown, the same tensions between local and national, between the party and the people, existed in Germany as in Italy. In his brilliant examination of the 'Hitler Myth', Ian Kershaw has demonstrated the degree to which there was a real disjunction between the workings—and the reputation—of the Nazi party among the majority of the population and the disposition of the same population to follow Hitler in his adventures.[8] Although many Germans were very critical of aspects of Nazism and looked askance at the way the Nazi party used the great powers it had assumed, they remained convinced for a long time that Hitler was a figure unsullied by the more criminal and corrupt operations of the party. Provincial politics within fascist Italy was no doubt heavily conditioned by the 'cult of the *duce*', which operated in much the same way. But just how much the 'Mussolini myth' compensated for other perceived deficiencies of Fascism 'on the ground' is one of the questions addressed below.

Inevitably, the counter-posing of myth and reality brings into play the question of the role of ideology. This has been the subject of a great deal of debate over the last two decades, and few would now be prepared to assert—as was once common—that Fascism had no ideology. The work of Emilio Gentile, among others, has served to show that Fascism had a very strong, and in some ways coherent, ideology;[9] and understanding fascist ideology is clearly fundamental for understanding the fascist project. The central tenet of that ideology—the need for

---

[8] Ian Kershaw, *Popular Opinion and Political Dissent in the Third Reich. Bavaria 1933–1945*, Oxford, Clarendon Press, 1983, and Ibid., *The 'Hitler Myth'. Image and Reality in the Third Reich*, Oxford, Oxford University Press, 1987.

[9] Emilio Gentile, *Le origini dell'ideologia fascista*, Bologna, Il Mulino, 1996 (first edn. 1975); also Ibid., *Il culto del Littorio. La sacralizzazione della politica nell'Italia fascista*, Rome & Bari, Laterza, 1998 (first edn. 1993); see also, for a more general approach, Roger Griffin, *The Nature of Fascism*, London, Pinter, 1991. But for an excellent critical assessment of the concept of political religion see Martin Blinkhorn, 'Afterthoughts', in (2004) 5(3) *Totalitarian Movements and Political Religions*, 507.

national palingenesis through the transformation of Italians—was immensely ambitious and no doubt attractive, at least initially, to many. Yet it is argued here that it would be mistaken to see Fascism—particularly provincial Fascism—as being exclusively driven by the pure light of ideology. The fascist movement developed and survived because of unavoidable compromises with non-fascist forces in Italian society—the monarchy and the Church being the most obvious examples—and such compromises could not but reduce the degree to which many aspects of fascist ideology could be followed in practice. And, while many fascists may have been 'true believers' in the fascist 'faith', following closely the dictates of the fascist political religion, many others had personal interests to pursue. Accusations of 'opportunism' or 'careerism' were frequently levelled at those who joined the movement after the March on Rome, or after 1927, and no doubt many such accusations were fully justified.

Ideology and self-interest are in no way mutually exclusive, of course, but one of the arguments developed in this volume is that of the distance that developed between the two during the course of the regime. This was a distance perceived particularly at the provincial level, where all too frequently private interest seemed to prevail over formal ideology to the great detriment of the fascist cause. Indeed, the relationship between a centre that decided and a periphery that implemented, between what Fascism was preaching in Rome and what it was practising in the provinces, between the 'national' public and the 'local' private, may hold one of the keys to the question of the eventual failure of the regime. In this sense, to use a distinction of approach no longer in vogue for the analysis of Nazism but possibly still appropriate to a discussion of Fascism, this study is more functionalist than intentionalist. It aims less to examine the coherence of fascist ambitions as expressed through the party's official statements than to look closely at the cracks in the fascist monolith revealed by fascist party practices. In current terminology, and at the risk of being accused of naïve empiricism, it aims to analyse what might be called 'real existing Fascism' in its provincial context and to determine the dynamic of the long-lasting regime from within that context.

Yet the party is not the whole story. There is also 'the people'—a generic and unsatisfactory term, sometimes rendered by the equally unsatisfactory 'ordinary people'. Here the term is used as a kind of shorthand to distinguish those in some way subjected to Fascism from the convinced fascists themselves (although, in totalitarian regimes, this distinction is never precise) who benefited, or thought they benefited, from the regime. It is the *relationship* between the people and the party (always a minority) which is examined in the second section of this study—a relationship which evolved over the years into a clear 'them' and 'us' on the popular side. Reference is made primarily to opinion in the 1930s—the years of the creation of the mass movement—when those attitudes prevailing in the second half of the 1920s, determined by the novelties of the regime and often reflecting optimism for the promised fascist future or, more cautiously, positions of wait-and-see—had been modified under the impact of economic crisis and the day-to-day experience of increasing party and state control. Popular attitudes towards the regime are described principally, through not exclusively, through the reports of police and fascist party informers. It is at this point that it becomes clear that the context in which that opinion was formed is crucial—the context of the corrupt and mal-functioning party analysed in the first section of the book. Popular opinion is seen as a more or less direct result of common perceptions of what the party repre-sented. It was as a consequence of these perceptions that the project of Fascism and the realities of the movement parted company.

Simplifying to the extreme, my thesis is that, if the people did not follow the example of fascist 'true believers', if the transformation of the Italians into New Fascist Men did not even begin to take place (had it ever been possible), this was because the people did not like what they saw when they looked at the local party and at the local fascist leaders. Nor did they appreciate the activities of the move-ment. Fascism was undoubtedly 'national' in many of its expressions, but its man-ner of expression betrayed it. The corrupt, privileged, and sometimes brutal fascist hierarchy earned itself the title of the 'caste'—unjust, untouchable, and (in a time of economic crisis when sacrifices were not evenly distributed) bitterly resented.[10] Theirs was neither an example to be followed nor an inspiration towards the reali-zation of new objectives. Again, personal experience has reinforced this image. On many occasions I have talked to elderly Italians about their memories of the regime. Some are prepared to concede a certain space to the broad ideas of the fascist move-ment, but with only very rare exceptions they all use the same term for the black-shirts they came into contact with on a daily basis—*gentaglia* (bad people; people to be despised).

It will no doubt surprise some readers that, in a book about 'the people' under Fascism, the question of consensus for the regime is not confronted directly—at least not on the usual terms of the ever-continuing debate, with the highly political overtones inevitable in a country which has had real difficulty in coming to terms with its fascist past. Renzo De Felice's contention that there was a widespread popular consensus for the regime (at the time—1974—very politically incorrect) divided Italy down the middle, in political terms, but stimulated neither then nor later empirical research aimed at verifying the truth of his assertion. In recent years his thesis seems to have been generally accepted, at least at a journalistic level, less because of fresh historical research than from a kind of self-excusing inertia among Italians which reasons that, if we all agreed about it at the time, Fascism cannot have been so bad after all.[11] In fact the word 'consensus' is used little here, not because the question of popular attitudes to the regime is not important, but because the term itself is inadequate to describe the complexities of popular atti-tudes towards and within a would-be totalitarian regime in which coercion, direct or implied, is always the conditioning context. The varieties of any would-be con-sensus are almost limitless, as are the difficulties of determining what exactly that consensus relates to. Where consensus ends and where coercion begins is equally

---

[10] Rather significantly, the term has acquired new popularity in Italy during the last few years, for example in the best-selling book by Sergio Rizzo and Gian Antonio Stella, *La casta. Così i politici italiani sono diventati intoccabili*, Milan, Rizzoli, 2008.

[11] See Paul Corner, 'Italian Fascism: Whatever happened to Dictatorship?', (2002) 74 *Journal of Modern History* 325–51.

difficult to decide within a totalitarian framework, which seeks to eliminate the workings of any kind of public sphere.[12] I have attempted to assess the changing situation across the years using (I hope) a less loaded terminology, although, by the time they get to the end of the book, I think few readers will have any doubts about where I stand on the issue.

In respect of this debate, one area where this study parts company with much that has already been written is in its suggestion that the wheels were falling off the fascist movement *before* the outbreak of the Second World War and that the crisis of the regime was not provoked by the disastrous course of the war for Italy but by a dramatic collapse of popular identification with fascism in the second half of the 1930s. Unlike many analyses of the evolution of the regime, therefore, I argue for a severe internal crisis even before the impact of war—something which may help to explain Italy's relatively rapid disintegration during the course of the conflict itself. The speed of disintegration is one of the ways in which fascist Italy differed most obviously from Nazi Germany and may point to a significantly different composition and consistency of popular support for the regime. In Italy, very obviously, different social groups detached themselves from the fascist regime at different times and this process will be examined, at least in part, in the pages that follow. Here, perhaps, it is important simply to clarify that the crisis of the regime at the end of the 1930s did not imply its necessary and imminent collapse. What it did mean was that a self-defined 'revolutionary' movement, dedicated to the transformation of the Italian people, might have relapsed, in other circumstances, into being a more traditional, authoritarian and dictatorial regime than its undoubted totalitarian pretensions would have initially envisaged.

This is not a text book, which is one way of saying that not everything found in the text is explained to first-time students of Italian Fascism. These may want to refer back to some of my main printed sources. Although I have tried to use the material in a different way, changing the perspectives and, where possible, listening to different voices, readers familiar with the subject will recognize that much of the material presented here is not new. Particularly in the chapters on the 1920s—essentially introductory to the main argument—it has been possible to make use of a considerable secondary literature. For the early period, up to the establishment of the regime in 1925–6, I have relied on Adrian Lyttelton's *The Seizure of Power*, a work which remains unsurpassed for both its wealth of detail and its overall interpretation.[13] Salvatore Lupo will find many traces of his more recent history of Italian Fascism,[14] as will Simona Colarizi in the reports of fascist informers.[15] The interpretation of institutional changes during the regime owes much to the classic

---

[12] On totalitarianism and the public sphere see Sheila Fitzpatrick, 'Russia under pre-war Stalinism', in Paul Corner (ed.), *Popular Opinion in Totalitarian Regimes. Fascism, Nazism, Communism*, Oxford, Oxford University Press, 2009, 24–6.

[13] Adrian Lyttelton, *The Seizure of Power: Fascism in Italy, 1919–1929*, London, Weidenfeld and Nicolson, 1973.

[14] Salvatore Lupo, *Il fascismo: la politica di un regime totalitario*, Rome, Donzelli, 2000.

[15] Simona Colarizi, *L'opinione degli italiani sotto il regime fascista 1929–43*, Rome & Bari, Laterza, 1991.

work of Alberto Aquarone,[16] and to the more recent studies by Guido Melis.[17] The second section of the book relies more on archival sources—necessarily, because there is very much less published work on the history of this period. Underlying many of my judgements are, inevitably, the volumes of Renzo De Felice's massive and invaluable biography of Mussolini,[18] while, as already stated, the rich production of Emilio Gentile has provided a basis for some aspects of my approach, particularly in respect of the totalitarian pretensions of the regime. Although we may appear to be saying very different things—Gentile showing why Fascism worked when it did, while I concentrate on why it did not when it did not—I would regard this volume as being in many ways complementary to Gentile's line of thinking—the other face of a complex and fascinating subject.

---

[16] Alberto Aquarone, *L'organizzazione dello stato totalitario*, Turin, Einaudi, 1965. Page numbers cited here are from the 1995 reprint.

[17] Guido Melis, *Storia dell'amministrazione italiana*, Bologna, Il Mulino, 1996; Ibid (ed.), *Lo Stato negli anni Trenta. Istituzioni e regimi fascisti in Europa*, Bologna, IL Mulino, 2008.

[18] De Felice, *Mussolini*.

PART 1

THE PROJECT, THE PARTY, AND THE FASCIST STATE

1

Postwar Palingenesis: Forming the Fascist Project

Apart from a dwindling number of neo-fascists, few would question that Italian Fascism was a fairly spectacular failure. The military collapse of Italy in 1943, the defeat of the puppet *Repubblica sociale*, the ignominious end of Mussolini—all served to seal the fate, not only of the regime, but also of the very idea of Fascism among most Italians. The Constitution of the new democratic republic made it plain that there was to be no going back. The revised postwar legal code envisaged tough sanctions against those found guilty of advocating Fascism, although this clause was to be invoked rarely in subsequent years. Yet the exact nature of the fascist failure was less than clear then and has remained unclear since. Then—as now—many Italians might well have been prepared to argue that failure was to be imputed exclusively to the mistaken military alliance with Hitler and to the fateful decision to join the Second World War. Even today it is common to hear people express the view that Fascism 'did many good things' and that, up to 1938 at least, Mussolini was really doing rather well. Indeed, in a journalistic canard, a prominent popular historian has argued that, if Mussolini had been lucky enough to die in 1938, he would now be up there with Mazzini, Garibaldi, and Cavour as one of Italy's national heroes.[1] By this reading, only military adventure and military defeat determined that Fascism was 'ultimately' a failure.

Success and failure, of course, are usually measured in relation to the original objectives. With the defeat in 1945 the central fascist goal of gaining great power status for Italy was finally frustrated—and of this there can be no doubt.[2] Nonetheless it would be reductive to define fascist objectives only in terms of international ambition. If we look beyond military issues to those which concern the fundamental transformation of Italian society that Fascism sought to realize, the degree of failure may be less apparent. After all, few would question that both Soviet communism and German Nazism transformed their societies radically, while both ended in failure. In the same way, in the Italian case it is legitimate to ask to what degree those fascist objectives of national transformation were realized, even given the final defeat. Was it, in fact, really only the war that brought Fascism down?

[1] Arrigo Petacco, *L'uomo della provvidenza*, Milan, Mondadori, 2006.
[2] On the international settlement, which saw Italy threatened initially with virtual colonial status, see John Lamberton Harper, *America and the Reconstruction of Italy, 1945–48*, Cambridge, Cambridge University Press, 2002.

Any consideration of fascist objectives is complex. These undoubtedly evolved over time, particularly during the course of the 1920s, as fascist leaders began to realize the full implications of what they had already achieved and what they might achieve in the future. Yet the extent and the nature of this evolution can be understood only in the light of a point of departure. This necessarily takes us back to the beginnings of Fascism—to 1919 and to the period of convulsive postwar readjustment. How did the first Fascism—that of 1919 and 1920—propose to change Italy and Italian society? Here again the answer is far from straightforward. Certainly the founding meeting of the *fasci di combattimento* in Piazza San Sepolcro in Milan on 23 March 1919 adopted a programme that presented a large number of radical demands, among which were the confiscation of war profits and the nationalization of war industries, expropriation of the property of religious orders, and a progressive tax on capital.[3] These were demands and proposals that reflected the generalized desire for dramatic change in the postwar world—change which people felt had to follow the horrors of the war and which constituted one of the central elements of popular mood in 1919, a mood often defined as *diciannovismo* ('[nineteen]nineteenism').

There are at least three problems with evaluating Fascism's original programme in order to determine fascist intentions. The first is that Fascism—even the Fascism of Milan—changed rapidly in its early years. Much of the March 1919 programme was no longer present in the fascist platform presented at the political elections of November 1919; even less was present in the policy document produced by the second national congress of the movement held in May 1920. This evolution was determined by important tactical changes in Mussolini's position as he struggled to gain a political foothold in a world reluctant to listen to him,[4] but they were also in part a consequence of what constitutes a second difficulty in defining early Fascism: that is, the movement's own reluctance to define its position. In fact, portraying itself as the 'anti-party' that opposed the established politics of the parties, Fascism presented itself as anti-political, and prided itself precisely on weak definition and lack of coherence—something that was, of course, politically very convenient. Mussolini's many statements—'We are revolutionary and reactionary, we are parliamentary and anti-parliamentary'—expressed the deliberate ambiguities of the fascist position perfectly.[5]

The third problem is created by the fact that many of the people who called themselves fascists in 1919 and for a good part of 1920—the fascists of 'the first hour', as they were called, who were not in Milan, but in centres like Bologna, Genoa, or Florence—often had relatively little contact with Mussolini and were inspired to activity less by rapidly changing published programmes in Milan than by a whole series of different motives, sometimes linked to grand ideas about the

---

[3] For the first programme see R. De Felice, *Mussolini*, vol. 1 *Il rivoluzionario*, Turin, Einaudi, 1966, 506–9 and Appendix 20.

[4] Mussolini's credibility was suspect. As a former socialist, he was viewed with suspicion on the right; as someone who had betrayed socialist pacifism in 1914, he was distrusted on the left.

[5] On Mussolini's political evolution in this period see, besides De Felice, Fabio Fabbri, *Le origini della guerra civile. L'Italia dalla Grande Guerra al Fascismo, 1918–1921*, Milan, Utet, 2010.

way the new postwar world should work, but frequently more connected to specific local issues. For these people—many of them returning army officers and
soldiers[6]—Mussolini was an emblem, a representative of alternative politics, rather
than a spokesman who had to be followed at every step. To speak of a common
programme, or a national programme of Fascism would, in the circumstances of
1919 or early 1920, be a great exaggeration, therefore.[7]

An example of the very vague inspiration of some of the early fascists is provided by the diary of the young Florentine *squadrista*,[8] Mario Piazzesi. His thinking is very typical of many of the young men of his time. Still at his classical high
school, Piazzesi was caught up in a politically turbulent 1919 and identified with
nationalist and anti-socialist organizations but found little to satisfy him in the
rather old-fashioned, 'parliamentary-style' speeches by local worthies ('beard
wearers'). Even the first local meeting of the *fascio dei combattimenti*, in October
1919, was a politically confused and audience-less fiasco, dismissed immediately
by the student as 'a waste of time'. What changed the picture for Piazzesi was his
participation in strike-breaking activities in Florence in 1920 and his contact with
a few former soldiers, who sold him the idea of the need to defend 'the demands
of the Victory...and of Fiume.' Anti-socialism and nationalism rather than the
figure of Mussolini seem to have been at the root of Piazzesi's initial activity.
Attention to what Mussolini was saying followed rather than initiated his political
activity.[9]

What is interesting, of course, and central to the question of how the fascist
movement formed, is the way in which people like Piazzesi translated a generic
and often rather confused message coming from Milan to meet their own particular circumstances. Reference by many to Mussolini was due in part to the reputation the future fascist leader had built up for himself during the war as the
representative of the soldier in the trenches, someone who had shared their suffer-
ings and had even been wounded in battle. The truth of this image has recently
been put in question,[10] yet the stance, ably constructed by Mussolini, meant that
he remained an inspiration and a point of focus to many returning soldiers, even
if they had little direct contact with him. Without knowing the details of his
programme, many were still ready to call themselves 'fascists' because of their
devotion to the person of Mussolini. Yet it is clear that Mussolini's attraction was
not simply personal. Putting himself forward as the spokesman for radical change,
he was able to exploit strong undercurrents of anti-democratic sentiment that had
been circulating for more than a decade among minority political groupings.
These sentiments pre-dated Fascism—indeed, many of them had their origins in
the decade before the war—but they formed an ideological humus which helped
Fascism to grow. In part, therefore, in 1919 Mussolini became the representative
of subversive intellectual and political trends he had had no hand in creating but

---

[6] Giovanni Sabbatucci, *I combattenti nel primo dopoguerra*, Bari, Laterza, 1974.
[7] These very loose connections are examined in detail in Fabbri, *Origini,* Chapter 1.
[8] The *squadristi* were the members of the violent fascist action squads.
[9] Mario Piazzesi, *Diario di uno squadrista toscano 1919–1922*, Rome, Bonacci, 1980.
[10] Paul O'Brien, *Mussolini in the First World War*, Oxford, Berg, 2005.

which served to make the radicalism of Fascism appear acceptable in certain quarters.[11]

Without embarking on a detailed account of these trends, it is sufficient to note that the rising tide of anti-democratic and anti-liberal thought prior to the war had found its proponents on both the left and the right of the political spectrum. The turn of the century had seen the birth of a new, aggressive nationalism around the figure of Filippo Corradini, whose denunciation of bourgeois society with its 'tepid' and complacent values resonated alike with revolutionary syndicalists and more right-wing radical adventurers, such as Gabriele D'Annunzio. Unlike the socialists, Corradini embraced the advance of industry wholeheartedly, arguing that the 'producers' should be at centre stage in a new imperialist thrust by what he termed the 'proletarian nation'. Like the revolutionary syndicalists, who took their inspiration from Georges Sorel, the Italian nationalists looked for national salvation through the appearance of a New Man, capable of confronting and dominating the challenges of a new world and replacing the mediocre personalities governing liberal Italy.

Equally subversive ideas came from the Italian avant garde in the years before the war. Debate about the relationship between Fascism and the constituent groups of this avant garde continues. There can be little doubt, however, that the various movements contributed to the process of undermining the foundations of Italian liberalism. Although they differed greatly in the remedies they prescribed for the situation in which Italy found itself, both the group around *La Voce* and the Futurists agreed on the diagnosis. In their eyes, Italy, under Giovanni Giolitti, was sliding into decadence, governed by a corrupt and inefficient political class without ideas or ambition. Both groups stressed—again in different ways—the need for national regeneration and for the realization of a New Italy, an Italy worthy of sitting as an equal at the table of the great powers. Central to the formation of the New Italy was, once more, the New Italian—a figure with very different characteristics from those which the *Vociani* and the Futurists saw in the Giolittian governing class.

An excellent example of the way in which elements of these ideas and proposals criss-crossed so as to become a mixture of denunciation of the old and advocacy of the new is to be found in the wartime writings of Agostino Lanzillo. Lanzillo was a revolutionary syndicalist who came from the South of Italy. Conscripted into the army, he had been wounded in the autumn of 1917 and spent his period of convalescence writing *The Defeat of Socialism*—a book, written in January 1918, which appeared in October of the same year.[12] His starting point was the benefits of the experience of war. The modern world, he wrote, suffering from 'social decomposi-

[11] On the various strands of anti-democratic thought, see Emilio Gentile, *Le origini dell'ideologia fascista*, 1st edn, Bari, Laterza, 1975; Adrian Lyttelton (ed.), *Roots of the Right. Italian Fascisms from Pareto to Gentile*, London, Cape, 1973; Roger Griffin (ed.), *Fascism*, Oxford, Oxford University Press, 1995; also Luisa Mangoni, *L'interventismo della cultura. Intellettuali e riviste del Fascismo*, Bari, Laterza, 1974, in particular Chapter 1.

[12] Agostino Lanzillo, *La disfatta del socialismo. Critica della guerra e del socialismo*, Florence, Libreria della Voce, 1918.

tion', had been 'purified' by the violence of war: 'A few days, or rather, a few hours were enough to destroy with the violence of a river that bursts its banks the whole castle of errors, of miseries, of falsity, of madness in which the modern world lived...' Turning to Italy he dwelt on the contrast between the old Italy and a new nation revealed by the Interventionist crisis of 1914–15, when Italy had been deeply divided about the need for Italian participation in the conflict. It was the difference between 'this Italy, all prejudices, bureaucratic, fearful, flaccid, unaware, and the new Italy, from whose eyes the European war has torn away all veils and rendered evident the decisive dilemma which history has imposed on the nation...'

Put succinctly, Lanzillo described the dilemma as 'deciding whether Italy were Europe or Balkan peninsular'. The moment was critical: 'Now is the time to understand the definitive and decisive worth of the movement of the young generations compared with the old—to strip away from the various questions every useless detail and every inessential complication, in order to pose in all its brutal truth the real problem of the future of the nation...' In opposition to socialist internationalism, therefore, the syndicalist's emphasis was on the nation and on national renewal. Insistence on the role to be played by the new generations in national renewal was also central to Lanzillo's discourse, in part because he saw that a defeated Germany was unlikely to lie down for long and that this would put further great strains on Italy. 'Perhaps this war will not end but begin a period of wars for national independence.' As a consequence, '[a]fter this war a new governing class must assume the guidance of the nation, renewing its political and administrative functions. To meet new destinies must be proposed new, young, generations—those who wanted and fought the war.' These generations would need a new ideology, adapted to a new civilization and to new challenges. Moreover, resolution of the problems facing Italy would require both conflict, essential for real renewal, and disposition to sacrifice—a quality it seemed the First World War had forced men to rediscover. Lanzillo concluded his (rather remarkably prescient) remarks with the observation that the future Italian society would be extensively militarized: 'through the great mass of men who will conserve in their lives the memory of the long agony of war... the military tradition will be conserved and nurtured.' But now, more than ever, that tradition would be linked to the discourse of the nation. 'Military consciousness means national consciousness... Love of the fatherland, which was just rhetoric for the older generations, is today a passion, pursued because of the blood we have shed and the mortification of the flesh that we have suffered in its name.'

Lanzillo was far from being alone in his mode of reasoning. His book, written, it is worth remembering, a full year and a half before the foundation of the first Milan *fascio*, is a kind of condensation of non-socialist, radical sentiments of the time.[13] Almost all the elements are there—the need for a new and much younger governing class, the myth of the New Man, the pride of place to be given to those who had

---

[13] The extent to which Fascism owed its inspiration to the experience (and the emergency legislation) of the First World War (and not to the socialist triumphs of 1919 and 1920) is examined most recently in Fabbri, *Origini*, Chapter 2, and in Roberto Bianchi, *Pace, pane, terra. Il 1919 in Italia*, Rome, Odradek, 2006. It is a persistent theme of the work of Giovanna Procacci; see, in particular, 'La società come una caserma. La svolta repressiva nell'Italia della grande guerra', (2006) 3 *Contemporanea* 423.

fought the war and to the values that the conflict had represented, the need for new institutions, and, above all, the centrality of the nation and the importance attributed to the destiny of a probably permanently militarized nation. Although Lanzillo's emphasis is on the dramatic consequences of the war itself, it is not difficult to see in his writings many of those ideas that had been developed before 1914 and that had, in a sense, been crystallized in the Interventionist crisis of 1914–15. There was not, of course, a straightforward continuity with the pre-war. Not all of the movements of the pre-war survived the conflict. *La Voce* disappeared and Futurism suffered from the deaths of some of its leading exponents, although several Futurists, including Filippo Tommaso Marinetti, were at the founding meeting of the *fasci di combattimento* in March 1919. But, while the extreme tensions of the conflict almost inevitably reinforced the nationalist right, it is difficult not to perceive in the writings of Lanzillo the extent to which the contact with war had consolidated many of the ideas propagated by those movements, rendering the voices of non-socialist dissent in the immediate pre-war period more incisive, more determined in their project of changing the reality of Italy.

It is not surprising that we find Lanzillo among those present at the inaugural meeting of the fascist movement in Milan in March 1919. The promise of the Piazza San Sepolcro gathering seemed to fit his aspirations for the future very well. But it is also apparent from his writings (and he published another book in 1919, shortly after the March meeting, similar in tone to the one cited above) that Lanzillo was there less because of specific policies proposed than because of a general mood that it seemed Mussolini might be able to represent. This mood was founded, first, on a rabid hostility to socialism and the Italian Socialist Party (PSI) because of its negative attitude to Italian participation in the war. Although, following the Italian defeat at Caporetto in October 1917, the PSI had somewhat abandoned its fence-sitting position of 'neither support nor sabotage', the nationalist hysteria that followed near-defeat had led many, both on the right and the extreme left (Lanzillo's background was that of revolutionary syndicalism after all) to classify the party firmly as the 'internal enemy' to be contested at every turn. In a similar way to that in which the German right would invent the 'stab in the back' legend after 1918, Italian Socialism was accused of having betrayed the nation. The second point was, in a sense, the reverse of the coin. Just as socialism had to be contested because of its alleged undermining of the war effort, so everything had to be done to preserve and build on the 'values' that had emerged from the war, most centrally that of the Nation. The 'valorization' of the conflict—the idea that people should not have died simply to allow others to return to the pre-war world of Giolitti or, worse, to see the socialists gain power—was a crucial element in the postwar psychology of people like Lanzillo. Certainly the masses had gained 'rights' as a result of their sacrifices, but any such rights had to be enjoyed within the confines imposed by anti-socialism and respect for the war.[14]

---

[14] A broader treatment of the ideas emerging from the experience of the war is to be found in Emilio Gentile, *Il mito dello Stato nuovo dall'anti-Giolittismo al Fascismo*, Rome & Bari, Laterza, 1982 and Ibid., *Il culto del littorio*.

These were in essence the two concrete objectives of the first Fascism—the defeat of neutralist and pacifist socialism that, in the eyes of the fascists, had brought Italy to the brink of defeat, and the defence of the war effort from those who denigrated it as 'useless conflict'. People could fix on these objectives as specific tasks (and would do so in subsequent years to great effect). What gave these goals particular force in the circumstances of 1919 and 1920, however, was the way in which they were encapsulated in a more general projection towards a brilliant new future. As is evident from many of the quotations from Lanzillo, there was a remarkable conviction among the early fascists that the world had to change in a dramatic way to accommodate the young, the dynamic, the new. The experience of 'total' war in Europe, with its apocalyptic aspects, produced not desperation but an explosion of expectation of change among those who had lived through it. There was simply no going back. Indeed change is too slight a word to describe these expectations. They were based on a chiliastic vision of the future, almost as though people were convinced that they could now take hold of history itself and mould and manipulate it to their own ends.[15] There was a strong idea of a new destiny awaiting the world and the Italian nation—a palingenetic rebirth—to be realized by those able to see that destiny and work towards it. Ideas current before the First World War, of renewal, rebirth, of resurrection almost, thus acquired a vastly increased force in the context of post-conflict 1919. Much of the enthusiasm of the early fascist movement derived, in reality, from the fact that the first fascists saw themselves on the threshold of a new world, to which they, and only they, possessed the key.[16]

This was very much, therefore, a response to a 'crisis of modernity' that some have seen as being at the origin of totalitarian movements. It was a response that not only denounced the past but also was couched in terms of the vision of a new, alternative, modernity.[17] If it was hailed as the moment of truth in revealing the way forward for society, the war had also served to lay bare the full squalor of the modern world which could now be changed. Again this is evident in the work of Lanzillo. He expressed what was in essence a sense of gratitude towards the experience of war because it had made obvious what people had been either unable or unwilling to see before. Capitalism was the principal accused, responsible for 'the great moral deviation of society, the progress of a conception of life...bestially individualistic and therefore not vital...' The product of capitalism—materialism—received the same treatment, seen as destructive of 'ethical health'. As a result, Lanzillo argued, the workers had been particularly harmed by the modern world: 'A century of optimistic democracy [and] of brutal materialism, have plunged the modern world, particularly the great mass of industrial workers...into a total negation of any idealism.'

---

[15] The same sentiments presaged the arrival to power of Hitler. Norbert Frei speaks of a concept of 'new time' prevalent among many fervent Nazi supporters in the early 1930s: N. Frei, 'Hitler's Popular Support', in Hans Mommsen (ed.), *The Third Reich between Vision and Reality: New Perspectives on German History*, Oxford, Berg, 1991, 59.

[16] For a lively exposition of the intellectual origins of Fascism, which, however, concentrates largely on the figure of Mussolini, see Roger Griffin, *Modernism and Fascism. The Sense of a Beginning under Mussolini and Hitler*, Basingstoke, Palgrave Macmillan, 2007, 191–216.

[17] An excellent examination of the German 'crisis of modernity' is to be found in Detlev Peukert, *The Weimar Republic*, New York, Hill and Wang, 1989.

People had lost their way. There had been a loss of any sense of the meaning of life, as people pursued the false goals of the modern world. By a strange logic, the war had actually put things right: 'Europe, surprised in its materialist enjoyment, has found its former virtues again. Death has lost its terrifying appearance and in all men...there is a rebirth of the sentiments of self-denial and sacrifice. The *epos* returns.'[18]

What is evident in this kind of discourse is the strong idealist and ethical element that lay at the heart of the vision of renewal. The old world was accused of having lost all true values. Although it promised a new world, Socialism was no more than an illusion—an expression of a tired and exhausted materialism. The first fascists argued that they were restoring values to a world that had lost them. They—the fascists—were the prophets, saved by their recognition of the new realities imposed by the war. This was very much what Hannah Arendt identified when she wrote of Fascism being a response to 'loss of world'—the individual's sense of alienation from the surrounding world that produced, in turn, 'loss of self' or personal identity.[19] Both losses were to be remedied by the discovery of the new fascist 'faith' in the community of the nation.

The strongly religious nature of fascist belief has, of course, been much noted by many historians.[20] In recent years political religions have become central to the study of totalitarianism.[21] Certainly, many of the statements of the first fascists are shaped in an unmistakably religious tone and obviously owe much to the Italian Catholic tradition. This kind of usage was not, of course, a novelty. Much of the language of socialism had been similar and, as George Mosse has shown, the combination of religion and politics has a long history that goes back well before Fascism.[22] In early Fascism the combination was very much linked to ideas of personal sacrifice—an aspect that, in the wartime and postwar context, gave a particular charge to early Fascism. Lanzillo's writings overflow with statements that betray this kind of orientation. His criticism of socialism was based on its alleged moral weakness; the socialists were 'devoid of faith and devoid of sincerity'. As a result, '[t]he proletariat lacks...faith, religious spirit'. Instead, he wrote, as a consequence of the experience of war, 'religion is reborn. A spiritual vision of life returns, healthy and strong'. Much influenced by the American philosopher William James, Lanzillo sought 'the moral equivalent of war' in what he envisaged in 1918 would be

---

[18] Lanzillo, *La disfatta del socialismo*, 187. On the mental processes involved in the elevation of war and killing to a higher moral plane, see Modris Eksteins, *Rites of Spring. The Great War and the Birth of the Modern Age*, New York, Doubleday, 1989.

[19] See the illuminating comments on Arendt's position in respect of 'loss of meaning' in Michael Halberstam, *Totalitarianism and the Modern Conception of Politics*, New Haven, Connecticut, Yale University Press, 1999, in particular 133–56.

[20] In a sense, it was no discovery. Mussolini himself defined Fascism as a religion on many occasions.

[21] For multiple considerations of the uses and abuses of the concept of political religion, readers need look no further than the journal *Totalitarian Movements and Political Religions*, since 2000 dedicated entirely to discussions and debates on this question.

[22] George Mosse, *The Nationalisation of the Masses: political symbolism and mass movements in Germany from the Napoleonic wars through the Third Reich*, New York, H. Fertig, 1975; for Italy, see Gentile, *Il culto del littorio*, Introduction.

the politics of the postwar. This meant that courage, the spirit of sacrifice, and 'faith' were to be the key characteristics of a politics based on will and action—all to be employed in defence of the Nation (which now gets a capital N). These qualities were the essential point of departure for national regeneration because, as Lanzillo put it (in what would turn out to be almost an obituary for Fascism itself), '[t]he idea should prevail over the real'.[23]

Many of these themes will be taken up in the course of this book. Here, I wish simply to note that the original fascist objectives had, in a sense, little to do with the published programme of March–June 1919. Institutional reforms and tax changes such as were advocated were intended to attract attention to the new movement (although they seem to have had little impact; for many it was a case of 'heard it before, heard it better'), but they were only a limited expression of a much grander objective, still to be fully formulated, which was that of the transformation of Italian society through a transformation of the Italians—of the way they thought and behaved. It is highly instructive to note that, in the eyes of Lanzillo, Fascism was to be, first and foremost, a moral and a spiritual revolution, weaning the nation away from its complacent self-satisfaction and prosaic materialism. It was intended to capture and preserve the qualities that had become evident for the first time in the trenches, where a new community with new values had been formed. These were values to be 'internalized' by the new society. The formation of the New Fascist Man and the new society was to be based on this experience.

Confronted by such an obviously utopian project, it might not seem necessary to say much more about the failure of Fascism. History—particularly the history of the twentieth century—suggests that attempts to transform human nature have usually ended in failure. The Soviet Union made the same kind of effort as fascist Italy, perhaps with much greater conviction than Fascism was ever able to muster, but the utopia inhabited by the New Soviet Man proved hard to create and such transformations as were realized were not durable. With the benefit of hindsight we now know that the objectives were unrealizable, although there is ample evidence that this did not seem so to many Soviet citizens at the time (nor did it seem so to an intelligent and alarmed observer like George Orwell). In the same way, history suggests that political religions may work for a time, but eventually let their proponents down, particularly in countries in which there is already a strong and well-established traditional religion. To explain the failure of Fascism, it would seem, we need to look no further than its initial, unrealizable, objectives.

Yet, between the initial objectives of the movement and the death of Mussolini in 1945 lies the whole history of Fascism. Less than the failure itself, which is obvious, it is the way in which Fascism failed that interests us here. The identification of broad, long-term, objectives is useful as a heuristic device; it provides us with something against which to measure the progress of the movement, the party, and the regime. But it should not be allowed to distract from the fact that the totalitarian project also had clear objectives that were, in a sense, intermediate as regards

[23] Lanzillo, *La disfatta del socialismo*, 27. *The Moral Equivalent of War* is the title of a book (1896) by William James, professor of psychology at Harvard before the turn of the century.

the ultimate aim of the realization of the new fascist society. The transformation of Italians was a *process* which required the achievement of certain goals if the final objective were to be reached. These goals involved the organization and regimentation of society in such a way as to produce, eventually, a nation united in a common purpose, persuaded of the values of Fascism, and dedicated to the realization of the national renewal. Mass popular participation in fascist activities was to be the means of achieving this common purpose. It is here that the fascist party comes into the picture. The formation of a convinced fascist society, politicized as never before, required the creation of an efficient political machine of a type previously unknown either in Italy or elsewhere. This was the single party—the all-embracing party with a monopoly of political activity. It was through the workings of this machine—through the operation of the party in guiding the people—that mystical aspirations would be transformed into the totalitarian reality of unity between people, party, and *duce*. Not just ideas were involved, but also actions, therefore. As Michael Mann has put it, 'Fascism was not just a collection of individuals with certain beliefs. Fascism had a great impact on the world *only* because of its collective actions and its organizational forms'.[24] The party was at the centre of these actions and forms, designed to change the world.

The construction of an organization capable of achieving this transformation was the essential precondition for success in the process of generating the fascist state, and in this respect the fascist regime was by no means simply a history of failure. The impact of the regime on both society and institutions was profound. At issue here, therefore, is the question of the way in which fascist ideas and objectives, undoubtedly seeking national palingenesis and strongly linked to forms of political religion, actually translated into practical politics—in the large cities, in the provincial centres, in the rural villages, and among the scattered population of the countryside. It is this 'translation' of an extraordinarily ambitious project into the reality of day-to-day politics that forms the principal theme of this book.

[24] Michael Mann, *Fascists*, Cambridge, Cambridge University Press, 2004, 12–13.

2

The Rise of Provincial Fascism: Periphery and Centre in the Years before 1925

Although the nation and the concept of national redemption were central to the thinking of many early fascists, in its origins the first fascist movement was anything but national in character. Initially centred on Milan, the movement showed little capacity to extend its influence to other areas during the course of 1919. Reports from supporters outside Milan during the summer and autumn of 1919 spoke of waning interest and declining support as people continued to look elsewhere for political inspiration. Certainly, the exploits of D'Annunzio during 1919 and 1920 did little to help Mussolini's cause. For several months after September 1919 it was the poet who held centre stage, probably much to Mussolini's annoyance, and this attention was reflected in the fascist movement's poor showing in the November 1919 political elections.[1]

2.1. CENTRIFUGAL FORCES

When the fascist movement finally emerged on to the national scene, in late 1920 and early 1921 and as a consequence of the rapid development of the very violent agrarian fascism, it did so in a piecemeal and uncoordinated way—something which simply reflected the extent to which the first Fascism was made up of a series of essentially local movements, centred on a town or, at most, a province, in which the aims of the fascists might be very different one from another, according to local circumstances.[2] The importance of the local had been made evident in Trieste, where a sudden explosion of the fascist movement in the spring of 1920 was to be attributed to severe tensions between Italians and Slavs, following the end of the war.[3] In the same way, while in Ferrara the 'enemy' for the fascists was clearly the

---

[1] For an excellent short summary of the national politics of this period, see MacGregor Knox, *To the Threshold of Power, 1922/33. Origins and Dynamics of the Fascist and National Socialist Dictatorships*, vol. I, Cambridge, Cambridge University Press, 2007, 268–81, 296–329.

[2] The most recent detailed treatment of the rapid development of the fascist movement in this phase is in Fabbri, *Origini*, but see also Gentile, *Storia*, Chapter 7. Note the extensive use of the term 'civil war' in Fabbri's study.

[3] Elio Apih, *Italia, fascismo, e antifascismo nella Venezia Giulia 1918–1943*, Bari, Laterza, 1966; Anna Maria Vinci, *Sentinelle della patria: il fascismo al confine orientale 1918–1941*, Rome & Bari, Laterza, 2011.

dominant socialist organization of the landless rural labourers, in another rural area not so distant from Ferrara—Cremona—the fascists turned their attention to the strong Catholic unions of agricultural workers because it was these that represented the threat to landowners in that province.[4] The same pattern was reproduced throughout much of northern and central Italy, and also in Apulia, the only area of the South where a strong fascist movement based on the operation of the brutal blackshirt action squads developed before 1922.[5] In Emilia, in Tuscany, and in Apulia, local issues dominated.[6] Unlike the Fascism of 1919, which had professed a more national vision, the new Fascism of 1920 took its inspiration from Mussolini and employed a national rhetoric, but utilized that inspiration and rhetoric to address what were essentially neighbourhood issues—issues often identified exclusively by the local fascists themselves. In so doing, the fascists did no more than reflect the nature of the liberal politics they were seeking to destroy—a politics that had been characterized by local networks and local issues, in which national questions had frequently struggled to gain attention.

This kind of expansion produced a movement that was initially fragmented and uncoordinated, not only geographically but also ideologically, and which often had great difficulty in raising its eyes from the horizon of a particular province. In a sense, there were many different fascisms. Even in late 1921 an observer could comment '[e]very region, every province, every village, has its *own* Fascism'.[7] Italo Balbo, the leader of the fascist movement in the province of Ferrara, stated significantly in his *Diario 1922* that his blackshirts paid little attention to national politics, simply following their noses in the local battles they were fighting: 'It is extraordinary how my *squadristi* do not know even the names of the ministers who have resigned or of those in office.'[8]

Understandably, even in these early years it is Mussolini who attracts the attention of historians as the dominant personality. But attention to his figure should not detract from the reality of an early Fascism that was anything but a monolithic movement driving all before it in unified and disciplined manner. In this respect we should try to avoid the temptation to read back into the early movement the image of coherence and unity that the regime was to try to create for itself in later years. Rather, from the beginning and despite the lofty rhetoric of national renewal, there is an almost curiously municipal character to much of the early Fascism, as if the movement were, at times, more concerned to unseat the local socialist mayor and his councillors or to regain control of provincial committees than to effect the national palingenesis. And in fact, very often, this was the case. In many areas, Fascism did little more than reproduce the interests and priorities of its most

    [4] Frank Demers, *Le origini del fascismo a Cremona*, Rome & Bari, Laterza, 1979.
    [5] Colarizi, *Dopoguerra e fascismo in Puglia*. Exceptionally for the South of Italy, the socio-economic conditions in the Tavoliere region of Puglia were similar to those in the lower Po Valley.
    [6] For an overview see Fabbri, *Origini*, Chapter 4; also Roberto Vivarelli, *Storia delle origini del Fascismo. L'Italia dall grande guerra alla marcia su Roma*, Bologna, Il Mulino, 1991, vol. 2, Chapter 4. Fabbri rightly notes the degree to which the socialist movement, although formally a national movement, had itself often been dominated by local rather than national considerations.
    [7] Guido Bergamo, quoted in Gentile, *Storia*, 321.
    [8] Italo Balbo, *Diario 1922*, Milan, Mondadori, 1932, 29.

influential local supporters, who saw in the new movement the opportunity to reassert lost influence and regain positions undermined by the turmoil of the immediate postwar years.[9] In a wider sense, it did no more than reproduce one of the characteristics of Italian politics since unification—that of local issues frequently assuming a greater importance than national questions.

It was this fundamental tension between the local and the national that was to constitute one of the main problems for the fascist organization throughout the 1920s and, to some extent, during the 1930s as well. Unity of a sort within the fascist movement was initially achieved because, even if local expressions of Fascism might be very different, the patriotic, nationalist, and anti-socialist impulses that informed the movement were shared by all. In the same way, the common denunciation of the 'old' politics of Giolitti was a unifying factor; political parties were attacked violently, accused of doing no more than divide the nation through perpetual argument, and parliament itself was vilified. In this sense the early Fascism represented a revolt *against* Rome, seen as generating corruption and inefficiency through the constant process of wheeler-dealing and political brokerage. Here the fascists had a point. A feature of pre-war government had been the way in which parliamentary majorities had often been built around the concession of favours to interest groups. A crucial vote on a major bill might be worth a bridge or a road in the province of the deputy concerned, who viewed national politics essentially as a resource and was frequently more concerned about his own backyard than about wider questions. Rome was seen by the fascists, therefore, as the great corrupter of politics, the place where deals were done and where favours were exchanged behind closed doors.

Contempt for the complex machinations of the centre was one of the characteristics of fascist attitudes in the provinces. Provincial fascists prided themselves on a direct and clear-cut method of dealing with problems—cudgels, pistols, and daggers, rather than words, were their preferred weapons. But there was a paradoxical aspect to these attitudes. Despite the constant repetition of national and patriotic themes in fascist propaganda, in many of the first expressions of Fascism there was a strong and conscious element of what can only be termed provincial subversion of the central state as such—a subversion that, even in the quest for a new nation, drew on a renewed affirmation of local autonomies and local identity. It was an irony of the situation that the anti-party, anti-parliament positions assumed by many fascists on the grounds that parties and parliament divided the nation, were expressed through a political battle that often had itself the appearance of an extremely divisive and largely local struggle, equally destructive of many elements of national cohesion.

To a great extent the tension between national and local was also the tension between the fascist ideal, of the kind elaborated by Lanzillo, which was undoubtedly

---

[9] In many areas of the North *comuni* found themselves without funds in the aftermath of the conflict. Landowners were particularly concerned about the attempts of new, local, socialist administrations to implement a direct tax on land and on wealth in order to improve the financial position of the *comune* and insert some element of social equity into the tax structure, based largely on indirect taxes. For the socialist programme of Perugia, for example, see Loreto Di Nucci, *Lo Stato-partito del fascismo. Genesi, evoluzione e crisi 1919–1943*, Bologna, Il Mulino, 2009, 56.

national in its vision, and political reality, which tended to have a local dimension. National palingenesis worked well as a theme as long as it was limited to words; it was less useful as a guide when it came to dealing with the realities of local politics, where manoeuvring, bargaining, and compromise were always part of the game. Provincial fascist movements found early on that provincial politics were far from being the simple confrontation implied by the initial battles against the local socialist or Catholic unions. These were not the only powerful groups in local politics and adjustments to other important local interests—often conservative interests—had to be made. When fascist 'new objectives' met up against 'old power', compromises often became unavoidable. Such compromises were usually justified on the grounds of immediate necessity, as being no more than the temporary means to a different end, and many of the early fascists undoubtedly reasoned in this way. But time would show them to be mistaken. As often happens, the means came to determine the ends—which is to say that the characteristics of the fascist regime were in many cases determined by the ways in which the fascists gained and held on to power. And, precisely because the fascist seizure of power was almost everywhere in the North and the centre primarily a local battle, reflecting local issues and involving local power struggles, the Fascism that emerged triumphant after 1925 was heavily marked by problems and solutions associated with regional and provincial movements.

This fragmentation was most evident in respect of agrarian Fascism, developing in the lower Po Valley provinces of Bologna and Ferrara in the autumn of 1920. Even if Mussolini had moved more explicitly to the right in the course of 1919 and 1920—the May 1920 congress of the *fasci* saw many of the more radical proposals of 1919 either abandoned or relegated to a lower priority—his awareness of the need to avoid closing the door to popular support remained constant. Thus it was not unexpected when, in late 1920, his first reaction to the operation of the brutal fascist action squads in the province of Ferrara was to welcome their formation as the new and specially characterizing element of the fascist movement but to disown their violence against the rural working class as being no more than the actions of a reactionary guard of the bourgeoisie. He was evidently alarmed about the complaint from a leading young fascist that, in Ferrara, the movement was made up mainly of 'priests and agrarians'. No doubt reflecting the views of Mussolini, Umberto Pasella, the secretary of the national movement and resident in Milan, accused the Ferrara *fascio* of following 'an entirely local rather than national policy' and warned that 'if you intend to give the *fascio* the character of an organization prone to the wishes of the employers, you will clash with the [fascist] programme, forcing the C[entral] C[ommittee] to take necessary but painful measures'. Yet, within days, the leadership in Milan had understood its mistake, making a complete about-turn in order not to lose the chance offered by the collapse of the socialist movement in the province of Ferrara. Rather than continue to reject rural reaction, Mussolini judged it better to endorse agrarian Fascism and to try to ride the tiger of provincial violence, expressed through the squads and rapidly acquiring the name of *squadrismo*.[10]

---

[10] For Ferrara, see Corner, *Fascism in Ferrara*, 128–30.

The Ferrara incident is indicative of many aspects of the emerging movement. It demonstrates well the degree to which local fascist organizations, springing up at the end of 1920 and the beginning of 1921, were often largely autonomous initiatives, usually invoking Mussolini as their inspiration but in no sense controlled by him. Provincial leaders were happy to call themselves fascist, pay their respects to Mussolini (often through no more than the occasional exchange of telegram), and then do what they deemed most suited to their own situation. This relatively autonomous origin of many local leaders was to have significant consequences in later years, as we shall see. Further, the embarrassment caused initially in Milan by the explosion of agrarian Fascism and the *volte-face* of the Milan directorate in respect of it shows the way in which Mussolini—the great opportunist—was always prepared to adjust his position, even radically, in order to take advantage of the prevailing political wind. But, above all, the Ferrara incident is indicative of a fundamental switch in the emphases of Fascism itself. Prior to late 1920 the Fascism of Milan had been violent at times, particularly when the demobilized *arditi* shock troops, loyal to Mussolini, had been involved in actions. Yet fascist politics had not been based almost exclusively on violence; there had been many, largely unsuccessful, attempts to attract support through policy statements and the traditional methods of the politics of the period. When Mussolini embraced the activities of the *squadristi* of Ferrara, he also embraced a Fascism characterized by a profound belief in the capacity of violence to resolve contentious issues, by a total intolerance of any opposition, and by a military approach to political questions. As a result of the successful onslaught of the fascist squads in the Po Valley, the precepts of action, violence, conflict, and intolerance became the controlling precepts of the fascist movement.[11]

Manoeuvre as he might in the following months and in later years in order to control and direct these tendencies, Mussolini was never able to do other than accept them as central to fascist thought and action. The imprinting which the movement received from the agrarian Fascism of the Po Valley was too strong to be removed. Thus, in many respects, it was the local movement that determined the way in which the national movement would present itself to the world in later years.

The fascist experience in the province of Ferrara made evident a further reality. As is well known, Fascism presented itself as the *new* movement, distinct and different from other groups, playing greatly on the aspect of novelty. Undoubtedly the first fascists gained a great deal of support from this self-representation, particularly among the young. But during the course of 1920 it was obvious to all that the movement was experiencing great difficulty in growing on its own. In the cities

---

[11] On the central role of violence in establishing a fascist 'identity' see Adrian Lyttelton, 'Cause e caratteristiche della violenza fascista. Fattori costanti e fattori congiunturali', in Luciano Casali (ed.), *Bologna 1920. Le origini del fascismo*, Bologna, Cappelli, 1982. More recent considerations on the role of violence can be found in Albanese, *Alle origini*, Chapter V, and Ibid., 'Dire violenza, fare violenza. Espressione, minaccia, occultamento e pratica della violenza durante la Marcia su Roma', (2003) *Memoria e ricerca* May–August, 13. See also now Michael R. Ebner, *Ordinary Violence in Mussolini's Italy*, Cambridge, Cambridge University Press, 2011.

and provincial capitals of the North it became clear that Fascism needed allies in order to develop as a credible political force. As a consequence, alliances were formed. To be useful politically, the allies were necessarily found among the more influential elements present in provincial society and, in the circumstances of 1920, frequently came from a kind of middle class mobilization that was emerging in the face of the apparently unstoppable rise of provincial socialism. Often—as in Bologna, for example—the new allies were middle-class patriotic and nationalist associations;[12] frequently they were the organizations of shopkeepers;[13] sometimes they were important economic interests centred around major industries. Often these alliances were decisive in the survival of the *fascio*. For example, it is clear that the turning point for the fascists in Ferrara came with the concrete financial and material support given to the action squads by the Agrarian Association in late 1920, support subsequently reinforced by the Association's use of its renewed control of the labour market to compel the political submission of the socialist leagues of the workers. Here the new was very much in cahoots with the old and, inevitably, alliances had their costs and produced their critics. In Ferrara, Italo Balbo justified dependence on his newly found friends by arguing that it represented a necessary, and indeed a desirable, compromise with the most solid and respectable representatives of provincial society—the people the fascist movement was trying to save from socialism.[14]

Obviously the patterns of development differ greatly from region to region, but some examples should serve to demonstrate the degree to which the early provincial movements were quickly linked to already-established centres of local power. In the rural areas of the North and the centre of Italy, there was almost nowhere which did not see the intervention of the proprietors in order either to launch or to strengthen the local *fasci*. Fascism permitted the landowners to wrap themselves in the national flag, linking self-interest and patriotism in a way not entirely possible before 1914. Sometimes the proprietors would hide behind a veil of anonymity, trying to give the impression that the fascists were operating autonomously, albeit admittedly in a direction favourable to the proprietors themselves. Rhetoric from the landowners about the courage of the young men, disposed to make the ultimate sacrifice on behalf of the nation, usually hid a much more self-interested and much more concrete link with the *squadristi*. Indeed, in some areas, when the local young men seemed a bit slow on the uptake—in Pavia and Alexandria, for example—the proprietors took the initiative and set up the *fascio* themselves.[15]

Often the determining factor in the exercise of influence was that of finance. The fascists needed somewhere to meet, which could be a cost; they needed weapons; above all the *squadristi*, many of whom were unemployed, often needed some

---

[12] Lyttelton, *Seizure* (1st edition, 1973), 57–61. On these themes see also Lupo, *Il Fascismo*, Chapters 1 and 2, and, more recently, Fabrizio Venafro, 'Il partito fascista a Bologna. Dalle origini al regime', (2007) *Italia contemporanea* December, 249.

[13] Jonathan Morris, *The political economy of shopkeeping in Milan, 1886–1922*, Cambridge, Cambridge University Press, 1993; Mara Anastasia, *Interessi di bottega. I piccoli commercianti italiani nella crisi dello Stato liberale 1919–1926*, Turin, Zamorani, 2007.

[14] Corner, *Ferrara*, 193–200.   [15] Lyttelton, *Seizure*, 70.

kind of payment. This last became increasingly an issue during the course of 1921, when being a member of the action squads turned more and more into a full-time occupation. A good example of the fascist movement representing a form of profitable employment was to come three years later. Allegations made against Italo Balbo at his trial in 1924 for the murder of the priest Don Minzoni spoke of the fascist leader's request for a monthly stipend of 1500 lire as a condition of becoming leader of the local *fascio*[16]—money which, if paid (as is likely), came from provincial landowners.[17] Fascism needed money to survive: it therefore needed moneyed supporters.[18]

This was true in rural areas, but it was equally true in places where industrial interests dominated. In industrial towns the strategy that had been so successful in the rural Po Valley—the strategy of open and violent attack on the landless workers—was less feasible. In zones of structural underemployment like the lower Po Valley the landless rural labourers (*braccianti*) who were killed, beaten, or exiled by the fascists could be replaced easily.[19] As the passage to Fascism in many of these provinces showed, desperation for work pushed people into the arms of the newly-formed fascist unions—the *sindacati fascisti*.[20] But skilled industrial workers were a different matter. They represented valuable assets for industrialists and they were not as easily replaced as the *braccianti*. Moreover, they were more use working than dead, injured, or exiled. The *fasci* were seen by businessmen and industrialists, therefore, as a means of restoring their control of the workforce—of breaking the unions, of exerting pressure on workers and intimidating them. The constitution of the fascist *sindacati* was a key aspect of this re-establishment of control. It was this that industrialists were prepared to pay for—but payment, of course, required results. Thus the *fasci* of the smaller towns of the Ligurian coast (not including Genoa), which had been strongly aligned with the radical Milan programme during 1919, were promised subsidies from local industrialists and newspaper owners in 1920 and promptly shifted to an anti-union stance. The influence of these local businessmen was such that, in a few cases, the *fasci* were controlled by them directly.

A really consolidated working class offered bigger problems. In the city of Genoa itself a movement similar to that which had occurred in the hinterland took place,

---

[16] See note 48 below.

[17] Corner, *Ferrara*, 251, note 1. Balbo is also alleged to have asked for a guarantee of a job in a local bank when the fascist 'battle' was finished. See also Giorgio Rochat, *Italo Balbo*, Turin, UTET, 1986, 44–5.

[18] Mimmo Franzinelli, *Squadristi! Protagonisti e tecniche della violenza fascista 1919–1922*, Milan, Mondadori, 2004; also, for a comparison of fascist and Nazi violence, Sven Reichardt, *Faschistische Kampfbünde: Gewalt und Gemeinschaft im italienischen Squadrismus und der deutschen SA*, Cologne: Böhlau, 2002 (Italian trans. *Camicie nere, camicie brune. Milizie fasciste in Italia e in Germania*, Bologna, Il Mulino 2009).

[19] The number of those killed by the fascist squads in the period before the March on Rome has never been established definitively. At the time, the socialist organizations spoke of some 2,000 deaths: the true figure may have been slightly higher. As was to be expected, given the relative lack of socialist response, fewer fascists were killed. Some estimates produce a figure of around 450. See Lyttelton, 'Violenza fascista'; Gentile, *Storia*, 475; also Fabbri, *Origini*, Appendix 1, who relies heavily on socialist documentation.

[20] See, in general, Ferdinando Cordova, *Le origini dei sindacati fascisti*, Bari, Laterza, 1974.

although much more slowly. An initial reluctance on the part of the fascists to alienate the dock workers because of their links with D'Annunzio (they had been among the strongest supporters of the Fiume occupation in 1919) eventually weakened and disappeared under the pressure of the shipowners, who had subsidized the fascist movement in the city from early 1921. As a result, the fascists turned on the dockers and a fairly lengthy process of breaking down the ship-workers' unions and cooperatives began, to be concluded only in the summer of 1922.[21] Similarly, in the steel-producing town of Terni in Umbria, the struggle was also long drawn-out because of considerable working-class resistance, and here again the victory of the fascists was realized only after collusion between the steel bosses and the fascists (who the bosses were financing), which involved the declaration of a lock-out of the factories in July 1922. This permitted the fascists, through a show of armed strength designed to intimidate even the most determined, to assert their hold on the workers' organizations at last.[22]

This kind of support from what can only be described as the economic establishment had its price. Many of the new financiers of the *fasci* belonged to the same middle class groups that had been roundly denounced by the fascists of 1919 as war profiteers and draft dodgers. Many were clearly identifiable as *notabili* who had formed part of the much deprecated old ruling group. Alliances struck by fascist organizations with the rich and the powerful provoked rifts within local movements precisely because they often made obvious a class orientation that the allegedly 'classless' Fascism of 1919 had sought to avoid. Political expediency was invoked as a justification for such alliances, but there was often embarrassment. Fascism was supposedly the new broom cleaning out the stables of cynical political manoeuvring and such alliances seemed to disprove this. Where possible, and not always with great success, the demagogy of the 'national' and anti-socialist cause was used to cover agreements with members of the local establishment.

The problems posed by this new, 'contaminated' Fascism would become immediately apparent in the summer of 1921 when Mussolini proposed a Pact of Pacification with the Catholic *Popolari* party (PPI) and the by now much-mortified socialist movement.[23] As a national political strategy it had much to recommend it, offering to broaden the base of Mussolini's support considerably and seeming to promise the constitution of that kind of mass popular movement to which the fascist leader aspired. Moreover, the Pact would have restored Mussolini's full control over the fascist movement itself—a control increasingly contested by the semi-independent agrarian Fascism. The proposal went some way to meeting the widespread accusations that fascist violence was too one-sided. D'Annunzio had declared that Fascism had become no more than 'agrarian slavery' and, in August 1921, even Mussolini himself referred to Emilian Fascism as being 'synonymous

[21] Lyttelton, *Seizure*, 68–70; also Alberico, *Origini* 81–138.

[22] For Genoa, Lyttelton, *Seizure*, 220–1; for Terni, Renato Covino, 'Dall'Umbria verde all'Umbria rossa', in Renato Covino and Giampaolo Gallo (eds), *Storia d'Italia. Le regioni dall'Unità a oggi, L'Umbria*, Turin, Einaudi, 1989, 569–70.

[23] On the evolution of the crisis surrounding the Pact of Pacification, Gentile, *Storia*, Chapter IV, 'La rivolta contro il *duce*', in particular 221, 287–8.

with terror'.[24] But the prospect of such a pact, which more or less envisaged the demobilization of the military wing of Fascism, was anathema to the provincial blackshirts, whose *raison d'être* was continuing conflict with the socialists and, to a lesser extent, with the *Popolari*. Opposition to the pact was strong, therefore, in the areas of the Po Valley where *squadrismo* had developed, where it was strongest, and where it was patently still necessary in order to maintain the political control of the fascists over the large numbers of now leaderless labourers. Making any kind of peace with the enemy carried the risk of nullifying all that had been achieved in the previous months.

But there was a further reason for opposition that should not be overlooked. At the national level many Italians had regarded Fascism as a movement that would run its course and exhaust itself within the space of a few months. Giolitti had certainly assumed as much in early 1921, inviting the fascists to join the national electoral bloc precisely in order to draw their sting. Perhaps, initially, many of the blackshirt *squadristi* had assumed as much themselves; the future of the movement was far from being immediately clear. But by the summer of 1921 the provincial leaders had already understood that their personal interests did not lie with a call to lay down their arms. The movement that had brought them to great prominence in such a short period of time—in many cases they had become the arbiters of provincial politics in less than six months—had to remain in existence as a fighting force if it was not to lose its relevance. In the province of Ferrara, to take one example, the fascist leader, Balbo, had quickly formed a close relationship with Vico Mantovani, the head of the Agrarian Association in the province, a leading freemason and a man with many important banking interests. In the uncertain context of 1921 this relationship promised Balbo, at the least, a previously undreamed-of career among the influential bourgeoisie of the provincial capital at the end of the fascist battle. The basis of the relationship was Balbo's command of the fascist squads, since it was the actions of the squads that had permitted the Agrarian Association to regain control over the workforce in the province. With the squads still active against the socialist leagues, Balbo remained one of the most important figures in the province; without the squads, he lost all importance to the Association and would no doubt have easily been pushed to one side. Mussolini's move to disarm the squads, part of the proposal for pacification, presented a threat to both political control of the province and personal position, therefore. Indeed, it is indicative of the strength and confidence of the provincial fascist movement at this point that certain of its leaders contested Mussolini's 'ownership' of the movement (in precisely those terms) and contemplated abandoning him rather than accept any kind of agreement with the socialists. It is not surprising that we find Balbo among the provincial leaders who opposed the Pact most strongly, even to the extent of considering approaches to D'Annunzio to replace Mussolini as *duce* of the fascist movement.

---

[24] At this point Mussolini argued that the squads should exercise a 'sense of limits' and that violence—'anti-human'—should always be 'intelligent' and not simply 'brutal'. Against all the evidence, he even suggested that ' fascist violence was an episode, not a system': ibid., 247, 250.

The struggle over the Pact of Pacification, a pact signed but never observed because of the opposition of the provincial leaders, was one of the first instances in which those elements that were to characterize so much of later Fascism came into play. The formal positions of the national movement (in the case of the Pact of Pacification, of Mussolini) were seen by the movement's supporters through the lens of the politics of provincial power. Often this, rather than the national question, was uppermost in their minds. This was hardly surprising. Local fascist movements inevitably and invariably produced local fascist leaders and few of these, given the momentum that Fascism quickly acquired, were prepared to renounce their positions willingly. The power they came to wield was far from illusory; not for nothing were they called the *ras*.[25] Thus, one of the problems faced by Mussolini in the early years—but, as we shall see, the problem, in a variety of forms, persisted throughout the regime—was that of a movement that had been born as a constellation of local rebellions and that, because of the personal ambitions of its local leaders, threatened to retain the characteristics of such a fragmented structure. It was no coincidence that one of the words used frequently in relation to provincial fascism in later years—that is the need to *spersonalizzare* local fascisms (to remove the personal element in the local movements)—first made its appearance in 1921.[26] In a sense this 'personalization' of the movement was a problem built into Fascism from the start, precisely because of its varied origins at the local level.

The circumstances of the early development of the fascist movement determined, therefore, that personal interest and public ideology should learn to live together. In the complex and agitated history of the provincial *fasci* during the years before 1925 many fascists continued to put forward a vision of Fascism as the instrument of national redemption. The rhetoric of national rebirth through a purifying struggle against anti-national elements remained strong. Indeed, it was reinforced by an increasing use of the myth of the Great War—in many respects the 'foundation myth' of Fascism—as a focal point for fascist devotion. At the same time, however, Fascism sought a clearer and, in some senses, more practical definition of its purpose, rendered necessary by its gradual appropriation of power and its contact with the reality of government. It was at this point that many of the tensions within the provincial federations came to the fore.

Often the rhetoric and the reality proved bad bedfellows. The high rate of depletion among the supporters of the *fasci* between 1919 and 1921, and again between 1922 and the end of 1924, was symptomatic of an umbrella movement within which different points of view vied for dominance, with losers often abandoning the field and new recruits filling the gaps. In many cases the 'dreamers' of 1919 (or, in Lanzillo's case, even before 1919) found that the new postwar world they had envisaged was slow in coming or was clearly not going to come at all. Lanzillo himself was disgusted by agrarian fascism, describing it as 'a cruel and implacable movement of interests', although he did remain within the party.[27] The case of

---

[25] A name taken from powerful North African tribal leaders.

[26] Mussolini, *Il Popolo d'Italia*, 20 October 1921; cited in Gentile, *Storia*, 359.

[27] Quoted in Lyttelton, *Seizure*, 55.

Pietro Nenni is well known: future leader of the Italian Socialist Party after 1945, he was one of the first leaders of the fascist movement in Bologna in 1919 but abandoned it quickly when he saw the direction it was taking. Many of the fascists of the original Ligurian group left the movement as a result of the obvious contamination represented by the subsidies businessmen were providing for their organization.[28]

Typical of these problems, once again, is the case of Ferrara, where a handful of the original group of fascists, residents of the provincial capital and usually of urban middle and lower middle class extraction, reacted strongly to the direction Fascism had taken in the province during the first six months of 1921. While satisfied with the defeat of the provincial socialist organization, they viewed the renewed hold gained by the Agrarian Association over the rural workforce, with all that that brought with it in terms of allocation of work and wage reductions, as a negative result of the struggle on which they had embarked. Moreover, they realized that their actions had served to weaken their own positions, as ambitious townspeople, because they had done no more than permit a reaffirmation of the control of the province by the agrarians. Their spokesman, the young industrialist Barbato Gattelli, shocked the provincial establishment with his call for 'cudgels to the right', meaning that the fascist cudgels, used up to that point against the socialist labourers and their leaders, should now be used against the landowners.

Gattelli's appeal reflected a strand of thinking that had been present in early Fascism, which liked to think of itself as anti-socialist but not anti-worker and certainly not pro-agrarian.[29] Balbo, understanding much more clearly than the dissidents the real relations of power in the province, ensured that this initiative was crushed quickly. It threatened the fascist hold on the province; as important— no doubt *more* important from Balbo's point of view—in inviting attacks on the Agrarian Association, it threatened his own position as undisputed leader of the provincial movement.[30]

In some respects this kind of conflict can be viewed as a manifestation of the differences between an 'urban' and an 'agrarian' Fascism—the first more dedicated to the ideas of 1919, the second to the realities of provincial control. With one or two notable exceptions, before the March on Rome it was the *diciannovisti,* the original urban fascists of 1919, who tended to get the worst of the argument. In many cases, contrasts within the provincial movements reflected the change occasioned in Fascism by the enormous impetus of *squadrismo,* the full impact of which was only felt during the course of 1921. From being a relatively elite movement (as many of the first fascists had envisaged), Fascism became a movement of the masses. The blackshirts, with their emphasis on military values and their belief in

[28] Alberico, *Origini,* 185–98.
[29] Gattelli could draw some encouragement from what was happening outside Ferrara. As late as September 1921, as the crisis surrounding the Pact of Pacification indicated, Mussolini himself was still playing with the idea of transforming Fascism into a kind of labour party, even suggesting that a future party might be called the 'national party of work': *Il Popolo d'Italia,* 8 September 1921, cited in Gentile, *Storia,* 327.
[30] Corner, *Ferrara,* Chapter 8.

violence and terror as the solution to all problems, and, above all, with their success, very much altered the internal balance of the fascist movement. The strong and decided reaction against the Pact of Pacification made evident that more moderate policies, aimed at a measure of reconciliation, were not to be taken into consideration.

At the same time, however, many of the struggles within the movement were less about the political line to be followed and more about personal position. Even in 1921, seniority within the movement was already an issue. In later years, the exact moment of adherence to the fascist cause was taken as a measure of sincerity. Thus, the man who joined in 1921 was likely to view the man who took the fascist *tessera* (party card) in 1927 as a mere opportunist. It was convenient to do so, not least because this served to conceal the fact that many who took up the fascist cause in 1921 were equally opportunist. What was happening in a great number of provinces both before and immediately after the March on Rome was a scarcely veiled struggle for power, as local leaders competed to assert their control and establish a power base within the movement. Small empires were being created ruthlessly and with great speed; and, often, as rapidly demolished. The degree of confusion was rendered well by an article in the newspaper *Il Secolo* in November 1921, in which the problems the fascist movement faced were analysed mercilessly: 'the trouble is that dynamism has rapidly been converted into confusion-ism and the union of free spirits into the most perfect disunion'.[31]

So-called 'dissidence' within provincial federations, so common in the early years, was a symptom of this competition. It was an indication that one group had found itself being pushed out of a controlling position by another group and now reacted by denouncing the political line adopted by its opponents. Barbato Gattelli, mentioned above, may have been genuine in his denunciation of agrarian Fascism (although it had taken him a long time to recognize his disgust). What is certain is that his position as one of the leaders of the local fascist movement had been dramatically undermined by Balbo's assumption of command of the provincial squads and by his subsequent success as military leader. To argue for a different political line was, therefore, to try to discredit Balbo and to reassert Gattelli's own position at one and the same time.

What is significant about dissidence—and there was hardly a provincial federation that did not experience something analogous to the phenomenon before 1925—is that, particularly in the smaller centres, it was frequently related to local power struggles rather than to major national issues. It assumed characteristics that were to become common in later years, when the infighting among local fascists would be referred to less as dissidence and more often as simple *beghismo* (struggles deriving from factionalism, the work of *beghisti*). In the early years, when the fascist movement was still finding its feet and manoeuvring among a large number of often equally flexible political movements and orientations, it was to be expected that there would be clashes and conflicts. To some extent Fascism had tried to be all things to all (non-socialist) men, and a progressive and greater definition of the movement

---

[31] *Il Secolo*, 3 November 1921, quoted in Gentile, *Storia*, 320.

could not but provoke tensions. Typically, the dissident movement in Ferrara claimed to represent a 'true' Fascism that had been betrayed by the increasing influence of the Agrarian Association over the provincial organization. Equally typically, the dissidents refused to recognize that, without the support of the Agrarian Association, provincial Fascism would probably never have got off the ground at all.

In public statements, the opposition of a 'true' (which often meant, in effect, 'provincial') to a 'false' Fascism was common. At the end of 1923 the young Roman fascist leader, Giuseppe Bottai, noted that he had received notice of the foundation of a *Centro Fasci Autonomi* which aimed at

> the defence of *true* Fascism against *false* Fascism (which is, naturally, that of the Party), of a league of dissident fascists, who are all *honest*, against the disciplined fascists, who are all *dishonest*, of a cohort of *pure* fascists to be formed around Benito Mussolini, to save him from the *impure* fascists who surround him... [Often, he observed in the same article, people were invoking the name of Mussolini *against* local federations] oppressed by the irresponsible tyranny of a local boss or fed up with his unbearable arrogance...[32]

Bottai's comments were clearly referred to the situation in the North and centre of Italy, where the creation of personal 'feuds' had become most apparent. The South of Italy presented a different picture, although there were some marked similarities with what had occurred in the North. With the exception of the Puglia region, the South had not witnessed an aggressively strong socialist movement in the immediate postwar years. As a consequence, *squadrismo* was much less a feature of the southern movement, which threw up leaders with few of the characteristics of the northern *ras*. Fascism—which, contrary to some accounts, did have its supporters in the South before 1922—had been less the movement of anti-socialist forces than that of those 'new' groups—young urban professionals or radicalized returning soldiers—who saw in Fascism the instrument with which to contest the political control of local landholding elites.[33] Reacting to the challenge and hoping to forestall the danger, the *notabili* of the elites often made their own approaches to Fascism, provoking local contests between rival groupings and often generating unlikely alliances. In these struggles, Mussolini and, after October 1922, the fascist government in Rome, often became the third point of a triangle, as leaders of local factions appealed to the influence of the centre in order to gain the upper hand against their immediate local rivals. Reference to Rome greatly increased after 1923 compared to what had been the practice before 1914—something which reflected a new situation in which there were new players. Even so, there was no hiding the fact that the 'national' was functional to what was essentially local. In the South, as in other areas of Italy, there were few doubts that what was in question was local control.[34]

---

[32] *Critica Fascista*, 1 December 1923.

[33] The role of the demobilized soldiers in Sardinia in the years immediately after the war is underlined in Sechi, *Dopoguerra*.

[34] For the characteristics of southern Fascism, see Chapter 5, 5.3 'Provincial factionalism in action', below.

The strength of local fascisms and the pretensions of the local leaders were to remain a constant source of problems for Mussolini throughout most of the 1920s. While the mass of the *squadristi* idolized him, he could never be sure that all his lieutenants were totally loyal to him. Unlike Hitler, and unlike his own position in the 1930s, Mussolini remained for many of his companions a *primus inter pares* who could be dispensed with if necessary. Reactions to the Pact of Pacification had made this obvious. Both before and after the March on Rome, therefore, he found himself manoeuvring against the political establishment without a base he could trust implicitly. The position was undoubtedly complex. On one hand, the fascist movement drew its strength from the force constituted by the local federations; on the other, attempts to control the same federations risked damaging the movement itself and rendering it vulnerable to attack. Precisely because of the way it had developed in much of the country (as a series of relatively autonomous rebellions and reactions), the fascist movement continued to express strong centrifugal forces. As one journalist put it in November 1921, '[t]hose who have talked about and discussed Fascism as if it were a national movement have been deceived or have deceived. There exist various regional movements, sometimes also provincial [movements], but a national Fascism, no.'[35] It is true that the logic of the local movements pointed to the control of the nation; but this was in large part because, without the control of the nation, the local movements would inevitably wither and decline. As Balbo said in his Diary, '[t]he local situations don't count if the entire life of the nation doesn't change'.[36] Power in Rome meant continued power in the provinces, where the forces of Fascism lay. Attempts by Mussolini to discipline these forces risked being tantamount to cutting off the branch on which he was sitting.

2.2. TOWARDS CENTRALIZATION?

The need for some kind of centralized discipline was recognized early on. In particular, the substantially new form of Fascism represented by the agrarian Fascism of the Po Valley seriously threatened to develop its own momentum and to ignore any attempts at control from Milan. From the point of view of the Milan Central Committee it also threatened to become a new Fascism that was working far too obviously for the interests of its financiers. Umberto Pasella, the secretary of the movement in 1919 and 1920, attempted to curb these tendencies, insisting that donations made to individual *fasci* should be handed over to the Milan committee, who would then see to their redistribution according to need. Control of the purse strings was considered a good way to realize influence over autonomous initiatives. Such a policy naturally provoked tensions when individual *fasci* and provincial federations saw money being taken away from them, and it is to be doubted that obedience was anywhere much more than purely verbal. Subsidies coming to the *fasci* from the large Agrarian Associations of the Po Valley or from small industrialists

[35] *Il Secolo*, 3 November 1921, quoted in Gentile, *Storia*, 320.   [36] Balbo, *Diario*, 20.

in Tuscany or Liguria could be made in a large number of ways that would elude the attention of the Central Committee in Milan. And, with much the same logic that determined the viewpoints of the local fascists, people giving subsidies usually did so for motives related to local issues and wanted to see their money spent on those issues. In reality, the often close personal relations between local fascist leaders and rich donors made centralized control from Milan virtually impossible.[37] This, of course, did considerably increase the risk that Fascism would be exploited by such donors, whose contributions were far from disinterested.

Discipline of a different kind *was* realized during the course of 1921 through a restructuring of the fascist organizations, but with rather unexpected results. As (in many of the northern provinces) the movement expanded from the provincial capital to the other, lesser, provincial centres, and as a large number of new provincial *fasci* were founded in the rural hinterlands, the original urban *fascio* often began to lose its dominant position within the province. As we have seen in Ferrara, real power shifted from the city fascists, frequently representatives of the Fascism of 1919, to the mixed bag of rural fascists—large and small proprietors, sharecroppers, landless labourers attracted by the fascist programme for land distribution[38]—who all had different interests from those of the city fascists and were frequently to be found among the blackshirt *squadristi*. Provincial federations were set up to incorporate the new *fasci*, inevitably much more influenced by the big landowners than the city *fascio* had been, and in many areas—usually justified by a call to discipline imposed by the new militarization of the movement—any kind of 'democratic' organizing of the federation was abandoned. Virtual local dictators were created through this process. It was not unusual for their provinces to be referred to as satrapies or feuds given that, in the majority of cases, the state had all but abdicated its authority and the prefect did what the fascist leader told him to do.[39]

As we have seen with the Pact of Pacification, the problem for Mussolini was that these local dictators—the *ras*—could not always be relied on to follow the political line of the leader, particularly when it threatened to affect their own interests adversely. The consolidation of the positions of such people at the provincial level, which was a consequence of administrative restructuring, risked making the question of the internal discipline of the movement more rather than less critical. Mussolini recognized this openly when, in September 1921, he wrote an article that, in later years, may well have come to haunt him for its continued accuracy. Lamenting a serious degeneration of Fascism, he went on to make a caustic analysis

---

[37] In his massively researched list of donors to the fascist cause between October 1921 and March 1925, Gerardo Padullo has found no contributions from the provinces of Bologna, Cremona, or Ferrara mentioned in the party records. This suggests that these provincial federations managed successfully to resist all attempts at central control of their finances. It is also worth noting that Padulla's list of donors to the fascist cause significantly includes few contributions from the South before October 1922. G. Padullo, 'I finanziatori del Fascismo', (2010) *Le carte e la storia*, quaderno n.1, 2010.

[38] Gaetano Polverelli, 'La posizione del Fascismo di fronte alla questione agraria', *Il Popolo d'Italia*, 27 January 1921.

[39] See, for example, Balbo, *Diario*, 20: 'The Prefect has to do what I tell him to do in the name of the fascists.'

of the situation, observing that, instead of being 'a proud movement of national unity in this poor Italy, murdered by a thousand *campanilismi*, it is disintegrating into a regionalism that acts on its own; this regionalism disintegrates into provincialism and this collapses into the communalism of Portolongone, which proclaims itself the axis of world history'.[40]

Both the Pact of Pacification and the formation of the *Partito Nazionale Fascista* (PNF) in late 1921 can be seen as manoeuvres dictated by Mussolini's need to control an unruly and fragmented movement. Defeated over the Pact, Mussolini managed to win the day over the formation of the party, even though the proposal faced tough opposition from many of those who had spent the previous two years denouncing the divisive effects of party politics, party cards, and party politicians and who believed, no doubt sincerely, that Fascism was best advanced by attempting to be something different from the traditional politics. Even with this victory, however, Mussolini's position was not fully guaranteed. The party statute stressed the need for 'order, discipline and hierarchy' which promised well for the fascist leader, but was equally useful as a tool for the affirmation of the provincial bosses within their own territory. As head of the party's new *Direzione* Mussolini's authority was re-established after the challenges made to him over both the Pact of Pacification and the formation of the party, but formally he was still obliged to consult the *Direzione*, in which many of the provincial bosses were represented. This meant that the problem represented by the provincial bosses, the tension between the local and often personal priorities of such people and the national vision, continued to exist even after the establishment of the PNF. Indeed, the problems constituted by the 'provincial Fascisms', as Mussolini termed them, would continue to exist for many years to come.

Some of Mussolini's difficulties lay in the fact that, in the move towards power, the military side of Fascism was the aspect that was most visible. The political manoeuvrings were less open—there were rumours of this and rumours of that—and were less capable of catching the public eye. The military side was essentially local. Balbo's March on Ravenna in September 1921 and his occupation of Ferrara in May 1922 were notable and well-publicized achievements, representing as they did the total subversion of the authority of the state, and there were many other such actions of only slightly lesser importance. These events inevitably threw the squads into the forefront of attention—and the squads were formed on a local basis. They sometimes acted outside their own province—the March on Ravenna by the Ferrara blackshirts is a case in point—but generally they drew their collective identity from their area of provenance. Their names, their immediate memories, their 'martyrs' were related to their locality. It was the 'Ferrara fascists' who attacked the Oltretorrente district of Parma in 1922, the 'Perugini' (from Perugia) who were called in to beat up the members of the dissident *fascio* in Ferrara in June 1923. Balbo himself recorded in his Diary for 1922 that the *squadristi* had a very local orientation, 'the fascist squad of a hundred or two hundred men operated in

---

[40] *Il Popolo d'Italia*, 25 September 1921. Portolongone is synonymous with 'the back of beyond'.

the shadow of its own church tower. It barely knew the local leader and had seen the provincial commander only in the distance.'[41]

In a sense even the March on Rome did little to change this. The actual March itself was more like a national rally of the squads than a genuine *coup d'état*; the real work was done in the provincial centres where blackshirt squads occupied town halls, prefectures, police stations, and post and telegraph offices, sometimes after fairly bloody exchanges with the army. Again, the degree to which the fascist movement was very much the sum of a large number of separate local movements, each acting within its own locality, was underlined by these actions. And, despite appearances of a victory in Rome, it was apparent, particularly to the provincial *squadristi* themselves, that the reality of the situation was that of a country in which a large element of control had *already* passed to the fascists in the central and northern provinces and that this was the determining factor in the King bowing to necessity and calling Mussolini to office.

2.3. THE *RAS* AND REVISIONISM

Mussolini, once appointed President of the Council in late October 1922, appreciated the need to discipline and control the unwieldy vehicle that had carried him to power. He still had to be careful that '*squadrismo* does not eat up Fascism'.[42] Power at the centre, achieved through the conquest of the provinces, had now to be used to control the provinces themselves. Continued violence risked being counterproductive, although it did allow the fascist leader to present himself to more moderate opinion as the only person able to keep the hotheads on the leash, standing between the survivors of liberal Italy and those straining to get at them. As always where fascist mass support was concerned, he had to try to play it both ways. A strong disciplined fascist movement could only reinforce his position, particularly in the choppy waters of coalition government and attempted 'normalization' after two years of virtual civil war; a weakened movement, shorn (through excessive control) of its dynamism and its volcanic and violent energy, might result in a jeopardizing of his negotiating stance.

Mussolini was well aware that, while it briefly revived hopes among some of the original 1919ers for an end to the domination of the squads, his own strategy of normalization, of attempted conciliation with Catholic and moderate liberal and democratic groups (there was even a suggestion of an invitation to reformist socialists to join his government), contrasted directly with the desires of some of his staunchest provincial supporters. Certain of the *ras* had understood that the term 'fascist revolution' was to mean something much more radical than the leadership of a parliamentary coalition. In a way, Mussolini had a warning of this discontent almost immediately after his assumption of power. Absent from Italy on his first (and last) visit to London in early December 1922, he learned that, instigated by

---

[41] Balbo, *Diario,* 88.   [42] Mussolini to Grandi, quoted in Gentile, *Storia*, 632.

Roberto Farinacci, the 'intransigent'[43] *ras* of Cremona and one of the principal provincial bosses, and Edmondo Rossoni, the leader of the fascist union organization, the squads and the fascist unions were threatening, on their own initiative, a general mobilization throughout northern Italy to oppose D'Annunzio's strange new plan for a national reconciliation based on a kind of grand alliance of workers—something that Mussolini had himself appeared to support. Not for the last time, Mussolini was forced to back-track in the face of his undisciplined, but very strong, supporters.[44] To appease them he ordered, in mid-December 1922, a police drive against D'Annunzio's legionaries and against parallel anarchist groups allied with them, to be followed in a matter of days by a similar action against the communist party (a warrant was issued for the arrest of Antonio Gramsci). This served to allay for a time the dissatisfactions of a 'revolutionary' provincial fascism, inclined to feel itself betrayed by Mussolini's top hats and morning dress and what it regarded as his exaggerated 'ministerialism'. But it did leave questions in many minds—Mussolini's foremost, perhaps—about whether the tail was not wagging the dog.

The necessity for action following the March on Rome was made evident by the conviction of many *squadristi* that, with a partially fascist government in power, they could act with even greater impunity than before. In some areas the violence of the squads had assumed a momentum of its own, which responded little to the calls for discipline issued by central authority. Immediately following the March, Giuseppe Bottai unleashed his squads against the workers of the Rome district of San Lorenzo, resulting in several dead and a large number of wounded.[45] Even worse, in December, were the infamous 'Turin incidents', in which the working class district of the town was besieged by *squadristi* who, very methodically, murdered and maimed at will. Although casualty numbers have remained uncertain, it is probable that more than forty people were killed in a single night. In both cases the police did nothing to stop the fascists.[46] These actions constituted an authentic reign of terror (something the literature often fails to attribute to Italian Fascism), albeit limited in time.

Following these events there were calls, even from moderate fascist supporters, for the squads to be disbanded. Instead, Mussolini's reaction was to announce the formation of the *Milizia Volontaria di Sicurezza Nazionale* (MVSN)—the fascist militia. Formally, the task of the new MVSN was far from clear. Its declared objective was decidedly and no doubt deliberately opaque—'to protect the inevitable developments of the revolution of October [1922]...'—but the intention was obviously to regularize the position of the *squadristi* (many were without any kind

[43] 'Intransigent' was the term applied to the more radical fascists, generally of provincial extraction, who sought a total transformation of the structures of the state and rejected compromise with the existing establishment. This position was often, though not necessarily, linked to violence; Italo Balbo, for example, was a proponent of violence, but in no sense an intransigent.

[44] Lyttelton, *Seizure,* 103.

[45] Lidia Piccioni, *San Lorenzo. Un quartiere romano durante il Fascismo,* Rome, Edizioni di Storia e Letteratura, 1982, 35–7.

[46] Lupo, *Il Fascismo,* 163–4.

of job after a year or more on the fascist trail) and to impose discipline, while at the same time leaving the ex-*squadristi* with a specific role (and a uniform) in local society.[47] In some ways this was no more than a sop but it was an essential sop. It responded to a wide feeling among the provincial blackshirts that they had not 'carried out the revolution', as they put it, in order simply to fade away unnoticed, and probably unemployed, into the provincial society from which they had emerged. Many could not have failed to see that their local leaders were often already well placed and that the March on Rome had done nothing to stem the flow of money coming from prominent financiers.

The creation of the MVSN had some effect on the situation, even if the new body met with some resistance from many *squadristi*. The time taken for the far-from-simple process of organization and reorganization served to some extent to take the wind out of the sails of an exultant *squadrismo* and to fudge the issue of the real implications for the future. Yet many of the characteristics of the squads remained after the formation of the MVSN—indeed, many of the squads remained in existence *de facto* and continued famously in acts of violence throughout 1923 and often beyond. Don Minzoni did not live to denounce his aggressors; Giovanni Amendola did, but only briefly.[48] Most significant was the continuing sentiment that *squadrismo* represented the true face of Fascism, bestowing on the *squadristi* a kind of moral authority within the movement that others seemed neither to possess nor to be able to challenge. It was an authority that grew out of the mysticism of violence, of risk, and of death which, when linked to the fast developing myth of the Great War, produced a legitimation of fascist actions which was to remain at the centre of fascist ideology throughout the regime. But it was a legitimation derived from the militants' own initiatives. They—the blackshirts from before the March on Rome—claimed the right to speak for Fascism, inventing for themselves a robust tradition almost overnight. This was an uncomfortable tradition for Mussolini. It lent strength to that kind of Fascism over which, before 1925, he exercised only uncertain control, precisely because its legitimacy did not derive from him and threatened on many occasions to assume a dimension of its own. However, in this respect, it is worth repeating that most of the ordinary *squadristi* were extremely loyal to the person of Mussolini. The problem, if anything, was that on occasions—considering themselves the 'most fascist' of the fascists—they seemed to take on themselves the task of defending Mussolini against himself.

---

[47] The MVSN—'serving God and the Fatherland'—was initially intended to be unpaid, except for officers and for those who served outside their *comune* of residence. For many *squadristi* who did not want to move, the Militia represented a solution to their problems in terms of status, but not in terms of money. See text of the decree proposing the formation of the MVSN in *Corriere della Sera*, 29 December 1922. The final version of the decree (RD 14 January 1923, n. 31) is reproduced in Aquarone, *L'Organizzazione*, Appendix 3, 332–3. Many of the officers were former army officers who enrolled for the pay rather than from any fascist conviction.

[48] Don Minzoni was a priest murdered by fascists in the province of Ferrara in 1923; Giovanni Amendola was a liberal politician, badly beaten in December 1923 and again, with fatal consequences, in July 1925. Amendola is generally credited with inventing the word 'totalitarian' to describe Fascism, a term ironically picked up and used with approval by Mussolini.

Although the creation of the MVSN was clearly a veiled move against the local leaders, the weight of many of the provincial *ras* continued to be felt just as strongly after the formation of the militia. Indeed, in some respects the fascist victory induced something of a crisis within the movement as the proponents of the various positions felt more secure in voicing their criticisms of the others. Institutional oscillation reflected these tensions, as a three- or sometimes four-way fight began between government, party leaders, MVSN, and provincial bosses. Moreover, the state bureaucracy, inherited from liberal Italy, was also beginning to make its presence felt. The fascist Grand Council's creation of the *high commissioners* early in 1923,[49] an attempt to give the provincial movement representation within a more formal structure (and thus to control them to some extent), showed the dangers of giving too much room to the provinces. The *commissari* were selected from among the most powerful *ras* and, together, in their reunions, they formed a formidable pressure group, even though, in the event, they could agree on little. The danger of institutionalizing a committee of his potential opponents rapidly became apparent to Mussolini, and it was small wonder that the *alti commissari* were disbanded in April. Significantly, however, the provinces had to be compensated and the new Executive Board, which replaced the old *Direzione* of the PNF, inevitably included several powerful provincial leaders, among them the intransigent hard-liner, Roberto Farinacci.[50] Despite the organizational juggling, therefore, the problem refused to go away.

It was the revisionist crisis of the summer and autumn of 1923 that made the lines of division even more obvious. The crisis centred around the figure of Massimo Rocca—one of the first fascists and a representative of the moderate, urban, wing of the movement. Rocca's campaign for a reform of the party structures—which would, in effect, bring about a greater discipline within the fascist movement and restore the central authority of the state—found support among others who wished to reduce the influence of the provincial leaders. It was, in a sense, a call for a renewed emphasis to be given to the more urban, political Fascism that had seemed to be swamped by provincial influences. Rocca put his finger on the problem when he pointed out that the fascist revolution had been 'carried out *by* fascists, but *for* Italy, and not *for* the fascists themselves'. He showed a clear appreciation of what was going on when he wrote of the 'parody of revolution' being enacted in the provinces and denounced the existence of 'pseudo-Mussolinis in miniature' and 'little provincial dictators' who aped the *duce*, unbeknown to him.[51] His position also reflected a difference of style between the elitist fascist and nationalist intellectuals and the 'cattle raisers' (Bottai's dismissive description of the *ras*) of the provinces.

Mussolini's immediate sympathies probably lay with the revisionists; a tightening of structures within a kind of 'normalized' authoritarianism was very much the

---

[49] The Grand Council of Fascism, formed of some twenty of the leading members of the movement, was created in December 1922 as a kind of parallel to the cabinet of government. It exercised relatively little influence during the regime, making itself felt most markedly on 25 July 1943, when it voted its creator, Mussolini, out of office.

[50] Lyttelton, *Seizure*, 182–4.

[51] Massimo Rocca, 'Fascismo e Paese', *Critica fascista*, 1, 7, 15 September 1923.

direction in which he was aiming to go. But, again, he could not go too far in their support. As always, it was something of a balancing act. Whatever the fascist politicians of Rome thought, the backbone of the movement lay in the provinces and could not be provoked beyond a certain level without great risk of rebellion and serious dissidence, which often involved veiled threats of secession from the movement. The menace of 'autonomous' fascisms lay only a little way below the surface and had to be respected.

A closer look at the revisionist crisis of mid- and late 1923 is instructive about what was going on within the fascist movement. Essentially, the revisionists wanted a return to *politics* after the years of violence and illegality; they put the state rather than the movement at the centre of their thinking. Their moderation and desire for compromise with a chastened establishment was not a renunciation of fascist supremacy, but it did imply that the original forces of provincial Fascism—rough-edged, undisciplined, and violent—should play a less important role in the future. Rocca even managed to observe that '[n]on-fascist Italy, everywhere and in every social class, is giving a good lesson in discipline to fascist Italy'.[52]

For the revisionists like Bottai, after the March on Rome the provincial fascists could only be counterproductive in the campaign to form a new state around a new elite. Writing in mid-1923, Bottai did not mince words in his attacks on provincial leaders. Recognizing the need for discipline but at the same time acknowledging some of the negative effects of appointments made from above, he described a situation which (he was not to know) would become all too common in the 1930s:

> ...at his *investiture* the dishonest man prepares his nest. He never abandons it again. He defends it tooth and claw. Cunning, like all villains who have made it, he gets hold of the disciplinary regulations and makes them his bible. Locked in the fortress of the hierarchy, he shoots out denunciations and proscriptions. When, every now and then, he makes contact with the people, it is never to discuss, to reason, to persuade, but— serious-faced—to review a *falange* of youngsters, closed in silence, which the newspapers call mystical in order to justify it in some way.[53]

Bottai was unable to hide his disdain for many of the provincial leaders:

> There is a fascist rhetoric which does more harm to our cause than a thousand articles of the opposition. It is the rhetoric of courage, shown off, dealt out, served in every kind of sauce. It is the clumsy rhetoric of the Sunday meeting, of the newspapers directed and written by illiterates. It is the unproductive rhetoric of men who, passing from a state of agitation to one of calm, feel they have lost their identity.[54]

Repelled by provincial power, he protested against 'the tyrannical, impulsive, and abusive use [of power] adopted by the greater part of the local chiefs'.[55]

---

[52] Ibid. In an article only two weeks later Rocca would refer to the provincial fascists as 'a new and authentic breed of subversives beautified by the tricolour...who demand the perpetuation of a provincial and feudal militia'; 'Diciotto Brumaio', (1923) 1(8) *Critica fascista*, October 1923.

[53] *Critica fascista*, 1 September 1923.

[54] *Corriere italiano*, 8 January 1924. Bottai here noted acutely the link between violence and fascist identity.

[55] *Critica fascista*, 1 October 1923.

Much aware of the *conservative* nature of many people's support for Fascism, the revisionists sought to bridle the provincial movement, with its 'peasants' and its 'yokels', but in so doing they risked throwing the baby out with the bathwater. Ultimately they were unsuccessful, defeated by the powerful interests stacked against them, but the movement did encourage some moderate fascists within the provincial federations to try to reassert themselves. Usually, however, they did so from a position of weakness, and Rocca's eventual expulsion from the party in May 1924 was a clear indication that the provincial *ras* could still make themselves felt when they wanted.

The ambiguities of the situation were made evident by the Acerbo electoral law of autumn 1923 and the run-up to the 1924 elections. In itself the law, which guaranteed a majority prize to the winning party, presented no problems to most fascists. Few doubted that Fascism would win that prize. What was much more a matter of contest was the electoral method. The more intransigent provincial leaders—Farinacci in pride of place—supported the idea of single member constituencies, clearly because this was a method over which they could exert the maximum control in the choice of deputies and thereby retain for the provincial federations a hold over the parliamentary workings of the party. Mussolini's insistence on a national majority-list system, in which the deputies were appointed from a central list drawn up in Rome, greatly reduced the possibilities of manoeuvre for the *ras*. Here was yet another instance of procedural measures being used to impose discipline. But even here, the party *direttorio* could not afford to go too far; it was, as everyone knew, the 'cattle raisers' who would be responsible for organizing the vote in the provinces and for securing a majority, and party officials would offend them at their peril.

A strong element of mutual dependence naturally determined caution on both sides. In the end it was the need for the fascist movement to mount a united (and very aggressive) front against liberal and, more particularly, Catholic opposition that produced agreement on Mussolini's position rather than any humiliating climb-down by the intransigents. Certainly the claims of the *ras* to be the leading edge of Fascism—the real men as opposed to the despised politicians—were put into perspective by the passage of the Acerbo law, although not decisively; if anything, it confirmed the deep-seated conviction among many of them that something had to be done about parliament itself. In the end, more threatening for the provincial federations was the neat little passage of an 'incompatibility clause' by the fascist Grand Council immediately after the 1924 elections, which stated that those provincial leaders who had been elected would have to resign their local party positions in order to take up their parliamentary seats.[56] Had the Matteotti crisis not intervened, there can be few doubts that great pressure would have been applied from the centre in the selection of new, more amenable, provincial party secretaries.

---

[56] The same circular that announced the implementation of the 'incompatibility clause', also denounced 'that litigious and paralysing localism, which is so often overrated and held to be the quintessence of Fascism': Lyttelton, *Seizure*, 188.

2.4. PROVINCIAL POWER AND PERSONAL POSITION

Although it was the Matteotti crisis that would make plain, and in the end to some degree resolve, the acute tensions between a centralizing, national Fascism and the fragmented Fascism of the northern and central provincial federations, it would be no exaggeration to say that these tensions had been one of the dominant features of the fascist movement from the moment of the explosion of agrarian Fascism in late 1920 and early 1921. Indeed, the crisis within the movement in 1923 was no more than an indication that such unity as there had been before the March on Rome had been created by the circumstances of the struggle for power. Once the objective was achieved, the movement revealed its various contending positions. What 1923 did show was that the provincial *ras* had no intention of disappearing when the battle appeared to be won. To do so would be to throw away all that had been gained. After all, fascist control had to be maintained if enemies were not to raise their heads again.

But by now there was also a strong personal element in the desire to survive. Verbal intransigence often served to obscure the evolution of a different reality in the provinces. The myth of national palingenesis was still on people's lips but, in many areas, the reality was about something else—and it was a reality that looked rather less to total breach with the past. The opportunities for personal advancement offered by Fascism to local leaders were too obvious to be ignored. The achievement of uncontested political power opened possibilities of private, as well as public, affirmation. Local bosses now enjoyed a dominant position in provincial society, important contacts with business and economic interests, the possibility of placing friends and relations in good local jobs, and a wide respect based on real power—something that generated both hope and fear among subordinates. It is from 1923 that reports begin to come in of provincial secretaries deciding on good salaries for themselves (L2,000–2,500 a month was quite usual, a sum that an agricultural labourer would be lucky to approach in a year), of the provision of cars and personal secretaries, of invitations to the best tables in town. Naturally some more dynamic and ambitious *ras* left for Rome, for national politics. Those who did invariably used national position to strengthen their hold on their province (provision of public works could be important here). But most did not. This was hardly surprising. A move to Rome could threaten the loss of the local power base, unless reliable lieutenants could be found. And it has to be remembered that hatred and mistrust of Rome and of the despised 'politics' Rome represented had been a component part of fascist rhetoric for years. No doubt the contempt for politics also represented a genuine uneasiness in many fascists, new to politics and unaccustomed to political ways, faced with the political protocol with which they collided whenever they had anything to do with Rome or its ministries. But essentially it was a confirmation of the fact that, for most people, local politics was about local position. It was in the local context that the fascist victory could best be exploited.

By late 1923, calls to order had had some effect in establishing discipline. To some extent agrarian Fascism—the really decisive new element in the picture—had been brought under control, and, with the creation of the MVSN, the *squadristi* had been shunted off to a side line, of uncertain destination. Even so, the provincial leaders and their followers continued to constitute a serious problem. Much of provincial Fascism—that part of the Fascism of the North and centre which looked to Farinacci as its spokesman—stood for the realization of 'integral' Fascism—that is, the complete fascistization of the state through the replacement of state officials within the state bureaucracy with fascists. This was the Jacobin face of Fascism and it called, often in a confused, unpredictable, and unrealistic manner, for a complete and in some senses 'revolutionary' break with the past. Mussolini understood well the extent to which this line risked being counterproductive within the country and might well have provoked a decisive backlash among moderate opinion; fascist forces were simply not strong enough to impose that kind of solution. At the same time the intransigents were useful to him as a weapon with which to threaten the liberal establishment. In political terms the continued existence of the threat of an intransigent Fascism was invaluable and he had to put up with it. It was this ambivalent position on the part of Mussolini that gave the *ras* their chance. Over time many of the leaders of provincial Fascism developed the conviction that national salvation and personal fortune were entirely compatible. Indeed, the logic of their argument was usually that the more they secured their hold on provincial politics, the more the national revival was guaranteed. Understandably from their point of view, the Fascist Revolution had become identified with their own persons. For the moment, at least, the rhetoric of personal sacrifice in the name of the national cause seemed to have taken a back seat, to be invoked with monotonous regularity as their only thought only on those occasions on which Mussolini decided to question their motivations.

The 'personalization' of the movement, by which personal fortunes and national revival came to enjoy a virtually symbiotic relationship for many of the local leaders, was very marked in the years before 1925. It was, in large part, a consequence of the way in which Fascism had grown from uncertain and imprecise initial precepts and without much formal structure. The local movements had invented themselves as they went along; it was the local movement that had thrown up its own local heroes and buried its own local 'martyrs'. These new leaders had enjoyed a great deal of autonomy in their actions and had few fixed points of reference outside their province beyond Mussolini himself. Almost inevitably, such people began to think that, in their province, Fascism meant themselves and their personal control of local politics. Identification of self with movement, by which (in the minds of those who nurtured them) personal aims and objectives assumed almost automatically a wider political significance, was a common feature of this period. The largely untrammelled power of the major *ras*—there were many minor *ras* in the hinterlands of the provincial centres as well—prompted the assertion of an individual interpretation of Fascism which, in this early phase, was invariably presented as the authentic voice of the movement. Moreover, it has to be recognized that 'personalization' was also a characteristic built into the fascist movement by Mussolini himself. In 1923 the cult of the *duce* was still some way off, but the identification of the movement with the person of Mussolini was already well established. And it was something that could be used and imitated. Personal contact with Mussolini could add greatly to the authority of the local bosses, who thus acquired something of his aura, and many of them did not hesitate to adopt the fascist leader's mannerisms and poses. This made for constant reiteration of ideas of authority, discipline, determination, and the exhibition of *decisionismo*—the capacity to decide rapidly and decisively. Here the input of personality was essential to the message. As a consequence the 'little Mussolinis' of provincial Italy became a common feature of the development of the movement, to increase enormously after 1925.

The degree to which the *ras* had occasioned a deviation from the original fascist project is related not only to their personal interests, but also to their contacts with the established and traditional controlling groups within provincial society. A few of the *ras* were, of course, representatives of these groups. In Tuscany the appearance of members of the local aristocracy at the head of the squads was not unusual. Dino Perrone Compagni in Florence is a case in point. The fascist leader in Piacenza, Bernardo Barbiellini-Amedei, came from a well-established local family. On other occasions it was common to find the sons of prominent local figures enrolled in the *fasci* and active in the squads. Apart from what were often undoubted patriotic motives, they were also protecting their inheritance. Perhaps as important, they could report back to their influential fathers on precisely what fascist intentions were. And it has already been noted that local fascist organizations often depended directly on such controlling groups for their financial support, and sometimes for other logistical aid (lorries, meeting rooms, and so on).

Undoubtedly, as the fascist movement increased its power at the local level, the degree to which financial contributions were strictly voluntary may be called into question. The 'invitation' to support the cause, sometimes made at the point of a revolver, was not easy to refuse. But money, given willingly or not, did provide access. This was one way, and a very effective way, in which the traditional elites moved carefully into a role in which they could influence the decisions of the new movement from a position external to the movement itself, without openly seeming to corrupt its much-vaunted purity. Having a strong local *ras* in their pocket was a strategy with which many prominent agricultural and industrial families sought to deal with the pretensions of the fascists, hoping, through the *ras*, to have some kind of representation of their interests in Rome. The local *ras*, of course, if he had any regard for his public appearance, would take the money but try to keep out of the pocket. In the early years, relationships of this kind were rarely very stable.

Provincial fascism, which affected to despise the traditional elite in many of its representations, nonetheless found itself involved with these people and, to some extent, conditioned by them. Many of the *ras* were aware that they were open to accusations of being bought off because of financial dependence and they continued in a show of hostility to the non-fascist *notabili*. In some cases this assumed the form of a genuine radicalism among *ras,* impatient with the compromises which others accepted and eager to assert a real independence within local society. For some, money was welcome, pressure less so. In Turin in 1923, for example, Cesare Maria De Vecchi appeared to be preparing to move against no less a figure than the

Fiat boss, Giovanni Agnelli, before the latter appealed personally to Mussolini and secured the removal of the local leader.[57]

This is an indication that on many occasions new men did clash with old elites as local fascists attempted to show who was now in charge. But often the radicalism was purely verbal and was little more than a show. Inevitably, as suggested above, the seductions of acceptance by the old elite were many. It was emblematic that Roberto Farinacci, the acknowledged leader of the intransigent wing of Fascism and a man who invoked the introduction of the pure and integral Fascism of a clean break with the past, should himself at this time be strengthening his ties with the Cremona business world; indeed, he was already looking for financial opportunities on a much wider scale.[58] And radicalism did have its risks. After all, in a sense, even the *ras* operated on a knife edge. Certainly, they were *the* essential feature of fascist control of territory in this early period, but too great a demonstration of radicalism, such as to turn the elites within a province against Fascism itself, could provoke a harsh reaction from the centre. In Naples Aurelio Padovani was expelled from the party for trying to use the *fascio* in order to attack the authority of the local client networks—an attack Mussolini opposed.

In this sense the traditional elites, particularly those with powerful economic interests, did have more than a few weapons at their disposal. It is for this reason that the growth of provincial Fascism after 1923 frequently saw a gradual re-emergence of traditional groups, something that undoubtedly threatened a 'contamination' of the radical thrust of the original fascist movement as the new men of Fascism were often absorbed slowly into local circuits of influence. As Bottai judged correctly, many provincial fascists were becoming 'conservative revolutionaries' because they opposed any change that might threaten their own positions; they were men who had succeeded in 'fixing themselves up'.[59] Such a transformation meant not only that many of the *ras* developed a very personal idea of what Fascism should be, but that in many cases they operated from a very personal power base. This could not but influence the overall advance of the movement after the March on Rome.

The revisionist crisis within the party in the second half of 1923 was fought in part over the role of the provincial bosses. Revisionism did its best to square the circle and find some kind of place in its scheme for radical provincial fascists—'we don't wish to save the Party against them, but with them' as Bottai put it—but it was hard-pressed to find a convincing solution. The differences were, in reality, irreconcilable as long as Fascism could not do without its local leaders. Again, it is in Bottai's writings at the time that the gravity of the problem becomes obvious. Declaring that 'it is not enough to suppress the local *ras*', he produced a remarkable denunciation of provincial Fascism:

> To talk about the abuses of the local bosses, of their unyielding refusal to understand the new necessities of these new times, to deplore the *marasma* of the provinces, where innumerable Marcelli [i.e. local bosses] fight over the crumbs of power and a lot of

---

[57] Lupo, *Il Fascismo*, 163–5.   [58] See below, Chapter 6, 6.4 'Party and personnel'.
[59] *Critica fascista*, 21 October 1923.

shirkers use their hands not to work but to beat people up; to shout out against the stupid presumption of those who declare '*I* am Fascism' and who refuse any kind of collaboration with men who are more able, more intelligent, better prepared; in short, to debate about the present degeneration of so much of Italian Fascism seems pointless.

This was hardly an argument about tactics; it was a scathing attack on everything Fascism had been up to that point. And it was an attack on the provinces and on the party still dominated by the provinces. Prophetically, Bottai finished his diatribe by calling for the 'total affirmation of the prevalence of the powers of the State over the powers of the party'.[60]

The moment at which the tensions between the various components of the fascist movement came out into the open was, of course, the crisis created by the murder of Matteotti.[61] As moderate support in the country moved briskly away from Mussolini, the current within the movement most identified with normalization and revisionism found itself exposed and without friends. Those moderate allies on whom any kind of normalization depended were no longer playing the game. Over the summer months, the depression which descended on the fascists of Rome was noted by many commentators. But, at the same time, intransigent provincial leaders realized that their positions were also threatened, as many (but not all) among the traditional elites turned their backs on them. In the provinces, intransigent fascists, alarmed by an apparently wavering Mussolini, began to argue more strongly for a 'second wave' of violence to suppress all opposition. The journal *Il Selvaggio*, directed by the Siena artist and journalist Mino Maccari and the expression of a part of Tuscan *squadrismo*, looked back to the good old days of antisocialist battles and declared that there had been enough politicking in Rome and that the time had come to go back to breaking heads.[62]

For the moderate fascists there were few obvious ways out of the crisis that did not look like capitulation to popular outrage. Conversely, the hard-line fascists—the majority of whom were to be found among the blackshirts, the MVSN, and the provincial *ras*—saw their opportunity, even though it was, to a great extent, an opportunity imposed by necessity. Given a choice between capitulation, with the loss of everything they had gained up to that point, and a 'second wave' of violent repression of all opposition, the intransigents inevitably favoured the second. Indeed, many of them had been invoking such a 'second wave' even before the crisis unfolded.[63]

The effect of the crisis was, at least in appearances, to put the political initiative back into the hands of the provincial *ras* and the leaders of the legions of the

[60] *Critica fascista*, 1 October 1923.

[61] The most comprehensive treatment of the Matteotti crisis is to be found in Canali, *Il delitto Matteotti*. Some new information on the context of the murder is provided in Ibid., 'The Matteotti murder and the origins of Mussolini's totalitarian Fascist regime in Italy', (2009) 14(2) *Journal of Modern Italian Studies* 143.

[62] Mangoni, *L'interventismo*, 93–121.

[63] On the 'second wave' see Lyttelton, *Seizure*, 237–68; also Ibid., 'Fascism in Italy: the Second Wave', (1966) 1(1) *Journal of Contemporary Italian History* 75.

MVSN. They were the people who could save Mussolini, but if they did this, it was clearly on condition that it would be their kind of Fascism that was to have centre stage in the future, and not that of the revisionist Massimo Rocca or the more intellectual Giuseppe Bottai, nor, even less, that of the hated moderate and monarchical Nationalists around their leader and, from June 1924, Minister of the Interior, Luigi Federzoni.[64] The Matteotti crisis pointed up the fact that, after more than a year in power in which Mussolini had manoeuvred in order to control the provincial movements, the real force of Fascism still lay with the provinces. The 'second wave' seemed inevitable if the fascist movement were to survive. Even *in extremis* Mussolini sought to avoid this conclusion because of the degree to which it would reveal his dependence on the violent wing of the movement. The so-called 'movement of the Consuls', of late December 1924, when, in a surprise move, a group of thirty-three powerful provincial leaders of the MVSN paid Mussolini a visit and warned that, if he did not react to the challenge, they would act alone, left the fascist leader with few options. The message was clear. They—the provinces— could (and would) do without him; he could not do without them.

---

[64] The Italian Nationalist Association, of which Federzoni was the leader, had fused with the fascist movement in early 1923.

3

Stabilization in the Provinces: the Party Adapts

3.1. THE PROBLEM OF THE INTRANSIGENTS

Whatever else we may think about him, there is no denying that Mussolini was a very astute politician; the lessons of the Matteotti crisis were not lost on him. After the March on Rome the fascist leader had attempted to strengthen his position by widening his political base, appealing to moderate opinion within Italy with the project of 'normalization'. Implicit in this project was a distancing of the *duce* from fascist violence. The nation-wide reaction to the murder of Matteotti showed that this policy was no longer an option. Mussolini had seen opposition to himself and to Fascism grow again in the country and he knew that, if he were not to abandon the field, it was necessary to react to a renewed and fairly generalized hostility, even among those who had been prepared up to that point to give him qualified support. Equally, he had seen his own lieutenants threaten him with independent action if he did not respond to the challenge and he could not ignore the implications of this for his own position. The final months of the crisis represented a kind of synthesis of many of the problems generated within Fascism in its early years. If the murder of Matteotti was not itself the work of provincial *squadristi*, it sprang nonetheless from very much the same kind of contempt for legality and love of violence the *squadristi* had always shown. Moreover, the reaction to the murder only provoked provincial Fascism into making clear the degree to which it endorsed political assassination as a method and the extent to which that kind of Fascism had never been fully controlled by the internal mechanisms of the party.

The calls for the realization of a 'second wave' seemed to presage a final explosion of the kind of Fascism personified by the provincial *ras*—an explosion that would consolidate their dominance in the movement beyond any further doubt. Mussolini's position was, at least to all appearances, that of dependence on a movement escaping progressively from his control, as the 'cattle raisers', fearful for their own futures, pushed for the realization of a Fascism that would finally be made in their image.

The Matteotti crisis made evident a further, underlying, problem within the fascist movement. This was the problem of legitimacy. The cult of the *duce* was not yet established and, while Mussolini was revered by many of his supporters, his authority was far from absolute. Grass-roots Fascism—the kind the intransigents and the *squadristi* personified—still claimed its own legitimacy, derived from the legacy of the war and the patriotic battle against Bolshevism. This was a legitimacy

arrogated to the fascists by the fascists themselves rather than through the concession of any leader. The foundation of the PNF in November 1921 undoubtedly
represented a move designed to channel and control this impulse towards autonomous action on the part of the 'provincial Fascisms' but it was far from being a
complete success. Equally, the rhetoric of the armed conquest of the state, realized
through the simulated *coup d'état* of the March on Rome, confirmed the belief in
the central role of the squads, suggesting that right lay with might. As everyone
knew, in the fascist case might lay with the squads in the provinces. Moreover,
Matteotti's murder highlighted the tensions between leader and led, revealing the
degree to which many provincial fascists considered Mussolini to be expendable. It
demonstrated the extent to which, seen from the point of view of the fascist rank
and file, Mussolini's right to decide the future of the movement could still be
questioned.

Why did Mussolini not simply dispense with his embarrassing radical supporters? Other dictators faced rather similar problems and showed themselves well able
to meet and defeat the challenge. In the Night of the Long Knives Hitler showed
little compunction when it came to the physical elimination of unruly companions. Stalin's treatment of former comrades in arms is all too well-known. Even
Chiang Kai-shek had few qualms about crushing his communist allies in the
Shanghai murders of 1927. Mussolini's approach was much more circumspect,
not—one suspects—because of any reluctance to use violence, but because he
could not survive without his intransigent wing. Much more than was the case
with the dictators named above, Mussolini's victory in 1922 had been only a partial one. The Matteotti crisis had served to show just how incomplete this victory
remained. The speed with which moderate support backed away from him, the
misgivings and oscillations of the so-called *quartarellisti* within the movement[1]—
all demonstrated the weakness of his position in the face of moderate opinion and
the forces of the liberal state. In a sense he was also weak within the party; he had
no SS to use against the provincial *ras*. Who was going to turn their guns on Farinacci? It was all too evident that, in circumstances of late 1924 and early 1925, the
fascist intransigents constituted the core support of the fascist leader without which
he risked being overwhelmed by a tide of opposition. They were his guarantee of
permanence in power. Mussolini's problem was that of retaining this guarantee
while, at the same time, avoiding being too conditioned by it. It was a balancing
act—which Mussolini performed with great skill. He decided to ride the tiger,
convinced that he could dominate the beast, but equally sure that the tiger would
continue to snarl and terrify his opponents.

Mussolini's response to the crisis and to the ultimatum of his leading followers—his speech to the Parliament on 3 January 1925—is generally seen as marking
the moment at which he began, successfully, to outmanoeuvre the intransigents
and reduce them, over a period of years, to relative impotence. It has sometimes

---

[1] Quartarella was the village outside Rome where Matteotti's body had been found. People who
wavered in their loyalty to Fascism or dissociated themselves from the movement after the discovery
of the body became known as *quartarellisti*.

been seen in terms of the triumph of the ordered and disciplined regime, reliant on the state, over the chaotic and undisciplined movement, represented by the party up to that point. Certainly Mussolini's decision to accept responsibility for fascist violence, to invoke a higher aim for Fascism as the justification for violence, and, at the same time, to announce the repression of all opposition, was a decisive move in the direction of dictatorship. It was also a determining stroke in the battle that had been going on for more than four years within the fascist camp, even though it would take more than a year for the full consequences of the decision to become fully apparent.[2]

3.2. STABILIZATION: ACT ONE. FARINACCI AS PARTY SECRETARY

That the 3 January speech was in fact a veiled attack on the party and the provincial *ras* who dominated it was far from being obvious in early 1925. Indeed, it is important not to overstate the degree to which the party was put in its place by Mussolini's proposed solution of the Matteotti crisis. It is true that the solution did put an unexpected emphasis on the role to be played by the repressive machine of the state, rather than that of the party, but when, in February, Farinacci was appointed as party secretary, it looked as though the party had won and that the moment of the intransigents had finally arrived. Many of the various provincial Fascisms whose hold on provincial politics had been consolidated in the previous three or four years welcomed the appointment of the man who was considered their representative and principal spokesman. Farinacci's elevation seemed to be a recognition that the party—and an intransigent party at that—had a fundamental role to play in the future of the movement.

Farinacci certainly read the 3 January speech as his own personal triumph. During late 1924 the pages of *Cremona nuova* (his newspaper) had resonated with threats against the opposition and appeals for the realization of a 'second wave' of violence.[3] On 18 December he had urged precisely the kind of challenge to the opposition that Mussolini was to issue in the Italian parliament less than three weeks later. In his view only the intransigents held the answer to the crisis: 'History and the facts have shown that the true soul of Fascism, that our intransigence, was right; it alone has saved Fascism and permits us now to renew the offensive everywhere.' After 3 January the tones became even more triumphant: 'The politics of the government will no longer be based on compromise, on abdications, on sentimentalism, but will be clearly fascist, just as we demanded in those times when

---

[2] For a general assessment of the significance of the speech of 3 January 1925, see Lyttelton, *Seizure*, 257–68; Renzo De Felice, *Mussolini il fascista*, vol. 2: *L'organizzazione dello Stato fascista 1925–1929*, Turin, Einaudi, 1968, 3–34.

[3] For Farinacci, see, in general, Matteo di Figlia, *Farinacci, il radicalismo al potere*, Rome, Donzelli, 2007; Giuseppe Pardini, *Roberto Farinacci, ovvero della rivoluzione fascista*, Florence, Le Lettere, 2007. More specific to these years is Lorenzo Santoro, *Roberto Farinacci e il partito nazionale fascista 1923–1926*, Soveria Mannelli, Rubbettino, 2008.

public opinion was against us...Not mistakenly, we wrote on several occasions that the Matteotti crime, so stupidly exploited, would lead to the burial of all the Matteottians.' Clearly the new party secretary did not feel there was anything for which he needed to apologize.

Yet, as party secretary, Farinacci undoubtedly occupied an ambiguous position. As Adrian Lyttelton has put it, he was very much in the position of poacher turned gamekeeper—the provincial tyrant given the job of controlling provincial tyrants.[4] Mussolini's decision to appoint a man he always disliked was a move designed to help the *duce* re-establish his hold on the party after the uncertainties of the Matteotti crisis. Farinacci's brief was to impose some kind of order and discipline on those areas of the movement in which indiscipline and illegality continued to characterize fascist actions and in which central control was persistently flouted. Although the Cremona leader's reputation was that of a self-willed provincial boss, this objective was far from being against his nature. As an intransigent and a supporter of an authoritarian and 'integral' Fascism, he appreciated the need for a single, strong, centralized party. For him, integral Fascism meant that the party should take the initiative, working towards a situation in which the state itself would become indistinguishable from the party in a total symbiosis of Fascism and nation. He was very far, therefore, from seeing the state as being opposed to the party, at least in theory. It was rather that, in his eyes, a party with genuine autonomy of action was the essential instrument for the realization of this kind of symbiosis.

At the same time, despite all his weighty discourses about discipline, his sympathies clearly lay with the provincial movements and with the kind of rough, violent, intolerant Fascism of the provincial squads. His very power base lay among these movements. Many provincial leaders looked to him as the archetypal fascist leader who feared no one. And Farinacci, as one of the most important of the *ras*, could not be indifferent to all those characteristics of provincial Fascism that typified the rule of the *ras*. In particular, he knew the degree to which his kind of Fascism depended on continuous conflict in order to survive—on the unpredictability of its actions, on lack of obvious control, and on exploitation of illegality in order to maintain its position in provincial towns. He knew only too well that, in many circumstances, too much stability could actually prove to be counterproductive, particularly for fascist morale. The realization of some kind of 'continuous revolution' required at the very least continuous activity.

Farinacci's answer to this problem was to call for discipline in the provincial federations but to insist that the kind of discipline imposed should reflect his idea of how the federations should function. Thus, while he worked for the realization of a centralized and vertical bureaucratic structure in the PNF and reorganized the party on lines that made it more responsive to central directives, he took his opportunity, in conjunction with this reorganization, to demonstrate to everybody that he was in no way a supporter of any policies of normalization, such as had been

---

[4] Lyttelton, *Seizure*, 271.

followed by Mussolini in 1923. In his early speeches as party secretary he repeatedly stressed the need to 'insert the fascist Revolution into the State' and to use the PNF to do this.[5] This was a vision of the party's place that had clear implications for Mussolini. The PNF, as envisaged by Farinacci, was to be central to Fascism. It was to be the motor of the movement, providing that input necessary for the total 'fascistization' of the nation. This was an interpretation of the role of the party that inevitably threatened to tread on Mussolini's toes. There was no suggestion that the fascist leader was himself expendable, but there was more than a suggestion in Farinacci's reading of the role of the party that PNF and *duce* would run as parallel—and equal—forces. Party secretary and national leader might have different functions, therefore, but by implication they were also of equal weight. Mussolini could hardly fail to notice this. From his point of view, Farinacci had his uses, but it was unlikely that Mussolini would stomach a kind of cohabitation of power for very long.

Farinacci's calls for a reaffirmation of the central role of the party dictated initially a renewed offensive against certain members of the provincial establishment who had shown themselves unreliable in the course of the Matteotti crisis. The campaign launched against the freemasons almost immediately after the speech of 3 January, even before Farinacci took over as party secretary, should be seen in this light. More important, aware that in many areas local fascist bosses had succumbed to the temptations of a kind of comfortable accommodation with the local bourgeoisie, he attempted to re-establish an autonomous authority for the *fasci*. In some situations this meant a renewal of the rhetoric of new *versus* old, with fiery denunciations of commercial and professional middle classes accused of thinking that, with socialism defeated, they could move back into the driving seat as if nothing had happened. Frequently this line of action meant rounding on the people who had been giving support to the movement up to that point. In many towns, in a recrudescence of *squadrismo* over the spring and summer, local gentry once again became targets for fascist denunciations and—on occasions—physical attacks. In other situations, this meant removing the fascists guilty of collaboration with the enemy; thirty-two *federali* were removed in the first months of Farinacci's secretariat and many of these *fasci* were passed to the control of special commissars sent from Rome to impose the party line.

What was at issue was less whether contact should be made with the traditional elites and the business world in itself—Farinacci himself had any number of (sometimes very shady) contacts, which would soon make him a very rich man[6]—than independence from any kind of political control and a re-establishment of a favourable negotiating position for Fascism after the apparent weakening of 1924. In particular it was seen to be essential to curtail, as far as possible, the activities of autonomous centres of power—such as the freemasons—within provincial life. Farinacci's aim was to show that a victorious Fascism was raising its head above

[5] Roberto Farinacci, *Un periodo aureo nel Partito Nazionale Fascista*, Foligno, Campitelli, 1927, 107.
[6] Lupo, *Il Fascismo*, 301–2.

those who sought to influence and manipulate the movement for their own ends. The message was that, if there were to be manipulation, it was to be fascist manipulation of others.

At the provincial level this campaign for fascist supremacy presented once again many of the questions that had been posed in 1923. In some respects Fascism was still well placed in its search for support. Many among the local bourgeoisie continued to look at Fascism essentially as the lesser evil. Whatever the faults of the movement it was better than having to deal with the apparently irresistible tide of socialism they had faced in 1919 and 1920. Socialist leagues and unions had now disappeared in most areas, replaced by fascist syndicates. By 1925 most socialist provincial and communal administrations had long since evaporated, either defeated or dissolved, and a revival of the socialist movement seemed unlikely.[7] Nonetheless, during the Matteotti crisis there had been ominous signs in some areas of new stirrings of opposition—particularly working class opposition—and this had undoubtedly provided food for thought. The continued existence of Fascism was seen to be a guarantee against any backsliding. The question the local elites asked themselves was, of course: how much was acceptance of Fascism worth in terms of cession of control of provincial affairs? And here, of course, the answer depended on how much Fascism asked in terms of control.

There was no single answer to this question. It is at this point, when Fascism was very clearly in power to stay, that manoeuvres for influence and position became the key part of the political game, even at the provincial level. Indeed, in many respects the years 1925 and 1926 were crucial years for the determination of the characteristics of the regime. People were aware that battles won or lost at this point might prove to be decisive for many years to come. It is for this reason that 1925 is marked with a large number of internal struggles within provincial Fascism.

This was not exactly the beginning of '*beghismo*', as it became known—the internal struggles within local movements among groups that competed for control had been going on almost from the start—but it was a feature that came very much to the fore in that year. Accusations of readiness to concede to the attack on Fascism—*quartarellismo*—continued to be thrown around long after the Matteotti crisis itself was closed. One of Farinacci's first declarations on taking up office as party secretary was aimed at the problem of local disputes.

> [We have] Forbidden, therefore, the miserable local questions, forbidden the sickening dissidences which have caused so much harm to the party, forbidden the ambitious and the profiteers, forbidden all spirit of indiscipline...[8]

Only a few days later, speaking to local fascists at Piacenza, he repeated the warning:

---

[7] On the dynamic of dissolutions, see Luigi Ponziani, 'Fascismo e autonomie locali', in Marco Palla (ed.), *Lo stato fascista*, Milan, La Nuova Italia, 2001, 317–28.

[8] Farinacci, *Un periodo aureo*, 41.

What has happened in so many other provinces has happened here as well...Passions and personalities have taken over...The future requires that what has happened in the past should not be repeated. Personalisms are forbidden! In the face of Fascism your rights and wrongs must disappear....[9]

As we shall see, this call to order had very limited results; Piacenza was to remain one of the most troublesome provinces in the following years. But Farinacci's reference to 'so many other provinces' is indicative of the degree to which the internal squabbles had become generalized at provincial level.

This was not true of all places. In a few provinces of the North any internal difficulties had largely been settled even before 3 January. Often this depended on the emergence of a figure sufficiently strong that other local fascists were unable to contest him any further. This was the case in Bologna where, after the fall of Gino Baroncini in 1923, Leandro Arpinati—a close friend of Mussolini—exercised undisputed control, just as it was true in Balbo's Ferrara. In Ferrara the substantial complementarities of interest between the Agrarian Association, the banks, and the fascist movement had been evident since at least 1922 and the protagonists all drew the obvious conclusions. On one hand it was convenient for Balbo because he was free to pursue his political career in Rome, precisely because he knew that his grip on the province was secure; on the other the powerful local interest groups recognized that, with Fascism, they had recovered their control of the province and that, with Balbo, they had a forceful and respected representative of their interests in Rome.

In this stabilization of 1925, much depended on how any particular fascist movement had developed up to that point. If, as in Ferrara or as in Genoa, important economic interests had been central to the development of the movement, it was unlikely that their positions would be challenged, even with the thrust to political autonomy of Fascism favoured by Farinacci. Local fascists might want greater freedom and, in certain circumstances, demand greater respect from established families and prestigious local institutions, but they were not normally in the business of digging their own graves by offending the people who really could pull the strings in the locality, unless, of course, they were sure of having equally influential friends on whom they could fall back.

In some provinces mutual interest was sometimes less obvious and cohabitation of political and economic power less easy. Once again, the key to the question was usually the way in which Fascism had imposed itself in the town or the province in the period before 1925. That interweaving of the political thrust of Fascism and the financial, commercial, industrial, and/or agrarian interests that was so common in the years after 1921 had in many cases produced serious tensions as the various interests competed for ultimate control. In certain places these tensions had been exacerbated by the pressures of the 1924 crisis of Fascism, creating local situations that were volatile and unstable. Internal rivalries within the *fasci* could also be important here. In the circumstances of relative fluidity that characterized

[9] Ibid., 43–4.

early 1925—the renewed affirmation of Fascism after the Matteotti crisis and of reorganization around a new and highly identifiable party secretary—local leaders frequently began to vie for the dominant position before the situation settled down.

Many fascist leaders took Farinacci's new attack on the provincial notables as meaning that fascist control should be absolute. They attempted to extend their influence to all areas of provincial life, provoking resistance from those most threatened. These last, usually not without means of their own, would resist as best they could. One course of action open to those attacked was to try to gain some kind of foothold within the fascist structure in order to condition the course of the contest. Thus, for example, it was possible to find the moneyed entrepreneurs of the province moving to positions favourable to the local leaders of the MVSN and entering into conflict with the direction of the local city *fascio*. Sometimes they would attempt control of the fascist *sindacati* and contest the line of the local party secretary (the *segretario federale*).

Obviously personal ambitions, jealousies, and enmities figured large in this context—the possibilities Fascism presented for social promotion were now evident to everyone. Provincial contenders for power would all have their local backers, often pulling in different directions, and the fascists themselves would thus come to represent different interest groups within provincial society. These alignments frequently produced very complex situations. On many occasions the fascist squads within the same province would support different local leaders. A competition for rights of jurisdiction between the *fascio* and the MVSN was common, again reflecting different interests. At times the squads, many of which had reformed in the summer of 1924, would criticize the role of the militia, or the militia, in a contest of competencies, would attempt to suppress the squads. Fights would develop between the various groupings, sometimes with dead and wounded on both sides.

Farinacci's year as secretary was really characterized by a series of contradictions. Clearly he felt the need to reinforce the hold of the movement on the country and to make plain to everybody who was boss. This was his opportunity to impose his 'fascistizing' line on the country and to counter a normalizing tendency, evident in 1923 and the early months of 1924, to compromise with non-fascist groups. The vacillations associated with the Matteotti murder had been noted and the lessons learned. The renewed attacks on the bourgeoisie were an obvious indication of this.[10] Denunciations of the occult influence of the freemasons and threats to recal-

---

[10] Farinacci would certainly have liked to go much further in his attacks on the bourgeoisie than he was permitted to go, as evinced from a letter of May 1927 to the lawyer and journalist Filippo Filippelli (cleared of the accusation of having participated in the murder of Matteotti but banned from practising as a lawyer). Farinacci wrote that he would ensure that Filippelli was readmitted to the professional body of lawyers, given the scandalous fact that 'well-known lawyers' in Milan, who had backed away from Fascism in 1924, were still practising. 'Compared with these, you have more right because you have part of the merit of having caused the disappearance of Hon. Matteotti—something which, as you know, has never caused me much sorrow'; ACS, Segreteria Particolare del Duce (SPD), b. 42, 18 May 1927.

citrant civil servants accused of 'sabotage', of deliberately slowing down the pace of the 'revolution', were a part of the operation ('[w]e have to propose this alternative to all state workers: either get out or submit to the Regime').[11] In his usual dramatic tones he advocated a purge of false friends through an unhesitating use of the surgeon's knife: 'cut and amputate without pity' was his recipe for success. But it was predictable that, as an intransigent and a provincial *ras*, he would not always oppose the realization of provincial domination through the actions of the squads. This was part of his make-up. As poacher turned gamekeeper, he still had a soft spot for the poachers; indeed, he clearly considered that they were all in the same line of business. This ambiguity ensured the continued use of violence. Here Farinacci's philosophy was typical of many more extreme fascists. Violence and conflict were not only necessary to the objective of victory but were also desirable because they were thought to produce an extreme clarification of position in a complex world. As more than one fascist would observe, the world was divided into the *bastonatori* (the beaters) and the *bastonati* (the beaten), and that was that.

From this point of view, Fascism was seen to depend on permanent conflict in order to maintain its spirit, its style of life, its 'revolutionary' dynamic. Violence was a necessary expression of this dynamic, not a means to a more pacific end. The problem facing the fascists, however, was that violence required a target, and identifying enemies against whom to use this violence was becoming less easy. The socialists and the unions were no longer a threat and therefore no longer an interesting target. Farinacci's renewed offensive against the local elites offered a possible solution, yet acting against the provincial bourgeoisie tended also to reveal the contradictory position of the movement. Fascism had not been a social or economic revolution; anything but in most areas. Violence could never provide any satisfactory answer to the fact that provincial societies were complex organisms and could not be dealt with by a simple division of the world into friends and enemies. Certainly there was an old (often physically old) political class deriving from the pre-war period that could be humiliated and destroyed, but in the end the social and economic elite had to be lived with. Without social and economic revolution, some kind of accommodation was inevitable. It was fairly pointless, therefore, to whip up the squads to renewed action against the old 'corrupt' elite if Fascism had no real intention of replacing it and, as the prefects repeatedly reminded central government, few people who were sufficiently competent to substitute it.

By 1925 the role of the squads could only be limited, therefore. Using the big stick could make the economic elite more amenable to compromise with the new force of Fascism. Violence, or the threat of violence, could make obvious to anyone who doubted that it was the *fascio* that called the shots and could avoid any renewed attempt at normalization. No less important, the hard line of the intransigent party secretary could assert a kind of 'primacy of politics in the national interest', thus putting the party at the centre of provincial administration. But it was still

---

[11] On this battle see Melis, *Storia dell'amministrazione*, 332–4. For the reorganization of the state administration see Sabino Cassese, *Lo stato fascista*, Bologna, Il Mulino, 2010, 37–44. The quotations in the text are from Roberto Farinacci, *Andante mosso 1924–25*, Milan, Mondadori, 1929, 185.

apparent that, at the end of the day, the problem of provincial control was one of political positioning and could not be solved solely through the violence of the squads. Indeed, the actions of a violent and undisciplined mass of fascists threatened to deny all authority to the local party secretary himself, frightening off the support which Fascism was bound to seek among key elements of provincial society.

This conundrum contained, of course, the problem implicit in the fascist 'revolution'. Indeed, in most revolutions, dynamism and discipline have proved to be difficult to reconcile. Continued violence was likely to be counterproductive and impede the realization of a broader political base for Fascism. Aiming to control directly neither the financial world nor the world of production, Fascism had inevitably to accept the necessity for compromises with these forces, which operated according to a logic that was not always easily and visibly accommodated to fascist political objectives of national revival and affirmation. This was exemplified by the fact that the large industrialists of the North usually insisted that the fascists should stop at the factory gates; intimidation of the workforce was one thing, interference with the organization of production another. The risk was that such compromises, necessary as they were, would take the wind out of the sails of the revolution, precisely because they required a greater control of fascist illegality. Mussolini, with many of his close supporters, was able to see that compromises were unavoidable, given the relative strength of the forces in play; the intransigents and the provincial *squadristi* found it much harder to recognize this reality.

The more time passed after the initial fascist onslaught of 1921, the more the distance between the revolutionaries and the realists increased. To some degree this was also a distance between the centre and the provinces. The centre required discipline in order to compose the essential compromises; the provinces thrived on indiscipline and relative anarchy. This contrast pointed up the fact that there was— and there always had been—an implicit contradiction between the centrifugal anti-political movement of the provinces and the attempt to create a rigid, vertical, centralized party structure in Rome. In historiographical terms the contradiction has often been seen as the difference between Fascism as 'movement' and Fascism as 'regime', with the second attempting to assert its control over the first, to the detriment of the dynamic elements within Fascism.[12] This was a difference that put the intransigent party secretary in a difficult position. Because of his background Farinacci was acutely embarrassed by the dilemma he faced. In Piacenza he asserted 'I felt a deep pain when I saw fascists of the first hour...arrested and searched'.[13] In a sense the PNF leader was guilty of wanting it both ways—he aimed to 'legalize the healthy fascist illegality' and bring it under control, while arguing that 'you cannot take our Revolution into a magistrate's office or a tribunal or an assize court. There is only one kind of justice valid for us: History!'[14] This kind of state-

---

[12] For a brief discussion of the theme see Renzo De Felice, *Intervista sul Fascismo* (ed. Michael Ledeen), Rome & Bari, Laterza, 1975, 36–46.

[13] Farinacci, *Un periodo aureo*, 44.

[14] Ibid., 71.

ment was tantamount to egging on the provincial leaders while calling for rigid discipline within the party, a position ultimately impossible to sustain.

Farinacci was dismissed as party secretary in early 1926. His defeat was occasioned by the 'events of Florence' (*i fatti di Firenze*) of October 1925, although he would leave office only several months later. The events, and the crisis they provoked, provided a kind of synthesis of the problems facing Fascism in 1925. The intransigent *squadristi* of Florence, headed by their disreputable and dissolute leader, Tullio Tamburini, became impatient with the slow pace of the 'revolution' and, in late September, unleashed a more or less private attack against alleged 'freemasons'—in reality members of the local bourgeoisie who had attracted the hostile attention of the squads. The actions extended to Prato, Pistoia, and many other towns in the area surrounding Florence. Several people were murdered,[15] many more beaten and badly injured. Significantly, the actions were undertaken in the name of party chief Farinacci, the intransigent—'the most fascist of all fascists' as they termed him—while Mussolini was implicitly accused of excessive moderation. Faced with a public outcry at the events (which had taken place 'under the eyes of 10,000 English and Americans', as a furious Mussolini put it),[16] the fascist leader took his opportunity and attacked Farinacci for following a party line that had, in effect, seemed to sanction actions of this kind. The Grand Council of Fascism decided, at Mussolini's bidding, finally to crush *squadrismo*. Mussolini forced Farinacci to swallow poison by making him announce that the squads were to be disbanded and that the wearing of black shirts and exhibition of the '*santo manganello*' (the 'sacred cudgel') were to be reserved for public events, and only then when authorized by the party itself. Tamburini and his close associates were expelled, despite the fact that Farinacci had sought to justify their actions. Tamburini himself was exiled to Libya, although he would reappear (and hold office) in the 1930s.

As was to be expected, Farinacci did not go quietly, accusing Mussolini of the 'the blackest ingratitude', given all that he—Farinacci—had done for the movement and for the party.[17] Mussolini replied in a dry and direct letter. Not to be outdone, he observed that, if gratitude were the issue, Fascism had greater cause to be grateful to him, the *duce*. Moreover, affirming that 'the difficulties' in the party had their origin in Farinacci's attitude as 'monopolizer of [fascist] purity', he requested that the Cremona leader should abandon his 'air of Anti-pope, biding his time', and, in a scarcely veiled warning, advised him that, if he behaved, 'your opponents will not have the pleasure of seeing you banned from political life'. The

---

[15] Some with particular ferocity. The lawyer Giovanni Luporini was stabbed repeatedly inside the fascist headquarters and then dragged into the street where he was shot several times. The trial of those responsible, held in November 1926, was hushed up, in the sense that newspapers were told they could report the fact of the trial but nothing else: see ACS, MI, PS 1926, b.156, 22 September 1926. See also, for these events, Marco Palla, *Firenze nel regime fascista (1929–34)*, Florence, Olschki, 1978. Palla notes how, at the fall of Fascism in July 1943, people's memories went back immediately to October 1925 and to 'the antifascists burned in an oven' (142).

[16] Lyttelton, *Seizure*, 283.

[17] ACS, SPD, b. 40, 8 July 1926.

final phrase of the letter was particularly ominous: 'Remember that people who leave the party wither and die.'[18]

3.3. STABILIZATION: ACT TWO. TURATI TAKES OVER

Controls over the provincial federations were undoubtedly tightened from the final months of 1925 onwards. The last months of Farinacci's period as party secretary saw a purge of *federali* considered insubordinate or seen to be exercising excessive independence of action. This was followed by a much more massive purge of the whole party by Farinacci's successor, Augusto Turati. Secretary between 1926 and 1930, Turati—from the northern province of Brescia—came from the syndicalist wing of the fascist movement and had achieved notoriety in 1925 when he had organized a strike of metal workers in Brescia, using the fascist syndicates against the bosses in an unprecedented (and not to be repeated) fashion.[19] On taking over as party secretary, he soon showed that the change of guard represented a radical shift of direction. It quickly became evident that, even though his principal concerns were also discipline, obedience, and stability, Turati's interpretation of what these words meant represented much more than a simple change of style.

Mussolini, talking to the journalist Yvon De Begnac several years later, would justify the change of secretary in a revealing way. He explained that he had always felt it necessary to keep a tight hold on his 'lieutenants', not so much because they tended to become too powerful in their own right, but in order to 'prevent the revolution from breaking up into local squabbles, village rivalries, district wars between troops of opposing factions'. In his eyes, Farinacci tended to favour this kind of degeneration: 'Farinacci is still the provincial [person] he always was. "Turati, on the other hand, had a very different influence"…he imposed on the party the pursuit of that unity of intent that…prefigured the beginnings of an effective unity.'[20]

The change of direction away from the line favoured by Farinacci reflected a different idea about the place the PNF should play in the overall fascist scheme of things, a different view of how the party should be used to realize that end, and a different assessment of the position occupied by the party at that point. Turati would not have quarrelled with Farinacci's idea of the centrality of the PNF in the reconstruction of Italy but he had fewer illusions about the capacity of the party, as it stood, to direct a thorough-going process of national transformation. Unlike Farinacci, he did not blame fascist difficulties exclusively on external enemies of the regime, but ascribed them also to deficiencies within the party structure itself. In Mussolini's view, again according to De Begnac, Turati had the virtue of seeing that 'the fault lay with the way the lieutenants used politics, first looking after their own interests, then those of the group in power'.[21] To meet this problem, Turati

---

[18] ACS, SPD, b. 40, 10 July 1926. The document carries a handwritten gloss, 'letter not sent'.
[19] See Kelikian, *Town and country*.
[20] Yvon De Begnac, *Taccuini Mussoliniani*, Bologna, Il Mulino, 1990, 461.
[21] Ibid., 462.

embarked on a fairly drastic revision of local leadership. The principal targets were those leaders who appeared too autonomous from the centre, those who had too-solid roots in the local community. A second factor provoking intervention was the question of the competence of provincial chiefs. Recognizing the many limits of the existing fascist personnel in the provinces—reports of the poor quality of many local fascists were common—Turati seems to have accepted that the party would have to be purged drastically if it were to find its proper place within the wider structure of the new fascist state and that it would then have to use more suitable, but above all more docile, recruits.

From Turati's viewpoint, the party was to be above all the instrument of the 'creation of a new way of thinking' among Italians. This was an objective firmly in line with that of national transformation. Unlike many other fascists, who seemed to consider the 'revolution' completed with their own personal affirmation, the Brescian leader was convinced that Fascism was in for the long haul before the process of transformation could be said to have been effected. The party, far from being simply an ancillary organism of the fascist state, was to have a fundamental role in the realization of this process of change; indeed, it was to be the essential element in the transformation of the Italian people. He recognized that Fascism, as it stood in 1926, was still an emanation of the 'old world', which had to be changed radically. In this respect his references to the original *squadristi* were not always flattering: 'fairly frequently I have to deal with the old men of the old world who are ugly even when they are good-looking...'[22] And he recognized that there was still a great deal to do. In some of his public addresses in 1926 and 1927 he explicitly rejected the idea that his listeners could pride themselves on being 'New Italians' as they liked to do. 'Every so often I hear people say, we are the new Italians. I doubt that new Italians have already been formed: perhaps they are not even born yet, or only just...'[23]

It was—precisely—to be the job of a stable, efficient, bureaucratic party to realize the *process* of transformation of the Italian character, thus creating 'new' Italians for the future.

> The Italians must have a new look, a new spirit. They must be men who are silent, tenacious, sure of themselves, who never lose their heads for any reason...every day educated not to expect roses from destiny...Getting up every morning and every day going to rest with the thought that tomorrow may be the hour of victory and of battle...[24]

As was evident, such people would not be exactly the mirror-image of many of the first *squadristi*, usually anything but silent and educated. It was logical, therefore, that the place of the *squadristi* should be relegated to that of glorious memory, as the new fascist guard of voiceless, determined, confident men gradually took their place. Turati's project for the PNF was designed to realize that objective and in this

[22] Augusto Turati, *Il partito e i suoi compiti*, Roma, Libreria della Littoria, 1928, 57.
[23] Ibid., 147.
[24] Ibid.

sense it cut directly and inevitably across the bows of many in positions of influence within the provincial federations.

Although the Brescian leader was undoubtedly numbered among the provincial *ras*, until 1926 he was a relatively minor figure and less linked by his past to the *squadrista* wing of the movement.[25] As a consequence he represented less of a challenge to Mussolini than had Farinacci and, having less need to play to his own public, was able to adopt a far less publicly aggressive posture in the pursuit of his policies. To some degree he comes over as a 'fascist in good faith'—something one would never be tempted to say of his predecessor. But if the style was different, and the objectives better defined, the immediate policies were surprisingly similar. In many ways Turati was a kind of simplified version of Farinacci, pushing the line of a disciplined PNF and attempting to repress unruly provincial federations. Where he differed from the *ras* of Cremona was in his vision of the task the party was to carry out in the future. He had no doubts about the role the fascist movement was to play in the total transformation of the country:

> The final destination of Fascism can only be reached on one condition: that we succeed in really permeating with our spirit all the vital points and nerve centres of national life. The regime will never be finally victorious…until that day when we know that, at every position of command, from general to corporal, there is a blackshirt with his spirit intact, the spirit of the Revolution, with mind and will well formed, according to the idea of the new Italian so clearly, genially, illustrated by the *duce!*[26]

To this end he began a gradual, but severe, imposition of discipline. In a cautious but extremely thorough process of revision of membership, more than 100,000 people were expelled from the party between 1926 and 1930 (about one-sixth of the total membership). Entire federations were disbanded after investigations carried out by central party representatives revealed indiscipline, criminal activities, and 'immorality'; many local leaders had their party card withdrawn.[27] Around forty provincial federations were controlled for some time by *commissari* sent from Rome to oversee affairs until the situation became more stable. The fascist press was also subjected to scrutiny, with many local and semi-independent newspapers (often the mouthpieces of local bosses) being suppressed in favour of a very few officially-recognized papers, *Il Popolo d'Italia* taking pride of place.

More rigid discipline was also imposed by an important new party statute introduced in the summer of 1926, which established that all appointments to office should be made from above, from the centre, thus effectively removing

---

[25] On Turati see Philip Morgan, 'Augusto Turati', in Ferdinando Cordova (ed.), *Uomini e volte del Fascismo*, Rome, Bulzoni, 1980, 475–519.

[26] Augusto Turati, *Una rivoluzione e un capo*, Rome & Milan, 1929, 131.

[27] Gioacchino Volpe, describing the expelled in his *Storia del movimento fascista*, wrote of 'opportunists, people who found it difficult to live quietly opposing Fascism or outside the movement'; of 'too many improvised leaders who, just as they were incapable of obeying, were equally incapable of commanding, too many profiteers': Rome, Ispe, 1943, 121.

any residual tendencies to the election of local leaders or to their appointment by 'spontaneous' acclamation, which had been common in some areas. The chain of command was made totally top-down, finally cementing that principle of disciplined obedience to hierarchy which was to be so much a central tenet of fascist orthodoxy and which, of course, firmly established Mussolini as the ultimate arbiter of everything. The provinces were thus subordinated to the centre; authority passed from the centre to the provinces and not the other way round. Mussolini summed up Turati's attitude very succinctly: 'Although he originated in provincial Fascism, he denied the provinces the right to take on the role of opposition to Rome. He took away the power of the lieutenants. He demolished their arrogance.'[28]

Turati's objective was that of a vast capillary structure of organizations with authority flowing outwards (and downwards) from the centre. The strong element of centralization represented by this approach was an affirmation of an implicit totalitarianism that interpreted all relationships of power and authority in terms of central control and provincial subordination. His aim was to initiate a process that had, of course, begun in the reverse direction. In his eyes, firm implementation of the policy would show that the unruly centrifugal nature of early Fascism had at last been dominated. Above all, after Farinacci's attempt to establish the autonomy of the party from Mussolini, Turati's approach abandoned any suggestion of dualism between party and *duce* and placed Mussolini firmly back in the driving seat. In this sense, Turati's period as secretary was the basic premise of the future cult of the *duce*.

Some fascist theorists would attempt to justify the elimination of elections with the argument that designation from above would mean that Fascism could finally put the right people in the right place and thus see an end to selection based on local client networks and private influence. It was to be a way of opening the path to a technocratic administration, based on genuine competence rather than personal acquaintance.[29] While it would be unwise to underestimate the strength of this thinking in some quarters—the idea of the corporative state was being developed rapidly in this period—there is little doubt that, far from realizing an authentic career open to talent, the intended consequence of the reform was to reduce the area for certain kinds of initiative on the part of local fascists—the undisciplined 'lieutenants' who gave so much trouble to central government. They had to be convinced that their role was to obey, to carry out orders emanating from above, rather than to think for themselves about politics or policy. The reform represented a further move in the direction of the emasculation of the party as a dynamic force in the evolution of the fascist movement. Inevitably, from this point on, local politics became more about organization, administration, and regimentation than about the direction Fascism should take. Local followers of the movement were very definitely not invited to express their thoughts about ultimate ends or to

---

[28] De Begnac, *Taccuini*, 466.
[29] Expressive of this point of view is Camillo Pellizzi, *Una rivoluzione mancata*, Milan, Longanesi, 1949 (now in a new edition, with introduction by Mariuccia Salvati, Bologna, Il Mulino, 2009).

permit themselves to 'interpret' Mussolini's thought, as Hitler's local leaders would do. There was to be no 'working towards the *duce*' in Italy.[30]

Certainly, as agents responsible for the implementation of directives formulated elsewhere, provincial leaders often had considerable room for manoeuvre. It was this room for manoeuvre that would continue to make local office attractive to many, as we shall see. But the direction indicated by the administrative reforms of 1926 and 1927 was that of the creation of a party that was essentially bureaucratic and administrative in its functions rather than anything more dynamic.[31] This direction was, of course, very much in line with the thinking which saw 'politics' as a dirty word, capable only of provoking division and argument. 'No politics, please' had been one of the original motivating ideas of the fascist movement, even though, at the time, it had hidden a very active idea of intervention in the political life of the nation.

From the point of view of fascist centralizers there was more at stake than simple desire for control. Between 1925 and 1926 the terms of the problem represented by the provincial *ras* had become clearer. Undoubtedly certain of the *ras* consti-tuted a challenge to Mussolini's authority—possibly the only real challenge remain-ing. Their insistence in reminding him that they had all carried out the fascist revolution *together* implied an equality of rank that Mussolini was increasingly unable to tolerate. Farinacci, for one, never tired of protesting total devotion to the *duce*, while always managing at the same time to suggest in some way that they were more or less equals (even when long out of office he would refer, in his letters to Mussolini, to the PNF as 'our party'). Despite manoeuvres, therefore, Mussolini and the provincial leaders remained implicitly in opposition to each other, the first attempting to assert an absolute authority which the second were reluctant to concede.[32]

Yet beyond this very transparent problem of hierarchy within the movement was a further question, already touched on at the beginning of this chapter. The *ras*, both big and small, owed their positions to the support they enjoyed in their par-ticular provinces and to the control they exercised in those provinces. They were, in this sense, very much linked to their territory and drew their legitimation, such as it was, directly from their relationship with that territory and from the consent of their local followers. Such legitimation was increasingly perceived by the centre as being contrary to the fascist vision of the nation. It was autonomous of the cen-tre and was not derived from what, according to fascist thinking, should have been the ultimate source of legitimation in fascist Italy—Mussolini and the fascist state.

---

[30] Ian Kershaw attributes the dynamism of Nazism to the fact that Germans competed to interpret Hitler's often rather vaguely expressed intentions when carrying out their duties, thus 'working towards the Führer' as best they could. See Kershaw, *Hitler 1889–1936: Hubris*, London, Penguin, 1998, in particular Chapter 13. Mussolini's icy reply to a challenge from the provinces, which advised him that his policies needed to be approved by a vote among the local fascists, indicated a very different atti-tude: 'My orders are not voted, they are accepted and executed without murmuring or reservation'; quoted in Lyttelton, *Seizure*, 284–5.

[31] Aquarone writes of a 'bureaucratic regimentation' of the PNF from this time on: *L'Organizzazione*, 165.

[32] On this competition see Gentile, *Storia*, 221–2.

In addition, in its reliance often on the influence of local client networks, this kind of local legitimation seemed to replicate one of the worst features of liberal Italy, in which local groupings had often been the determinant of politics. More than simply representing a fragmentation of authority, therefore, the provincial leaders who affected independence and built up what were essentially private power bases (often realizing considerable financial autonomy as well) were acting in defiance of what was seen increasingly as one of the fundamental precepts of fascist rule—that all power derived from the centre and was handed down to the provinces.

As Turati's period as party secretary proceeded, certain priorities in the action of the central authorities of the party became more evident. It became clear that the party line was less that of enforcing ideological conformity in the provincial federations than that of achieving some kind of lasting stability. In Turati's eyes stability required obedience to Rome and therefore discipline within the federations, but he did not insist on any obligatory adherence to any one view of the meaning of Fascism. Thus disciplinary actions and substitutions were less determined by the position local leaders and their followers occupied on the spectrum of party opinion—intransigents or moderates—or by their social position—petty bourgeoisie or elite—than by the degree to which opinions or social position threatened local stability in the provincial context. The purges and expulsions carried out at the behest of the party secretary were a response to situations in which the authority of the centre appeared to be contested in one way or another—either directly by local bosses still intent on showing that they and not the despised 'Romans' were in charge, or less directly by precarious local equilibria which put discipline at risk. Particular attention was paid to 'personalisms'—that is, to the tendency in some provinces for Fascism to be excessively identified with the local leader and for one man to identify the destiny of Fascism with his own destiny.

The message conveyed from Rome was that local *segretari federali* should accept subordination to Rome and not try to emerge too prominently on the local landscape if they wished to retain their positions. Evidently the fear was that local bosses would in some way interfere with the line of command, interposing their wishes and thoughts between orders from Rome and the province they controlled, in this way frustrating fascist attempts at centralization. Thus the campaign to 'depersonalize' the fascist movement saw the removal of some people—Alezzini in Padua was a case in point—who had in fact been very successful in realizing some kind of internal equilibrium in the province but had made the fatal mistake of attracting too much attention to their efforts among the party hierarchy.[33] It was significant that Turati would often replace prominent local leaders with fairly undistinguished figures, presumed to be more amenable to central party requirements. Moreover, expulsions and rotations of provincial leaders had the side-effect (not unintended) of permitting increased control to the prefect, often the permanent feature of a shifting situation. This, too, tended to weaken the authority of provincial leaders.

---

[33] Alessandro Baù, 'Tra prefetti e federali. Note sul Fascismo padovano degli anni trenta', (2007) 46 *Storia e problemi contemporanei* 51.

The net effect of this attack on provincial autonomies was undoubtedly to improve—at least in the short term—the control of the party over the provincial federations. In itself the initiative of the national party secretary was very significant and did represent a change in the relationship between centre and periphery. The campaign against 'personalisms' and the utilization of party commissars to re-establish order in the more unruly provincial federations on terms acceptable to Turati constituted a move in the direction of greater national control of difficult local situations. There is little doubt that a fairly dramatic centralization was taking place as the central party authorities first expunged the remnants of liberal local government structures and then extended their tentacles in such a way as to discipline the local fascist federations. And, just as the centre increased its hold on the provincial federations, so these federations strengthened their control of the local capillary organizations. An example of this was the massive restructuring of the fascist leisure organization—the *Opera Nazionale Dopolavoro* (OND)—which, from being a loose affiliate of the fascist unions in 1925, passed to the direct control of the party in the course of 1927–8.[34]

This process of centralizing authority was an essential prerequisite for the 'fascistization' of the provinces and the intention was clear to everyone. There was no longer the sensation, as there had been with Farinacci, that the party secretary was acting in one way but thinking in another. Instead, Turati broadcast the unmistakable message that the party should become an efficient political machine, running on lines laid down by the centre and without the intrusion of personal interests or ambitions on the part of individuals thrown up by the provincial movements. Hierarchy, discipline, and obedience were the key words relayed from the centre. The degree of reception is, of course, a different question.

3.4. THE VIEW FROM THE RANKS

For the ordinary rank and file fascists of the provinces, particularly for those who had been with the movement since 1921 or 1922, the new party line communicated a message that many had difficulty in understanding. This difficulty was related to their perceptions of what they had experienced and achieved in the first half of the decade. To appreciate their predicament fully it is essential to understand the extent of the control that many fascists had established within their provinces before the process of disciplining the party began in earnest in the second half of 1925. Faced with disciplinary measures, many former *squadristi* would recall the earlier period of almost total dominance, when they had enjoyed a largely uncontested sway over provincial affairs. Theirs was a memory of very personal control in which their authority had been little short of absolute, essentially private power used in a very public way. Many fascists who remained active in their provinces retained this personal conception of Fascism,

---

[34] Victoria De Grazia, *The Culture of Consent. Mass Organisation of Leisure in Fascist Italy*, Cambridge, Cambridge University Press, 1981, 38–44.

derived from their own experience. Fascism was essentially about *their* relationship with power in *their* province or town. Recalling this period in later years, they often found themselves in an ambiguous position, torn between a desire to reproduce what they considered to be the 'true' Fascism of the first years—the Fascism of the 'movement', when they had been the principal protagonists, when privileges had far outweighed duties—and the obligation to obey the Fascism of the 'regime'—the Fascism which seemed to have lost the crusading dynamism of the early years. Such people were inclined to reason in one of two ways. If they continued to hold office, they would often consider that, in the end, their contribution to Fascism had given them the right to exercise power on a largely personal basis and for personal ends; if they found themselves out of office, then they bitterly resented the power of the 'opportunists', the 'fascists of the sixth hour', who had usurped their positions and who (by definition) misused the authority that Fascism bestowed upon them. Either way of thinking was likely to be destabilizing.

This kind of reasoning was to characterize much of provincial Fascism in the course of the 1930s. In the years 1925–6 it was just beginning to become evident as the consequences of increased centralization were felt in the provincial federations. The call to order was not always well received among those accustomed to imposing their own discipline on others, often by very direct methods. Again, the degree to which fascist violence was part of a broader fascist ethic must be stressed. The *squadristi* regularly attached adjectives such as 'purifying' and 'cleansing' to the word violence and saw its employment as containing its own justification. Because of what was considered its moral function, violence was seen as totally legitimate—something essential to the cause of national transformation. Limitation of the use of spontaneous violence against enemies represented a severe curtailment of what many *squadristi* regarded as being almost the most positive aspect of Fascism, therefore. It was a limitation that threatened their very identity as fascists, outlawing that aspect which had helped form the strong bonds between the original fascist groups. Discipline posed real problems to which the *squadristi* could not find answers. How were you to deal with your enemies if the state now dictated that the beatings which were the expression of fascist intolerance of all opposition were formally illegal? Where was your power of intimidation now? The curtailment of violence represented the removal of something that was central not only to fascist 'style' but also to the fascist mission.[35]

As early as 1921 the anarchist Luigi Fabbri had recognized the importance of violence as a constituent element of the fascist movement: 'Fascism will lose all its sombre prestige and all its force as soon as it stops being violent.'[36] This was exactly

[35] On the characteristics and interpretation of fascist violence, see (in addition to the works quoted in Chapter 2 at note 11) A. Aquarone, 'Violenza e consenso nel Fascismo italiano', (1979) 1 *Storia contemporanea* 147; also A. Lyttelton, 'Fascismo e violenza: conflitti sociale e azione politica in Italia del primo dopoguerra' and J. Petersen, 'Il problema della violenza nel Fascismo italiano', both in (1982) 6 *Storia contemporanea* (pp 965 and 985 respectively).

[36] L. Fabbri, *La contro-rivoluzione preventiva*, Bologna 1921, quoted in Gentile, *Storia*, 321.

what the *squadristi* feared. For the *squadristi*, violence *was* politics; it was not a means to an end—something that would disappear as the politicians took over. The assurance that the state authorities would assume the task of repressing opposition and that Fascism was now synonymous with the state was of only limited reassurance to them. It might mean that the 'revolution' was guaranteed (although many doubted this because for them the revolution was intrinsically linked to violence) but, at the same time, it could also mean that those people in the provinces who had 'carried out the revolution' were being ordered to demobilize and stand aside for others, many of whom had very obviously jumped on the wagon of the winners.

Inevitably, the ordinary *squadristi* suffered from the same problem as the more violent and undisciplined of the provincial *ras*. The more successful they had been in destroying any opposition to Fascism, the less they became indispensable for the perpetuation of the movement. Some *squadristi* had difficulty in seeing this; many had no interest in seeing it. The collusion and complicity of certain fascists with criminal organizations had become apparent during 1925 (this seems to have been one of the features of Tamburini's Florentine fascist organization) and such people had no intention of renouncing privilege which was also profitable. Extortion ('voluntary contributions to the cause') and racketeering seem to have been fairly common.[37] As part of Mussolini's attack on Farinacci, as we have seen, the action squads were formally disbanded following the *fatti di Firenze* and, in addition, provincial federations were instructed to remove suspect elements from their membership lists. As a result, many of the more dubious figures were expelled. Formal disbandment was only a limited solution, however, in part because in some places the squads continued to exist under other names (some renamed themselves 'sporting associations', or 'welfare societies', more or less openly cocking a snook at central authority), but also because—at least for a few years after 1925—the groups continued to meet in the same bars and cafés and could be reconstituted as action squads within a matter of minutes if the command came from a local leader.

At the local level, it was extremely difficult to put the genie back into the bottle. Giuseppe Bottai would speak much later of a fatal 'illegitimate legitimacy' that developed within the fascist movement at this point, undermining any ordered progress of the movement.[38] He was referring to the fact that people thought that participation in the fascist battle had left them with acquired rights, often the rights to bully and threaten others with impunity. Taking these rights away from them was far from easy. It was an operation likely to provoke not only disturbances of the peace but also instability in the provincial federations as leaders and led sometimes pulled in very different directions.

---

[37] In some places, immediately following the March on Rome fascists had gone to the local banks and demanded 'loans' for considerable sums: see De Felice, *Mussolini il fascista*, vol. 1, *La conquista del potere*, Turin, Einaudi, 1966, 406.

[38] G. Bottai, *Vent'anni e un giorno*, Milan 1949 (the phrase cited is from the new edition, Milan, Rizzoli, 2008, 62).

It is worth pausing a moment to consider the position of many *squadristi* in the mid-1920s.[39] If they had fought in the First World War they were likely—by 1925—to be between 26 and 35, possibly a little older. By that year many of them would have seen ten years of almost continuous military action, first in the army and then in the paramilitary organization of Fascism. Possibly many of them would not have had any other kind of employment, either before the war, when they were too young, or after, when they faced the unemployment of the period of reconstruction. The fascist movement had pulled these people through the trauma that demobilized soldiers throughout Europe had suffered in the early 1920s, giving them a role, a purpose, and an identity when their fellow soldiers in other countries were begging on street corners or standing in dole queues. For those who did not find their way into the fascist militia—and this was one way of avoiding the crisis—the attack on the squads constituted a real betrayal of what the *squadristi* had fought for and, more immediately, presented serious problems of day-to-day survival. An anonymous letter from Padua to Mussolini in the early 1930s made this point well, talking—critically—of a group of local *squadristi* 'who have always exploited the fact of being fascists and are full of debts and want jobs because they say they have made Italy'.[40] In a sense, the disbandment of the squads represented for these people a kind of personal 'mutilated victory' and placed high on the agenda the problems of demobilization that had been put off for five years. Like Hitler's SA later, because of their restlessness, and because of the debt the fascist movement undoubtedly owed them, the *squadristi* represented a serious problem for the higher echelons of the party.

From 1925 onwards, in many places, very frequently the *fasci* became the focal point of fierce local battles as people jockeyed for power, position, and privilege. The status of local heroes may have been an issue in some cases, but in most the documentation makes it clear that control of the local *fascio* had much wider implications than simple personal status. People fought for control of the *fascio* because, increasingly after 1925, it was the local *fascio* that asserted its right in the provincial context to make appointments and to decide dismissals. Farinacci had done nothing to discourage these pretensions. On the contrary, his continual repetition of the intransigents' line appeared to justify it: '...we have the right to request that everything is fascist, that everything is at the service of the fascist regime...' And the reality of provincial life meant that much was at stake. The control of the local banks, boards of administration, the direction of the local *consorzi*, the presidency of the *consigli provinciali*...—these and many other positions were central to the exercise of power in the province and could become objects of bitter struggle. Moreover, they were, in many cases, highly

---

[39] For an in-depth treatment of the role and significance of *squadrismo* within the fascist movement, see Roberta Suzzi Valli, 'The Myth of Squadrismo in the Fascist Regime', (2000) 35(2) *Journal of Contemporary History* 131. Interesting insights are also to be found in Cristina Baldassini, 'Fascismo e memoria. L'autorappresentazione dello squadrismo', (2002) 5(3) *Contemporanea* 475.

[40] ACS, Min. Int., PNF, SPEP, b.11, Padua, undated, but early 1930s.

lucrative positions in themselves and with great potential for patronage. Not for nothing would Mussolini observe in later years that, only seven or eight years after the 'revolution', his chiefs of staff had grown old, had lost political energy and the 'shine of revolutionary youth', and—the cause of this precocious fading—had grown rich.[41]

[41] De Begnac, *Taccuini*, 467–8.

4

Party and State

4.1. PARTY AND STATE: HIERARCHIES OF AUTHORITY

While national party secretaries attempted to discipline unruly provincial party organizations and achieve some degree of stability within the movement, local party leaders—the *segretari federali*—were frequently facing attack from another direction. Despite the advent of Fascism, the Italian state had by no means faded away. Its principal representative at provincial level—the prefect—remained very much a force to be reckoned with.

The relationship between the prefect and the *segretario federale* of the *fascio* at provincial level was the sharp end of what was, in other places, a very theoretical debate taking place in the late 1920s about the exact roles and relationship of party and state. In these years the abstract and often incomprehensible philosophizing about the nature of the fascist ethical state was just beginning to gain momentum, but its clear thrust in the direction of the unitary, organic state had obvious implications for the place of the party. The regime found itself in the awkward position of having to stress the centrality of the party within the structure of the regime, while at the same time attempting to control and limit any kind of autonomous interpretation of that role. Government directives reflected this attempt at control. Yet, while in one measure after another it was made evident to local PNF leaders that their position was subordinate to the state, their precise role within the province remained difficult to define. Subordination to the state meant subordination to local representatives of the state and it was at this point that a conflict of competencies became apparent. It was a conflict that made evident the fact that the regime was much more than just the PNF because it represented the fascist state and not just the party. Although clearly a question of hierarchy—a word fascists claimed to respect—these were hierarchies local fascists sometimes found hard to understand.

In 1927 Mussolini had left little room for doubt about his position: '...I will never give the head of a prefect to any federal secretary'. He went much further in 1929, when he stated that '[t]he head of the province [the prefect] can issue orders to all those peripheral forces in which the State and the regime find expression; to the party, therefore, and to the federal secretary, who assumes the function and the precise physiognomy of subordinate collaborator of the head of the province, of a real and proper functionary *extra ruolo* of the prefecture'.[1] In the same speech he

---

[1] Edoardo and Duilio Susmel (eds), *Opera Omnia di Benito Mussolini* XXII, 381, quoted in Aquarone, *L'Organizzazione*, 163.

reiterated his thinking about the role of the PNF, stressing the 'solemn subordination of the party to the State' and insisting that it was essential not to confuse 'the *Partito Nazionale Fascista*, which is the primordial political force of the regime, with the regime itself'.[2] Local fascist leaders could have been forgiven for thinking that, had Mussolini made a similar statement in 1922, his political fortunes might have been very different.

Prefect and *segretario federale* were the main protagonists in the local disputes over definition of roles, but there was a further figure—usually somewhat out of the limelight—who was influential in the struggles. This was the local chief of police. It was to be of great importance in the conflict of competencies within the provinces that the police remained outside the control of the party. Mussolini's appointment of the extremely able Arturo Bocchini as chief of police in November 1926 (Bocchini was prefect of Genoa at this point) was to prove a master stroke, in as far as the new chief remained independent of party influences and, until his sudden death in 1940 (from over-eating), solidly faithful to Mussolini (even though, no doubt simply from professional habit, he could not resist keeping a file on the *duce* himself). The reform of the legislation on public order in late 1926 and the formation of the Division of Political Police (*PolPol*, of which the OVRA—the infamous secret police with responsibility for rooting out anti-fascism—would be a part) kept the mechanisms for repressing opposition firmly in the hands of state functionaries rather than fascist officials.[3]

Had the party gained control of the police it would undoubtedly have greatly increased fascist powers at the provincial level.[4] In fact, fascists *qua* fascists had few formal and autonomous repressive powers. People would be 'arrested' by local fascists and taken to fascist headquarters for questioning and worse, but if further (official) action was to be taken against the accused it had to pass through administrative channels related to the *Questura* (local police headquarters) and the Ministry of the Interior. In a sense, the party did have its own police force: the *Uffici Provinciali Investigativi* of the MVSN, formed in November 1926, operated in most provinces, had investigative powers, and ran their own informers. Moreover, as emanations of the party, they were not dependent on the Ministry of the Interior. Relatively little is known about the functioning of these offices but they seem to have had little real impact, partly, perhaps, because, in the event of successes against local 'subversives', the UPI were, in any case, not able to charge people directly, but had to pass through the channels provided by the *Questura* and the prefect.[5]

   [2] *Opera Omnia*, XXIV, 141–3, quoted in Aquarone, Ibid., 164.
   [3] See Giovanna Tosatti, 'Il Ministero dell'Interno e le Politiche Repressive del Regime', in Guido Melis (ed.), *Lo Stato negli anni Trenta*, Bologna, Il Mulino, 2008, 137f.
   [4] But see the important article by Jonathan Dunnage, 'Ideology, clientelism and the "fascistisation" of the Italian state: fascists in the Interior Ministry Police', (2009) 14(3) *Journal of Modern Italian Studies* 267.
   [5] On the police under Fascism see Mauro Canali, *Le spie del regime*, Bologna, Il Mulino, 2004; Ibid., 'Repressione e consenso nell'esperimento fascista', in Emilio Gentile (ed.), *Modernità totalitaria. Il Fascismo italiano*, Rome & Bari, Laterza, 2008, 65–7; see also Jonathan Dunnage, 'Surveillance and Denunciation in fascist Siena, 1927–1943', (2008) 28(2) *European History Quarterly* 244.

Day-to-day policing remained largely the responsibility of the *Questura*, there-fore, and the *Questura*'s dependence on the Ministry of the Interior guaranteed close collaboration between local police chief and prefect. The powers of the pre-fect were greatly increased by the introduction of the new law on public order of 1926 which, in effect, restored to the prefect many of the discretionary repressive powers he had enjoyed during the exceptional circumstances of the First World War.[6] In this respect, it should be noted that it was the prefect, and not the *federale*, who could send people to *confino* (domestic exile) after consulting with the Minis-try.[7] This restriction was possibly little assurance for the accused, given that, fol-lowing Federzoni's resignation in late 1926, Mussolini was always his own Minister of the Interior, but it did mean that people who fell foul of the local *fascio* were not totally at the mercy of local bullies. The state still had a role to play in their fate. Mussolini's policy was that of a gradual fascistization of the police rather than their subordination to the party. Unlike in Nazi Germany, therefore, where the party controlled the police and where Nazi police units could operate with relative impu-nity under the cover of the infamous protective custody regulations, people in Italy (with one or two notable exceptions) did not just disappear after being driven away in the large black car.[8]

The disposition of the repressive mechanisms of Fascism further emphasized what no *segretario federale* could fail to see—that, in questions of provincial admin-istration, central government had placed the prefect firmly in command, and that this represented, after years of confusion, a reaffirmation of central governmental intervention in local affairs. Made explicit by the Circular of January 1927 in which the prefect was defined as the 'supreme authority of the state' at provincial level, the primary position of the prefect had been apparent, for those disposed to see, since January 1925. The Ministry of the Interior, under Federzoni, had fought a long battle during 1925 and 1926 against fascist illegality in the provinces, incur-ring the bitter hostility of Farinacci for its pains. In telegram after telegram the

---

[6] On the theme of continuity of emergency legislation between war and Fascism, see Giovanna Procacci, 'Osservazioni sulla continuità della legislazione sull'ordine pubblico tra fine Ottocento, prima guerra mondiale e Fascismo', in Piero Del Negro, Nicola Labanca, Alessandra Staderini (eds), *Militarizzazione e Nazionalizzazione nella Storia d'Italia*, Milan, Unicopli, 2002, 83–96. The 1931 adjustment of the law further extended the powers of the prefect.

[7] *Confino* (domestic exile to a remote part of Italy) was an administrative sanction; its implementa-tion did not pass through the law courts, therefore. The same is true of the other commonly used weapons—the *diffida* and the *ammonimento* (warnings, of different degrees of severity)—which served to advise people that the authorities were watching them closely and that more severe punishment might easily follow continued 'misbehaviour'. On the history of *confino*, besides Tosatti cited above, see an excellent summary in Barbara Cardeti, *L'internamento civile fascista: il caso di 'Villa Oliveto' (1940–1944)*, Florence, Edizioni dell'Assemblea, 2010, Chapter 1; also, for a detailed analysis, see now Ebner, *Ordinary Violence*.

[8] It should be noted that police repression of opponents of Fascism was particularly extensive in the years 1927–32. The *Casellario politico centrale* (the police archive recording names and activities of political suspects, which dated back to 1894) was totally reorganized in 1927. In both 1929 and 1930 more than 12,000 new files were opened each year—far more than ever before. This is highly indica-tive of police, rather than party, activity, and was undoubtedly in part the result of a much improved and extended network of police informers. See Nicola Rapone, 'L'Italia antifascista', in *Storia d'Italia*, vol. 4, *Guerre e Fascismo*, ed. G. Sabbatucci and V. Vidotto, Rome & Bari, Laterza, 1997, p. 519f.

Minister urged prefects to make it clear to the local fascist organizations that acts of violence and intimidation were not to be tolerated. In particular, prefects were invited to move against those who attempted the reconstitution of the action squads (as happened during 1925, Tamburini in Florence being the most obvious example). Here Federzoni demonstrated concern for what was, in fact, the traditional concern of the Ministry of the Interior for the maintenance of public order, but his actions served to underline the fact that fascist illegality constituted a deliberate and explicit threat to the authority of the state and that the state was no longer prepared to tolerate that threat.

The prefect's position was asserted by more than simply contesting the lack of discipline of the fascist rank and file. In general terms, in the period 1923–29, the resolution of that dualism represented by the conflicting roles of party and state was realized largely at the expense of the PNF and in favour of the prefect. The centralizing thrust of the regime was directed in particular at the many semi-autonomous provincial and communal institutions that had survived undisturbed from the political and economic structures of the defunct liberal state and that, under socialist control in the years after the war, had presented the opportunity for a real challenge to the authority of the state. Remembering red flags on communal balconies, Federzoni, as the Minister of the Interior, spoke of the necessity to defend the state 'against that splintering and localist tendency which aimed to make the *comune* the instrument of the conquest and the destruction of the State'. Local autonomies were dramatically reduced (in part by the abolition of the elective principle) and ministerial control became the norm.[9] Such a thrust was not necessarily damaging to the authority of the party; it might have served to clear the ground for a greater fascist control of provincial and communal life. In point of fact, however, the destruction of many of the elements of local autonomy in the quest for centralization was carried out in a way that, with few exceptions, did nothing but emphasize the reduced status of the *segretario federale* in relation to the local representative of the state administration—the prefect.

In certain parts of Italy the administrative adjustments consequent on the fascist seizure of power had, in any case, favoured the prefect in his contest with the local party chief and seen the equilibrium of local control move decidedly towards the representative of the state. In many areas, particularly of the South of Italy between 1923 and 1926, this shift of balance was accentuated by the widespread use of ministerial *commissari prefettizi* and *commissari regi* in *comuni* that, for one reason or another, were distinguished for bad management or had become ungovernable. Where (often long-standing) tensions between the feuding groups had become too strong to permit a sitting administration to operate, the local council would be dissolved and a ministerial commissar put in its

---

[9] Ettore Rotelli, 'Le trasformazioni dell'ordinamento comunale e provinciale durante il regime fascista', in Sandro Fontana (ed.), *Il Fascismo e le autonomie locali*, Bologna, Il Mulino, 1973, 85. It is worth noting that in 1927 the *segretario comunale*—the principal and frequently very influential administrative figure of the *comune*—became a state employee, dependent on the Ministry of the Interior, rather than simply a dependent of the *comune*, as he had been up to that point. He referred to the prefect, therefore, rather than to the fascist mayor (the *podestà*).

place. The commissars, who had considerable powers, were intended to express neutrality and impartiality in local struggles and were used not only to replace inefficient (and/or sometimes socialist) administrations but also to discipline unruly fascist groups and local party bosses who had become too prominent for their own good. They represented, at least in theory, a way in which fascist central authority could break up the hold of local elites and make itself felt at local level. Even so, the commissars selected by the Ministry were frequently local people—a fact that was indicative of the capacity of local interests to influence even this kind of appointment. In practice the commissars often found it very difficult to resist local pressures and to act independently in their mediation functions. Intended as a cure for situations 'seriously characterized by localisms and personalisms', at times they risked becoming victims of the same forces.[10] As a result, they often became heavily dependent on the prefect (financially dependent even) and usually served to reinforce the position of the prefect *vis-à-vis* the local party leaders.[11]

That this reinforcement of the ministerial appointees represented a reversal of roles in many local contexts is beyond doubt. As one fascist put it in 1929:

> In the cities, the towns, the villages, the *fascio* dominated in the past, and, within the *fascio*, the most combative and intransigent elements—the nostalgia for the cudgel and for the beatings was common; now the prefect dominates, the police chief, the officer and the second officer of the *Carabinieri*...[12]

For many fascists, it was hard to take. One of the delights of fascist provincial leaders in the months before the March on Rome had been that of making life difficult for the prefect, provoking and goading the state official whose every move usually did no more than reveal his impotence in the face of the fascist squads. It was common for the provincial *ras* to boast that 'the prefect does what I tell him' and many accounts confirm that, before the March on Rome, prefects often followed the fascist line, sometimes out of sympathy for the fascist cause but often because they had no confidence that central government would support strong repressive measures and therefore found themselves with little choice. Domination of the prefect was one of the measures of the exceptional nature of a situation which, from a formal and legal point of view, should have looked very different. It did no more than reflect the fact that, in many provincial contexts, the local fascists had assumed full control, arrogating to themselves many of the functions of state administration.

The laws and decrees concerning provincial and communal administration, put into operation after 1925, undid this *de facto* dominance, much to the chagrin of many a *segretario federale*. The most striking example of this restoration of state authority is represented by the institution in most *comuni*, in 1926, of the fascist

[10] Luigi Ponziani, *Il Fascismo dei prefetti. Amministrazione e politica nell'Italia meridionale 1922–26*, Catanzaro, Meridiana libri, 1995, 72.
[11] Ibid., 65–7.
[12] Letter from Torquato Nanni to Rinaldo Rigola, Easter 1929, quoted in Aquarone, *L'Organizzazione*, 164–5.

podestà in the place of the elected mayor (and the elected communal council).[13] The *podestà* was to be responsible for the entire administration of the *comune* and was, therefore, a very important local figure, particularly from the point of view of financial administration, which involved distribution of public funds. What was significant was that he was nominated by royal decree on the basis of the indication of the prefect to the Ministry of the Interior. In his appointment, the local *federale* was to be consulted—indeed, the prefect would often be presented by the *federale* with a list of possible candidates—but the role was essentially consultative. Subsequent to the 1927 circular, many *federali* would contest the prefect's privilege in this respect, sometimes very successfully, but the formal position was clear.[14] Moreover, the decree creating the role of *podestà* stated that he was to be assisted in his functions by a *consulta municipale* (a kind of town council), one-third of which was to be made up by members designated directly by the prefect, and two-thirds by people representing local fascist unions, economic organizations and so on.[15] Both the number and the nature of these organizations was also left to the decision of the prefect, as was the choice of the representatives the organizations proposed to him. It should be further noted that the administrative decisions of the *podestà* were subject to the approval of the prefect.

In many respects the *podestà* was dependent on the prefect, who had the authority to revoke his appointment, and this dependence made the real terms of the new hierarchy obvious. Prefects were not above underlining heavily the extent of their control. In Siena in 1928, for example, the prefect sent out a confidential circular to the *podestà* of the province in which he put them in their place very firmly. He began by reminding them that 'the *podestà* is a state functionary, and, as such, is directly and immediately dependent on the Prefect'. Perhaps revealing what had, up till then, been the tendency, he made clear his resolve to prevent the formation of any 'local dictatorships' and repeated that the subordination of the 'most important *podestà* to the smallest Prefect' meant that they—the *podestà*—should not take part in any kind of 'reunion, demonstration, ceremony promoted or called by other persons or agencies' if they had not previously informed the prefect and obtained his permission. He ended by tersely requesting acknowledgement of receipt of the circular from all involved.[16]

In the same way, the prefect rather than the party chief was to be found as chairman of many of the local administrative committees. For example, the *Consigli provinciali per l'Economia*, which (as organs of the new corporative state) replaced the local chambers of commerce in 1926, were to be directed by the prefect. This

---

[13] The term cast back to the communal period in Italian history. The word *podestà* is both singular and plural.

[14] Pressures from the party were such that the right of the *federale* to intervene in nominations was formally recognized in November 1941. This was just one aspect of the significantly increased role being assigned to the PNF in the later years of the regime.

[15] Interesting observations on the membership of the *consulta* in Turin can be found in Luca Angeli, 'L'istituto podestarile. Il caso di Torino in prospettiva comparata (1926–1945)', (2001) 52 *Passato e presente* 19. Angeli stresses the degree to which the body, which did very little, was a kind of stooge for local financial and industrial interests, with the workers' role reduced to next to nothing.

[16] ACS, PNF, SPEP, b.21, Siena, 13 August 1928.

control gave him enormous power in dictating appointments and mediating between the various economic interests of the province. From late 1928 these bodies would even have responsibility for the control of food prices. In a different sphere, it was the prefect, and not the *federale*, who could decide which newspapers and magazines could be presented for sale in the province and which not. This was a power invoked usually with the excuse of the maintenance of public order, but it was often used to suppress broadsheets of local fascist factions when their campaigns found the prefect against them. In this way, as in many others, a wide interpretation of the administrative powers of the prefect could be used to condition the evolution of the local fascist party.

There was a further point that illustrated even more the degree to which Fascism after Matteotti had adjusted its sights. According to the law of 1926 the position of *podestà* was to be unpaid; only in very exceptional circumstances was the prefect permitted to allocate a salary from public funds. This measure, rather demagogically designed to discourage corruption or pursuit of private financial interest, meant that the *podestà* was often, at least in the early years of the institution, selected from among the wealthy members of the local community—from those who did not need to be paid.[17] The first directives from Rome insisted that the person appointed should be a local figure of standing. Thus local aristocrats, together with prosperous landowners and retired military personnel, figured largely among the people singled out for office. There was a strong possibility, therefore, that the *podestà*, frequently not a member of the party (although obviously a person sympathetic to Fascism), would have a different social origin from the *segretario federale* of the local *fascio* and was likely to be conservative in political orientation. Thus, not only did the *federale* not have the last word in the nomination of the *podestà*, but he could on occasions find himself dealing with the kind of person who, only a few years before, had been the object of fascist attentions as one of the local establishment to be excluded from any role in local political life.[18] In this case, as in the case of the operation of many prefectorial commissars in the South of Italy, measures directed at the streamlining and 'depoliticization' of provincial and communal administration often smacked of restoration.

In the face of these powers of the prefect and, to a lesser extent, of the *podestà*, what was the role of the *segretario federale* and the local PNF? Was nothing left for those who had (in some cases) followed the movement with such dedication from the beginning? Here a note of caution is in order. Despite all that has been said above, it would be a great mistake to think that, after 1927, the *federale* was no

---

[17] See Marco Palla, 'I podestà di nomina regia nella provincia di Forlì', (1993) 1 *Memoria e ricerca* 69–101; also Ponziani, *Prefetti*, 202–7. Luca Angeli, 'L'istituto podestarile', notes that the pattern changed from region to region, with the presence of ex-*squadristi* and party members being more marked in Emilia-Romagna than in Turin, Tuscany, or the South, where the elevated social position of the *podestà* was always more evident. Angeli concludes that 'neither the *podestà*, nor their collaborators, can be considered a class of professional politicians' (38).

[18] In 1929 Michele Bianchi would interpret the fact that only 12 per cent of the 6,095 *podestà* were paid as an indication that people took the position for the prestige rather than the money. He made no comment on what the figure revealed about the social origins and economic position of the vast majority of the *podestà*. See Rotelli, 'Le trasformazioni', 89–90.

longer a very important provincial figure and that the party had become no more than a home for ageing and nostalgic *squadristi*. As the local contests for power would make more than clear in the following years, there was still a lot that was worth fighting for and many *federali* were far from recognizing defeat in their attempts to assert their control. All was far from being totally cut and dried after January 1927. There would be many cases in later years of the *federale* gaining the upper hand over the prefect. In particular, *federali* would return again and again to the question of the appointment of the *podestà*, insisting on a right of veto (which in practice they often gained) and even on a prerogative in proposing candidates.

Certainly, the largely unrestricted power of the *federale* had been severely curtailed in the course of 1925–7, particularly in relation to his capacity to intervene in the administration of the province and the various *comuni*. He could no longer be the independent, fire-eating *ras* of the early years, ignoring both Rome and the prefect. But he did have some very significant functions determined by his position as local party leader. He was *ex officio* the head of the *fascio* of the provincial capital—no mean position. He appointed the heads of the *fasci* in the various *comuni* within the province and determined many of the appointments to the various capillary organizations emanating from the *fasci*. As local party leader, he had responsibility for appointing the leaders of the *Gruppi universitari fascisti* (GUF) (the fascist university students' organization) in his area, and, after 1931, of the *fasci giovanili di combattimento* (FGC) (the more general fascist youth movement). He had considerable powers of patronage, therefore. Moreover, he was responsible for discipline among local fascists (including, according to the party statute, members of the MVSN, the *Balilla* youth groups, and the fascist union organizations) and could pronounce expulsions, something which could easily mean the end of a person's political life.

Most significant, he presided (from 1927 until a revision of the structures of the PNF in 1937) over the *Comitato intersindacale* of the province—an organism which was intended to put into action on the local level the corporative idea of collaboration between employers and workers and which brought together, under its wing, all the different economic organizations of the province. As the organism responsible for negotiating labour agreements and mediating in disputes, the *comitato* was at the centre of provincial affairs; as its president, therefore, the *federale* was in a position of great influence with industrialists, landed proprietors, banks, fascist union leaders, and with the workers they represented. During the years of the economic crisis, beginning in 1927 when the revaluation of the lira produced deflation within Italy, this position was to be of great importance in determining the ways in which wage reductions were to be effected and how, for a brief period in 1927–8, certain food prices were to be controlled—both areas in which party intervention could have an important impact on local economic life.[19] The influence was extended

---

[19] Philip Morgan, ' "The Party is Everywhere": The Italian fascist party in economic life, 1926–40', (1999) 114(455) *English Historical Review* 85. The difficult business of price controls was passed to the *Consiglio provinciale dell'economia* in 1928, to be resumed by the PNF from 1934 until 1937, when the *comitati intersindacali* were abolished.

in 1928 when employment exchanges were set up in all provinces, presided over by the *federale*. Party control of employment was a particularly important stick for beating both employers and workers, according to circumstances and alliances.

Yet, although the *federale* still had considerable power and although the party was given an important controlling role in the economic affairs of the province (and would keep this role until 1937),[20] the real significance of the restructuring of authority that had taken place between 1925 and 1927 was that the local party secretary had been made to understand that he was no longer a free agent. His job was to respect and implement initiatives that had their origin elsewhere. It is true that implementation of policy often opened the road to interpretation of particular policies, which in turn permitted the use of a *federale's* own judgement and discretion when it came to application. For example, arbitrating between employers and workers could be done with greater or lesser reference to particular political criteria. Thus one *federale* might be seen to favour the employers consistently, while another would make efforts to protect the workers. Even so, the function was essentially an executive function and could not be viewed otherwise. In fact, Mussolini, in his 1929 speech partially quoted above, attempted a positive definition of the role of the party while at the same time making clear that the local party secretary had no decision-making capacity:

> The party is the capillary organization of the regime. Its importance is fundamental. It gets everywhere. More than exercising authority, it exercises an apostolate and with the sole presence of its regimented masses it represents the element defined, characterized, controlled in the midst of the people. It is the party with its mass of supporters that gives to the authority of the State its voluntary consensus and the incalculable support of a faith.[21]

This was strong stuff—possibly, one suspects, because it was intended to compensate for powers that, if not totally lost, had nonetheless been severely limited. Even so, certain of the words the fascist leader chose were very revealing of the functions the party was to assume within the context of the fascist state. 'Capillary', 'everywhere', 'regimented', 'followers'—these were words which indicated the essential functions of the party at local level and defined the parameters within which the local *federale* should work. In practical terms, devoid of the rhetoric, Mussolini was explaining that the party was to organize, educate, and regiment the population, preaching the fascist message in order to provide the necessary foundation of popular consensus on which the regime was based. This was far from being an unimportant role; indeed, it was central to the creation of the totalitarian state and constituted one of the major novelties represented by Italian Fascism. If the Italian people were to be transformed in some way by Fascism, this was going to happen

---

[20] In 1937 the two main provincial councils—the *Consiglio provinciali per l'economia* and the *comitato intersindacale*—were rolled into one with the formation of the *consigli provinciali delle corporazioni*. In each province this council was headed by the prefect, with the *federale* having a position on the council, together with representatives of the employers and the unions; see Aquarone, *L'Organizzazione*, 218.

[21] *Opera Omnia* XXII, 381, quoted in Aquarone, *L'Organizzazione*, 163.

only through the operation of the party at the grass-roots level. And this, through the many organizations and associations formed by the regime that involved so many people in one way or another, was what the party attempted during the 1930s.

Evidently, given the way in which the party managed to extend its influence into so many areas of normal life, this was a function that gave considerable power to those responsible for the administration of the fascist machine. In fact, in most respects the party's bureaucratic powers increased during the course of the 1930s, keeping it firmly at the centre of provincial life. The party remained the arbiter of many local situations and membership of the party constituted an essential qualification for many administrative posts. Yet it is important to recognize that it was essentially a bureaucratic and organizational role that was being allocated to the party. It was the *administration* of Fascism at local level and it was not what many provincial fascists had imagined to be the objective of the fascist battle. As Nanni put it in 1929 in the letter cited above, 'with the system of appointment from above...even the political secretaries and the *podestà* are becoming *functionaries*, purely and simply'.[22] Certainly local fascists had some rewards. But even as they basked in the reflected glory of the local symbols of fascist modernity—the *casa del fascio*, the new railway station, the monumental post office—they could hardly fail to realize that their role was that of management, not of decision. As they organized, regimented and educated, threatened, intimidated, and cajoled, many of the first fascists were bound to reflect on the fact that they were now merely cogs in a motor the driving force of which lay elsewhere. It was no longer possible to imagine that the party—particularly the provincial party—was the leading edge of the revolution.

4.2. PARTY AND STATE: HIERARCHIES CONTESTED

The question of appointments determined one of the characteristic features of provincial politics from 1926 onwards—the contest between *federale* and prefect. This was a contest that, in many areas, seriously affected the efficient working of the party machine. Formally, there was no question to be answered; the 1927 circular decreed that the prefect was the ultimate authority of the state within the province. But fascist leaders were reluctant to accept this state of affairs, precisely because of their assumption that fascist control of the state meant, very logically, *their* control of the locality. They attempted to implement, at the local level and to their own benefit, the authority principle they themselves recognized in respect of Mussolini, and this almost inevitably brought them into conflict with the prefect.

Federali found some justification for their claims to ultimate authority in the fact that central government frequently fudged the issue of who should command when it came to provincial administration, reserving some functions for the prefect and others for the party leader in an obvious attempt to square the circle and appease both sides. As a consequence, in many provinces the relationship between party and state continued to be essentially unresolved. Relations between the two

---

[22] Nanni, as note 12 above.

authorities remained unsettled, with complaints being made from both sides that the other was overstepping the limits of his authority.

This was to be a persistent problem. An example drawn from as late as December 1940 illustrates the kind of relationship that often developed between prefect and federal secretary. Following reports of inactivity, the *federale* of Reggio Emilia complained to a fascist inspector, sent to sort out the differences in the province, that the prefect 'had had little respect for him up till then; that, in order to humiliate him, he had tried several times to exclude him from the public and administrative life of the province;... that he had consistently shown little deference towards the party; that he had obstructed him with all the means he had'. The inspector then went to the prefect, to get his side of the story, and was told that the *federale* was 'a gossiper, a liar, a professional squabbler; that he had not known how to approach the *squadristi* of the place; that he had humiliated the *fascio* of Reggio by making inopportune comparisons with the *fascio* of Florence...; that he had not known how to choose his collaborators, to the extent that there were at least five members of the Federal Directorate who had been expelled from the Party...' Such contrasts were typical of many provinces, with prefect and *federale* both convinced that each could do the job of the other better.[23]

A way out of the problem appeared to be the creation of prefects drawn from the ranks of loyal fascists. In this way, it was assumed, prefect and *federale* would be bound to see things in the same light. Before 1925, however, there were few inducements to prominent fascists to put themselves forward for the job of prefect; real power in so many provinces still lay elsewhere. In fact, from 1923 onwards a few fascists were nominated prefect, thus apparently meeting the intransigent fascist demand that, in the fascistization of the new Italy, state officials should all be fascist.[24] The results were generally unsatisfactory, however, and it was only with the elevation of Farinacci to party secretary in February 1925 that the pace of substitution increased. Even so, the appointments were relatively few. Of the eighty-six new prefects appointed between 1922 and 1929 only twenty-nine were recognizably fascist.[25] The others were drawn from the established career service of the Ministry of the Interior. Moreover, apart from the fact that, in many cases, the new men were sent to fairly unimportant peripheral provinces, the creation of fascist prefects proved to be no solution to the problem of a dualism of authority in the provinces.[26]

---

[23] Perry Willson charts the way in which the very active women's organizer in Reggio Emilia, Laura Marani Argnani, in 1929 went over the heads of the local fascist leaders, who had refused her funding, and appealed directly for support from the prefect. Although she was, in this case, successful, there can be little doubt that the long-term consequences of such actions were to increase the tensions between fascist and state authorities. See Willson, *Peasant Women and Politics in Fascist Italy; the* Massaie rurali, London, Routledge, 2002, 192.

[24] In the first meeting of the Grand Council of Fascism—the directing body of the movement—on 11 January 1923, Mussolini asked the PNF to provide him with seventy-six fascist prefects and seventy-six fascist police chiefs (one for each province). The request was not followed up in any serious way.

[25] Aquarone, *L'Organizzazione*, 75.

[26] Melis, *Storia dell'amministrazione*, 355–7, concludes that, despite the entry of some fascist prefects, '[t]he key prefects of the *ventennio*, that is those nominated to the most sensitive and prestigious situations, continued to be, essentially, men of the administration' (355).

Experience soon showed that the fascist prefects were frequently those who quarrelled most with their local *federale*. This demonstrated that the differences between prefect and *federale* were not ideological, in the sense of the difference between the fascist and the non-fascist, but were much more simply about who should command and where. Precisely because they were fascists, fascist prefects tended to think that they could do both jobs and that the federal secretary was essentially redundant. Typical of the fights between prefect and *federale* was that reported in an official *Nota Riservata* of 16 October 1930, which warned the party secretary that the prefect of Modena—in this case a career prefect—was likely to cause trouble.

> The prefect of the Province [of Modena] Ernesto Perez thinks that the activity of the *segretario federale* is excessive and that it invades his area of responsibility. For the present, nothing to worry about, but it is probable that, very shortly, it will be necessary to intervene.[27]

A simple distinction between administration (prefect) and political activity (*federale*), invoked by some, proved totally unworkable. This was only to be expected when, for example, it was the prefect who directed the *Consigli provinciali per l'Economia* and the *federale* who controlled the *Comitati intersindacali*; the overlap in functions was obvious and created a dualism which frequently degenerated into 'an open struggle'.[28] As already mentioned, differences between prefect and *federale* usually arose when it was a question of appointing people to important jobs in the province—directorates, boards of administration, unions, councils of the various economic organizations, and so on. There were demarcations laid down in the formal competencies of both prefect and party leader, but these were often not respected and each would try to expand into all the space available.

This contest was not simply a question of accumulating personal influence. Prefect and *federale* would be likely to have different criteria for appointments, the first looking primarily to administrative and technical competence, the second to loyalty to the party, to the fascist 'mission', and—as we shall see—to more personal considerations. In fact, the two men had very different interests and objectives. While the PNF *federale* was concerned (in theory) with the affirmation and continued health of the party at local level, and was therefore usually ready to stand by his supporters, even when unruly and undisciplined, the prefect's main interest was in asserting the dominant position of central government and in the maintenance of public order. And public order was defined by the statute book and enforced by the Ministry of the Interior, not by the squads and the PNF, as many prefects would have occasion to observe during the course of the *ventennio*. From June 1924, when Federzoni became Minister of the Interior, efforts had been made by the Ministry to recoup authority that had been lost to the fascists and prefects were made to understand that the imperative of public order was to be taken seriously. Precisely for this reason, prefects' career prospects depended to a great degree on their success in maintaining good public order and this remained their main

---

[27] ACS, PNF, SPEP, b. 8, Modena.   [28] Aquarone, *L'Organizzazione*, 217.

priority, often overriding any special regard to be paid to local fascists and their activities.

It was no doubt this priority that, in large part, determined that even 'fascist' prefects, appointed from the ranks of the party and not from the career track of the civil service, would frequently become attentive followers of state rather than fascist imperatives. In the same way that career prefects would carefully understate intractable problems in their particular province or emphasize excessively their own activities in solving local problems, prefects coming from the fascist movement would stress the fact that it was they who were keeping local fascists under control. What is striking is the degree to which the new men took on so rapidly the imperatives of the state and appeared to put in second order those of the PNF, frequently irritating those fascists who considered themselves the real makers of the 'revolution'.

Intervention by prefect could have a profound influence on the efficiency of the local party. On occasions a strong prefect could assist a weak or inexperienced *federale*, but not too much. A prefect concerned to assert his authority would try to make sure that he had a relatively weak and pliable *federale* to work with—a position that might have negative repercussions on the working of the local party machine because the weak *federale* would not command respect among local fascists. Conversely, a strong *federale* might find his path blocked repeatedly by protests from the prefecture. The result, in Philip Morgan's words, was 'a party leadership which lacked standing and authority among the membership and a loss of drive and initiative in party activity'.[29]

The situation of open or latent conflict in many provinces was not helped by the creation of the figure of the *podestà*. As we have seen, the *podestà* was the non-elected equivalent of the mayor in the *comune* and as such had very significant administrative functions, not the least of which was allocating government contracts for public works. The intention behind the creation of this figure was to avoid the confusions and divisions of local elections and the excessive influence of local lobbies. The *podestà* was to be an impartial administrator, national rather than local in his legitimation and therefore not beholden in any way to the provincial elites. Intentions notwithstanding, for several years after the appointment of the first *podestà* in 1926, the office became a further cause of conflict between prefect and *federale*.

This conflict was a serious problem because in large provinces with many *comuni*, it represented an almost permanent source of friction. In one or another of the *comuni*, a *podestà* would almost always be either coming or going. The prefect would often attempt to appoint a local man, in the hope that a figure of some prestige in the area would be able to administer with authority. Moreover, he would attempt to appoint someone with whom he himself felt he could work. By so doing, he inevitably stimulated infighting among groups within the *comune*, eager to put their own candidate forward (and to denigrate the rival). In this way the

[29] Philip Morgan, 'The prefects and party–state relations in fascist Italy', (1998) 3(3) *Journal of Modern Italian Studies* 241; the quotation is from page 261.

podestà often became a pawn in the battles already being fought between factions, not only at provincial but also at communal level, and also in the conflicts between prefect and *segretario federale*. To quote Philip Morgan again, 'the *podestà* was sucked into the vortex of the local internal political battles and became one of the richest prizes to be contested in the incessant squabbles between rival groups and families'.[30]

Provincial societies were very far from accepting in supine manner the imposition of central control, therefore. *Federali* contested the prefect in many spheres of activity and national directives often met with little respect in the provincial setting. The intended centralizing and de-provincializing function of the *podestà* was rarely strong enough to withstand provincial pressures. At most it could be said that provincial battles were now fought out with some reference to prefect and central authority, even though these were not always decisive in the evolution and the outcome of the struggles.[31] Provincial—and communal—realities retained a powerful capacity to condition choices.

Over the years the dualism of authority within the province—state and party— caused some to argue that the roles of prefect and *federale* should be amalgamated, saving both time and money, and avoiding the conflicts which only served to make life difficult for everyone. Farinacci was a strong supporter of the idea, clearly tending to give priority to the role of the party. Most argued the opposite. As evidence of arrogance and malpractice by the *federali* gathered, rather timid suggestions were heard from some quarters to the effect that it was the local party secretary who was, perhaps, superfluous. In 1933 an informer in Rome, commenting the arrest of several *gerarchi* in Milan, remarked that some people were saying that it was 'now opportune to reduce the importance of the role of the Federal Secretary and just leave the prefect in command...thus avoiding this kind of power-sharing'.[32] Four years later, observations that went even further came from an informer in Perugia. Local people were advocating that the provincial federations be wound up completely, with power passing exclusively to the prefecture. This request was provoked by constant friction between the two authorities and a clearly perceived duplication of functions. The activity of the *federale* was judged to be 'useless and often damaging' to the initiatives of the prefect, 'often limited by the fact of having to get the opinion and the agreement of the federal secretary'. This conflict produced a situation in which the prefect, if he wanted to make important appointments, was forced to 'ask the federal secretary, whose opinion often has precedence'. The best way to avoid these contrasts, which frequently blocked all activity, was to eliminate the figure of the *federale*, particularly as prefects were judged to be 'all fascists'.[33]

Disagreements over appointments aside, there was undoubtedly more to the contrasts between prefect and *federale* than differing views of their respective func-

---

[30] Philip Morgan, 'I primi podestà fascisti: 1926–32', (1978) 3 *Storia contemporanea* 407.
[31] Baris, *Il Fascismo in provincia*, 46–7. If matters got out of hand, the prefect could request the appointment of a *commissario*—an external (and temporary) solution to the problem.
[32] ACS, MI, DGPS, Polizia Politica, b. 219, 28 June 1933.
[33] ACS, Ibid., 6 February 1937.

tions. Turf wars were an important motive for hostilities, but it is difficult not to feel that the public fights that often developed between the two officials reflected a largely unspoken hierarchy of legitimacy that went beyond the words of the 1927 circular. The prefect knew that he had a long and very distinguished tradition behind him, stretching back to 1861. He was accustomed to command respect from those he dealt with because he was the representative of the state. At provincial level there was no higher authority. With perfect legitimacy he could speak of the King as his ultimate referent, given that he was nominated by royal decree. Fascist *federali*, on the other hand, could not quite aspire to the same kind of authority. Despite all the rhetoric about the nation and Fascism being the same thing, the violent origins of the fascist movement—and the implicit threat of violence that remained in many provinces well after 1925—suggested a more dubious claim to respect. Fascists held power because they had conquered power; their legitimacy was self-asserted and therefore open to question.

Often the social and political origins of the *federali* worked against them. Self-selected in a sense, many had distinguished themselves by their use of violence rather than by their use of words or administrative skills. Moreover, they liked to stress the fact that they were the 'new' men. Sometimes it showed. Most were new to political life and fairly rough at the edges. In certain official contexts the uncouth new could not quite replace the old; all too often they lacked the aplomb, the *dignitas*, the style of the traditional. There is often a distinct sense of *de haut en bas* in the manner in which prefects treated the fascist officials. Although from a later period, the following description of the *federale* of Piacenza by the prefect who was supposed to work with him is not untypical. The opinion is referred by a third party, reporting the prefect's phrases. It should be noted that this is a fascist prefect speaking—a fact that is suggestive of the way people changed when they changed roles.

> 'The people who command are the Prefects. The *federali* have to do what the Prefects tell them'—'The Prefect will not protect the *federale* any longer'—'You, *federale*, are a person of modest education and capabilities'—And referring in general to the preparation and capabilities of the *federali* of the country: '...of the ninety-seven *segretari federali* in all Italy only around twenty are up to the job of educating the young people.'[34]

The local politics of Fascism was clearly not going to thrive with this kind of conflict going on in so many places. In fact, the greater social prestige attached to the position of prefect may have been one of the reasons for which the fascist prefects appear to have distinguished themselves by taking their distance from their colleagues within the party. Yvon De Begnac observed, of the fascists who had been made prefects:

> Some of them behaved very well; but the mass of the political functionaries were careful to transform themselves, the day after the decree nominating them, into severe supporters of the rights of reaction...In this way we got to the paradox of fascist

---

[34] ACS, PNF, SPEP, b. 14, Piacenza, 8 January 1938.

prefects who quarrelled with fascist *federali* solely because both thought the slice of power they had was too small.[35]

In fact, quarrel as they might (often in public), *federali* and fascist prefects tended to suffer from the same problems. As men with little or no experience of administration, their shortcomings were all too obvious to those who had that experience. Worse, these limitations were often magnified by the tendency of the newly arrived to show off in public, frequently making themselves ridiculous. This was true at the highest levels. De Begnac (not an observer unfavourable to Fascism) again:

> The writer of these pages has met almost everywhere these 'elect' [the new men of Fascism], coming from a world of absolute ignorance of our history and our culture, and achieving a rank completely outside the possibilities of their social education. The writer of these pages has seen consuls, consul generals, and ministers, coming from the fascist movement, who have caused hilarity in foreign cultural circles and cast discredit on the Revolution they had used in order to get themselves a high salary.[36]

4.3. POOR PERSONNEL

De Begnac's observation touched what was to be a permanent open sore of the regime. Beginning as soon as the second half of the 1920s and continuing throughout the 1930s, the poor quality of the fascist supporters available for administrative and political positions at the local level attracted attention. This deficiency further added to provincial problems. Not only were the provinces disrupted by the struggles between the central party directorate and the local bosses, between the same local bosses and the prefects, and between the *podestà* and either or both of the other two authorities, but the fascists involved were increasingly perceived to be inadequate to the task.

The question of the quality of fascist personnel made itself felt initially in respect of the appointment of the first fascist mayors in 1926, because the educational requirements for office were found to exclude a surprising number of the people linked to the movement. The same problem extended to many other positions. Prefects looked for ability and political fidelity in the people they appointed, but when they found, as they often did, that the two did not always go together, they looked for the first rather than the second. This kind of preference offended fascists who considered themselves candidates for office, but their opinion of themselves was often not shared by others. In report after report, prefects and other government officials emphasized that a fundamental problem was the lack of competent fascists able to undertake tasks of provincial administration, organization, and leadership.

Both the anonymous *fiduciari* (police and party informers) and the prefects persistently recounted that good men were in short supply. They would often add

---

[35] De Begnac, *Palazzo Venezia. Storia di un regime*, Rome, La Rocca, 1950, quoted in Aquarone, *L'Organizzazione*, 74.
[36] Ibid.

that those local fascists who were in command were not up to the job either. In their eyes, the 'new men' of Fascism did not have either the education or the personal qualities to replace the old guard. To return for a moment to the question of the *podestà*, it is revealing that, according to the figures of Luigi Ponziani, in only 40 per cent of the 926 southern Italian *comuni* with a population of less than 5,000 did the first *podestà* complete the full five-year period of office. By 1931 the others had either resigned or been sacked. Of the 367 who did complete their term, only 269 (less than 30 per cent of the original group) were proposed for reappointment. And these were not just teething troubles. It is interesting to note that the number of substitutions (or of the nomination of a *commissario* by the prefect to take the place of a *podestà*) was actually accelerating in 1929 and 1930.[37] This rate of change does not look exactly like the formation of a new ruling class, but it does suggest a rapid rate of depletion among those few who had been thought worthy of being part of it.

The same difficulty seems to have afflicted the fascist syndicates. Although the unions constituted an area where some able and committed people did operate, often coming from a socialist or revolutionary syndicalist past, the overall picture seems not to have been very different. In an article in *Critica fascista* in 1928, a critic of the unions, Gaetano Roma, denounced the 'absolute mediocrity' of most union leaders, who were—he wrote—self-appointed officials with neither ability nor particular competence in union affairs. An accompanying editorial (presumably by Bottai himself) endorsed the opinions of Roma wholeheartedly.[38]

In their reports to the Ministry, prefects frequently returned to the question of poor *cadres*. For example, in 1926 the prefect of the province of Salerno despaired of finding 129 good *podestà* for the 129 *comuni* of his province. He wrote that his job was 'difficult because suitable people are few or missing altogether'.[39] In Padua in 1931 it was reported that there were problems because of the 'difficulty of finding people who are able and ready to accept responsibility' while, in the same province in 1932, it was stated that the *federale* was hampered in his work by the fact 'of not having a sufficient number of able people available to whom he can entrust jobs involving direction. That depends...on the absenteeism of local people...'[40] In Siena in 1931 the prefect lamented 'the fact that [the] best prepared people and those most suited to carry out any political or administrative activities...withdraw, abstain (as far as is decently possible) from any act of support or of collaboration with the Federal Secretary'.[41] In the same way the prefect of Ferrara

[37] Ponziani, *Prefetti*, 209. Note Ponziani's conclusions (209–10) in relation to Southern *comuni*, the study of which 'confirms...the persistent difficulty of Fascism in maintaining a political and social control on the local *comuni* which was not tendentially coercive and...the obstinate insistence of men and social and economic circles in many *comuni* to consider the administration of their *comune* as an independent variable in respect of national politics, even in the face of a total change of regime'.

[38] Gaetano Roma, 'Dirigenti sindacali', *Critica fascista*, 15 February 1928, quoted in Ferdinando Cordova, *Verso lo stato totalitario*, Soveria Mannelli, Rubbettino, 2005, 91.

[39] Ibid., 191.

[40] ACS, PNF, SPEP, b. 11, Padua, 'Estratto della relazione del mese di maggio 1931'; 'Estratto della relazione del mese di febbraio 1932'.

[41] ACS, PNF, SPEP, b. 20, Siena, 12 February 1932.

wrote, in 1934, that 'among such a mass of people [in the province] there are very few who show themselves to be suitable for public office, particularly from the point of view of their intellectual capacity'.[42]

A later report, this time from the prefect of Piacenza, provided a perfect illustration of the problem. He was, admittedly, no friend of the *federale* and was therefore disposed to criticize the party, but his attempt to explain why things were going so badly in his province during 1937 did point to fairly typical shortcomings.

> The solution to the problem of the rejuvenation of office holders…depends on the preparation of *cadres*, which is in large measure beyond the competence and the possibilities of the Prefecture, being principally the job of other organizations. This sector is characterized by the most depressing squalor. In the course of the last fifteen years there has been no sign at all of the emergence of people able to take on jobs of a certain importance. All the people now used in the public administration belong to the category of those brought in from outside, not of those formed by Fascism.[43]

Here the prefect made clear the distinction between technical competence—a phrase the fascists liked to bandy around a great deal—and allegiance to Fascism. What he was at pains to underline was the fact that the two were not to be found together and that the regime was not generating new and able administrators.

The shortage of able fascists at the local level was to be a problem that would bedevil the fascist regime during its entire existence. Formally, of course, the fascist movement had committed itself to a revolution in the social composition of those in authority. The creation of a new governing class was high on the agenda of the movement from an early stage and had been reflected, not only in Farinacci's frontal attack on the civil service in 1925, but also more generally in the frequent references to the creation of the fascist 'new man'. Part of the credibility of the fascist movement was posited on the degree to which it could distance itself from the despised class of silver-haired men that had dominated Italy before 1922 and mobilize new forces. The functioning of many of the capillary organizations in the provinces depended on this kind of mobilization among the provincial petty bourgeoisie. Without an army of willing helpers—some paid, some volunteers—the fascist revolution was likely to lose its impetus.[44]

The difficulties the regime experienced in this respect were, at least in part, of the movement's own making. As we shall see in the next chapter, many of the original pre-March on Rome fascists had fallen victim to the internal party squabbles of the 1920s; others had become disillusioned with the movement and had decided to call it a day. These two paths away from Fascism, not always unconnected, were a testimony to the evolution of the movement over the course of the 1920s—an evolution that had provoked both dissidence and disillusion among many of the

[42] ACS, MI, Direzione Generale Amministrazione Civile, Affari Generali e Riservati, b. 150, 18 June 1934, quoted in Roberto Parisini, *Dal regime corporativo alla Repubblica Sociale: Agricoltura e Fascismo a Ferrara 1928–1945*, Ferrara, Corbo, 2005, 22.

[43] ACS, PNF, SPEP, b. 14, Piacenza, Prefect Montani to Minister of Interior, 1 May 1937.

[44] Cf. De Grazia, who quotes the complaints of the *federale* of Trento in 1931 about the 'scarcity of school teachers…almost the only element on which we can rely in the small municipalities' (*Culture of Consent*, 40, note 49).

faithful as Fascism reneged on many of its more radical positions (republicanism is an obvious example) and became immersed in the compromises of power. The first dissident movements—as early as 1921—indicated that conceptions of what Fascism represented could be very different. Differences were frequently insurmountable and people were pushed to the margins or expelled if they persisted in expressing opinions contrary to those of the directing group either in their own locality or in Rome. On occasions it would become clear to blackshirts that enemies within the local fascist group had gained the upper hand to the extent that there was no point in remaining within the movement. Many would take no further part in fascist activities because of this.

There was, therefore, a continuing process of adjustment throughout the first half of the 1920s which left many casualties in its wake. And, as suggested in the previous chapter, the massive purges of party members between 1925 and 1931—realized first by Farinacci and then, to a much greater degree, by Turati and Giovanni Giuriati, who followed him—tended to hit the local activists whose very commitment to some of the more radical aspects of Fascism had forced them into positions of conflict with the central party directorate. The purges were a necessary blood-letting from the point of view of party discipline and the authority of the party hierarchy, but they cost the fascist movement dear in terms of dynamism and, more immediately, in terms of efficiency.

For local fascist organizations, a further factor in reducing the quality of the personnel available was represented by both the requirements and the strategies of the centre. It was no surprise that Mussolini called to himself in Rome many of the fascists who had, in some way or other, distinguished themselves for their ability at the local level. These were assigned to some of the ministries and to posts of undersecretary and formed the administrative hub of the PNF (Bianchi, Lantini, Arpinati are examples). To some extent they could be paraded as the representatives of a new fascist governing class and, again to some extent, they did perform that function. The call to service at the centre was not always determined by exclusively functional considerations, however. It is obvious that in some cases—the case of Renato Ricci of Carrara, for example—the appointment to Rome was a way of removing a difficult or undisciplined fascist from his local power base in order to better control that person at the centre. From Mussolini's point of view, it was preferable to have ambitious followers pursuing their careers in Rome than in their provincial homelands, where such careers risked being disruptive and destabilizing. The strategy of ostensible promotion was used to sort out a series of local difficulties in 1929, when a number of troublesome provincial fascists found themselves elected to parliament on the fascist list and then discovered that this honour was incompatible with their holding any kind of office at provincial level. *Promoveatur ut amoveatur* was a useful device for Mussolini, but it did tend to make discipline, or the lack of it, rather than ability, the paramount criterion for advancement.

But not all the problems of personnel within the movement were created by tensions or conflicts among fascists. It was natural that, after several years of intense political activity, some people would withdraw to do other things, from economic necessity, for family reasons, or even, perhaps, from boredom. The initial activism of a fascist movement that had seen itself as the midwife of a new history was increasingly frustrated. Permanent revolutions require permanent activity and this was not always forthcoming; beating up socialists in the 'punitive expeditions' was probably more exciting than organizing a tug of war among schoolchildren.

However, a certain detachment from fascist militancy did not always depend on a critical position in respect of the evolution of the movement. Disillusion and disgust there may have been in some quarters, but it was far from being all resentment after 1925. Many prominent local fascists used their prominence to good effect, finding lucrative positions in local society and ceasing active militancy in the movement as a result. An attractive *sistemazione* was one of the main reasons for the defection of some of supporters in the course of the 1920s—of those who had never really envisaged any kind of permanent political career but who had nonetheless managed to make themselves noted in their immediate surroundings. Many of the first fascists lost their radicalism when they found their way into good jobs in local administration, in business, or in banking, largely as a reward for services rendered. Such people were not lost completely to Fascism; they furnished a sympathetic environment within which the provincial federations could work. A bank manager who was also a former *squadrista* might make all the difference in hard times—but these employment choices did take good people away from the direct running of local Fascism.

In this respect a particular note should be reserved to the fascist militia, the MVSN. A large number of the *squadristi* passed to this organization after its formation in early 1923 and after the various attempts at the dissolution of the squads throughout 1925. The effect of the formation of the MVSN was certainly that of slowly but progressively drawing the sting of *squadrismo*, as had been the intention, but it also had a further effect of creating a world to some degree separate from other aspects of provincial administration. The militia assumed an internal logic of its own, with committed fascists working within that fairly restricted paramilitary logic and, it may be suggested, often happy to be away from the much more troubled waters of the provincial fascist federation. This too represented a loss to the more political wing of Fascism and it served to limit further the catchment area from which personnel could be drawn. People from the MVSN were drafted into party jobs at times, but there was always the risk of divided loyalties.

As the regime progressed in its institution of other new fascist organizations, from the fascist unions to the OND, to the state-run *Opera Nazionale Maternità ed Infanzia* (the pre- and post-natal organization for women) and *Istituto Nazionale Fascista Previdenza Sociale* (the state social insurance institute), the space for the employment of fascists increased. In this sense, Fascism clearly represented a vehicle of social promotion. Militants who were lucky found secure jobs in many of the local fascist organizations, looking after leisure activities, youth groups, unions, or the early expressions of fascist welfare. While appointments in the state bureaucracy were frozen, for financial reasons, between 1926 and 1933, there was what Guido Melis has termed 'a veritable explosion' in employment in the new state-run institutes of the public administration (the *parastato*) in the late 1920s and, to a much greater degree, in the 1930s.[45] Again according to Melis, the people who flowed into these jobs were often fascists of the early years of the movement, having various types of formation—they were self-taught intellectuals, former syndicalists, people recently graduated in political science, many with specific skills in communication and organization. To some extent they represented a new elite, rewarded for their allegiance to the fascist movement.[46]

This kind of preferential employment was not at all surprising. Jobs for the boys was a fairly natural consequence of the kind of local control exercised by the movement and fascist leaders had little difficulty in defending the practice, sometimes making pointed allusions to the pork-barrel politics of Tammany Hall in order to justify themselves. Many active fascists moved sideways, as it were, into the institutions of the *parastato*, finding security because of their fascist credentials but being able, at that point, to cease worrying too much about any continuing militancy. Although it is difficult to find any concrete information on this question, there is more than a suspicion that people moved to these jobs because they were much better paid than intermediate positions within the party structure.[47] In any case, as we shall see, the more important fascist officials in the party often found other ways of making ends meet.

The picture then is of a weakening of the momentum of the provincial fascist movements, in part because a considerable number of the more committed fascists were finding other things to do which distracted them from further militant activity. The traffic was not all one way, of course. As we have seen, many joined the movement in 1925 and early 1926, before enrolment was partially closed and made much more difficult by the extension of a whole series of checks and controls.[48] Many of these who had stood on the sidelines in previous years found it convenient to profess fascist sentiments and to join the party as a step on the road to a good job. A large number of these were public servants of one kind and another, who were encouraged to join the party from 1926 onwards, partly in order to provide a moderate counterweight to the radical fascists of the intransigent wing of the movement. These state employees joined essentially to protect jobs they already held and in the hope of furthering a career already begun. Theirs was an essentially formal adhesion, therefore; they hardly represented new blood, capable, in terms of fascist dynamism, of replacing those who were leaving or being forced to leave the party. Many joined because they recognized the value of the fascist party card. Indeed, there were frequent criticisms of the new arrivals—the '27ers'—who, like the so-called 'March violets' who flooded into the Nazi party in 1933, saw personal advantage in proclaiming their loyalty. The really determined of these would not be content with a new *tessera*, dated 1927 or 1930, however. It is from the late 1920s that the market for fascist virginity opens, with people producing false testimony to their early allegiance and buying documents showing, ostensibly, that they had been fascists since before the March on Rome or even

---

[45] On this expansion see below, Chapter 6.5.   [46] Melis, *Lo Stato*, 105–6.
[47] Alessio Gagliardi, 'I ministeri economici negli anni trenta', in Melis, Ibid., 160.
[48] See Aquarone, *L'Organizzazione*, Appendix, doc. 12.

from the 'first hour' in Milan. The numbers of those apparently present at the Piazza San Sepolcro meeting in March 1919 rose to remarkable heights.

To some extent the adjustments in membership of the mid- to late 1920s represented a real change in the social composition of the movement. Although the consequences of the changes have still to be fully assessed, it is clear that, with the control and partial suppression of the radicalism of the intransigents and the *squadristi,* a certain kind of populist and Jacobin element within Fascism was weakened. This element—the fascists of 1920 and 1921—had been the most radical component of the fascist movement, the most dynamic, and—in terms of social composition—had had a popular component to it. In the main the new recruits expressed no such radicalism, coming from different social classes (urban petty bourgeoisie, bourgeoisie), and were in general much more conservative, often combining the rhetoric of the 'revolution' with a firm practical defence of established social positions.[49]

The change in social composition was not necessarily a replacement of 'good' fascists with 'bad', but it did represent a significant shift in the direction of the movement and would not be without further consequences in later years. Whatever their reasons for joining at this stage, it was unlikely that the new members were going to make a decisive contribution to the progress of the party, in the sense of engineering a radical transformation of Italian society. The fascist movement may have been a vehicle of social mobility for many, but the emphasis was much more on *entering* provincial society than on changing the characteristics of that society in any fundamental way. Lyttelton notes, among the new recruits, 'a mass of state employees, of postal workers, of teachers and the like, anxious to protect their careers by joining the dominant party', and observes that the link of these people with the state was to be of great importance in furthering the subordination of the party to the state machine.[50] A much increased presence of the provincial lower middle class, many of them 'unproductive' public servants of one kind or another and therefore dependent on the state, was not exactly a recipe for revolution. Indeed, it is from this point that Aquarone sees the beginning of a progressive bureaucratization of the PNF, as it abandoned any strictly political activity to dedicate itself to the task Mussolini had assigned to it: 'to constitute the educational and formative aristocracy of the Italian people'.[51]

The conformists made their appearance at this point too, keeping in step with the winning team, but with no great initiatives to propose. In many cases the self-interest of the newly enrolled was blatant; but personal ambition or the protection of position was hardly the best starting point for disinterested service to the party. Such people always remained vulnerable to accusations of opportunism, of trying, as one commentator put it, 'to monetarize the *tessera*' at the first occasion.

An exception might seem to be constituted by what was called the fascist 'call-up' (the *leva)*—the practice, from 1927 onwards, of admitting to the party (or the

---

[49] In this respect see Mariuccia Salvati, *L'Inutile salotto*, Turin, Bollati Boringhieri, 1993.

[50] On the changing social composition under Turati, see Lyttelton, *Seizure*, 303–4; also Mariuccia Salvati, *Il regime e gli impiegati*, Rome & Bari, Laterza, 1992, 107–10.

[51] Aquarone, *L'Organizzazione*, 165–6.

MVSN), even during the periods when enrolment was closed for all others, those *Avanguardisti* who had reached the age of 18 in the previous year.[52] The rite of passage, held once a year on 23 March (the anniversary of the founding of the fascist movement), saw between 60,000 and 80,000 adolescents admitted each year, a sufficient number, it might seem, to permit the rapid formation of a new ruling group. Yet there is little evidence to suggest that the influx of new young people had much effect on the movement, at least in the early years. The first groups admitted by the *leva* had, after all, undergone few years of indoctrination before being enrolled in the party—certainly insufficient to permit them to form a new administrative class of convinced fascists. And motivations for participating might well be mixed. Parents would encourage their children to take part in fascist activities because of the benefits such activities would seem to offer under a dictatorship, while at the same time continuing to preach a different kind of politics around the kitchen table. Much later—and therefore with increased significance—a police informer would comment on the fact that young people were still more influenced by the demo-liberal ideas of their parents than by the blatant propaganda of the regime. Suspect motivation of the youth admitted to the party provoked generational conflict almost from the start. Young people were immediately subjected to the criticisms made of the more mature recent recruits—that Fascism was seen as being nothing more than the opportunity for a quick career. The people making such criticisms—the 'old guard' (who were in fact still relatively young, given the youthful character of early Fascism)—clearly had no intention of making way for the new arrivals, who found, as a consequence, their path forward firmly blocked.

This last point is amply backed up by a statistical analysis of the ages of *segretari federali* provided by Didier Musiedlak.[53] Dividing those holding office in March 1939 into age groups, he finds that the great majority (more than 93 per cent) fall in the 30–50 group, the average age being 38. Although this does suggest a relatively young political class, it does also indicate that very few of the generation born after 1910—people who would have been reaching maturity in the 1930s—had moved into positions of power. Despite the invocations to open the ranks to the young—'*Largo ai giovani!*' ['Make way for the young!'] was one of Mussolini's 'marching orders' of 1932—little had been done to accommodate the up and coming fascists. This impression is confirmed by a further analysis of the ages of the 150 *segretari federali* nominated between March 1939 and the fall of Fascism in 1943. Although the number of those in the 20–30 age group does increase—they move from 3 per cent to 9 per cent of the total—the overall picture is that of a slight ageing of the group as a whole. The average age has risen from 38 to 39 and

---

[52] This practice was modified in 1931 with the creation of the FGC, which admitted those young people between 18 and 21 from the ONB (*Opera Nazionale Balilla*) who had not become members of the GUF. Formally the *fasci giovanili* and the GUF were administered by the party, while the ONB (until it too passed to the PNF in 1937) was run by the Ministry of Education and was, therefore, a state rather than a party institution.

[53] Didier Musiedlak, *Lo stato fascista e la sua classe politica 1922–1943*, Bologna, Il Mulino, 2003, 479–81.

those between 40 and 60 constitute almost 50 per cent of the whole, as against some 33 per cent in the earlier analysis.

The formation of a generation able to take over from the 'old guard' was seen by many as one of the most important tasks facing the regime and was the task entrusted to the party, but there seems to be little evidence of this imperative in the nomination of local party secretaries. In fact, on average, *federali* were getting older, not younger. Even allowing for distortions created by the war (many young people would be away at the front), it seems clear that the cohort that had created and sustained the fascist movement between 1920 and 1925—people born between 1895 and 1905—continued to keep hold of the reins of power, something which was perfectly understandable given that they were still, in 1940, relatively young in absolute terms but also very young in comparison with other European political elites. This last consideration indicates the degree to which the slogan 'Make way for the young!' was, in a sense, pure demagogy. Instances of groups of 40-year-old politicians willingly handing over power to an even younger generation are few and far between, particularly in Italy.

5

Provincial Battles: Problems in the Party

That provincial federations faced considerable problems in the early years of their existence is hardly surprising. The fascist experiment represented a radical change from previous forms of political organization in Italy. As it developed, it offered new possibilities, but it also trod on a good many toes. Local elites, sticking closely to their favoured bars, restaurants, and theatres, might look down on the new men of Fascism, but they could hardly ignore the threat these people represented. In their reactions, they often betrayed the ambiguity of their position towards the regime—uncertain whether to contest it or to join it. At the same time, the new men of Fascism often displayed the same kind of ambiguity, tempted by traditional privilege but also irritated by the presumption of superiority that accompanied it.

Yet many of the difficulties the provincial movements faced after 1925 were related less to this confrontation between the old and the new at provincial level than to problems within the federations themselves. As we have seen in previous chapters, fascist centralization of authority met resistance from local leaders, even after 1925–6; when it came to it, *segretari federali* were reluctant to concede ground as they vied for power with the prefect. These contests had inevitable consequences for the efficient working of the federations, constantly fighting turf wars with all around them. In this context, the new men of Fascism predictably found life hard going—but they were not above making difficulties for themselves. One major problem was that, all too often, the new men could not agree with each other, forming factions and, at times, attacking each other with a vigour they had previously reserved for their socialist enemies. A closer look at these struggles tells us a great deal about the varying fortunes of provincial Fascism.

5.1. INFIGHTING AND FACTIONALISM

As we have seen, even in the late 1920s the fascist movement was already beginning to experience those problems of regeneration that would become so much more evident in the following decade. As the prefect cited in the previous chapter complained, recruitment of suitable people, able to do a good job within the local fascist federation, was extremely difficult. Why this was so was not immediately obvious, but on occasions the prefects' reports do go further than simple denunciation of the fact and give some indications of why, in their view, able and intelligent people were not staying with the movement or deciding to join it.

The first reason generally given was the negative effects of the fairly constant atmosphere of conflict that characterized political life in many provinces. This explanation obviously included the institutional problem we examined in the previous chapter—the struggles for control between prefect, *federale*, and, to a lesser extent, *podestà*. Frequent confrontation between these figures alienated sympathies and discouraged participation. But the really damaging conflicts were those constituted by the infighting that became endemic among the fascists themselves in many provincial federations—the *beghismo* mentioned in Chapter 3.

At its most obvious level political infighting represented simply the struggles between rival local leaders, competing for the position of provincial control that they had always assumed the fascist victory would give them. Personal ambition is a theme few of the reports on infighting fail to mention. Such contests could represent much more, however. People could clash about differing visions of what Fascism was meant to achieve at local level; moderates and intransigents could find themselves at loggerheads here. At the same time, apparently simple personal rivalries could mask deeper divisions between classes, interest groups, and lobbies within a town or province. Agrarian, industrial, and commercial interests might enter into conflict—over levels and distribution of local taxation, for example—and try to find support for their different positions by forming currents within the local *fascio* or among the men of the MVSN. Often political infighting has elements of all these possibilities—the local man wanting, for instance, to assert his hard-won control of the province in order to push his view of fascist transformation, and accepting the support of the local industrialists in order to realize his ambitions. To a degree this was normal political behaviour but, in the context of local politics, it immediately exposed the subject to accusations of ambition, political incorrectness, and kow-towing to economic interest.

By the late 1920s, political infighting already had a long history. In the early days it was often the consequence of arguments about the direction Fascism should be taking and about the local federation's relations with the local establishment. The example of the dissident movement in Ferrara in 1921, mentioned in Chapter 2, is not untypical. The desire to turn the *santo manganello* against the landed proprietors revealed a very ingenuous understanding of Fascism on the part of some of the first fascists and could not but provoke schism within a provincial movement funded by the same landed proprietors. The bitterness of these struggles should not be underestimated. In Ferrara the schism continued, on and off, until 1923 when Balbo lost patience and called in the notoriously brutal *squadristi* of Perugia to settle accounts once and for all. Even so, the defeated refused to lie down and die, emerging every now and then to make declarations embarrassing to those in control.

That this kind of situation was not unusual is indicated by the instructive letter sent by Francesco Giunta, general secretary of the PNF, to all provincial federations in December 1923. At this point the fascist movement was still in the phase in which it recognized the validity of elections to office at local level. In the letter Giunta invited the federations to hold elections for the various offices, as envisaged by the 1921 Statute of the party, but to do their utmost to avoid the use of violence between fascists in the electoral assemblies—something evidently common enough to justify his letter. In particular, he stated that people should not attend electoral meetings with firearms—fascists must have been shooting at each other on a regular basis—and warned that, if groups of fascists already expelled from the party were to attempt to take part in the meetings (in an obvious attempt to regain control of the federation), they were to be arrested by the *Carabinieri* or members of the MVSN.[1]

Few federations escaped the kind of infighting revealed in this letter, although the reasons for the internal struggles were often very different. In certain southern federations, for example, the fascist organization would be split about the extent to which it should continue to represent the interests of the demobilized soldiers, how far it should collaborate with existing elites or about the need to appeal to Rome to act against such people. In other places there might be arguments about the action to be taken against the freemasons or against the local clergy. Personalities also played a large part, with egos that had expanded enormously during the fascist seizure of power clashing over the rewards of victory.

These differences produced a tense situation in many provinces, with the formation of factions within local fascist movements. *Beghismo* (political infighting) was the expression of these factions, made up of the always much-maligned *beghisti*.[2] Usually linked in the ultimate analysis to people rather than to policy (after all, after 1925 local fascists were not invited to formulate policy, given the top-down nature of the fascist decision-making structure), the groupings contested power relentlessly, sometimes getting hold of crucial jobs, sometimes being forced into opposition.

It is significant, in terms of the relative weight given to local and to national politics in the interpretation given to Fascism by its provincial adherents, that in many areas the factions which formed *within* the local fascist movement often reproduced existing divisions within local society—divisions going back well before the advent of Fascism. In these cases it is possible to sense the way in which Fascism was, in a way, a superimposition on local rivalries, which continued to exist despite the allegedly unifying mission of the movement and which showed themselves to be stronger than the fascist message. After its initial and to some extent unifying dynamism had worn off, the fascist movement became the vehicle through which previous, often traditional, rivalries were fought. Long-standing struggles between families, between professional groups, even between areas of a town, would be reproduced under fascist control—but presented as contests about which group could best claim to be the rightful representative of Fascism. In Cosenza, for example, the factions involved in contests to appoint the various *podestà* formed along social and economic divisions that were fairly rigid and had

---

[1] Aquarone, *L'Organizzazione*, Appendix 7.

[2] The problem was the central issue at a meeting of the PNF Directorate in August 1924, where Roberto Forges Davanzati spoke of 'that quarrelsome tendency which has gravely obstructed the work of the provisional Directorate'. He went on, 'the relationship between centre and periphery will benefit the more, the less we bring up personal questions…' See *Il Popolo d'Italia*, 7 August 1924.

long been present in local society.[3] Similarly, at Cassino, in the newly created province of Frosinone, the appointment of the first *podestà* in 1926—requested as a matter of urgency by local fascists to provide a way of *suppressing* divisions within the movement—generated the formation of factions within the fascist organization that reproduced fairly exactly the old divisions between 'blacks' and 'whites' long present in the area.[4] Ironically, therefore, Fascism, born to stamp out factionalism, became the new terrain on which the old factionalism was now contested. In Cassino, as in Cosenza, the office of *podestà* (created in order to be an independent figure above faction in the effort to defeat faction) became the bone of contention in local factionalism.[5]

Despite the national victory represented by the seizure of power, in the years immediately following the March on Rome, and particularly after 1925, many fascists were more concerned with establishing their control on the ground than with arguing about the direction the national movement should take. It is evident that they were often doing this in a partial vacuum, in as far as—at least in 1925 and 1926—the relative positions of *fascio*, MVSN, *podestà*, prefect, and police chief still had to be worked out and this had to be done after several years in which local fascists had become accustomed to doing very much what they liked, regardless of the authorities. This led to numerous turf wars, many of which would provoke long-lasting divisions within the fascist movement and between the fascist organizations and the state authorities.

Typical is the clash between the MVSN and the *Carabinieri* in Rovigo in late 1926. Probably following instructions of the official *fascio*, the *Carabinieri* had arrested several disident fascist militiamen for illegal possession of arms and munitions. The arrest provoked a strong reaction from the local Consul of the MVSN who went to the barracks of the *Carabinieri* and gave the guilty officer, who argued that he was only doing his duty and enforcing the law, a dressing-down in the following terms.

> What law against the Militia? There will be trouble for anyone who touches my men. I don't need instruction from you, I am your superior officer and, if you carry on like this, either I go or you go, together with some nobody who is protecting you and who in any case is inferior to me.

As the commander of the *Carabinieri* observed, commenting on the incident, the Consul had no right to ask for explanations from the *Carabinieri*. The fact was, however, that he did so, convinced that, as a fascist officer, he had greater authority. It evidently appeared to people like this Militia Consul that power was up for

---

[3] G. Sole, 'Lettere anonime e lotta tra le fazioni nel Cosentino 1926–43', (1986) 15(4) *Rivista di Storia Contemporanea* 586.

[4] Baris, *Frosinone*, 45.

[5] Slightly different, but illustrative of the perpetuation of old divisions, is the example of the *comune* of Bagnara (Reggio Calabria) where local rivalries were expressed through allegiance to one of the two orchestras—one socialist (and anti-fascist), one Catholic (and pro-fascist). The prefect attempted a fusion of the two 'in order to destroy definitively all residues of the old mentalities' but his efforts failed miserably as the two *maestri musicali* fought bitterly over who should conduct the newly formed orchestra: ACS, MI, DGPS, PS 1927, b. 157, 28 January 1927.

grabs. The experience of previous years of local fighting had given the impression that the winner would take all—and Fascism had won. The problem, from the point of view of the fascist organization, was that within every province there were almost always several people like this Consul, each convinced that he alone was the winner and determined that others should stand aside before him.

There were few provincial federations that did not see infighting of some kind. In contrast with the municipal politics of liberal Italy, prefect and central government would often intervene to try to resolve local differences—this was a significant aspect of fascist centralization—but often with limited results. In many places the worst was over by 1927, as unruly *ras* were controlled from Rome, party discipline asserted through expulsions, and *podestà* appointed to oversee developments. Yet, as we shall see, rancour and hostility often lingered on. The expulsion from the party of 100,000 fascists between 1926 and 1930 created 100,000 potential dissidents, and their effect was certainly felt. New unofficial groupings, which owed their inspiration to ousted leaders, were often formed among the discontented and the expelled. The formal motivations for difference were many but there was little doubt that what was always being contested was the exercise of local power.

One problem prefects and police chiefs faced in their attempts to come to terms with local struggles was that local alliances were rarely stable. The crisscrossing currents of provincial life often produced surprising reversals of position. Thus yesterday's intransigent might appear today at the head of the agrarian lobby, strenuously defending established interests. The ability of local fascists to manoeuvre is sometimes little short of remarkable. It testifies perhaps to the primacy of power over principle, but also suggests that survival was a key determinant of provincial manoeuvrings. Positions could be reversed with great speed if necessary, as people transferred from one group or one leader to another. Such transfers paved the way for accusations of betrayal, lack of coherence, opportunism, sell-out, and general incomprehension of the meaning of Fascism—very much the language in which provincial politics was waged during the course of the *ventennio*.

Political infighting was a phenomenon that the regime was never able to dominate completely. It was apparent in many places during the period that goes roughly from 1926 to 1932, but can often be seen both before and after those dates. In many federations good years were usually followed by bad and any lasting stability was hard to achieve. Internal struggles were endemic to the movement and, as we shall see, one of the principal reasons why Italian Fascism failed to build up a real popular momentum in the course of its twenty years in power. Continuing internal conflict was one of the paradoxes of the fascist movement. As we have already observed, the original fascist attack on the political system of liberal Italy had been centred on the divisiveness of political conflict, which allegedly undermined national unity and dramatically weakened the national cause. 'Politics' had become a dirty word precisely because of its association with competition and division. Fascism, with its emphasis on national unity in the Italian state, liked to portray itself as the solution to the problem. Yet under the cover of the overarching panoply of the national fascist movement, conflict and division persisted.

Inevitably the terms of division were changed. The ideological chasm that had separated socialism, Catholicism, and liberalism in 1920 and 1921 had been bridged—or at least covered over for the time being—and the internal battles of Fascism were regularly fought in terms of every fascist being 'more fascist than thou'. Even so, the bitterness of the internal struggles should not be underestimated. People were often fighting for their political lives, and for many the political life was synonymous (to them) with continued existence. Disgrace exposed them to possible exclusion from everything. As one fascist put it, when pleading to be allowed back into the party, his request meant a desire to be readmitted not only to political activity but 'to life itself'.[6] This was an often repeated theme. More than one appellant against expulsion from the PNF would protest that such a fate would mean total ruin.[7]

5.2. THE RESPONSE OF THE PARTY

The clash, after 1925, of the strongly centrifugal nature of the first Fascism with the heavy centralizing pressures of the newly founded regime inevitably produced tensions within the provincial federations. In a sense, Farinacci, as party secretary, was almost a personal embodiment of these tensions; the independently minded provincial *ras* attempting to pursue a policy of centralization of authority. Turati's appointment (he was essentially a second-level fascist leader before he became party secretary) is probably to be attributed precisely to the fact that he had no really strong provincial identity and was better able, therefore, to enforce central authority on the undisciplined provinces. His call for the 'de-personalization' of provincial politics corresponded exactly to the desire to destroy the power of the provincial bosses, and the large number of expulsions effected under his secretariat testified to a genuine intention to call the provinces to order.

The new 1926 PNF Statute was clear about the way discipline should be enforced within the party. Starting from the premise that '[e]very Secretary of a *fascio* must know the moral record of every member and the way he earns his living', the Statute established that wayward fascists were to placed under investigation by the Directorate of the *fascio*. Three possible punishments were envisaged—censure, either permanent or temporary suspension from the party, and expulsion. The accused had the right to appeal, but if the sentence were to be confirmed by the central authorities, the exclusion was to be total: 'the fascist who is expelled from the Party is a traitor to the cause and must be excluded from political activity'. This was understood to mean not only party functions, but also those related to the public administration.[8]

---

[6] Corner, *Ferrara*, 248, note 5.

[7] Dante Germino, *The Italian Fascist Party in Power. A Study in Totalitarian Rule*, Minneapolis, University of Minnesota Press, 1959, 35.

[8] Quoted in Aquarone, *L'Organizzazione*, 390–91.

Expulsions and other disciplinary measures had predictable consequences, how-ever. These should have been obvious to Turati because, if the scale of expulsions after 1926 was new, the fact of expulsion, and its consequences, had been under the eyes of everyone since the early years of the movement. If ambitious, the expelled rarely just walked away from the movement. It should perhaps be stressed once again that the local party structure was the only point of access to a political career, even a fairly modest local political career. Being on good terms with the party opened many other doors among the local business and professional com-munity as well. Membership of it could not be abandoned lightly, therefore. Tura-ti's measures, particularly his battle against Farinacci and the Farinaccians, meant that—by the end of the 1920s—in a large number of provinces there was usually more than one pretender for local power. He was almost always a displaced former leader, guilty perhaps of 'indiscipline', 'misunderstanding of Fascism', or 'moral turpitude', but certainly of having formed losing political alliances or of speaking out of turn. Convinced that he had right on his side and that his moment would come, the disgraced leader, together with a cohort of faithful followers (also expelled or suspended), would constitute a thorn in the side of the local directo-rate, arguing, criticizing, and refusing to abandon the field. Indeed, one of the key features of political infighting was that disgraced militant fascists lived with the conviction that the immediate battle did not represent the whole war and that the struggle was never really over. 'Political resurrection', as Mussolini put it, was always a distinct possibility.[9]

This conviction was entirely understandable. Over the course of the years proce-dures for appeal against expulsion from the party saw many people reinstated. Certain particularly awkward local leaders—Barbiellini-Amidei of Piacenza is an example—were expelled, reinstated, and then expelled again within the space of a few years. Where position depended to such a great extent on personal relations and on political alliances, any change in the triangular relationship between pre-fect, *segretario federale*, and the central directorate of the PNF could provoke the realization of vendettas or, conversely, attempts at pacification, both of which might determine a reshuffling of the cards at local level. Only a few of the most prominent fascist leaders were independent players; most were dependent on someone more powerful above them. Barbiellini, mentioned above, owed much to Farinacci, and the Cremona leader's fortunes greatly conditioned his own.

It is symptomatic of the situation in many provinces that a change in party sec-retary in Rome could completely alter local equilibria. Thus, when Turati was removed in October 1930, many of those he had expelled from the PNF during the previous years were readmitted to the party by his successor, Giovanni Giuriati. Particularly in the northern provinces, where the battle against Farinacci had been waged so strongly, those who had benefited from Turati's purges found themselves purged in turn. The process was even more dramatic than it had been under

---

[9] Mussolini used this phrase in a telegram to the Prefect of Genoa, in which he protested that the laxity of the authorities encouraged people to think that a pardon was always just round the corner: ACS, MI, DGPS, PS 1927, b. 156, 25 July 1927.

Turati—there were now 120,000 expulsions. Farinacci, pushed to the sidelines under Turati's period as secretary, took the opportunity to re-emerge as a leading national figure. Those who had been favoured by Turati became targets and the wave created by the change of guard at the centre rippled out to touch most provinces. Some of those considered too likely to continue to serve the former secretary loyally, even when he was out of office, were expelled from the PNF almost immediately on Giuriati taking office. Even Turati himself was not safe from attack. Bereft of influential supporters and facing the many enemies he had made while secretary, he was expelled from the party little more than a year after his dismissal, formally because of newspaper articles betraying attitudes considered too critical of the regime, but in reality because he dared to voice those opinions as though still a person of authority, entitled to argue the toss with Mussolini himself. In the meantime, Giuriati had been replaced by Achille Starace as party secretary and Starace had begun a new attack on Farinacci and on those who had found favour under Giuriati.

The message given out by this kind of procedure of expulsion and readmission was, of course, that no decision of the Directorate of the PNF in Rome was to be considered final. This was in contravention of the spirit of the new 1929 Party Statute, which (precisely in order to try to dispel this impression) had added to the phrase relating to the position of the expelled fascist '[h]is position cannot be revised, except in the case of error, resulting from new facts or new evidence and only following an order from the *Duce*'.[10] Although this phrase was reproduced with the same emphasis in the 1932 revision of the Statute, it was all too apparent, for those who had suffered disciplinary measures, that life under Fascism was to be seen as a question of swings and roundabouts. Those expelled could usually live in hope of readmission; all that was needed was for there to be a shake-up in Rome within the party, or the arrival of a new prefect, or the dismissal of the current *federale*, and the possibilities of a revision of previous procedures became a reality. Moreover, if you played your cards well and were lucky, your rivals might themselves be expelled or suspended as part of the same operation. And if no change of prefect or *federale* was imminent, then personal 'godfathers' might be convinced to intercede with central power.

As the result of such interventions, expulsions—always solemnly declared to be irrevocable at the moment of their proclamation—were frequently revoked. Revisions of the party Statute had further emphasized the concentration of power in the figure of Mussolini and on occasions he could be induced to intervene on the basis of old friendships. The archives are full of wailing letters to the *duce* written by those who claim to have suffered some kind of injustice and who ask to be restored to office and to favour. Whatever they thought of the party, people never had any doubts that Mussolini could make and Mussolini could break.

Put very simply, for the expelled, it was always possible to live with hope. And hopes for the future were not reserved exclusively for the expelled. On the basis of the wheel turning or being made to turn, even those who remained in the party,

[10] Quoted in Aquarone, *L'Organizzazione*, 511.

but without what they considered adequate recognition of their contribution to the cause, could reasonably expect a change of fortune sooner or later. This constant uncertainty about the future was a fair recipe for disaster. Uncertainty produced insecurity and suspicion among both friends and enemies. The continuing possibility of reprieve or of a return to favour worked against the formation of a really disciplined party among provincial fascists. It suggested to many that, in the final analysis, party discipline meant discipline for others but not for themselves.

Central in many provinces to this instability, as we have already noted, were the former *squadristi*. Like the Nazi 'old fighters' for Hitler, they represented a particularly difficult problem to resolve because they could claim, with evident justice, to be the foundation on which the fascist edifice had been built. For many *squadristi*—especially those who had not decided to seek a career in the MVSN—the creation of the dictatorship simply meant that pay-back time had arrived. Yet, as Federzoni's instructions to the prefects in 1925 had made clear, the kind of Fascism they represented—the activism, the violence, the intolerance, and the indiscipline—could find little place in the post-1925 vision of fascist stability. Many *squadristi* found it difficult to understand that the qualities required for the 'punitive expeditions' against the socialists were not those needed for normal administration in quieter times. As we have seen, the squads were officially disbanded on more than one occasion in the mid-1920s but the spirit of *squadrismo* and the memory of the exploits of the squads continued to condition the thinking of a large number of young men. Many former *squadristi* imagined that they deserved plum jobs in local administration or within the PNF. When they had difficulty in finding work, this idea fed the sense of resentment that they had been in some way 'passed over' in favour of those 'less fascist' than themselves. Often they had few formal qualifications, given the disturbed life they had led during the 1920s, but they refused to recognize this fact. They complained about selection for jobs on the basis of '[p]olitical *clientele*, nepotism, family relations and such things' rather than their fascist virtues. Many—according to one report of 1933—were 'in an extremely uncomfortable moral and economic position'.[11]

One problem was that, with the expansion of the public administration and the *parastato* under Fascism, the regime *was* handing out a large number of jobs and the excluded were aware of this. In mid-1930, for example, the prefect of Venice wrote that '[i]n recent days there have been protests of discontent among the Old Blackshirts, who complain that they are neglected and unemployed and that, in preference to them, jobs and positions in the Party are given to people of recent and doubtful fascist faith'.[12] Similar problems had arisen in Padua in the late 1920s, where a group of ex-*squadristi*, led by one Ferdinando Baseggio, continued to create trouble, again arguing that good local jobs were being taken by people 'of the sixth hour'. By 1931 some of the *squadristi* had been given jobs—'in recognition of their political merit'—in the administration of small *comuni* in the province, but they remained unsatisfied. 'Putting them in those jobs fired their desire for

---

[11] ACS, MI, DGPS, Polizia Politica, b. 219, Rome, 13 December 1933.
[12] ACS, MI, DGPS, AGR, b. 378, PS 1930–31, 22 August 1930.

important positions, absolutely incompatible with their intellectual, moral, or professional, capacities.' Baseggio himself, although considered by most to be immoral, a bully, and a liar (he claimed a very improbable personal friendship with Mussolini), was bought off with a newly created position as head of an office with responsibility for finding work for the ex-*squadristi*. He immediately appointed around thirty of them to jobs as night watchmen, but the whole group, Baseggio included, continued to argue that they deserved much better. What they wanted were positions of authority. The Fascist *commissario federale*, appointed to sort out the difficulties in Padua, resisted these pressures, stating that the ex-*squadristi* were 'incapable of taking on the responsibility for delicate positions of command', adding, rather contemptuously, that the old *squadristi* 'threaten a lot, but do very little'. They had, he repeated, 'no capacity for authority, very little desire to work'.[13]

This was a picture repeated over and over again in the provinces. Increasingly, as the years passed and their destiny became ever clearer, the old fascists began to constitute 'a party within the party', often disrupting efforts at a local stabilization.[14] Many continued to make reference to Farinacci—in their eyes a kind of prince across the water waiting to be recalled to his rightful position. Because of their unruly nature, in many provinces the ex-*squadristi*—or at least a part of them—constituted a perpetual cause of protest, demonstrated by the fact that most disgraced leaders would continue to have a phalanx of former *squadristi* in tow, all convinced that continued agitation would produce tangible results.

Factionalism, fed by aspirations to control and perpetuated by conviction that today's misfortunes could be righted tomorrow, had its inevitable effect on the authority of the party. It was perhaps a sign of the lack of definition of roles and competencies that personal contacts remained extremely important within the movement, despite a formally very rigid hierarchical structure. Those local fascists temporarily out of power, but still in the PNF, would form a usually very disloyal opposition to the group running the local federation, generally appealing to national party secretary or directly to Mussolini in an attempt to go over the heads of the local party officials in order to gain sympathy for what they considered to be their unmerited exclusion. The expelled would form a group of 'outs' who—often very vociferously—contested the authority of the 'ins'. On occasions they would attract the violence of their fellow fascists. If they refused to capitulate and continued to be really troublesome, they could be persecuted by the police, acting on the orders of the *Questura*, and even threatened with *confino*. Indeed, many did end up in remote places with ample time to reflect on their misdeeds.

Yet it was significant, in terms of the way people looked at the authority of the party, that those expelled for indiscipline or 'moral turpitude' (the generic, and very frequent, cause of expulsion) usually continued to consider themselves loyal fascists, even without the *tessera*, and argue that it was Fascism—obviously, in its local incarnation, ruined by their opponents—that was out of step rather than they themselves. In support of this position, expelled local leaders might still be considered more 'legitimate' leaders in the eyes of their followers than those supposedly

[13] ACS, PNF, SPEP, b. 11, Padua, 18 June 1931.   [14] Germino, *Fascist Party*, 46.

impartial 'outsiders' sent, in some cases, from Rome to replace them. While this attested to the profound local roots of many fascist movements, it also implied an attachment to a kind of generic Fascism, usually centred around the figure of Mussolini, that was in a way larger than the PNF. The assimilation of Fascism to the PNF was far from being automatic, therefore, and those who fell foul of the party would still protest their loyalty to Mussolini and to Fascism.

In some ways this kind of position inevitably referred back to the early days of Fascism, when the party did not yet exist, and when there was a kind of broad equality within the movement. These were the days when ordinary *squadristi* would use the familiar 'tu' form of address with Mussolini, as if they were all comrades in arms of the same standing. The 'trenchocracy' of the First World War to which the early movement appealed was intensely egalitarian. That the sentiment should still have some sway towards the end of the 1920s speaks volumes about the lack of respect attributed by some to the local PNF federation. The federation may have been central to many aspects of provincial life but it was not the sole determinant of fascist allegiance. For many, hierarchy—one of the key words of Fascism— became difficult to swallow when it was referred to local rankings. The discipline of hierarchy which they recognized was linked to the *duce* rather than to those who claimed to speak for him. It is difficult to think of Nazis, expelled from the NSDAP, behaving in the same way or, indeed, being permitted to behave in the same way.

5.3. PROVINCIAL FACTIONALISM IN ACTION

As prefects reported frequently, in many provincial federations factionalism threatened the efficient functioning of the party machine and worked to bring the party into disrepute. But there was often little they seem to have been able to do about it. Examples drawn from provinces in both North and South of Italy serve to confirm this diagnosis and show the extent to which factionalism dogged certain provincial fascist movements for the whole of the *ventennio*.

Savona—on the Tyrrhenian coast above Genoa—was made a province in 1927 but had been an area largely independent of Genoa for some time. The fascist movement in the province had been divided between various groups since at least 1922. As in many other places, these factions were the successors of previous competing networks of interests, indicative of a degree of continuity between liberal and fascist politics. In the words of a local fascist, the causes of conflict were

> unbridgeable splits, mainly for financial reasons, between various groups who previously belonged to the popular or liberal parties, or to that of the subversives. After 1922 these rivalries were transplanted into fascist circles, fomenting those eternal squabbles which have been the joy of the city for so many years.[15]

The chaotic situation had become more defined, if not more stable, with the appointment of Alessandro Lessona as *segretario federale* to the newly formed

[15] ACS, PNF, SPEP, b. 20, Savona, undated but 1933.

province in early 1927. Not a native of Savona (but still a Ligurian), he found that he had to deal with a resident group of fascists around the figure of a war hero, local leader of the action squads, and ex-Consul General of the MVSN, the high-sounding Francesco Giuseppe Amilcare Dupanloup. By the time Lessona arrived on the scene Dupanloup had already been expelled from the party for indiscipline, but continued to have strong popular support among 'the greater part of the dock workers, a large *number* of dissident fascists, some student intellectuals, some soldiers and a group of the discontented'.[16] These, after fruitless attempts to unseat Lessona on the grounds that he had joined the PNF after the March on Rome and was really the representative of well-established financial interests, formed a dissident *fascio* 'with secret membership' and withdrew into their own private and unofficial organization. In 1929 Lessona was made under-secretary at the Ministry for the Colonies in Rome and was thus obliged to give up the position of *federale*, which he left to his lieutenant, a certain Dr Celle. 'With him the old appetites revived',[17] and the *Dupanloupiani* renewed their attack, hoping to be able to satisfy those appetites. This attack was again repulsed—Lessona had the support of party leader Turati—and some of the more prominent attackers, unfortunate enough to have state jobs, found themselves 'telegraphically' transferred to obscure places in southern Italy. Two others were even sent to *confino*.[18]

The situation changed—typically—with the fall of Turati as party secretary in early 1930. The supporters of Dupanloup succeeded in persuading the new secretary, Giuriati, to send a special commissar to Savona in order to attempt a revision of positions within the local federation, in this way succeeding in unseating the supporters of Lessona 'who barricaded themselves in the command of the Militia'.[19] The apparent victory was reversed, however, immediately on the fall of Giuriati in December 1931. The new PNF director, Starace, insisted on the return of a representative of the Lessona faction (Lessona was by now Minister for the Colonies) and the post of provincial party secretary was assigned to a man no one thought up to the job but whose main quality was that he was 'a person in whom the Hon. Lessona had absolute confidence'.[20]

Efforts were made in 1932 to reach some sort of a reconciliation in order to end the paralysis of the local movement. A revision of all party cards was begun, with the readmittance to the party of many of those suspended or expelled. But, by 1933, any hope of compromise had disappeared and the two groups were again on a war footing. The documentary sources make it clear that the contest was never resolved. A party informer reported in 1934 that the supporters of Dupanloup were as strong as ever, many of them hoping for their leader's reinstatement in order to realize their 'hopes of a career...promotions and favourable treatment'.[21]

---

[16] ACS, Ibid., informer, 26 September 1934. Since 1919 the port workers, like those of nearby Genoa, had been national-radical rather than socialist in orientation, largely because of the influence of their leader, Giuseppe Giulietti.

[17] ACS, Ibid., undated but 1933.   [18] ACS, Ibid., report of January 1932.

[19] ACS, Ibid., undated but 1933.   [20] Ibid.

[21] ACS, Ibid., 26 September 1934.

This reversal of fortune never happened, provoking an angry protest in 1936 (just a month after the proclamation of Empire) from a follower of Dupanloup:

> In Savona they are pursuing anti-fascism, anti-*squadrismo*. The veterans of a war and of a revolution are excluded from political life: passed over, spied on, put on trial, for their patriotic and civic past; derided for having been part of the glorious *squadrismo* of the Blackshirts of the Revolution, targeted, persecuted in their work and in their families...[22]

Protests such as this were insufficient to change matters. Further reports show that the condition of the provincial federation remained difficult, permanently undermined by the feuding between groups. In the second half of the 1930s intervention by central party authorities in the province, which saw a fairly continuous rotation of office holders, seems to have been unable to heal divisions and achieve a reorganization of provincial Fascism.[23] In January 1936 a new *federale* reported a totally chaotic situation caused by internal conflicts,[24] while in February 1940 a local fascist noted that '[t]his city still divides according to the dispute (Lessona, Dupanloup)'.[25] Still later, in December 1941, yet another new *federale* was induced to give a summary of the *ventennio* in Savona. It was short and to the point: 'Nothing has been done in 20 years of Fascism'.[26]

A similar picture of factionalism emerges from many other provinces. One of the worst hit in the late 1920s and early 1930s was the province of Piacenza.[27] Here again it is clear that the apparently purely personal conflicts between local leaders were in fact an expression of contrasts between different interest groups. The aristocrat, former army officer, and *squadrista*, Bernardo Barbiellini-Amidei, created problems throughout the 1920s because his idea of Fascism—radical, activist, and strongly linked to the formation of a mass base for Fascism through the realization of 'integral syndicalism'—cut across the bows of the powerful agricultural and industrial interests in the province which, after the initial years of battle against provincial socialism, had every interest in returning to a more moderate and conservative Fascism that would guarantee their positions in respect of their workers. The factions formed reproduced to some extent a contest between agrarian and urban Fascisms and, as such, was also a struggle between the more dynamic part of the old, pre-fascist, elites on one hand, including several new entrepreneurial figures thrown up by the war, and the movement of the *squadristi* on the other (although, as in Ferrara, even the *squadristi* split between the two sides in the course of the 1920s, as many were enticed into the camp of the agrarian interests).

---

[22] ACS, Ibid., Rinaldo Rinaldi ('membership card 1919') to *federale* of Turin, Piero Gazzotti, 23 July 1936.

[23] To follow rotations and discover where *federali* were sent, see the invaluable work of Mario Missori, *Gerarchie e statuti del PNF Gran Consiglio, Direttorio nazionale, Federazioni provinciali: quadri e biografie*, Rome, Bonacci, 1986.

[24] ACS, PNF, SPEP, b. 20, Savona, *federale* Burtoni to Starace, 8 January 1936.

[25] ACS, Ibid., *federale* to Muti, 24 September 1940.

[26] ACS, Ibid., note for the secretary of the PNF, 13 December 1941.

[27] Fabrizio Achilli, 'Classe dirigente e dinamica interna nel fascismo piacentino degli anni venti', in Istituto mantovano di storia contemporanea (ed.), *Fascismo e antifascismo nella Valle Padana*, Bologna, Clueb, 2007, 95–104.

Barbiellini, as we have seen, was expelled from the PNF in 1924 and then readmitted in 1925 when Farinacci, who viewed the Piacenza leader with favour, became party secretary. But even the support of the centre was insufficient to give the provincial *ras* the upper hand. The powerful economic interests—the banks, those that controlled the *Federconsorzio* (the national organization of agricultural producers, centred on Piacenza), the provincial *Consorzio agrario* itself, and the various *Consorzi irriguo* for schemes of land drainage and land improvement—managed to keep the ambitions of the young leader at bay. This capacity to resist was a fair indication that, even with the creation of the regime, established elites still possessed powerful weapons that could be deployed against the local *ras*, if the central directorate of the party did not intervene to prevent them from doing so. Here it is also significant that, in the operation of controlling the activities of the *federale*, it was the young *fascist* prefect, Carlo Tiengo, who played the major role, supporting the agrarians and the industrialists and using his powers to take key decisions out of the hands of a protesting Barbiellini.[28]

By 1929, when Barbiellini was again expelled from the PNF—this time for contesting publicly the authority of the prefect—it looked as though the alliance between strong local economic interests, a fascist prefect (behaving, as usual, more like a career prefect than a fascist), and an unsympathetic party directorate had succeeded in crushing the radical impulse represented by Barbiellini and putting the province on an even keel. To underline the apparent success, Turati went in person to Piacenza to declare that the problems were over and that the province had recognized the 'the necessities of the revolution above all personal concerns'.[29] In the case of Piacenza it would seem that the necessities of the revolution were broadly similar to the needs of the powerful economic forces in the province, who had succeeded in convincing the PNF secretary that Barbiellini, for all his fascist virtues, was an embarrassment to their economic interests and thus a threat to provincial stability.

What looked like a striking victory for fascist centralization of authority was not quite as impressive as it might seem, however. Certainly the local man had lost out, but the effects of the struggles of the 1920s would continue through into the following decade in fairly typical fashion. Even though Barbiellini was banned from setting foot in the province of Piacenza after 1929, he retained his body of supporters within it, particularly among a part of the old guard of *squadristi,* and these continued to give trouble. Prefects persistently supported his opponents, but only to limited effect. By 1931 the informers' reports speak of the 'extremely serious crisis' of provincial fascism 'troubled since the end of 1923 by serious internal disagreements'.[30] The crisis appears to have been provoked by the actions of the *segretario federale,* Franco Montemartini, who—a faithful supporter of Barbiellini until 1927—had abandoned his mentor and, encouraged by the prefect, had thrown in his lot with the more conservative Fascism of the provincial elite. His retention of

---

[28] ACS, PNF, SPEP, b. 14, Piacenza, reports for months of February and April 1931.
[29] Turati, quoted in Achilli, 'Classe dirigente', 101.
[30] ACS, PNF, SPEP, b. 14, Piacenza, report of April 1931.

the position of *federale* into 1931 was too much for the members of the fascist old guard, who reacted to their exclusion by complaining about persecution and denouncing to the party secretary in Rome the fact that, according to them, Montemartini had surrounded himself with his friends—'profiteers', 'elements of extremely limited fascist faith, known as political fixers in the old regime, of exquisite social-democratic and popular extraction'.[31] This was the typical accusation levelled at a political enemy—that of representing the 'old' politics in contrast with the 'new' Fascism. In this case the 'new' succeeded in obtaining the removal of the *federale* (but only after a few weeks: the central party directorate did not want to appear to be acting directly as a result of the denunciation) and the appointment of a new man, the noble Carlo Anguissola. It did not take long, however, before he too was being accused of much the same sins as Montemartini. He had, for instance, failed to appoint a new local party directorate, simply accepting those appointed by his predecessor, thus frustrating the ambitions of Montemartini's critics. To make matters worse, precisely at the same moment and with what can only be called exquisite timing, the PNF secretary in Rome decided on the readmission to the party of Barbiellini, who was immediately celebrated with a banquet in nearby Milan arranged by his local supporters (he was still banned from Piacenza). It was reported that, at the banquet, 'the dissidents are spreading the word that a battle against the present *Segretario federale* Anguissola will begin very shortly'— which it clearly did.[32] After less than two months an informer wrote that '[i]n a few words it can be said that the situation is on the way to being what it was before, if not worse'.[33]

The situation did not, in fact, precipitate until Anguissola fell out with the (fascist) prefect in 1932 in a typical who-should-do-what contest that resulted in the *federale* being replaced. Even so, tensions remained high. A rumour in early 1933 that the new *federale* had decided to allow Barbiellini back into the province was sufficient to trigger an immediate reaction from the more conservative fascists who had kept control of the local PNF directorate. 'The news, spread among the higher-class fascist circles, has been commented variously and disapproved by the majority of the components of the Provincial Directorate.'[34] The rumour proved to be untrue and Barbiellini stayed away, but the battle continued. A further report of October 1933 observed that the *federale* was encouraging 'this reflowering of *beghismo*' by his actions and went on to suggest that '[t]he disquiet revived in these days and a certain renewal of personal antagonisms look just like preparations for an election, with attempts at cannibalism in the family included'.[35] All this infighting left its mark. Prefects and *federali* (all 'imported') followed each other with monotonous regularity during the 1930s, keeping order but not effecting a real pacification. In 1937 the prefect noted that people were shunning Fascism 'for fear of being involved in the factional struggles' that seem by that time

---

[31] Ibid.   [32] ACS, Ibid., informer's report, 2 July 1931.
[33] ACS, Ibid., report for month of August 1931.
[34] ACS, Ibid., report for month of January 1933.
[35] ACS, Ibid., 22 October 1933.

to have been accepted by all as undesirable but inevitable, part and parcel of provincial Fascism.[36]

Compared with the province of Savona, the different element in the story of factionalism in Piacenza is the way in which interest groups, to some extent representing an old political elite, were able to form an alliance with the central fascist authorities—the Ministry of the Interior (through the prefect) and the central PNF directorate—in order to unseat a radical local leader who threatened the stability of fascist control of the province. It was a way of using Fascism against Fascism and was very eloquent of the different imperatives of centre and periphery within the movement. This was a picture more common in the South of Italy where—as we have noted in Chapter 2—the first Fascism had fought its battles more often against the control of traditional local elites than against strong socialist movements. Entrenched interests would react to the challenge of Fascism in one of two ways: by attempting to use their many levers of provincial power in order to take over the local federation or at least to condition its activity, or else by appealing to influential friends within the fascist sphere in Rome in the hope that Rome would act against a local fascist movement threatening the continued hold over the area by the local *notabili*. Often the achievement of the former was realized as a result of the latter.[37]

This kind of triangle of conflict set up a wonderful terrain for factionalism—and squabbles internal to the fascist movement were very much the order of the day in the South as well. The *fascio* of Taranto was reported in 1926 to be reduced 'to infinite little groups, without any belief, inspired only by personal or electoral ambitions'.[38] The prefect of Salerno complained, in the same year, that 'there are very few *fasci* where there are not two or more factions active and which, therefore, do not go through crises of dissolution, suspensions, and restructuring of the Directorate, etc.'[39] These squabbles had rather different attributes when compared to those of many northern provinces, where the battles were generally fought between local fascist leaders and reflected the permanent tensions between the 'ins' and the 'outs'. While this also happened in the South, the phenomenon of *rassismo*—the emergence of one or more powerful local leader or *ras*—had been much less accentuated and the emphasis in the southern provinces was usually much more on the conflict between the 'new' and the 'old'. In the first Fascism of the South—that before 1922—the movement had drawn support from the very strong organizations of returning and demobilized soldiers formed in the years immediately following the end of the war. By no means all the soldiers flowed into the fascist groups, however, and an initial division was often constituted between fascist ex-combatants and their former comrades who remained opposed to the movement.

---

[36] ACS, Ibid., Prefect Montani to MI, 1 May 1937.

[37] 'The appeal to the centre is the path chosen during the years of the regime by those factions that find themselves in opposition, very ready to make references to the codes of national-popular culture with accusations of clientilism, shady business deals, and corruption': Salvatore Lupo, 'L'utopia totalitaria del fascismo (1918–1942)', in Maurice Aymard and Giuseppe Giarrizzo (eds), *Storia d'Italia. Le Regioni dall'Unità ad oggi. La Sicilia*, Turin, Einaudi. 1987, 388.

[38] Ponziani, *Prefetti*, 196.   [39] Ibid., 191.

With the exception of Naples and the Tavoliere delle Puglie, *squadrismo* had been limited in the South and the desire of the ex-soldiers for radical change was directed less against a largely non-existent socialist movement and much more against the traditional landowning elite. But even within the *fasci* there would be conflicts about the line to follow in respect of this elite. As in the North, these conflicts produced confused situations, in which a local fascist movement would find itself deeply divided, with one side favouring a radical attack on the traditional networks of power and the other adopting positions that effectively protected their interests. The relative strengths of the two groups would often be determined by the degree to which the 'old' controlling groups—landowners and prominent businessmen—had managed to infiltrate and even 'occupy' the local fascist movement, putting the 'new' people—students, ex-combatants, urban professionals—in difficulty. Infiltration of this kind became evident immediately after the March on Rome when many among the traditional southern elites realized that, if nobody was going to defeat the fascist movement, then they had better join it. Thus, for example, in Reggio Calabria '[i]mmediately after the March on Rome, the first of a long and uninterrupted series of crises took place, engendered mainly by the frantic and disorientated fight among the people of the old regime, who wanted to take control of the Party'.[40]

In the South, in very broad terms, the conservative thrust of established groups tended to get the better of younger and more radical elements. In this way the fascist movement (often aided by the prefect) became the vehicle that permitted these groups to continue their domination.[41] The manner of realization of this operation of *trasformismo* was usually through the control of the local administration. As in other areas of Italy, therefore, fascist struggles were local struggles, in which the prize, as always, was the control of the *comune* and the province rather than the triumph of an ideology. In the words of one prefect, '[t]he rise of Fascism in the province of Avellino has not had any effect except [to provoke] local struggles, for and against the administration of the *comune*, but not for or against an idea that might animate and revive the masses and act as a guide them in politics'.[42] Whereas in the North and the centre of Italy, the strength of fascist radicalism might tilt the balance of an accommodation between traditional forces and new in favour of the latter, producing situations in which new men did emerge as arbiters of local politics and administration, in the South the established elites were much more successful—at least through the 1920s—in stealing the clothes of the fascist movement in order to hide the many elements of substantial continuity with the past. As Luigi Ponziani has put it, through such a procedure these people became 'national and fascist' in appearance (a not unimportant consequence), while remaining profoundly local in practice.[43] In this kind of operation, where the affir-

---

[40] ACS, PNF, SPEP, b. 17, Reggio Calabria, undated report, probably 1931.

[41] These are the conclusions of Ponziani, *Prefetti*, 12. See also pages 182–3: 'The renewal of the local administrations in the years 1923–26 resulted, therefore, ... in the confirmation or the restoration of the power of the traditional ruling class, which, through the recognition of Fascism as the party of government, gained—for the future as well—the acceptance of its leadership'.

[42] Prefect Efisio Beccaredda, quoted in Ibid., 169.　　[43] Ibid., 16.

mation and stabilization of the movement in the South was the priority rather than the pursuance of any confused and destabilizing radical change in social relations, the elite might often find important allies in Rome (and in Rome's local representative, the prefect).

The realization of a formal fascist control, often through the use of the *commissari*, was not achieved without the regime having to pay—inevitably, in order to achieve a certain level of consensus—a high price in terms of accommodation with essentially conservative existing elites, therefore.[44] Loyal and intransigent followers of Mussolini, who had believed that Fascism would bring a renewed and 'modernizing' energy to the South through the destruction of the hold of the traditional ruling class, frequently found themselves disowned and abandoned by the centre, precisely because real change was bound to be destabilizing of existing social relations.

Naples saw many aspects of this process in the course of the 1920s. Aurelio Padovani—a typical early fascist figure in that he was young, a former army officer, a *squadrista*, and a proponent of radical political change—inspired the first fascist movement in Naples and represented a real challenge to the existing liberal elite. His attacks on the local *notabili*, his insistence on the theme of cleaning up local politics, and his opposition to the fusion of his local fascist movement with the much more conservative Neapolitan Nationalists (a fusion envisaged in the agreement at national level in early 1923) provoked the wrath of Mussolini, who, more interested in stability than in social revolution, expelled him from the party in 1923.

Padovani's opposition to what was left of Neapolitan Fascism was soon made explicit; he viewed it as yet a further example of a window-dressing exercise that would simply leave the old elites in power. Almost immediately on his expulsion, most of the local fascists left the party with him and the Naples *fascio* appeared on the point of collapse. Yet—again very typically—those who left found they had nowhere to go. Readmitted without their leader at the end of 1923 (after Rome had already done its deals with the traditional elites), many crawled back into the party—this time with a new front man, Vincenzo Tecchio, who had always been a supporter of the expelled leader. Padovani himself remained on the sidelines with a few of his dedicated supporters, protesting his loyalty to Fascism but, predictably, creating a faction to contest the positions of his former friend, Tecchio—positions in reality very similar to his own. During 1924 the two groups clashed continuously: 'In that period there were serious incidents every day; there were dead and wounded'.[45] Nor was the division healed by Padovani's rather mysterious death in 1926 (he was killed together with some of his supporters when a balcony on which they were standing collapsed), given that his supporters continued to believe that he had been murdered and determined to honour his memory by refusing to re-enter the ranks of the orthodox.[46]

---

[44] Ponziani notes the way in which Michele Bianchi, the fascist *quadrumvir* from the Apulian region and very much the arbiter of fascist politics in the South, insisted on the inclusion of a strong element of the old elite in the fascist electoral list for the elections of 1924 (Ibid., 118).

[45] ACS, PNF, SPEP, b. 9, report PNF Naples to secretary of PNF, 23 December 1939.

[46] For these events, Raffaelle Colapietra, *Napoli fra dopoguerra e fascismo*, Milan, Feltrinelli, 1962; see also Paolo Varvaro, *Una città fascista: potere e società a Napoli*, Palermo, Sellerio, 1990.

At this point, two competing fascist movements came into existence, one official and one dissident, but each with its own newspaper and each with a strong body of support. The official movement, headed by the lawyer Nicola Sansanelli and backed up by the establishment newspaper *Il Mattino*, recognized the authority of the PNF secretary, Turati, while the second, where we now find Tecchio heading the reunited ex-Padovani group, 'enjoyed the protection of the former Secretary of the Party, Roberto Farinacci' and identified with *Il Mezzogiorno*, directed by the former priest and rabid anti-semite, Giovanni Preziosi. Here, as in many other places, it is evident that some kind of proxy war was being fought, as local contestants sought reinforcements in higher places and national figures tried to reinforce their positions at the centre by reference to the strength of their local support.

Turati ordered and eventually succeeded in obtaining the suppression of *Il Mezzogiorno*, but when Sansanelli was replaced as *federale* in 1929 (he was nominated to parliament), his supporters refused to recognize the legitimacy of his replacement and broke with the official *fascio*. Thus, three groups were now in existence, each contesting the other two. As a result, we find a confidential report of 1930 in which it is stated that '[t]he political situation in Naples has suffered, and suffers, from the well-known dispute between the opposing groups: on one side Preziosi, Avv. Tecchio and others; on the other Hon. Sansanelli and friends; both groups *against the* federale'.[47] The result was paralysis. As a later report recorded, this division 'has had no other result than to render the life of the Party sterile, without bringing to the city and the province any enjoyment of the provisions of the *duce*'.[48]

These examples provide us with many of the elements of factionalism—the struggle for power between local fascist leaders, backed up by their followers who hoped to profit from their leader's success; the strong and continuing support for a local man *vis-à-vis* the man from even a few kilometres away (Lessona, in Savona, was guilty of having been 'imported' from Chiavari, a town on the coast just below Genoa); the fragile and temporary nature of expulsions and suspensions from the PNF; the conviction that fortunes could change and that the influence of the centre could be used against local enemies; the disgust of those, particularly the former *squadristi*, whose faction had been defeated but who nonetheless remained convinced that theirs was the authentic Fascism.

Obviously no two provinces were the same, but it is possible to find many of the elements that characterized Savona, Piacenza, or Naples in most provinces during the course of the regime. What marks out Savona, perhaps, is the fact that the same dispute permeates provincial activities for almost two decades despite repeated interventions from the centre. In other provinces, very often, the competing groups would change over time, as alliances changed, but usually the essential elements of the struggle remained constant. It is also worthy of note that the documentation covering the entire period in Savona never makes any reference to differences of policy or political programme. The contest is framed entirely in terms of personalities

---

[47] ACS, PNF, SPEP, b. 9, Naples, report dated October 1930.
[48] ACS, Ibid., 23 December 1939.

and of the pursuit of the interests and positions of the feuding groups. This is a general characteristic of the way in which factionalism is presented and reported. The qualities of the people involved are brought into question, their history within the fascist party, their attitudes during the Matteotti crisis ('*quartarellismo*' is a common accusation made throughout the entire *ventennio*), their relations with disgraced leaders, and—as we shall see—their personal morality. Explicit contrasts over what might be termed 'policy' are rarely an open issue.

Even so, in most provinces it is possible to see, often by reading between the lines of factional exchanges, the way in which factions had been formed as the result of differences in the interpretation of what Fascism should mean in the local context and, more particularly, of which interest groups Fascism would favour.

A good example is provided by the battle that broke out in 1926 in the locality of Bondeno, in the province of Ferrara, between the local *fascio* and the MVSN. Here the prefect had been forced to first disarm and then disband both the *fascio* and the local command of the fascist militia because they had been about to come to blows. 'The bad feeling between the two factions is very deep-seated... there could be serious incidents,' reported the chief of police. The tensions were not new. Both prefect and police chief recognized that the causes lay in a conflict between groups representing different interests: 'the struggle for the conquest of public office derives exclusively from pursuit of interest'.[49] It was, in fact, the usual struggle coming to the surface once again and, as always in Ferrara, the agrarian interests were at the centre of the dispute. These, together with the important local sugar-producing industries, were attempting to gain control of the fascist unions in order to avoid respecting agreements that had been drawn up at provincial level—agreements that had guaranteed the landless workers a certain number of days' work each year. Recognizing that pacts had been broken persistently by the employers, the local *fascio* had reacted to this attempted takeover of the unions, asserting its right to run them and presenting itself as the defender of the workers. This, in turn, had provoked the intervention of the MVSN, firmly on the side of the large farmers and industrialists, as was to be expected in a province dominated by Balbo, who had ridden to fame and fortune on the back of a local *squadrismo* financed by the agrarians.

It seems that *fascio* and militia had few qualms about fighting each other over the question, and were prevented from doing so only by the prompt action of the prefect and the introduction of massive police reinforcements to the centre of Bondeno. Insults were traded between fascists and all attempts at mediation resisted. In this manifestation of factionalism, therefore, the positions of *fascio* and MVSN *vis-à-vis* each other were still very much at issue. Personal rivalries played a large part in the struggle, as undoubtedly did the fact that well-paid and influential jobs were at stake in both industry and the fascist union organizations. But, as usual, vested interests hid behind the clash of local personalities. Moreover, it is highly instructive that the contest was lived as a strictly local issue. The chief of police had attempted to placate the radical blackshirts of Bondeno by suggesting

[49] ACS, MI, DGPS, PS 1928, b. 198, 10 July 1928, police chief to prefect, Ferrara.

that they might be called away to become part of Mussolini's prestigious *Battaglione Moschettieri* (prospected but never realized). This offer had no effect because the interested parties considered that 'it had nothing to do with the political situation in the *Comune*'.[50]

That, in one way or another, all were trying to use the movement for their own ends, did not escape the prefect, who defended his repressive actions with the words '[i]n this way those inhabitants will understand that Fascism and the Militia do not serve the particular interests of the agrarians, the sugar producers or the shopkeepers who base their business on politics, nor those who aspire to positions of authority'.[51] The list did not leave room for many others.

It is worth reminding ourselves briefly of why people fought between themselves like this and what was at stake. Of course, personal prestige, lucrative employment, the possibilities of a further career were all important factors. Employment was one of the most obvious areas in which local political power could be put to good use. The main point of supporting one leader against another was that prospects for placement were attached to victory. As we have seen, (and as we shall see in more detail in the following chapters) a word from the *federale* was enough to get family and friends jobs, either in the public or fascist administrations or with private companies. Client networks were set up in this way, reinforcing the position of the key official, but also excluding others unfairly. Nepotism was rife—a new *federale* in Reggio Calabria admitted that, before his arrival, nepotism had been the order of the day.[52]

But there was also a further consideration, in a way the reverse of this picture. We have already seen, in the protest of one of the excluded of Savona, something of what could happen to dissidents. The writer complained bitterly that he had been 'made a target, persecuted in work and family...'[53] A statement made in 1929 by the former *ras* and ex-*federale* of Reggio Emilia, Giovanni Fabbrici, serves to make the point even better. Fabbrici was a supporter of Farinacci and, like many others, had been forced to stand down in June 1927 as a consequence of the purges effected by Turati. A notorious eater of prefects, he had also been told to keep quiet. In early 1929 he was accused by the prefect, the former blackshirt leader Dino Perrone Compagni, of having encouraged one of his supporters to criticize the system of appointment by designation during a fascist assembly, and to praise the old elective system. Fabbrici reacted strongly to these accusations, pointing out that, had he wanted to create trouble, he would have done it before and done it better, but also complaining that since his dismissal he had been subject to police surveillance, that he had had to give up all his other public positions, including a presumably profitable link with the local savings bank, and that he had been deliberately hampered in his professional activities as a lawyer. Moreover, 'I was forced to assist, with great displeasure, [in] the systematic persecution of fascists who were

[50] ACS, Ibid., prefect Ferrara to Minister of Interior, 10 July 1928.
[51] ACS, Ibid., 27 June 1928.
[52] ACS, PNF, SPEP, b. 17, Reggio Calabria, 24 May 1940.
[53] ACS, PNF, SPEP, b. 20, Savona, Rinaldo Rinaldi to *federale* of Turin, Piero Gazzotti, 23 July 1936.

considered my friends...Several friends of mine from the first Fascism were expelled from the Militia in this way, while other fascists, employed in the public administration, were warned not to have any contact with me...'[54]

In other words, if defeated, dissidents were not always allowed to carry on with normal life until their turn came round again. Prefect, police, and sitting *federale* could make life very difficult for them if they so wished. Dissidents might be harassed by the police and jobs could be lost or put at risk, not only for the dissidents themselves but also for family and friends. Conversely—and this was what kept battles alive and dissidents active—if you were a part of the faction currently in favour, fresh opportunities might suddenly appear and the repressive forces at the disposal of the winner could be used against your enemies. In the case of Reggio Emilia (but the same could be said for most provinces), it is to be noted how far the prefect is the deciding voice in determining the fate of one group and in giving often decisive support to another.

The constitution within many provinces of a group of difficult, discontented fascists was a persistent problem for the authorities, both state and party. Precisely because of their continual declarations of loyalty to the cause, the discontented were difficult to ignore or to suppress. Various strategies could be adopted in relation to the 'outs' but none was without its down-side. Thus, in the *comune* of Celle Ligure (Savona), where, in 1931, a special commissioner had determined the readmission to the party of a group of expelled fascists in order to keep them quiet, the *podestà* protested that the original expulsions had been justified and the readmissions foolish. He pointed out that the majority of those readmitted had criminal records and quoted from the Judicial Record of the Civil Court of Savona, listing their crimes. Among these were 'theft', 'grievous bodily harm', 'repeated threats', 'confidence tricks', 'living off immoral earnings' (this was somewhat disingenuous: the man had procured prostitutes for the local *fascio*), 'attempted murder', and so on. As the *podestà* concluded, the readmission of such people provoked a very unfavourable reaction from those still within the party.[55]

In an analogous case a year earlier in Milan, the prefect was forced to resort to a very pragmatic climb-down. A group of fascists, expelled 'following the purges carried out by Hon. Starace', were making trouble and had to be neutralized. The prefect suggested that those who had shown themselves reasonably disciplined during the process of expulsion should be readmitted to the party, while the others—the undisciplined, who were unemployed—should be given 'material assistance with modest and profitable jobs'.[56] (This was a fair indication of the way in which expulsion from the party could also result in problems in obtaining employment and could provoke economic difficulties. The expelled might, in reality, be less concerned

---

[54] ACS, PNF, SPEP, b. 18, Reggio Emilia, Prefect Perrone Compagni to Turati, 16 February 1929 and *Memoria* of Giovanni Fabbrici to commissario Pierazzi, 24 February 1929.

[55] ACS, PNF, SPEP, b. 20, Savona, Podestà Verando to Minister of the Interior, 25 June 1931.

[56] The animator of this group of expelled fascists, Enrico Cagna, not himself expelled, had incurred the wrath of the Milan *fascio* for having taken part in a demonstration of solidarity for Arturo Toscanini in early June 1931 at the time when the conductor was being persecuted by the Fascists because of his refusal to play the fascist hymn 'Giovinezza' at La Scala.

about their politics than their pockets when they made their protests.) The prefect argued that it was better to satisfy their needs in some way, therefore:

> ...it appears that even the local town hall favours their being fixed up with licences for small-scale commercial activities. For example it seems that the well-known Gattai Bruno has already been given—in his wife's name—the licence for a large fruit and vegetable kiosk in Corso Sempione.[57]

Bruno Gattai, and no doubt many others like him, must have thought that creating trouble for the prefect paid dividends. The fact that the licence was given to his wife was clearly an attempt on the part of the authorities to deflect the anticipated complaints that a troublemaker had been bought off while loyal fascists remained without such rewards.

5.4. PURE, UNDILUTED CANNIBALISM

It is difficult to look through the reports on provincial fascism in the late 1920s and early 1930s without finding repeated evidence of divisions, infighting, and factionalism within the provincial movements. Indeed, as Emilio Gentile has written, 'the internal life of the party was *always* conditioned by those circles in which it had developed'.[58] In many areas contests would be resolved or suppressed, often by the imposition of a central party commissar whose job it was to impose discipline on those who refused to give up their claims to power. At times the commissars could be fairly brutal in their decisions, particularly with expulsions, and they often created a great deal of local resentment through their judgements. The resentment would then continue to simmer and would surface several years later. But pacifications were also achieved, sometimes by compromise, sometimes by inducement (the discontented could be bought off fairly easily if, for example, a local government agency needed a new director—or another usher), or by the disgracing and—usually—exile of one of the contenders. The problem was that, as we have seen, these solutions were rarely considered to be definitive. As soon as the commissar was removed and a new *federale* appointed, ambitions would be rekindled and resentments remembered. The whole process of internal struggle would begin again. Thus the characteristic of many provincial federations was frequently that described at the time as 'cannibalism'[59]—the capacity of a provincial fascist movement to self-destruct around the personal squabbles of pretenders to power. What we have seen in Savona, Piacenza, and Naples was pure, undiluted, '*cannibalismo*'.

---

[57] ACS, MI, DGPS, PS 1930–31, b. 378, Milan, 21 July 1930.
[58] Gentile, *Storia*, 318, my emphasis.
[59] See, for example, ACS, PNF, SPEP, b. 20, Savona, undated but 1933: '[t]here have been episodes, in various periods, of real "cannibalism," in which, of course, the least guilty have come off worst'. The persistence of this tendency is confirmed by the extremely succinct statement of fascist objectives given by *federale* Giuseppe Frediani on his arrival in Pavia in 1936: 'No cannibalism, no politics', quoted in Lupo, *Il Fascismo*, 24.

Such continuous bitter contests were anathema to many, exhausting for most. Prefects reported that the internecine quarrels of Fascism alienated a lot of people, precisely because the petty and personal causes of conflict were so evident, and that they discouraged participation in the movement. In many cases this represented a loss of potential supporters; in others it signified the alienation of those who had already given a great deal to the movement. Even those with an active fascist history sometimes became tired of perpetual argument and withdrew from the fray. As the prefect of Siena wrote in September 1931, the internal struggles·of the local *fascio* had provoked 'the continuous, silent but eloquent, alienation of people who, up to now, had been active, authentic, fascists—representatives of the majority of Siena blackshirts'.[60]

Three quotations illustrate very well the various negative aspects of provincial Fascism. All relate to the 1930s and all point up the fact that factionalism had an extremely debilitating effect on the local movement. The first comes from Savona in January 1932, from where a fascist official—probably a commissar sent from Rome to sort out the local situation—reported that '[f]or too long the Fascism of the province has been distracted from its true mission and consumed by sterile and damaging internal struggles, which have alienated the masses and made them diffident'. The second—a prefect's report from 1937—relates to the situation in Piacenza, where questions surrounding the 'historic' local leader of Fascism, Barbiellini-Amidei, produced a decade of suspensions, expulsions, constant infighting between fascist groups, and, ultimately, complete paralysis. Again referring to the lack of able people to run the local administration, the prefect observed:

> This painful phenomenon...has its origins here in the disagreements which have often taken the shape of true tragedy, with the result that a great many well-prepared citizens have been and still are distant from public life because they are frightened of being involved in factional struggles. The period of the well-known troubles has been followed—and it has lasted several years now—by a period of listlessness...[61]

The third—an unsigned and undated memo from 1939 or perhaps 1940—describes the disastrous situation in the province of Modena. The informer makes the same point about the difficulty of finding suitable people, but adds further explanation and in particular shows the way in which a *federale* appointed from the centre did not always improve the workings of the federation to which he was sent:

> The crisis...which had already begun a few years ago, got worse with the appointment of *camerata* Feltri as *federale*. His appointment, proposed by the top echelons of the Party at the time, seems to have provoked the alienation of those who for some years had decided everything in both city and province. This outcome was welcomed because Modena Fascism had felt the weight of these *gerarchi* whose sectarian and ambitious activities were not adapted to the times. But after this purge, as we could call it—a purge many had hoped for—there followed an exaggerated and stressful campaign centred around one man, which resulted in the alienation of people of all ages who might have been able to make a disinterested personal contribution and

---

[60] ACS, PNF, SPEP, b. 21, Siena, report for month of September 1931.
[61] ACS, PNF, SPEP, b. 14, Piacenza, 3 June 1937.

carry out some intelligent activity, to the extent that all Fascism is now encapsulated in the figure of the Federal Secretary because those excluded have been hit so hard.[62]

These reports are in no way exceptional. They go a long way to suggesting that, in many provinces, if you could, it was better to avoid having anything to do with the local federation. Many, of course, could not.

What stands out from the examples provided by these provincial situations is the inability, in many cases, of the PNF officials in Rome to dominate the provincial problems. The repeated replacement of the *federale* in Savona during the course of the 1930s demonstrated that, in certain circumstances, fascist centralization could go only so far in calling people to order. During the 1930s the PNF attempted to use a rotation of younger fascists—many drawn from the GUF—as *federali* with the intention of inserting into the local context people not conditioned by local squabbles. The hope was that it would prove possible, with the second generation of fascists, to create a new group of 'professional' administrators, efficient, impartial, and implacable in their decisions. However the effects were only limited. A continuing problem facing the new, younger, *federali* was that they were considered by the older fascists to be without authority. They suffered precisely because they were often young and inexperienced—and, in some cases, because they were seen as the representatives of Rome. Frequently treated with great condescension by 'first hour' comrades, they inevitably had no glorious past as a First World War hero or intrepid *squadrista* on which to rest their reputations and were forced, therefore, to rely for their authority on the prefect or on the reputation of the central party secretary. In the period during which Starace was secretary, this was not a happy position. Resulting insecurity often produced overreaction. A police informer in Rome in 1935 reported that stalwarts within the party were saying of those 'without a beard yet', '... these youngsters, who have been raised to the dignified position of leaders of the province, feel they are the *duce* and behave as if they were the *duce*, covering the party with ridicule... Unfortunately we are in the hands of the last-comers and the breast-fed'.[63] A later communication from Florence to Rome in 1938, spoke of the 'scarcity of prepared people among those coming from the youth organizations' and complained about the 'small number' of good young people available for party jobs, compelling the party to use 'unsuitable' people.[64]

Thus, the new, younger men—one component of the 'professional fascists'—were often considered to be ill-prepared for the task which confronted them.[65] But, quite apart from the degree of preparation of those despatched from Rome to control the more troublesome provincial federations, young 'imported' *federali* risked being thrust into the embrace of the prefect, something which could very quickly limit their freedom of action. A further problem was that they found that they had,

---

[62] ACS, PNF, SPEP, b. 8, Modena, *Pro-memoria*, undated but either 1939 or 1940.
[63] ACS, MI, DGPS, b. 219, 7 May 1935.
[64] ACS, Ibid., b.109, 2 January 1938.
[65] Marco Palla, 'Fascisti di professione: il caso toscano', in Gabriele Turi (ed.), *Cultura e società negli anni del fascismo*, Milan, Cordero, 1987, 31–49.

inevitably, to work with the local fascists and that this usually implied some kind of choice between groups. A *federale* appointed from outside the province in order to resolve factionalism could rarely arrive at independent decisions or form non-factional directorates. Young *federali* needed local support if they were to succeed. It was, as we have seen, the job of the *federale* to nominate seven local fascists to form part of the provincial Directorate; he also had to nominate the Political Secretary of each *fascio di combattimento* and propose the names of five people to form the directorate of each *fascio*. These were decisions that, in a big province with many *comuni*, could often involve a large number of people and really required someone with intimate knowledge of the province. Advice was essential, but it was not always disinterested. Moreover, a change of guard inevitably left a sizeable group of the discontented, ready to obstruct the activities of the new arrival. At best, a new, non-local, *federale* would establish some kind of truce between conflicting factions, hoping to survive without loss of face until 'rotated' once again.[66] Always hailed as the definitive 'pacification of spirits', these truces rarely lasted for long. Once factions had been formed—and they were usually formed in the 1920s—they became very difficult to suppress, testifying to the extent to which local factors conditioned the working of the fascist party machine.

Certainly, not all provincial federations were fissured by factionalism in the pattern presented here; not everywhere was characterized by cannibalism. The strong, local leader, of national importance, could provide an exception to this picture and the situation was sometimes different in those few provinces in which a leading figure managed to establish his authority from very early on and maintain it in the face of challenge. This was the case of Balbo in Ferrara, for example, and also of Costanzo Ciano in Livorno. Both were figures of national importance who were able use their weight at the centre in order to consolidate their positions within their own province or city. In this respect, the card Balbo played, almost from the start, was that of the concession and subsequent control of public works. His ability in procuring government money for land improvement and for infrastructures within the province of Ferrara made him a key figure both for the landed proprietors and for the unemployed, even before the March on Rome. In later years he was able to build on this position of strength. The presentation in Ferrara of important national conferences and prestigious art exhibitions, and the restoration of local buildings and monuments, induced people to speak of the new Renaissance of the province.

What was notable about Balbo's hold on power was that, when away from the province, first at the Air Ministry and later as Governor of Libya, he continued to rely on a group of loyal local fascists, many of whom had been his supporters since 1921.[67] Personal, even family, links remained central to his control. Once initial

---

[66] Lupo notes that the young *federali* were often essentially *commissari* in another form (*Il Fascismo*, 388). As with the *commissari*, the stability achieved by the 'professional' fascist administrators tended to be no more than temporary.

[67] Parisini charts the progress of the fascist syndicates through the late 1920s and into the early 1930s, showing the degree to which the personnel of Fascism changes little during that period: *Ferrara*, 9–136.

dissidence had been eliminated, the province remained remarkably stable, with the operation of local power firmly in the hands of people who made constant reference to their leader. Because of this loyalty and constant reference, Balbo was able to act as a link between the fascists and the traditional bourgeoisie of Ferrara, carefully mediating between the requirements of the day-to-day appearances of authority—the perquisite of the uniformed fascists—and the more amorphous realities of economic power, which remained largely with those who had held it before the advent of Fascism. The confirmation of this ability to procure funds on one side and to mediate between interests on the other came in the late 1930s with the project to develop petro-chemicals for the new industrial zone in the area of Pontelagoscuro—a radical departure for a province previously centred, even in its industries, on agriculture.[68]

Costanzo and Galeazzo Ciano retained control in Livorno through methods not unlike those employed by Balbo.[69] Here again close personal loyalties were important for the maintenance of command, family connections even more so than in Ferrara. The Ciano family had a head-start on Balbo, of course, because of Costanzo Ciano's distinguished record in the First World War, which made him something of a local celebrity. During the years of the regime, both he and his son, Galeazzo, would operate principally away from Livorno—the father in Rome until his death in July 1939, the son in the diplomatic service and then in Rome—but both were able to depend on a very faithful group of local fascists, which remained fairly constant in its composition throughout the *ventennio*. As in Ferrara, the local group of fascists busied themselves with the administration of the city while the acknowledged and never-contested leader brought government money to Livorno in an effort to stimulate the local economy. As in Ferrara, there was a project for the development of an industrial zone to diversify from excessive reliance on a port declining in importance. Stability depended on the fact that the Ciano family, using its considerable influence, was able, like Balbo, to mediate between fascists and an established local elite, ensuring what sometimes seems like a clear division of competencies. National prominence was used to consolidate and protect provincial control by the fascists, therefore, but not—as some intransigents of the 1920s would have hoped—to unseat the traditional bourgeoisie. The two groups were able to operate in parallel, reflecting a substantial identity of interests between old and new.

Both examples given here indicate that the party would work best when directed—even at a distance—by a man with strong local support and a solid local power base. 'Imported' *federali* almost inevitably suffered because they could not meet these conditions. But—and this was the Catch 22—the existence of strong local leaders often presented problems for central government because their local power base encouraged independence of action. The campaigns aimed at the '*spersonalizzazione*' of the provincial *fasci* had been aimed to prevent autonomous and

[68] Rochat, *Balbo*.
[69] On Livorno see Toby Abse, *Sovversivi e fascisti a Livorno: Lotta politica e sociale (1918–1922)*, Milan, Franco Angeli, 1991; more recently, on the regime, Mazzoni, *L'ombra del fascio*.

personally determined initiatives. Events surrounding Balbo—precisely—illustrate this problem. In 1934, Balbo's supporters asked quietly of their leader if they should 'move' in his defence when he was transferred from the Air Ministry to the Governorship of Libya (effectively, a political demotion). What they planned is unknown but it was clearly autonomous, independent action in support of a single figure. Balbo appears to have reflected; he then told them to behave themselves.

In Balbo's case, his personal connections with 'his' province permitted him to survive as a first-rank leader, even when abroad. A host of others were less lucky. And, in those provinces where such leaders were removed, or where a single leading figure had never emerged, local rivalries would always resurface, preventing the formation of a strong and stable party structure. In effect, this was something of a conundrum which the fascist movement never really succeeded in solving. In one way or another the thrust towards fragmentation in Italian political life persisted in coming to the fore. The imperatives of cohesion and national unity, of single-mindedness in the pursuit of a single national goal, even if mouthed by all with conscientious monotony, took second place to more immediate local concerns of position and control.

5.5. PNF AND NSDAP COMPARED

The conventional view of dictatorship has little room for this picture of a surprisingly dysfunctional party organization—permanently unstable at provincial level because of personal tensions and conflicting group interests. Dictators are supposed to be able to deal with these things. It may be instructive to ask why Nazi Germany was not so troubled by the kind of local infighting seen in Italy. In the rural provinces the Nazis certainly had their problems with the traditional elite and ran into a large number of conflicts in their attempts to transform aspects of provincial life.[70] But there is little sense of local Nazi leaders fighting incessantly among themselves for power or even of using a local power base in order to contest the authority of the centre. One reason, undoubtedly, is the example provided by the Night of the Long Knives; radical contesting of Hitler's line meant risking a rapid and violent response. This was true throughout the history of the Third Reich. The existence, and dominant position, of the SS after June 1934 constituted a powerful disincentive to indiscipline among second-level leaders. Hardly comparable in any way with the fascist militia, the SS was not regionally based and, as a national corps, had little time for local squabbles.[71] These were not unknown, of course. Local Nazi officials did compete among themselves, particularly in defence of their often poorly defined roles *vis-à-vis* each other and in relation to Berlin ministries. Petty rivalries and feuding were very much the order of the day. And state officials would try to protect their jurisdictions from encroachment by arrogant party

---

[70] See Jill Stephenson, 'Popular Opinion in Nazi Germany: Mobilization, Experience, Perceptions: the View from the Württemberg Countryside', in Corner (ed.), *Popular Opinion*, 106–46.

[71] I thank Jeremy Noakes for this observation.

leaders, sometimes provoking bitter local struggles. But in Nazi Germany there is—overall—little sense of the *damaging* effects of permanent factionalism at the local level that is present in Italy.

An important difference between the two movements lies in the original inspiration of the Nazi movement which, from the beginning, was nationally rather than regionally orientated. While Italian Fascism was in many ways a revolt against the centre, a revolt that brought to the surface of political life in Italy those powerful centrifugal forces that had never been totally controlled in liberal Italy, the Nazis' anti-state attitudes were much less an affirmation of local autonomy from central government and much more a reflection of the desire to form a new, strong state along the lines of the defeated Empire. Where the provincial *ras* of Fascism became uncertain about their loyalties in the 1920s because of the tensions between local power and central state authority, provincial Nazi leaders never had any doubt that the national and the racial imperatives should dominate.

Here the position of Hitler—the strong imposition, and recognition, of the leadership principle—was certainly very important. This principle was less apparent in Italy. As we have seen, for a long period in the 1920s Mussolini was unable to establish the same kind of domination of his movement; his opponents within the party continued to be essential to his control of the country. It was important that in many cases fascist leaders had established their claims to position before and not after the seizure of power. Mussolini remained to some extent in their debt and found it difficult to discipline them beyond a certain point, as the continuing friction between *federali* and prefects, even after the circular of 1927, demonstrated amply. This relationship of dependence was to change with time, but by the time the cult of the *duce* was in full operation in the 1930s much of the damage had long been done. Factions had been formed and each faction continued to insist that it had Mussolini on its side.

Mussolini himself seems to have oscillated between irritation and indecisiveness on many of the questions relating to factionalism. Perhaps what is striking in much of the documentation of the local struggles of the late 1920s and 1930s is the degree to which the problem is left to the PNF secretary, who seems to have had relatively little authority in the provinces, and the extent to which Mussolini himself remains aloof from the questions of discipline and factionalism among party members. He scribbled pencil notes to Starace and to his police chief, Bocchini, making (usually very brief) suggestions about discipline and replacements. This was very different from invoking the intervention of the SS.

A further reason for difference lies in the role assigned to the party in the two regimes. In Nazi Germany the party commanded, the state carried out those commands administratively.[72] This may be an overly simplified summary of the situation, which was, in effect, a very confused polycracy, but there can be no doubt that, after a series of measures which effectively eroded the powers of the state organs immediately following 1933, the party became the senior partner in the party–state relationship. It had, therefore, ultimate authority, even in the local

---

[72] See Richard Overy, *The Dictators*, London, Allen Lane, 2004, 134.

context. The leadership principle, the requirement of unconditional and unquestioning obedience to higher authority, passed from the centre to the locality through the party and permeated local as well as national affairs.

The complex system of regional and local government set up by the National Socialist regime in the course of 1933 and 1934 was designed, at least in part, to curtail the risk of the formation of regional autonomies, competing with the centre for control. Significantly the Reich Governors appointed initially to the *Länder* and the *Gauleiter* who controlled the *Gaue* administrative districts were much less 'local' men than the *ras* were in Italy. The *Gaue* districts were in any case usually much larger than the Italian provinces; even leading Nazis who were natives of those regions were much less liable to be influenced predominantly by local affairs, therefore. The *Gauleiter* were also much more permanent fixtures, not constantly 'rotating' like the *federali* of the 1930s in Italy. Moreover, the functions of Nazi officials were made to include those of overseeing the state administrative offices in the region as well as the organization of the party. In certain regions the creation of the figure of the *Reichsstatthalter* effectively combined both party and state roles in the same person, thus removing the dualism of power so evident in the Italian provinces.

In short, the impression is that the local leaders in Germany had their eyes much more on Hitler, much less on local contests for power, and that they felt fairly constantly that Hitler's eyes were on them. Indeed, if we accept Kershaw's theme of Nazi officials 'working towards the Führer', the kind of competition among local leaders generated by the confused and badly defined structures of the polycratic Third Reich would seem to have been beneficial to the regime—a source of continued dynamism and vitality rather than a recipe for paralysis.

Many elements of the Italian situation were the exact opposite. Mussolini's manoeuvres between 1925 and 1927 aimed at the reduction of the role of the party. The defeat of the intransigents effectively resulted in a kind of castration of the PNF, reducing its dynamic function while at the same time provoking profound and sometimes permanent divisions within the local movements. His confirmation of the prefect as 'the supreme authority of the state' within the province tended inevitably to push the PNF into that bureaucratic, administrative function it continued to occupy throughout the 1930s. This was still an important role within the fascist scheme of things but it did mean that key decisions concerning provincial life were more likely to emanate from the prefecture than from the *casa del fascio*. The Italian party simply had less authority—deliberately so—than its German counterpart and found itself competing, often on unfavourable terms, with other authorities at the local level in a way a Nazi *Gauleiter* would have found unthinkable.

In a rather paradoxical way, therefore, it was precisely the reduced importance of the local party organization in Italy that opened the path to continuous factionalism. Lack of dynamism produced loss of direction. Had Farinacci won his battles with Mussolini and succeeded in placing fascists in all positions of command within the state structure, it seems likely that a much more rigid system of discipline would have been imposed on the party. For the PNF to carry out its essential functions in running both fascist and state organs, as Farinacci wished, the degree of factionalism witnessed in the Italian provinces would have been intolerable. Instead, the secondary role of the party in respect of the state authorities permitted local questions and local differences to continue to manifest themselves without attracting an immediate (and violent) response from the centre. It was very much the case that party and state continued to run on parallel tracks, with the state in some respects unimpeded by the consequences of provincial factionalism (as we shall see in Chapter 6, the state found its own, different, ways of penetrating provincial life) and with the party always convinced that a solution to factionalism could be found—after all, the quarrelling groups all proclaimed themselves loyal fascists—and unable to see the consequences of such factionalism for the long term.

That the secondary political role assigned to the PNF had severe consequences on its working (and would make it less efficient than the NSDAP was to prove) was apparent surprisingly quickly. As early as 1929, Torquato Nanni, whom we have already had occasion to cite, was denouncing the condition of the party. The dominance within the provinces of the prefect and the police had produced a 'police state', he complained—not necessarily negative, providing it was short-lived. Instead it had become the norm, with results that the centre had failed to appreciate.

> If Mussolini could see the local situations like any lowly mortal...he would realize that...air and light are not circulating...; that the party, the fascist movement, have now been reduced to a narrow bureaucracy; that the soul of the fascist masses, excluded from any responsibility, never consulted and by now tired of parades that do not galvanize and do not stimulate enthusiasm, is losing the conviction and the hopes of its best years.[73]

This was a recognition of crisis already emerging within the PNF at the end of the 1920s. Nanni's criticisms, appearing remarkably early considering that many policies were still in the process of implementation in 1929, represented themes that many others would dwell on during the course of the following decade.

[73] Letter from Nanni to Rigola, Easter 1929, quoted in Aquarone, *L'Organizzazione*, 164–5.

6

The Provincial Party: Activity and Reputation

How important were the tensions within the provincial fascist movements? Was it of any real importance that prefect and federal secretary often crossed swords over the limits of their respective jurisdictions? Did factionalism really matter? Or were the tensions simply something internal to the party—something confined to the few who counted, or sought to count—which had no real effect on the workings of the fascist organizations? After all, most political parties see some degree of infighting, but this does not necessarily prevent them from working successfully as parties. To return to the example of Nazism, rivalries, betrayals and backbiting play a prominent part of the story of the NSDAP, even at provincial level, but few would put in doubt the capacity of the party to control the situation in Germany and to advance the Nazi cause.

6.1. BOUNDLESS NUMBERS, ENDLESS ACTIVITY

From some points of view, the same must be said of fascist Italy and the fascist party. Despite problems, the show did go on, and, in many respects, it was a very impressive show. Even though the party had its difficulties, as we have seen, it did continue to permeate provincial life to an ever-increasing degree. The many capillary organizations, which expanded their reach during the course of the 1930s, affected individual experience at school, at work, and when simply passing leisure time doing nothing in particular. These were the years in which Achille Starace was national secretary of the PNF and, if he had many defects, lack of organizing energy was not one of them. The very powerful tools the party had at its disposition in terms of economic regulation in the province—wages and prices depended to a great degree on the *comitati intersindacali*—and in terms of welfare made it a constant point of reference for everyone. The local party might not be political dynamite after its effective subordination to the centre, but, as a bureaucratic-administrative machine, it did often have a 'totalitarian' presence and was impossible to ignore.

In this sense the regime effected a mobilization of the population on a level that had never been seen before. People participated massively in fascist-sponsored activities and many of these activities were the direct responsibility of the party. Some of the numbers are quite remarkable. By March 1940 the PNF had more than 3.5 million enrolled and around 20 million Italians—little short of half the total population—were involved in the various capillary organizations, unions included. The *Gioventù italiana del Littorio* (GIL: the fascist youth organization) claimed a membership of over 8 million in October 1940—more than the Hitler Youth at the same time. In terms of the extension of its operations there can be no doubt that the party stood at the head of a mass organization of which Italy (and most of Europe) had not seen the like. At least in formal terms, fascist Italy was well on the way to the realization of the totalitarian state.

Many historians of Fascism have very correctly insisted on the elements of novelty in the fascist movement, beginning with the single party itself and extending to the many capillary organizations of the movement. At the provincial level it was the party that was at the centre of many of these novelties—often representing unpractised forms of new collective activity. Indeed, activity is almost the keyword for the provincial fascism of the 1930s. After all, Fascism was not just 'faith', it was also meant to be—perhaps above all—action. Fairly predictably, the more the provincial federations were relieved of any serious political function, and the more they became bureaucratic and administrative organs, the greater was the tendency to concentrate all their attentions on activities.

This tendency is best illustrated by reference to certain local party documents. During the 1930s provincial party leaders were required to send in monthly, or sometimes bimonthly, reports on what had been going on in their province. The sheer concentration on numbers—on counting—is striking. Numbers of meetings held, people involved, uniforms worn, quantities (of many things) collected, quantities distributed, roll-calls made, bicycles ridden, motorcyclists trained, children holidayed, picnics eaten, and so on—it is all recounted in an obsessive avalanche of numbers, month after month. In Taranto, for example, the *federale* proudly reported the Christmas and New Year activities of the *fascio* for 1934–5. He listed the benefits to the poor:

> The *Befana Fascista* was celebrated on 6 January and over 3,000 packs of various clothes and shoes were distributed. On 7 January the distribution points for the popular meals were opened, handing out 3,700 rations a day of bread and soup. Up to the end of February, 1,982 families have been assisted and the rations allocated to the meal distribution points have increased to 8,200 units, as well as the 380 food subsidies in the form of food parcels handed out to needy families who for social level cannot go the distribution points.[1]

Assistance—sometimes complementing, sometimes substituting for traditional Catholic assistance—was undoubtedly one of the regime's strongest cards. Assistance might be distributed unfairly, it might be very limited in extent (the above was essentially a soup kitchen), it might be heavily paternalistic in tone, but, in hard times—and the 1930s were hard times—many could not do without it. It constituted, therefore, a wonderful instrument of social control for the regime.

A second card the party could play—and again a very strong card—was the organization of people's leisure time through the *Opera Nazionale Dopolavoro*.

---

[1] ACS, PNF, SPEP, b. 23, Taranto, Report for January–February 1935.

Founded in 1925 and passing to the direct control of the PNF in 1927, the OND, or *Dopolavoro*, as it became known, rapidly expanded its activities to become one of the central pillars of the regime's relationship with the population. Again, it thrived on numbers. For example, in Siena and province, where the leisure organization initially had problems interesting people, the 30 centres and affiliated branches of 1927 had become 204 by 1937; activities passed from the 93 'events' of 1927 to the 10,900 claimed in 1935 for the period 1927–1934.[2] A further and fairly typical report relates to the activities of the fascist leisure organization in Piacenza in 1935. It was evidently important to leave nothing to the imagination. Thus Starace was informed that, in May–June 1935, the activities of the *Dopolavoro Provinciale* alone had been:

1 game of *tamburello*
27 games of bowls
4 tug-of-war contests
2 canoeing competitions with 17 crews
2 games of football
1 athletics meeting
12 target-shooting competitions
7 plate-shooting competitions
19 excursions with 1,088 participants
21 tourist events with 2,851 participants
3 tourist motorcycling events with 66 participants
22 tourist cycling events with 2,962 enrolled
7 walking events with 125 enrolled.[3]

Clearly a lot of people were doing a lot of things—and with great and almost frenetic frequency. Cohorts of organizers were involved, found mainly among the middle and lower-middle classes—local schoolteachers (particularly elementary schoolteachers),[4] other state employees, and some lower-level professional people. This was new. In many areas of Italy the personnel of local politics—bureaucratic-administrative politics—did change radically with the advent of Fascism. Tommaso Baris has shown the ways in which a new administrative class emerged under Fascism in the province of Frosinone (below Rome), to some extent contesting, to some extent complementing the authority of the traditional elite.[5] And Vittorio Cappelli has described how, in Calabria, 'a small army of those in the liberal professions (lawyers, doctors, professors), as well as pharmacists, elementary school teachers, council workers, but also the unemployed and the rootless, assembled under the banner of Fascism, seeing in it the possibility for themselves of finally gaining

---

[2] 'Il dopolavoro provinciale senese nel primo decennio di vita', in *Rivoluzione fascista*, 27, 5 May 1935, quoted in Stefano Cavazza, 'Il palio e le tradizioni popolari senesi durante il fascismo', in A. Orlandini (ed.), *Fascismo e antifascismo nel Senese*, Florence, Olschki, 1994, 265.

[3] ACS, PNF, SPEP, b. 14, Piacenza, 'Relazione Attività Bimestre Maggio–Giugno XIII'.

[4] Perry Willson emphasizes the central role of primary school teachers in organizing the *massaie rurali* in many areas: *Peasant Women*, 88, 191–2.

[5] Baris, *Frosinone*, various. While the author stresses the appearance of the 'new', he is also careful to show the ways in which the traditional elite managed to retain a great deal of control over the situation.

political power'.[6] The same phenomenon can be seen in the North. In July 1935 a meeting of local fascist organizers in Turin alone saw almost 1,500 people present.[7]

In this respect, the fascist movement seems—for a certain period at least—to have succeeded in involving a large part of the population in activities that, while apparently unpolitical, could be directly associated with their political sponsors. The inculcation of the fascist 'life style', based on vigorous activity, was meant to occur at this point. Young people in particular could be induced to associate pleasurable activities and enjoyment with the party, which could be presented as a viable alternative to the closed and authoritarian structure of the family. In this kind of operation sport was a very strong aggregating factor and the fact that it was the responsibility of the local fascist organization served to give a political gloss to new forms of leisure activity.[8] Local studies of Turin show that sport was a very effective means of creating a favourable impression of Fascism among the young.[9] A tug-of-war was a tug-of-war, but, under the aegis of the *Dopolavoro*, it became, at least in theory, a fascist tug-of-war.

Many found the paramilitary aspects of the youth organizations equally stimulating, at least for a time. Playing at soldiers and drilling with smart uniforms and wooden rifles fired the imagination of children and of some adolescents and was likely to be particularly seductive after the victory in the Ethiopian campaign. Children's comics featured young fascists in exotic African adventures, where, inevitably, they always came out on the winning side of their battles with the grass-skirted natives. It is worth remembering in this context that around 80,000 young people passed from the *Balilla* and the *Avanguardisti* to the *fasci giovanili*, the PNF, and the MVSN each year through the process of the fascist 'call up'. The level of indoctrination achieved among these young people was of great importance for the regime, therefore.

The capillary network of fascist organizations, developing increasingly during the 1930s under the aegis of the PNF undoubtedly represented a real penetration of Fascism into the lives of ordinary people. Numerous testimonies of the time refer to the ways in which fascist propaganda was present in the school and university, at work, and at play, and there can be little doubt that it had an impact on a great many people. The regime made an enormous effort to saturate people's space and time in such a way as to make Fascism a constant physical and psychological presence. The level of saturation was significant for town dwellers—perhaps a little less so for the rural population, where 'fascist' socialization was more difficult—and does constitute an aspect of what was a partial nationalization, or at least a 'socialization', of the masses under Fascism around national models of activity and consumption.[10] Without any doubt, the party did manage to place itself at the

---

[6] Vittorio Cappelli, 'Politica e Politici', in Piero Bevilacqua and Augusto Placanica (eds), *Storia d'Italia. Le Regioni dall'Unità a oggi. La Calabria*, Turin, Einaudi, 1985, 542.

[7] ACS, PNF, SPEP, b. 25, Turin, 6 July 1935.

[8] See, among others, Simon Martin, *Football and Fascism*, Oxford, Berg, 2004; Maria Canella and Sergio Giuntini (eds), *Sport e fascismo*, Milan, Angeli, 2009.

[9] Maurizio Gribaudi, *Mondo operaio e mito operaio*, Turin, Einaudi, 1987.

[10] Raffaele Romanelli even uses the phrase 'nationalization of the periphery', although this seems a little excessive; (1988) *Meridiana* 4. See also Salvati, *L'Inutile salotto* and Marco Palla, 'Relazione introduttiva', in Orlandini (ed.), *Senese*, 36.

centre of people's attention and constitute a common frame of reference. The message conveyed through the varied activities was that the paternal party was interested in you and was on your side—a total political novelty for large parts of the population, effectively excluded from any form of political socialization before the advent of the regime. The message was even more evident, of course, with the assistance handouts, where nothing was given without a heavy statement about the virtues of Fascism and the generosity of the *duce*.

With increasing frequency after 1932, when a decidedly populist tone was introduced to the political arena with Mussolini's command to 'reach out to the people', the capillary organizations, and particularly the OND, made use of local festivals and regional folklore in their efforts to follow this order. In theory, the accentuation of regional and provincial peculiarities ran contrary to ideas of centralization, but fascist organizers were sufficiently astute to realize that cultural manifestations of regional or specific communal identity were very different from affirmations of political separateness and could be used to strengthen a sense of national belonging. As Stefano Cavazza has shown, the use of the traditional popular festival—sometimes taken over by the fascist organizations, sometimes revived, sometimes invented, even—did represent a powerful weapon, combining public participation and popular enjoyment with—often fairly gentle—indoctrination, in which the national, the patriotic, and the fascist were fused (and confused) in an effort to create a single entity.[11] For his part, Mussolini—like any politician—in his tours of the provinces would often make reference to attractive or flattering local characteristics—'plucky Tuscans', 'proud Piedmontese', etc. The celebration of the particular was one of the ways in which the fascist leader attempted to suggest an identity of outlook between the national fascist movement and local or regional sentiment.

Typical of this kind of fusion of national and local was the insertion in 1934 of the *fasci littoriali* symbol (the Roman rods and shield—the symbol of authority) among the many sacred and profane images depicted on the Palio of Siena (the banner awarded to the winner of the annual horse race).[12] The insertion represented the careful interweaving in Siena of long-established tradition and the immediate requirements of the regime. Local history, religion, and Fascism were amalgamated as if each found its proper place in the company of the others, thus stressing complementarity rather than contrast. For the local fascists, this fusion looked like legitimation by association; for the local aristocracy and bourgeoisie it looked more like the assimilation (but only up to a very carefully controlled point) of a potentially subversive movement. Precisely whose interpretation was correct is hardly a question of debate, however. Siena might integrate aspects of Fascism into

---

[11] Stefano Cavazza, *Piccole Patrie. Feste Popolari tra Regione e Nazione durante il Fascismo*, Bologna, Il Mulino, 1997. See also Vittorio Cappelli, 'Identità locali e Stato nazionale durante il fascismo', (1998) 32 *Meridiana* 53. On the relationship between Fascism and 'civil religion' in Siena, see Gerald Parsons, *The Cult of Saint Catherine of Siena. A Study in Civil Religion*, Aldershot, Ashgate, 2008, 50–74.

[12] A fascist symbol had appeared on the 1927 banner, but it was not until 1934 that fascist symbols became some of the dominant elements.

its traditions and put the symbols of the regime on its banners, but it did remain firmly and distinctively Siena. People would pay some lip-service to Fascism when the movement was associated with traditional forms of local socialization, such as the Palio horse race, but the traditional component remained by far the more powerful element. In the case of Siena this meant that a long-established political and economic elite not only retained its authority, but even managed to utilize fascist forms of mobilization to reinforce its own position.[13]

The attempt at synthesis did represent, in a sense, a form of mediation between regional and national imperatives, in which the celebration of the particular was employed as a means towards the reinforcement of the whole. Nazi leaders were to use this tactic with great success, deliberately encouraging regional consciousness as an 'authentic' part of German national identity.[14] Mussolini and his provincial imitators may have been less successful, however. Their point of departure was, very obviously, different from that of any Nazi leader; Italian national sentiment was still in the process of formation and was in no way as developed as in Germany. Regional and local divisions, suspicions, and hostilities, still ran deep. To a person from Milan, a Sicilian was a threat, not a promise. A common saying in Siena was 'better to have a death in the house than a Florentine on your doorstep' and variants of this were reproduced in many places. Unifying the local and the national was difficult, therefore. It was impossible to find an Italian equivalent of the German *Heimat* to which to make appeal. If, in Germany, the concept of *Heimat* served to unite the national and the local in emotional terms, 'bridg[ing] the gap between national aspiration and provincial reality', it did so as the result of a century-long process of political education and indoctrination.[15] In Italy, homes and hearths were still strongly regional and local in their emotional significance, and without the national overtones implicit in *Heimat*.[16]

Even the much-worked fascist concept of 'ruralism' had little real cohesive force for the nation. The appeal to the solid and traditional rural values of the Italian peasantry may have made an impact on some city dwellers, nostalgic for the world they had (just) lost, but it was unlikely to cut much ice with those—the vast majority of the population—who knew first-hand what rural life was really like.[17] In any case, rural values and traditions varied so much throughout the peninsula that they

---

[13] See Daniele Pasquinucci, 'Classe dirigente liberale e fascismo a Siena. Un caso di continuità', (1991) 184 *Italia contemporanea* 443. Eloquent of the situation was the way in which, in 1936, the fascist *federale*, Aldo Sampoli, made a renewed attempt to control the old elite. He was transferred to another province immediately.

[14] Confino, *The Nation as Local Metaphor*, cited in the Introduction, above.

[15] Celia Applegate, *A Nation of Provincials. The German Idea of* Heimat, Berkeley, University of California Press, 1990, 13. Applegate writes (11) that '*Heimat* was both the beloved local places and the beloved nation'. The problem the fascist regime faced was precisely the lack of any deep-seated sense of 'the beloved nation' among the majority of the Italian population.

[16] For a critical reading of Confino, which suggests that the concept of *Heimat* is not appropriate for an analysis of developments in Italy, see Rolf Petri, 'La *Heimat* dei tedeschi', (2000) 6 *Memoria e ricerca* July–December, 136.

[17] Memorable in this respect is Eugen Weber's description of the modernization of rural France: 'Many grieved over the death of yesterday, but few who grieved were peasants.' *Peasants into Frenchmen*, 478.

had little unifying force. One of the problems with Mino Maccari's *Strapaese* move-ment of the mid-1920s, which had claimed to refer to 'authentic' and 'genuine' Italian provincial values and to defend them against national and modernizing incursions, was that it seemed to refer to a model (the Tuscan model) with which relatively few Italians could identify.[18]

For this reason, emphasis on regional characteristics carried the strong risk of accentuating, rather than reducing, divisions. The risk was particularly high in a Fas-cism that had developed initially as a series of local movements, autonomous of the centre. Too great an emphasis on the local features of the movement could generate once again those centrifugal sentiments the regime had been at such pains to try to suppress. The accentuation of the regional, and the local, had potentially ambiguous interpretations, therefore, and was very far from working in a single direction.

Nonetheless, between organized leisure and local festivals, there can be no deny-ing the level of fascist activity, much of it centred around participation and pleas-ure, and much of it novel for those taking part. In 1938, for example, official figures speak of 685 folklore groups in operation, putting on a total of 5,535 shows during the year—a remarkable number.[19] However, before this rather idyllic pic-ture of a caring, 'fun' party takes hold completely, it is worth remembering that there were strong inducements to collaboration with the fascist organizations. As we shall see in the next chapter in relation to reactions to the Ethiopian war, popu-lar participation in many fascist activities was not always entirely spontaneous. The obsession with numbers noted above meant, of course, that someone, somewhere, was counting, and counting meant that registers were kept, names recorded, pres-ences checked. The party, when it worked well, kept a very close eye on the popula-tion, particularly on those enrolled in one of the many fascist organizations—which, by the mid-1930s, meant most people. The neighbourhood groups (*gruppi rionali*) were very important here, working in close contact with the residents of a small area within the town or city and providing an essential channel of communication between federation and population. The Federation of the PNF of Reggio Emilia, for example, printed a four-page form—the *Cartella di Famiglia*—to be filled in by the party officials for every family with which the Federation came into contact. It required all the usual details of the members of the family (date and place of birth, etc), but also registered details of place of work, type of job (permanent or tempo-rary), salary earned, rent paid for housing, past military history, membership of fascist organizations, and eventual membership of the MVSN. A separate page was left entirely for notes about 'political conduct—morality'.[20] This kind of control of the population, often effected through the *gruppi rionali*, carried with it an implicit threat of reprisals for non-collaboration. The party was aware of your existence

---

[18] On *Strapaese* and *Il Selvaggio*, see Mangoni, *L'interventismo*, 136–60.
[19] Cavazza, *Piccole Patrie*, 137, who quotes the figures of Aristide Rotunno, *Vita culturale e dopolavoro*, Milan, Turati, Lombardi, 1938. Mabel Berezin states that the Verona branch of the PNF put on 727 public events between 1922 and 1942—an average of 36 a year: Berezin, 'The Festival State: Celebration and Commemoration in Fascist Italy', (2006) 4(1) *Journal of Modern European History* 62.
[20] ACS, PNF, SPEP, b. 18, Reggio Emilia.

and, in fact, knew a lot about your personal circumstances and those of your family. As one fascist report observed (with pride),'... those enrolled in the Party are today effectively controlled not only in their political, but also in their personal and private, activity'.[21]

Attention to the family unit, rather than just to the individual, was also significant. If you stepped out of line, not only would you suffer but it might be your children who would be passed over when it came to new possibilities of employment. If you behaved, then perhaps your son or daughter would be among the next group of workers taken on at the local factory.[22] Fascism could be a vehicle of social mobility for upwardly aspiring people, particularly for young people eager to escape family control, but, in the same way, the party could also destroy your chances if it chose to do so. As in most one-party regimes, bureaucratic control of the population, combined with considerable power over the allocation of—usually scarce—resources, permitted the establishment of a formidable regime of sticks and carrots from which few could escape.[23]

The large numbers of Italians involved with the various fascist organizations no doubt reflected—at least in part—this kind of regime of enticement and obligation. Numbers, when related to totalitarian regimes, are notoriously difficult to interpret and Italian Fascism is no exception. What did being a party member mean? Pressures to join the party had been strong for certain categories of worker ever since at least 1925. As we have already seen, a large number of public sector workers flowed into the PNF between 1925 and 1927—many from conviction, but some no doubt to protect their jobs and to improve prospects of promotion. There were protests when enrolment was closed in 1927; people were evidently aware that not being a party member could damage them. And there was perplexity when enrolment was re-opened in 1932: was it a good idea to enrol (and pay the party subscription of 10 lire) or was it possible to survive without the party card?[24] Around half a million people made up their minds and joined between the re-opening of lists and the beginning of 1933. That there were advantages in membership was made clear in early 1933 when enrolment was suddenly closed again. There were complaints that the regime had created two categories of Italian—those in the PNF and those not—and that this kind of discrimination was unjustified and damaging to those who had not managed to join in time.

The whiff of the initials PNF standing for *Per Necessità Familiare* becomes very much stronger in this period, as membership of the party became a discriminating

---

[21] ACS, PNF, SPEP, b. 25, Turin, 6 July 1935.

[22] Evidence of this kind of discrimination in selection is provided in Davide Tabor, 'Operai in camicia nera? La composizione operaia del fascio di Torino, 1921–1931', (2004) 17(36) *Storia e problemi contemporanei* 39.

[23] For a more detailed treatment of this theme see Corner, 'Italian Fascism: whatever happened to dictatorship?' 325–51.

[24] Not everyone was perplexed. An informer from Pisa reported the total indifference of the population to the re-opening of enrolment: 'The news...has passed unnoticed by the mass of the working people, who are those who should provide the largest contingent if we are to be able to say that the Party really has the consensus of the country': ACS, PNF, SPEP, b. 14, report on the political situation, January 1932.

factor in the question of employment. In gradual steps, enrolment in the party was made obligatory for many categories of worker during the course of the decade.[25] Numbers reflect this, with significant increases between 1936 and 1939 and a rise of 1 million (to more than 3 million) between November 1939 and the same month in 1940 as criteria for enrolment were considerably relaxed and people, in great economic difficulty at that time, sought the assistance and security of party membership. In the same way, the further rapid increase in membership during the war years is more likely to be a reflection of rapidly growing difficulties (which could be faced only with the benefits the party card provided) than of any sudden increase in dedication to the cause.

The question whether membership of the party is to be seen as evidence of fascist conviction is, of course, impossible to answer categorically. Membership could reflect opportunism, necessity, conformism, complicity, or commitment and no doubt all these motives were present in different ways and to different degrees among the card-carrying fascists. And, just as all the enrolled might not be convinced fascists, there were, no doubt, many outside the party who sided with the regime and with Mussolini. Evidence of this kind of ambiguity is found in many of the documents relating to 'Insults to the *duce*'. From these it becomes clear that party membership was no guarantee of a respectful attitude towards the party and the fascist leader. For example, a newspaper seller in Ferrara (described as an 'Israelite'), was reported, in 1935, to be heard to say, every time there was a picture of Mussolini on the front page of *La Stampa*, '[a]s long as this idiot [is in power], we shall never sell any newspapers'. He had been in the party since 1933. Two young men, enrolled in the *Fascio Giovanile di Combattimento* and, according to the prefect of Catania, from good fascist families, had been found gouging the eyes of Starace and Mussolini out of all the photos in the OND magazine *Gente Nostra* (and this in the OND building). In another incident, again in 1935, the prefect of Florence recounted that, in conversation with her butcher, a certain Annunziata Masolini had been heard to call Mussolini 'Baldy', going on to speak out against the *duce* and the approaching war, and explaining to the assembled shoppers certain methods of avoiding the conception of children to serve as soldiers, in terms too obscene to reproduce here. She was not a party member, but she had compelled her two sons to enrol in the party, despite her very evident opinions about the *duce*.[26]

An even more illuminating example is provided by a long report (seven pages) from the prefect of Cosenza, relating the reasons for the arrest of a certain Luigi Bevacqua in April 1935. Fifty-three-year-old Bevacqua had taken his long-time mistress, Rosa Maretta, to a cheap hotel near Cosenza. Before going to bed he had

---

[25] Perry Willson records the way in which female workers in the northern rice fields were obliged to take the fascist union card from 1935 onwards if they wanted to work. This pushed them towards almost 'automatic' membership of the *Massaie rurali* or the *Giovani fasciste*. See Willson, *Peasant Women*, 183–4.

[26] ACS, MI, DGPS, AGR, b. 10, 1935, 'Offese al *duce*', Florence, 7 March 1935. In her defence Masolini claimed she had been referring to the butcher as 'baldy'. Unfortunately for her, the police reported that the butcher had a very flourishing head of hair.

noticed an envelope, containing photographs, in the handbag of Maretta, who refused to show him what they were. During the night the woman left the room and Bevacqua took advantage of her absence to look in the envelope, finding photos of family members, an effigy of the Madonna, and a picture-postcard of the *duce*. He tore the postcard of the *duce* into little pieces and threw it into the chamber pot, which he hid under the bed. Much later in the night, Maretta, apparently with the intention of drowning a flea, pulled out the chamber pot and found pieces of her picture of the *duce* floating in it. She screamed, and in the ensuing confusion denounced her lover to the police.

Bevacqua turned out to have been enrolled in the PNF since March 1923 and had an excellent record within the party. Rosa Maretta was described as a prostitute and was not a party member. But she was found to have no fewer than seventeen photos of the *duce* in her possession, together with a gold medallion carrying a picture of Mussolini. When questioned, she made her case against Bevacqua even more forcefully by revealing that, two years earlier, her companion had spat at a portrait of the *duce* on the wall of a bar. He did not deny the event, but said that he had tripped while sneezing, with unfortunate consequences for the portrait (the police, with a very straight face, noted that the picture in question was more than two metres above the floor).[27]

No doubt many cases are less colourful than this; nor is it possible to generalize from isolated incidents. But the example does show the difficulty of assessing the significance of numbers. The seemingly good fascist destroyed a picture postcard of the *duce* and was apparently in the habit of spitting at his image, while the prostitute carried with her numerous pictures of Mussolini, together with her family photos and a picture of the Madonna. If anything, it serves to point up the fact that there was often a great difference between what people were doing—their formal behaviour—and what they were thinking. This is a theme which will be developed later.

6.2. DISLOCATION AND PARALYSIS

Leaving subjectivity aside for the moment, the numbers enrolled in the organizations make it clear that, for one reason or another, the fascist movement came to occupy an important position in the lives of most Italians. As Mussolini had instructed in 1929, the party had to be 'everywhere' and came close to being so. For this reason it was important that the party should be respected and give a good account of itself. It is here that we return to the question of how provinces were run under Fascism—to the themes of factionalism, of the relations between *federale*, *podestà*, and prefect, and to the more general problems relating to the fragmentation of command in the provinces.

For the party organization to work well at the local level, some kind of continuity of operation was necessary. Continuity did not mean that changes of personnel

---

[27] ACS, Ibid., Prefecture of Cosenza, 27 April 1935.

could not be effected, even on a fairly frequent basis of rotation; in fact the regime argued that a revolution required constant change in order to avoid 'going rusty'. But it was important that such changes should not represent a radical shift in the orientation of the local movement. The problem presented by factionalism was precisely this. The alternation of competing groups, hostile to each other and determined to weaken the other as far as possible, signified continual changes in the priorities of the local party organization. We have seen that factions rarely represented solely the individual and personal interests of the local leaders; rather, they were formed around wider interest groups within the local community, or represented other forms of division, sometimes pre-dating Fascism itself. The most obvious example of such difference is that between urban and agrarian interests in many of the Emilian provinces, but a rapid investigation of factionalism in almost any province usually throws up a story of contests between currents, lobbies, factions, and clubs that goes well beyond the persons of the warring would-be leaders. In this sense, the much-publicized 'depersonalization' of local politics, pursued after 1926, was unlikely to have had much effect if it had stopped simply at the removal of a single leader. Indeed, removing people from office often created precisely the formation of antagonistic currents we have already witnessed. It should be remembered, in this context, that in his brief period as party secretary between 1925 and 1926 Farinacci removed a significant number of *federali*, while Turati, in the course of his four years as secretary, replaced an even greater number. Even if stability, rather than ideological conformity, was the objective of these changes—particularly those of Turati—an inevitable result was the creation of a mass of the resentful excluded among both leaders and led.

The victory of Montemartini over Barbiellini in Piacenza, therefore, had much wider implications than that of the destiny of the two contestants, as did that of Bastianini over Feliciani in Perugia, or Sansanelli over Padovani and Tecchi in Naples. The list could be almost endless. But the fact that such victories were rarely final, as we have seen, meant that these provinces were left in a situation of permanent turbulence, something which encouraged radical oscillations of position as each side attempted to destroy the other. There was no way in which the workings of the local *fasci* could not be affected by these kinds of tension. Constant change, or threat of change, or expectancy of change produced uncertainty and loss of momentum. The battles fought in Savona between Lessona and Dupanloup had just this effect, as one desperate local fascist explained in 1933:

> The situation is such that, in reality, there is no person or fascist who does not ask himself if it is possible to carry on in this way. And this state of affairs has been going on since '22! And, to give a few statistics, it can be said that in around four years, after the departure of Lessona [in 1929], there have been seven—repeat, seven—*federali*. A few too many![28]

Savona was exceptional, but not so exceptional. Many provinces saw changes at least every two years, some with much higher frequency—Reggio Calabria had

---

[28] ACS, PNF, SPEP, b. 20, Savona, anonymous letter of 1933.

eighteen *federali* in twenty years. The rotations indicated the continuing conviction of the party Directorate that local tensions could be resolved by a change of
personnel. But such a conviction was often based on a real misreading of the local
situations by the Directorate and suggests that the nationalizing and centralizing
ideology of Fascism sometimes served to produce an undervaluation of the centrifugal forces of Italian localisms—almost as if the centre believed that the repeated
enunciation of the idea of unity was sufficient to create the fact. In reality, the
histories of many provincial fascisms make it clear that the effect of continuous
changes of personnel was to increase rather than to decrease factionalism. Resentments increased with every rotation. Moreover, the very fact of change stimulated
hopes among the excluded that the new man could, in turn, be overturned.

The effects of simmering factional disputes in so many provinces were many, but
two in particular should be noted. The first was to hinder the efficient functioning
of the party machine. This was an effect which became more marked as the 1930s
wore on, but it was apparent even in the early 1930s in some areas. To return to
Savona again, the same fascist quoted above went on to say that, as a result of continuous uncertainty, he could see everywhere 'a loss of direction among the fascists'. He also noted the detrimental effect on fascist economic and recreational
organizations and, in particular, on the capacity of the provincial fascist movement
to raise money for its activities. Lack of any stability meant that those local sources
of finance on which the federation depended had dried up, presumably because
people could not be sure who they were giving their money to. As a consequence
the federation—like many federations in the 1930s— was dramatically in debt.[29]

In a later report, of 1936, yet another new *federale* felt obliged to defend himself
at the outset of his period of office by describing in detail the chaos he had found
on his arrival in Savona. The *fasci giovanili di combattimento* 'were a parody from
all points of view'; 'there was no discipline' and punishments had been necessary
for local commanders who, to their partial justification, 'had no funds and no
rooms in which to carry out regular activities'. The neighbourhood groups were
'non-existent' and the federation had L.300,000 of debts.[30] The good intentions of
the new broom do not seem to have been matched by facts, however. In February
1940 a local fascist wrote '[t]he work of the various *federali* who have followed each
other in Savona in recent years has been absolutely negative: the Party has not
made a step forward among the masses… the GIL is disorganized and its administration… has a debt of around half a million [lire]….As far as propaganda is concerned, even less has been done'.[31] The same writer noted that the various Catholic
organizations were flourishing. Much of this disastrous situation was ascribed to
the continuing tensions between the supporters of Lessona and those of Dupanloup, tensions never resolved.[32] By the end of 1941 the *federale* was forced to confess to a situation of 'desertion in the province' from the fascist point of view, with

[29] Ibid.
[30] ACS, Ibid., Savona, *federale* Nino Bertone to Starace, 8 January 1936.
[31] ACS, Ibid., signed letter to unidentified Guido, Savona, 19 February 1940.
[32] ACS, Ibid., *federale* to Muti, 24 September 1940.

the 'GUF lacking leaders and enthusiasm', with the organization of the GIL 'inadequate' ('entrusted to a priest and a nun').[33]

Similar situations are evident in many areas in various periods. In the province of Rieti, near Rome, for instance, in 1931 a confrontation had developed between two groups—one representing the established elite and the other a number of professional people and employees, many of them former *squadristi*. The confrontation had provoked paralysis. The *federale* wrote that '[t]he struggle revolving around personal resentments between two groups... shows no sign of abating and tends to become more bitter... This creates a state of nervousness which is reflected in the solidity of the provincial fascist group. As a consequence of this situation, it has not yet been possible to constitute either the Directorate of the federation or that of the *fascio* of Rieti'.[34] In the same way, in Reggio Emilia, where we have seen the struggle being waged between the historic—but deposed—leader of local Fascism, Fabbrici, and his successor Muzzarini, the condition of the local movement was described in 1929 as experiencing 'for some time a damaging stasis which has led today to a profound crisis of depression and loss of direction'. Assemblies had not been held for years and activity had reduced to zero. Frustration among the former *squadristi* was on the point of provoking open revolt, expressing 'spontaneously, uncontrolledly, the exasperation of the fascists'.[35] The prefect had few doubts that the troubles were caused by Fabbrici, convinced as he was that 'Fabbrici has stopped being interested in politics only in appearances, carrying on instead with his underhand system of agitation and undermining'.[36]

Factional struggles were in no sense limited to the early years of Fascism. Often they would spring up in rather unexpected fashion in the 1930s, with results just as damaging as those of the 1920s. The serious consequences of local squabbles were reported from Padua in early 1931, when a party special commissar wrote a memo to Rome about what he had found in the province he had been sent to reorganize. Classically Padua had been fairly stable, run by a *fascio* closely linked to the agrarian interests and therefore well able to control the territory. But in 1929 Turati removed the *federale*, Alezzini, on the grounds that he had become too dominant, and by so doing upset a delicate equilibrium established in the province between remnants of the *squadristi* and the agrarian-fascist bloc. (Here, as in many places, 'depersonalization' had a very negative effect.) For around three years, confusion reigned (Padua saw six new prefects and five new *federali* between 1929 and 1931)[37] and the results of this were reflected in the commissar's report. He did not mince his words:

> Situation of the Political Federation. Total disorganization, lack of any single directive and of all coordination. Everyone has always done what they wanted: the last three months of factionalism have made things worse. There are no federal services, organized

---

[33] ACS, Ibid., Notes for the secretary of the PNF, Rome, 13 December 1941.
[34] ACS, PNF, SPEP, b. 18, Rieti, extract of the monthly report, October 1931.
[35] ACS, PNF, SPEP, b.18, Reggio Emilia, report on the political situation in Reggio Emilia, undated, but 1929.
[36] ACS, Ibid., prefect Perrone Compagni to Turati, 16 February 1929.
[37] On Padua see Baù, 'Tra prefetti e federali'.

offices do not exist... the personal files of the enrolled in the *fascio* are non-existent... The papers of the Federation have been stolen... the sporting associations are not active... the GUF and the *fasci giovanili* have been criminally involved in the most recent little local battles...

As in many other provinces, local infighting seems to have reduced Padua Fascism to a state of confusion and disarray. The commissar did not despair totally—'the situation is not rosy, but it can be restored'—but warned that he would have to build up a completely new political class.[38] His success in doing this was only limited, it seems. An inspector wrote at the end of 1931 that no one was doing anything because 'until a definite structure has been given to the Federation, any measure adopted is considered provisional: there follows from this a limitation of initiatives, less enthusiasm about objectives and little confidence in actions'. This was all to be attributed, he wrote, to the persistence of 'the old squabbles based on misunderstandings and on the personal ambitions of the local leaders'.[39]

This state of affairs continued into the mid-1930s, with a brief pause during which a minimum of apparent consensus was found around the figure of a young local sculptor, sufficiently uninspiring to raise nobody's hackles. In reality it seems that the reduction in friction probably owed more to a reduction in the activity of the *fascio* than to any miraculous meeting of minds. Inactivity meant that the *fascio* trod on fewer toes and that the important decisions were left to those who had always taken them in the province—the agrarian, ecclesiastical, and commercial interests. In March 1934 the leader of a provincial neighbourhood group in Padua wrote to Adelchi Serena, the vice-secretary of the PNF, to complain that the local party was not doing anything beyond simple and uncontroversial assistance activities. 'Today the activity of the Party can be carried on with relative tranquillity only in the area of welfare', because, he explained, any other kind of initiative was impeded by the local administration, by the banks, and by various other institutions. There was no cooperation on anything because of disagreements between leaders: 'There is no collaboration between administrative and political authorities; in the villages there is frequently disagreement between the *podestà*, the political secretary, the Militia, the ONB, etc and almost always the priest or the local land-owner takes advantage of this to continue his domination undisturbed'.[40]

By 1937 the situation had, if anything, worsened, again because of divisions within the *fascio:* 'In the Federation they work only in order to keep an eye on each other, always in fear that they may lose their comfortable positions'.[41] An inspector for the PNF, writing his report in March 1941, was no more optimistic. The global situation might have altered dramatically with the outbreak of the Second World War, but in Padua little had changed. He wrote of 'a stagnant situation for many long years, despite the succession of many *federali*; few new men have emerged'.[42]

---

[38] ACS, PNF, SPEP, b.11, Padua, Rapporto sulla situazione fascista di Padova, 27 March 1931.
[39] ACS, Ibid., Relazione del mese di dicembre 1931.
[40] ACS, Ibid., letter, unsigned, 11 March 1934.
[41] ACS, Ibid., anonymous letter, 20 March 1937.
[42] ACS, Ibid., PNF Inspector Giorgio Suppiej to Adelchi Serena, 6 April 1941.

The report of a new *federale* in October 1941 was strikingly similar to that of ten years earlier, quoted above. 'The confusion is incredible...; political secretaries practically inactive; in eighteen centres there is an unbearable situation of discord between *podestà* and political secretary;...everyone is divided up into different currents.' The *federale* had little hesitation in attributing blame: 'the most serious problem in the Province is constituted perhaps by about a hundred people—would-be politicians and *éminences grise*—who have been the principal cause of local squabbles and up till now have controlled everything'.[43] Nobody, it seems, had been able in ten years to call these people to order.

The most powerful lever at the disposition of the local party organization was, in theory, that it could act as intermediary between provincial interests and central government. For many different kinds of operation—economic, administrative, legal—the local PNF was necessarily one of the main points of reference. A word of recommendation put in by the *federale* at the relevant Ministry during one of his frequent visits to Rome could make all the difference to any kind of application or request. In the same way, but in the reverse direction, the favourable disposition of the *federale* to a local organization could condition the way in which government directives were in fact applied at the local level. Even in a rigidly hierarchical, top-down dictatorship, mediation, intercession, and implementation still had their parts to play. Indeed, from some points of view, they became more rather than less important in a regime which had destroyed representative bodies.

These functions, which should have constituted the strong suit of provincial fascism, placing the party at the centre of the provincial scene as an indispensable point of reference and passage, were very much weakened by the internal factionalisms of the provincial movements. The fact that factionalism was usually not limited to the restricted circle of the party and MVSN functionaries but extended out from the provincial centre, wedge-like, into provincial society, often produced situations in which segments of local society—those out of favour—were unable to make their voices heard through the vehicle of the provincial directorate and, as a consequence, refused to consider it as the appropriate intermediary. Non-collaboration with the *fascio* and a resulting exclusion from important decisions was often the result. It was, of course, precisely because of this kind of exclusion that people fought so hard to avoid it and to win control of the local federation. Declarations of national unity, proclaimed by the single party at the national level, could not hide the reality of a provincial society still divided by class, by social position, and by interest, with its component parts desirous of a political representation that reflected their own particular interests and not those of others.

Factionalism often reflected personal struggles, but was rarely totally unconnected with tensions latent in provincial society. It was almost inevitable, therefore, that in many provinces the party would have difficulty in functioning in a stable and productive manner. *Federali* always had one eye on their backs, wondering where the next attack was coming from. This uncertainty was frequently exacerbated by the tensions between the different authorities. The conflicts between

---

[43] ACS, Ibid., *federale* Eugeno Rolandi to Aldechi Serena, 23 October 1941.

federale, prefect, and *podestà*, which we noted in Chapter 4, could only contribute further to this instability. People who found that they were not getting a favourable reception from the *federale*, because he was a representative of the opposing faction, would turn to the prefect or the *podestà* in the hope of getting some kind of satisfaction. It could, of course, happen in the other direction, with people who knew that they had made little progress with the prefect over a particular question turning to the *federale* in the hope of his intervention. In either case the effect was to short-circuit the hierarchy of authority in the province, passing over one or other of the principal exponents of local power.

The frictions created by this fragmentation of provincial power were a frequent source of instability and could lead to a virtual paralysis of local activity, as each authority obstructed the actions of the other. Very frequently local politics became a contest of personality between the authorities, with the stronger man coming out on top. Thus, although the 1927 circular had made it clear that the prefect was to be considered the supreme authority in the province, many *federali* simply refused to recognize the fact and continued to insist on their right to the final word on everything. In some provinces they would succeed in dominating the prefect. At that point there would be complaints from both prefect and a part of the population that the *federale* was too powerful and had taken to himself powers not rightfully his. In others the positions would be reversed. In yet others the *podestà* would make an appearance, usually as an ally of either prefect or *federale* and therefore subject to exactly the same kind of criticisms. Often heads would roll as the result of the intervention of Rome—even prefects were removed at times. Almost always the end result would be a decline in local activity among the fascist organizations.

Numerous documents make reference to tensions within the local federations generated by these kinds of problem. The conflict between *federale* Gazzotti and prefect Baratono in Turin in 1938 has been described by Lupo, who notes the way in which the 'proletarian' *federale* attempted to use his undistinguished origins as a weapon against the whist-playing, 'old, Giolittian, antifascist, blunderbuss' of a prefect.[44] The difficulties we have already seen in Reggio Emilia came to a head in 1940, when an inspector had to be sent from Rome to verify the situation. The *federale*, in bed (as usual, it seems) because of rheumatism, complained that the prefect 'had tried several times, in order to humiliate him, to cut him out of the public and administrative direction of the province; that, with a recent circular, he had forbidden the *podestà* to receive orders or make contact with the political secretaries; that, in short, more than help his initiatives and therefore assist his function, he had obstructed it with all his means'. Passing to talk with the *Questore*, the inspector heard a similar story. The police chief 'has confirmed the tension existing between prefect and *federale*, tension which is truly damaging to provincial interests and paralyses all the activity of the Party, making the work of the *federale* inefficacious, so that...it ends up by being not only without results, but produces results which are totally negative'. Interestingly, the inspector found that the prefect had gained the support of the local *squadristi* (seduced by the agrarian faction)

---

[44] Lupo, *Fascismo*, 383–5. The description of prefect Baratono is obviously that of Gazzotti.

against the *federale*, reinforcing his hand enormously, but also, perhaps because of this, provoking the conclusion that 'the prefect is trying to exert excessive pressure on the *federale* and on his activity'.[45]

A further, and almost classic, exposition of the problems created by the lack of clarity in the distribution of authority between provincial institutions is provided by the report of the *federale* of Piacenza, written in January 1938. Clearly on the defensive, the *federale*—the Consul of the MVSN, Bruno Biaggioni—first sang the praises of 'his' provincial fascism, explaining that 'the usual problems—the factious groups, the whispering campaigns, the anonymous letters—have disappeared for some time' from the province, but then went on to admit that there was a small matter unresolved:

> The neglect with which many vital problems of public administration are carried out (or rather, not carried out) suggests a responsibility of this Federation which it does not have. The intolerable inactivity of the administrative organs, both communal and provincial, has been the subject of harsh criticisms levelled at the Federation, which has always found an intransigent resistance in those offices directly responsible. Moreover, this state of affairs causes demoralization which cannot but be reflected unfavourably in the political arena.

In short, provincial fascism was not working—but it was not his fault.

The fault lay, according to Biaggioni, with the *podestà* and the prefect. The *podestà*, a former military figure, 'has given and continues to give proof of the total lack of collaboration with this Federation, of the refusal to respect even the most modest request made of him'. The prefect Montani—a fascist prefect—was, in his view, even worse:

> he refuses to tolerate the fact that this federation carries out and busies itself with administration and indicates points of misunderstanding or—worse—suspicions of corruption; he refuses to tolerate any position on the part of the Federation that gives rise to 'difficulties' that might disturb the peaceful slumber of the administrators...

This alleged interference on the part of the prefect had produced complete standstill in the province: 'The prefect complains that the Federation doesn't do anything, but he doesn't take into account the absolute lack of collaboration—or rather the negative collaboration with the Federation, shown by the obstacles placed by the prefectorial authorities in the path of every initiative of the *federale*...' Typically, there was even a female aspect of the problem, because, according to Biaggioni, 'the wife of the prefect... on more than one occasion has nullified the work of the provincial secretariat of the *fasci femminili* and of the leaders of other organizations where she is active'. He rightly identified the root of the problem in what was evident to everyone, the creation of 'real and proper dualism between party and provincial communal administrations'. The solution, for the *federale*, was obvious—the replacement of the current prefect (rather surprisingly, he asked for a career prefect, not a fascist), for whom—or rather, for whose wife—he reserved, at the end of the report, a final poisoned arrow: 'You could find out

[45] ACS, PNF, SPEP, b. 18, Reggio Emilia, report on inspection, 12 December 1940.

about certain positions of the prefect's wife from *camerata* Barbiellini.' Apart from the direct sexual innuendo, this was tantamount to saying that the prefect was dealing with the twice-expelled enemy.[46]

6.3. LOSS OF REPUTATION

But if the various kinds of factionalism, the *beghismi,* the disputes between prefect, *podestà,* and *federale,* and their respective supporters, reduced many provincial *fasci* to virtual inactivity for long periods of time, there was a second, equally damaging, consequence of these battles which was related to the manner in which the various local struggles were fought. Attacks were usually personal attacks, which sought in some way to put in question the ability or the integrity of the person charged and suggest that such a person was not suited to an important position of office in the province. As such, attacks were not related to major differences about the direction of national politics: you do not find local fascists fighting each other because one is in favour of the Concordat with the Vatican and another thinks that it represents a betrayal of the Risorgimento, or because one is in favour of the Ethiopian war and another sees it as an unjustifiable aggression. Major national political decisions are almost never the subject of public argument. This is hardly surprising; provincial fascists were not there to discuss, they were there to obey, as Mussolini had occasion to remind them on more than one occasion. There was never any doubt that all major decisions were taken in Rome and handed down to the *federali* and the prefects for execution. The meaning of the defeat of liberal democracy and the establishment of a hierarchically organized dictatorship had been just that. The job of the local party organization was to muster support for central government decisions, not to question them. Persons, rather than policies, dominated provincial discussions, therefore.

This much is fairly obvious. But—and this is important—local federations did retain some room for manoeuvre. Thus, if it was not possible to contest openly the political direction of party directorate and central government, it was possible to criticize the way in which the *federale* was implementing—or not implementing—central directives. Factionalism inserted itself in the picture at this point. Denunciations would be made in order to discredit those in power in the eyes of the local population, but also—and perhaps more significantly—in order to catch the attention of central party officials in the hope of intervention from Rome. People played out their battles with this in mind. Accusations had, preferably, to be of a kind that would interest the Rome Directorate and provoke a reaction. They did not necessarily have to be true. Mudslingers knew that the accusations they peddled were often utilized by the central authorities as an excuse to intervene in local conflicts, even at times when the stories were known to be unfounded.

A constituent part of factionalism, therefore, was the production by one faction of lists of accusations, couched in terms of fascist rectitude and of failure to observe

---

[46] ACS, PNF, SPEP, b. 14., Piacenza, Report of Bruno Biaggioni, 8 January 1938. Biaggioni lost his batttle. He was replaced as *federale* in late January 1938.

the standards required by such rectitude. Given the type of material, the truth of the denunciations is often to be doubted (although at times confirmed by party inspectors and other third parties) but that is hardly the important point. What is important is that these were the terms on which provincial politics was played out. Whether true or not, the accusations were the weapons used by all parties in efforts to discredit the rival—prefect against *federale* and vice versa, *podestà* against either of the other two, or both, and so on, in a triangular dance of denunciation. Whatever their origin, they became common currency, and—in one way or another— they served to give the party a bad name.

The simplest accusation levelled at an opponent in office was one of inactivity, of not implementing anything; the *federale* was just not doing his job. More often the accusation would be of activity that suggested individual and autonomous initiative on the part of the accused—something Rome would certainly frown on. This autonomy would often be related to bias in the way the *federale* was carrying out his functions. Allegations would be made, for example, that he was paying too much attention to one group in local society—the agrarian lobby, the shopkeepers, the ex-*squadristi*, the banks, the fascist unions—and not enough to all the others (in particular, obviously, the one making the protest). Unjustified bias was a frequent line of attack which would often see the guilty party accused of 'incomprehension of Fascism'—a serious charge between fascists, which meant, when interpreted, that the accused's idea of the way Fascism should work did not correspond to the idea held by the accuser and—it was hoped—of the national party secretary. This kind of accusation was the nearest people could get to contesting what might be called 'policy'—the direction local Fascism was taking—and could undoubtedly represent a significant difference of opinion. Many *squadristi*, particularly those coming from the movement of the early years, had a very different idea of the way Fascism should work from that of the newly established provincial elite.

'Incomprehension of Fascism' could be related to another common accusation— of lack of fascist 'faith'. The accused, it would be alleged, was not a 'true believer' in what Mussolini had described as the political religion of Fascism. It was one way of suggesting that a person was insufficiently committed to Fascism and lacked total commitment in the cause. 'Faith' was a word much bandied about in the power struggles of the kind described in the last chapter. The writer of a letter of denunciation and his friends were always witnesses to the true faith, their enemies were usually said to be totally unable to understand even the meaning of the term, or else they were accused of having betrayed the concept. 'Faith' became a kind of coded message, encapsulating the possession, or the lack, of all those qualities that, it was assumed, went towards the making of the good fascist. What those qualities were was usually not made explicit, presumably because their identification could have made it easier to contest their presence or absence. Such accusations would frequently be combined with others asserting the analogous and often-related crime of retaining links with the 'old' politics of liberal Italy. An incomplete fascist faith was usually attributed to continuing contamination by the evil 'politics' of the past, as if the persistence of the 'old' constituted a kind of hidden fifth column within the fascist ranks, still to be exposed and exterminated.

Even so, accusations of this kind could not just stop there. Precisely because of the vague nature of the concepts, the lack of faith or the contamination by the 'old' had to be exemplified; the failings had to be justified with reference to some objective correlative. Attacks often began by asserting that, because of an imperfect idea of the meaning of Fascism, local leaders and *podestà* had not known how to select the right people to assist them. These criticisms found their way into official reports. Thus Bofondi, *segretario federale* of Reggio Emilia in 1933, was accused of having surrounded himself with freemasons, profiteers, 'incompetent people',[47] and 'unworthy elements'.[48] Focarile of Taranto had 'surrounded himself with people who, in general, are in poor consideration';[49] Pizzirani of Padua ('a crude person, with little energy') had 'made the mistake of choosing collaborators who are old "believers" but of little worth and low prestige...';[50] Faraone of Reggio Calabria was unable to do anything because 'dragged into the scandalous process involving the Trezzi Company by his own collaborators'.[51] Of the *federale* of Reggio Emilia in 1940 it was said 'he did not choose his collaborators very well, in as far as at least five members of the Federal Directorate were people who had been expelled from the party'.[52] The ex-*squadristi* of Savona complained that the *federale*, Biaggioni, had overlooked them, choosing the wrong people and not even selecting local people: 'the *gerarchi* and the collaborators of Biaggioni are in part "imported." With only a few exceptions, those local people chosen are the usual dimwits'.[53] These were accusations that, superficially, put in doubt the ability of the local fascist leaders to judge people for what they were worth and, more to the point, to judge collaborators' commitment to Fascism. In reality they were often oblique accusations of incompetence or of abuse of power on the part of groups surrounding the *federale* or *podestà* and acting with him.

In fact, it was rare for the accusations to be limited to the simple assertion of poor judgement. Any *beghista* worth his salt would look for something much more damning to say about his opponent. Here a variety of devices would be used. The most common was that of putting in doubt the opponent's fascist credentials—not in terms of 'faith' but in those of seniority within the movement. It was of great benefit to be able to number oneself among the early fascists and, with the passage of years, the number of 'fascists of the first hour' increased enormously.[54] However, the tendency of many ambitious blackshirts to backdate their moment of entry

[47] ACS, PNF, SPEP, b. 18, Reggio Emilia, 'Sulla situazione generale in Reggio Emilia', 29 December 1933.

[48] ACS, Ibid., 2 March 1934.

[49] ACS, PNF, SPEP, b. 23, Taranto, report February 1931.

[50] ACS, PNF, SPEP, b. 11, Padua, report on inspection of Federazione di Padova, 29 and 30 March 1941.

[51] ACS, PNF, SPEP, b. 17, Reggio Calabria, report of informer, 16 May 1934.

[52] ACS, PNF, SPEP, b. 18, Reggio Emila, report on inspection, 12 December 1940.

[53] ACS, PNF, SPEP, b. 20, Savona, 10 February 1940.

[54] As Turati observed in 1929, 'just as happened for Garibaldi's Thousand, who after a few years had trebled...so it is for the first fascists': ACS, SPD, MDRF, 28 January 1929.

into the movement, or to boast about participation in punitive raids that had never taken place or at which they had not been present, left them open to unmasking and denunciation. The problem here was that, from relatively early in the history of the movement, this kind of falsification had been common. By the 1930s, with all the new entrants, the expelled, the suspended, the readmitted, the situation regarding seniority within the movement had become so confused that it was difficult to discover the truth. A large number of people could be suspected of either exaggeration or falsification. There was, after all, no single register of party activists that could be considered credible and definitive. The arguments about who was really present in Piazza San Sepolcro on 23 March 1919 made this obvious. Precisely for this reason, the tendency was to give credit to accusations of falsification, or at any rate, not to consider them immediately to be unjustified. Everyone knew that it was possible to invent—and document—a glorious fascist past, just as everyone knew the potential benefits of doing so.

The problem became particularly acute from the first half of the 1930s when the party card—the *tessera*—represented a pass towards many kinds of employment. The card carried the date of enrolment in the movement and people would try to buy a *tessera* with an early date on it. In illustration of this it is worth quoting a fascist informer who wrote in 1937 that he had assisted at a conversation at the Bologna train station: 'It's true that enrolment is closed, but if you are ready to spend 500 lire and make the journey to Rome, I can get you one [a *tessera*]; I know an office in Rome which does this kind of thing and I can get you the date [of enrolment] you want'.[55] *Federali* who were accused of lying about their past were often on very difficult ground, therefore. It was often their word against that of others and the suspicion of dishonesty combined with shameless ambition would linger.

Further complaints reflected the fact that there were few controls on the *federale's* exercise of power. It was common for *federali* to be accused of unreasonable arrogance in the performance of their duties. Such charges became increasingly common during the course of the 1930s, during Starace's period as secretary of the PNF and when local fascist potentates evidently felt more secure. One offended ex-*squadrista* in Pisa protested against the way his local leader was treating him and his companions, simply because they had asked for some kind of recognition of their status: '...we are arrogantly threatened with exile, suspension [from the party], disciplinary measures; as a consequence we have to keep quiet in order not to lose our humble jobs... [We are] forced to have recourse to the cowardly, but unavoidable, anonymous letter in order not to have to submit to sabotage by the *gerarchi*, loss of our jobs, and other disgraceful measures'.[56]

Police and party informers made no attempt to hide the fact that *federali* were often considered to be arrogant, sometimes to the point of making themselves ridiculous. One informer made a long denunciation of this issue in September 1936, writing that there were two big problems in the provinces, 'adulation and

---

[55] ACS, MI, DGPS, Polizia Politica, b. 109, informer, 24 March 1937.
[56] ACS, PNF, SPEP, b. 14, Pisa, anonymous letter to Muti, 22 November 1940.

exhibitionism'.[57] The first arose from the fact that the citizens looked to the *federali* for personal benefits and favours. Incredibly servile adulation of all forms—in conversations, in public speeches, in newspaper articles—became the order of the day, therefore. This kind of attention caused the various *'gerarchetti'* [minor *gerarchi*], as they are termed in the report, to get inflated opinions of themselves—something that provoked exhibitionism: 'really authentic exhibitionism...can be seen on the days of the official ceremonies, when some *gerarchi* give themselves Napoleonic airs and graces and attract the attention of everyone in the street with their shouts, complaints, commands, and discourteous behaviour even towards anyone who just happens to be going by'.[58] A later report also felt obliged to make reference to Napoleon. From a short note of October 1937, it seems that arrogance even extended to the language of dress:

> People have noted, in both LUCE newsreels and more directly during meetings and ceremonies, the strange mania for exhibitionism shown by certain leaders, particularly in the provinces, who never miss the chance to show off in the most Napoleonic poses possible, exhibiting uniforms of the latest style...in many cases there has been a degeneration to a uniform that no longer has anything commanding or military about it but which would suit much better those dandies with a lisp who frequent Via Veneto.[59]

In the light of these comments, it is not difficult to see the way in which resentments within the provinces could build up, particularly among the 'excluded'—those who believed they had as much claim as the sitting *federale* to command in the name of Fascism.

Sometimes people would attack what was in some respects the reverse side of arrogance. This was not exactly laziness; rather, it was what could be described, with understatement, as a certain nonchalance on the part of the *federale* or the *podestà* in respect of his functions. It sprang from the 'I and only I command here' mentality of many senior fascists, convinced that they need not bother to do their job because they thought that nobody could touch them for not doing it. They were accused of never being in the office at the times in which they were supposed to receive members of the general public, or of deliberately shifting the office hours so that nobody would come (one was alleged to have set office hours from 11 until midnight in order to avoid disturbance). Another frequent accusation was—as we have already seen—that of spending too much time at the table. If Mussolini himself was fairly ascetic, his *federali* were repeatedly denounced (anonymously) for being seen too often in the best restaurants in town; few had any doubts about who was paying the bill. Misuse of official cars also brought criticism: 'the car of the Federation, with its special permit, takes the wives of the *gerarchi* around while the

---

[57] ACS, MI, DGPS, Polizia Politica, b. 109, 16 September 1936.

[58] A sickening servility towards those in power is one of the characteristics of the regime at all levels. It is enough to read the prefaces and dedications to many semi-official publications to appreciate this and also to recognize that the servility was in no sense confined to the lesser ranks of Mussolini's followers.

[59] ACS, MI, DGPS, Polizia Politica, b. 109, Rome, 11 October 1937.

rest of us walk'.[60] The *federale* of Taranto was accused of spending too much time fox hunting (the denouncer enclosed an impressive photo of the accused, suitably dressed for this activity).[61] Some *federali* were permanently on holiday, if their critics are to be believed: 'It turns out that the *segretario federale* concentrates all his activity to the game of *tamburello* and to trips to the beaches of the Adriatic where... under the pretext of visiting the summer camp, he passes long days in attractive female company'.[62]

A variant on these themes—although this time the targets were the president of the province and the prefect—was provided by an anonymous letter, sent from Perugia to the *duce*: 'Here in Perugia... they spend public money in a barefaced and scandalous way; the president of the province, together with the prefect, throws money around in dinners and trips (even to Rome), using a huge Alfa-Romeo, which cost more than L.70,000, and is seen publicly with vulgar floozies; between dinners and hunting trips the prefect is always out...'[63] And some *federali* were said to be always drunk: 'In Savona, the third port of Italy, a drunken barber is in charge, making an obscenity of the Party and disgracing the uniform'.[64]

Campaigns, evidently not disinterested, against sitting fascist authorities would be mounted on these bases, even though much of the behaviour described was relatively innocuous. By such behaviour, however, the *federali* inevitably offered their flanks to criticism by those who had a different idea of what a fascist *federale* should do and how he should behave. The regime spent a lot of time and money propagating the image of the perfect fascist and it was not difficult to use this image against those who actually held local power. In particular it was, once again, the ex-*squadristi* in many provinces who would organize campaigns of protest against the local *federale*, accused of having a very lax attitude towards his duties. As we have already seen, these attacks, no doubt on occasions justified, often served to cover the real source of anger—the fact that new men, who had not 'made the revolution' like the *squadristi*, had been put into position above their heads. As the 1930s progressed, those who considered that they had merited recognition from the party, but had not received adequate recompense—those who thought that they had earned the right to reward ('tangible recognition' is a constantly repeated phrase)—constituted an increasingly serious problem for many local organizations. Finding themselves often pushed to one side by new men with (in their eyes) dubious fascist credentials, the *squadristi* represented a thorn in the side of many *federali*, perpetually claiming the privileges of primogeniture and denouncing the legitimacy of those who had stolen their birthright. What was particularly irritating about them was the fact that they always assumed that, because of their past history, they held the moral high ground and that those who had followed them, sometimes at considerable distance of years, were inevitably inferior.

[60]   ACS, PNF, SPEP, b. 20, Savona, 'A group of decorated *squadristi*', 13 December 1939.
[61]   ACS, PNF, SPEP, b. 23, Taranto, informer, 5 November 1938.
[62]   ACS, PNF, SPEP, b. 14, Piacenza, 13 September 1937.
[63]   ACS, PNF, SPEP, b. 13, Perugia, 27 July 1938.
[64]   ACS, PNF, SPEP, b. 20, Savona, 13 December 1939.

This serves to remind us once again of one of the central themes of this book—that the local struggles were about the control of power at the provincial level, with all that this implied; that Fascism had been from its outset an uneasy alliance between interest and ideology and that many fascists had seen the movement, almost from the start, as a vehicle for social (and economic) promotion. Even the first *squadristi*—those who were strongly motivated by patriotic sentiment—were not slow to recognize that their victories could be used to achieve some favourable position. On one hand this ambition could be justified as the necessary guarantee of the continuation of the fascist revolution; on the other it could be seen as the just reward for personal risk and dedication. This was precisely the position that determined disillusion in the later years, when many found that they had gained nothing and then directed their resentment against those who had found better fortune within the movement.

The fundamental objective underlying most examples of factionalism was, of course, the destruction of the reputation of the opponent and with him, of the group he represented. All the criticisms and accusations mentioned above aimed at the realization of this objective. An attack on the personal integrity and professional ability of the opponent would usually be applied, by extension, to the group that the opponent headed. Thus, for example, the ex-*squadristi* would be denigrated because their leader was said to be a violent ignoramus and a persistent frequenter of local brothels. By association they would all become subject to the same charges. It was this which led to the provincial wars between groups, some of which we have charted in earlier chapters. Sustaining the stratagem of the open confrontation was the hope that, if enough noise were made, if rumours of discontent could be sufficiently widely diffused, some kind of intervention from on high could be provoked, with a consequent change to the advantage of the critics and rumour-mongers.

Inevitably, therefore, the spokesmen for the factions would frequently go beyond charges of incompetence, arrogance, and laxity, and make much more serious accusations, often concerning the private life of the accused. The first of these was 'moral turpitude'—immorality, sometimes referring to corruption but often to sexual misbehaviour. Increasingly present as an accusation during the 1930s, sexual misbehaviour represented an area in which the critics had to tread carefully, however. The first Fascism, particularly early *squadrismo*, had had what can only be described as a fairly robust attitude towards sexual activity—an attitude consonant with its military characteristics. The local brothel had been a frequent port of call for *squadristi* on return from their punitive raids on the socialists—and *machismo* was, of course, one of the characteristic attitudes of Fascism, beginning with the *duce* himself. Denunciations of sexual immorality had to be levelled not at sexual activity per se, therefore, but at particular kinds of deviation. Mistresses, wives of colleagues, call-girls, and under-age partners often made their appearances here, together, more rarely, with rumours of homosexuality.[65] Any kind of behaviour

---

[65] For fascist attitudes to homosexuality see Lorenzo Benedusi, *Il nemico dell'uomo nuovo: l'omosessualità nell'esperimento totalitario fascista*, Milan, Feltrinelli, 2005; also Ebner, *Ordinary violence*, 193–7.

that seemed at odds with the official fascist 'morality', or which was distracting the *gerarchi* from their official functions, was fair game.

A hint of this is already seen in the reference made above to the *federale* of Piacenza, accused of spending all his time on the beach playing quoits in 'attractive female company'. This particular denunciation did not stop there, however. No doubt benefiting to some extent from the sexual fantasies of the writer, it went on to accuse the *federale* of adultery and of using his office for amorous encounters:

> It is extremely well-known in the whole town and province that one of his most strenuous activities consists in visiting the wife of the *Fiduciario* of the local fascist group 'Filippo Corridoni', geom. Ercole Manfredi, without taking into account that the use of the Offices of the federation for romantic encounters is not a mystery for anyone—the public watches the privilege of precedence, and the interminable interviews, given to persons of the female sex known for their easy ways.[66]

Here we have character assassination fascist-style—the *federale* is said to be irresponsible in filling his position, to be a philanderer, and to pursue (immoral) private interest in public places while the public waits. The hoped-for conclusion was that moral rectitude would surely require his replacement.

Federale Biaggioni of Savona—the 'drunken barber' referred to above—came in for even heavier treatment, this time from more than one source. An anonymous letter of March 1940 (signed 'Saluti Fascisti Arriba Espana'), mentioned him in passing (the attack was in fact directed at another *gerarca*): 'the *federale* is without any morals; he runs after under-age girls night and day and his wife creates scenes everywhere'.[67] Another anonymous letter went into greater detail about the affair.

> How should we judge a Federal Secretary who takes advantage of his rank as Commander of the GIL to take girls to hotels—girls entrusted to the Fascist authorities by their families for their education and moral preparation? Who more than him, by similar behaviour, can permanently destroy the serenity of a family, respect for the Fascist cause, and the future of a inexperienced girl...? Only a few days ago he used the car of the Federation to take a girl to a hotel in Voltri where the fact that she was without any identification gave rise to problems. The gallant *federale* began to shout, invoking his rank as a *gerarca*, which seemed so unlikely to the hotel keeper that he called the police station... For the rest of the story it is enough to ask the police.

Why had the girl allowed herself to get into this position? Not for love, according to the correspondent, but because she had been 'seduced...by the prestige of a rank as high as it is unworthily worn'.[68]

This last—exploiting rank—was a further accusation, common to many other such stories. *Gerarchi* were charged with using their position to exact sexual favours from women who in some way depended on them. One *gerarca*, Compiani, again in Savona, was said to have set up an evening business school for girls, in which 'those most favoured pass by his office, during school hours, and those who satisfy

[66] ACS, PNF, SPEP, b. 14, Piacenza, 13 September 1937.
[67] ACS, PNF, SPEP, b. 20, Savona, anonymous letter to 'Mutti', 13 March 1940.
[68] ACS, Ibid., anonymous denunciation, 29 November 1939.

his pleasures find work'.[69] The most straightforward statement of this use of rank came from a man in Padua who explained to Starace in 1935 how best to get a job from the local *federale*: 'You have a son who wants a job? He needs to have a pretty mother or a sister'.[70]

Not just *federali* were subjected to these attacks; *podestà* and aspiring *podestà* could also be targets. In the race for nomination to the post of *podestà* of Perugia in 1934, an informer spoke of 'a bitter fight' worthy of the 'demo-liberal era' and described the 'lively contest in diffusing insinuations, calumnies about the two most likely to get the job. A spectacle... not exactly suitable for the Regime... the men lose their dignity as fascists in a struggle characterized by squalor'.[71] Further South, when invited to look into accusations concerning the habits of the *podestà* of Stignano in 1931, the *Carabinieri* of Reggio Calabria reported that he was widely known to have seduced at least eight young women (who were named) in the course of the previous ten years, some married, others from the same family, buying off husbands and arranging marriages when the women became pregnant. He was apparently so much feared that no one dared to stand up to him.[72]

But if the sexual mores of many *gerarchi* seem to have left them open to attack, no self-respecting denunciation of a fascist official—*federale, podestà*, or even, at times, prefect—was really complete without some reference to the personal dishonesty of that official. The most common accusation of this kind was of using public office to further private financial interest, that officials were not only filling their bellies in continuous long lunches but also filling their pockets at the same time. In 1934 in Savona the 'out' faction began spreading rumours that the federation was on the make: 'People in fascist circles in Savona are saying very unsavoury things about Baldieri [the local leader] and he is accused of making illicit profits, together with other members of the Federation. More precisely Baldieri is accused of having made a considerable sum this year simply from the administration of the fascist summer camps'. This suspicion had even provoked a campaign of wall-writing, centred on the invocation: '*Duce*, tie the hands of the profiteers'.[73]

Usually it was a question of what was known as '*affarismo*'—questionable business deals in which the political position of the *federale* or *podestà* had been put to good use and made to produce returns. Accusations of this kind were particularly potent, it would seem, because so many of the fascist officials used their positions to 'enter' local society, rubbing shoulders finally with the rich and economically powerful and becoming rich and powerful themselves. The reports about high living make obvious the degree to which Fascism was also social escalation for people of relatively modest origins. Power gave opportunities for trade-offs and exchanges in which political influence could be bartered for financial benefit. As Lupo shows in respect of Farinacci—railway employee turned lawyer, with very dubious profes-

---

[69] ACS, Ibid., Notes for the secretary of the PNF, Rome, 13 December 1941.
[70] ACS, PNF, SPEP, b. 11, Padua, letter to Starace, 15 November 1935.
[71] ACS, PNF, SPEP, b. 13, Perugia, 3 April 1934.
[72] ACS, PNF, SPEP, b. 17, Reggio Calabria, Capitano Landolfi to *federale* of Reggio Calabria, 8 March 1932.
[73] ACS, PNF, SPEP, b. 20, Savona, informer, 26 September 1934.

sional credentials—considerable wealth was the reward for political influence. For his personal intervention in a question concerning public works in 1933, Farinacci was promised L.50,000 for his legal advice when the concession was approved and a further L.50,000 a year for the duration of the project. Arpinati was correct to say to the Cremona leader 'I don't think that even you believe that you would have become the great lawyer Farinacci if you were not former Secretary of the Party'— but he was only stating what must have been obvious to everybody.[74] When people could see so readily what was going on in some quarters, it required little imagination to accuse political enemies of such activities, even if untrue.

The exploitation of public position for private profit was one of the accusations that became more frequent as the regime wore on—probably a sign of an increased interweaving of provincial business and political circuits during the 1930s.[75] Opportunities for making money were many, particularly in hard times. In 1940 an anonymous writer from Pomigliano d'Arco (Naples) accused the *segretario federale* of the cynical exploitation of unemployment in the area. According to the informer, the *federale* had been selling jobs to desperate unemployed workers, 'L.500 for a labourer, L.1,500 for a bricklayer, price to be agreed for apprentice mechanics, etc (as well as gifts and other things)'.[76] Similar cases were reported from other areas. Sometimes abuse of position might involve government money to be spent in the province, the allocation of which would flow through the hands of the *federale* or the *podestà*. The system of tenders—the assignment of contracts for government-financed works—gave great influence to the *federali* and could be used to personal or family advantage. The *federale* of Modena, Feltri, was replaced in 1940 after a series of scandals involving mixing marble dust in the flour to make it weigh more (his cousin was the principal mill owner of the province), selling 'red' petrol reserved for agricultural uses illegally to others (he was the manager of the local AGIP agency), and giving contracts for state-financed building work to his brother-in-law.[77] This kind of behaviour may have been common practice. An anonymous letter from Pescara accused the *federale* of building up a considerable fortune by allocation of contracts to a front-man: 'in reality the contracts are his'.[78]

Some local leaders exploited their positions for personal financial advantage to such a degree that protests were made against what was known as the 'accumulation

---

[74] Lupo, *Fascismo*, 302. Farinacci's professional and business deals were the subject of an official enquiry in 1931 during Giuriati's secretariat. The results, going back to 1924 and showing many cases of enormous fees being paid for the Cremona leader's support, were not acted on, officially because of 'lack of evidence' but presumably because of the scandal public revelation would have provoked. See Musiedlak, *Lo stato fascista*, 193–5. The papers of the Segreteria Particolare del Duce contain a copy of letters sent by Farinacci in 1928 in which, for modest interventions in a civil case, he asked first L.30,000 and then L.25,000 more: ACS, SPD, CR (1922–43), b. 40, 18 October 1928. The letters had clearly been filed in order to be used against him, should need arise.

[75] Bottai recounts the case made against Gazzotti of Turin, 'rich in episodes of speculations, of shady business deals, of squalid love affairs'. Quoted in Lupo, *Fascismo*, 384.

[76] ACS, PNF, SPEP, b. 9, Naples, 18 July 1940.

[77] ACS, PNF, SPEP, b. 8, Modena, report from informer, 16 January 1940 and report of inspectors, undated but January 1940.

[78] ACS, PNF, SPEP, b. 14, Pescara, anonymous denunciation, 16 January 1940.

of positions', by which a single person would occupy a whole series of lucrative local jobs—chairman of this and president of that with salaries to match.[79] Popular agitation against this kind of injustice prompted party action in the early 1930s, when a directive was sent out from Rome warning against the continuation of the practice. *Federali* were expected to fall into line and renounce the rich pickings their political power and influence made available to them.

This injunction prohibiting accumulation of positions formed part of the general move of the early 1930s to control the excesses of the local *gerarchi*. Mussolini was well aware that many were getting themselves a bad name and bringing Fascism into disrepute at the same time. His instructions to the local *fasci* to 'reach out to the people' were made in this context, representing the realization that, in a time of crisis, an elitist fascism was failing to make headway against popular opinion because it seemed too often to set itself apart from the rest of the population. In the same way the famous *Consegna* of 1933—a series of instructions concerning the correct comportment of the *gerarchi*—were an effort to restrain the exaggerated behaviour of the local leaders.[80] The true fascist, it was stated, should be modest, honest, ascetic, and of manifest morality.[81] This was 1933; yet the accusations made against the *federale* of Piacenza that we noted earlier in this chapter relate to 1937. They are accusations—womanizing, not doing his job, wasting his time playing games—identical to those made frequently of certain *federali* before the *Consegna* and to many made subsequently. In short, there is little evidence to suggest that the directives of the centre, intended to realize some kind of clean-up in the activities of provincial leaders, found any kind of reception in the provinces.[82] Things went on much as before—as, indeed, was to be expected. Mussolini might say what he liked in Rome but, on their own territory, the *federale* and his close supporters were those who commanded. The fascist authorities, because of the

---

[79] An informer gave an example of what was going on: 'Mr X...can get L.3,500 as secretary of the federation, L.1,500 as Director or President of the local savings bank, L.1,000 as a permanent collaborator of the local newspaper; he can pick up L.1,000 in payment for attending certain meetings and L.1,500 as travelling expenses, and, in some not rare cases, L.2,000 as a parliamentary indemnity. Total L.10,500'. However, the informer went on, if you ask him how much he earns, he will reply 'L.3,500': ACS, MI, DGPS, Polizia Politica, b. 219, 13 December 1933.

[80] Mussolini had evidently become aware of these common criticisms of the provincial *federali* when, in July 1933, he issued the *Consegna* to his followers. This was a series of instructions designed to ensure modest and unassuming behaviour by leading fascists. They were to go on foot when possible and not by car (the car, when used, was to be a popular and not a luxury model); they were to avoid expensive restaurants and not be seen too often at the theatre; they were to dress modestly; they were to respect office hours, and so on. There is no evidence of the *Consegna* having any effect at all, although they did, of course, provide a standard against which many continued to criticize the fascist hierarchy. (See, for example, ACS, MI, DGPS, Polizia Politica, b. 109, Florence, 15 July 1933.)

[81] Camillo Pellizzi considered that the 'reforms of custom' announced by Starace at the end of 1932 'reformed customs (for the better) very little; in many areas they made things worse', bringing to an end the possibility of those structural and social reforms that had been the *raison d'être* of Fascism: *Rivoluzione mancata*, 92.

[82] In his personal diary entry of December 1938, Paolino Ferrari denounced the fact that '[t]here are—despite the forbidding of the accumulation of jobs—men who direct innumerable institutes, who occupy the most diverse positions of command, who control the most disparate activities of numerous large institutes...' He doubted their capacity to do so many jobs 'even if they have the genius of Leonardo': ADN, DG/89.

kind of power they exercised at the local level—personal, discretionary, beholden to no electors—were in a position of dominance that invited constant abuse.

Some *federali* evidently found it impossible to resist the temptations before them. Favours would be accorded to friends and followers following due payment, the concession of privileges to supplicants would receive a reward; the prompt and helpful intervention or the conniving blind eye were equally worthy of recompense. In any case the 'winner takes all' logic of Fascism was not one that made for moral scruples. The desire of the local *ras* to 'command' had clear political meaning—it was one of the messages of dictatorship—but, from early on, command had also suggested an economic dimension. Italo Balbo—a poor ex-student at the beginning of 1921—was a rich man by 1924. For many fascists the victory of the movement had been about achieving the advantages of command and it was in no way surprising that some would turn these advantages to financial gain.[83] Many made no secret of their new fortunes.

Public power was continuously used for private gain. This abuse was indicative of a further and deeper issue. Many fascists simply had great difficulty in distinguishing between the public and the private; doubts relating to conflict of interest did not arise. In their eyes they, as fascists, had taken over the state; in the new fascist state what was public was theirs, therefore. The privatization of authority that had occurred with the fascist takeover, even though modified radically by Mussolini's manoeuvres after the Matteotti crisis, remained the model for many fascists. The violence of the early years, when the fascists did very much as they liked, had left its mark. A position of dominance was to be exploited because it had been won on the field of battle.

This manner of thinking produced two moralities, visible in the local contests for power. One was observed by the winners—essentially, might is right—and seemed to justify a great deal of nefarious activity. The other—invoked by the losers in attempts to unseat their rivals—was based on the image of a 'pure' Fascism and of 'pure' fascists betrayed by those in power. A change of guard could, of course, produce a reversal of roles in this respect as well—the terrain was very mobile. What does emerge from the documents is that people found no lack of material for the denunciations of dishonesty and *affarismo*. Personal enrichment and nepotism remained the principal targets. From Rome came, in late 1937, a request for the abolition of the PNF in order to eradicate 'that kind of nepotism that has been created among the fascist hierarchy, among whom so many have become shamelessly rich'.[84] A group of 'elderly fascists' in Naples—clearly belong-

---

[83] Didier Musiedlak provides ample evidence of fascist enrichment, beginning with Luigi Federzoni, son of a teacher and Mussolini's Minister of the Interior in 1925–6, who was elected president of the Senate in 1929 and coolly raised his yearly salary from L.25,000 to L.125,000 without asking anyone's permission. By 1939 his salary (together with allowances) had risen to L.263,000. When tried after the end of the war, he was reckoned to be worth between L.7 and L.8 million. Other examples of evident enrichment are not hard to find. In 1942 Giuseppe Bottai bought a 42-room villa for L.4 million; in the same year Alessandro Pavolini bought two farms near Florence for L.4 million. During the 1930s, as the popular song testified, the state employee's dream was to have L.1,000 a month. See Musiedlak, *Lo stato fascista*, 173–5 and 204–5.

[84] ACS, MI, DGPS, Polizia Politica, b. 219, 14 December 1937.

ing to the 'outs'—wrote to the new PNF secretary Ettore Muti in late 1939, complaining that the party had repeatedly consigned the city to '*federali* who like luxury too much and who have a well-padded wallet in place of a heart, to councillors who love themselves and try all the time to enrich themselves and their families...'[85] They pleaded with the party secretary to intervene and put people like themselves—honest fascists—in power. This was a very typical stratagem of attack—the accusers claiming more years in the movement and a more rigorous interpretation of the meaning of Fascism.

Rumours were often started about the probity of local party administration. People could see money going in to the federation—often it was their money—but at some times it was difficult to see how it came out, while at others it was all too obvious. An official enquiry into the federation of Parma in 1931 discovered a kind of '*camorra* dedicated to shady business deals and to profit', led by the *segretario federale* Pizzi and the *vicesegretario*.[86] Another answer to the enigma of provincial finances is provided by the inspection of the Pisa Federation in 1941, which revealed that large sums of money were unaccounted for in the registers and had simply disappeared, that the party was extorting contributions from local industrialists with threats, and that 'grants' had been made to individuals with no justification. Party officials were paying themselves unwarranted 'subsidies' (this was a recurrent item in many party balance sheets). Official cars were used without any documentation of their missions and the GUF (which had a separate account) was regularly paying out large amounts to individuals for no documented reason and spending money on trips, on hotels that were unjustifiedly smart, and on meals that were unjustifiedly lavish.[87] In this case, disciplinary action was taken; the malicious voices that had called for the inspection had cause for celebration.

A very similar situation was revealed by a party inspector, Tommaso Bottari, sent to Taranto in mid-1941. He found that local party finances were in total confusion, with large sums of money donated to the federation by local firms and by private individuals being used without any proper accountability. Again, 'subsidies' were being paid to party members and even to people who did not exist, and expenses were being claimed to support the 'expensive high living of the *Federale* Jannelli'. Other points came in for criticism. The *federale* had carried out the obligatory inspections to make sure that price controls were being respected but, to keep the shopkeepers on his side, he had been careful to send someone ahead of him to warn that he was coming. In this way he was seen to be doing his job but not doing it, and the shopkeepers rewarded him accordingly. The inspector did not mince words about the consequences of such behaviour. All party activities were 'in crisis', some 'at a complete standstill', the capillary organizations 'abandoned, as in the past', and the federation reflected the 'lack of attention', 'disorder', and 'abandon' that had characterized the fascism of Taranto 'in previous years'. The total disarray the inspector found was ascribed—significantly—to the fact that 'in the province

[85] ACS, PNF, SPEP, b. 9, Naples, 13 December 1939.
[86] Quoted in Musiedlak, *Lo stato fascista*, 193.
[87] ACS, PNF, SPEP, b. 14, Pisa, administrative inspection, 5 May 1941.

the laws and the dispositions of the centre were given little consideration, particularly by those who should have carried them out'.[88]

6.4. PARTY AND PERSONNEL

Clearly we are here in the sphere of defamation, whispering campaigns, and gossip—which is not to say, of course, that many of the accusations may not have been based on fact. Certainly, few *federali* seem to have heard of Caesar's wife. It was precisely this kind of material that fuelled factionalism in the smaller provincial centres. In many, perhaps most, cases, it was small town stuff. Denouncers often insisted that the scandal they were revealing was known to everyone in the area, suggesting a fairly restricted compass for rumour. But the big cities were not immune. Milan saw its infighting in 1929 with the denunciations surrounding the figure of Mario Giampaoli and the accusations made against him of racketeering, and both Naples (as we have seen) and Palermo were frequently in the throes of personal campaigns waged between rival groupings, often with surprising savagery.

It was evidently not possible to say that your rival or your political enemy was a good, but mistaken, man; he had to be destroyed. And this meant destruction of reputation. This objective explains the extreme bitterness of many local struggles. It explains the fact that, on many occasions, local fascists would come to blows or even exchange gunfire. In the non-pluralistic politics of local Fascism there was a 'winner takes all' element to provincial power struggles which ensured that anything would be used if necessary to guarantee victory—and defamation of the opponent was high on the list. The fact that it was difficult to contest political orientation by reference to different political criteria—a problem in dictatorial regimes—meant that personal questions remained paramount. Thus, in the absence of clearly stated political differences—all contestants would declare themselves loyal fascists—the repeated struggles between local figures were fought almost entirely on the basis of attempts to destroy the reputation of the rival. This meant that the fascist dirty washing was continuously being aired in public. The intimate language of local Fascism was the language of calumny—a fact that could not be without wider consequences.

One immediate and very evident consequence of feuding and rivalries was the sapping of energies and the weakening of activities in the various local fascist formations and affiliates—the youth organizations, the fascist unions, the leisure and after-work structures. We have already seen something of this in the various reports from the provinces of Savona, Padua, Piacenza, and Taranto. Apart from the time wasted in formulating or replying to attacks, local leaders were frequently so insecure as to be unable to do their jobs properly. Constant changes of direction undermined any concerted effort at popular mobilization. Much provincial activity was based on the work of volunteer organizers—people whose dedication required

---

[88] ACS, PNF, SPEP, b. 23, Taranto, Inspector of PNF Bottari, undated, but from mid-1941.

stimulus and direction. Where squabbles produced paralysis, the lead, the inspiration so necessary for many of the provincial activities, was lacking and if, as the prefects suggested, local fascist organizers were in any case often of poor quality, this lack of leadership could not but worsen the situation. Informers' reports describe predictable consequences. As noted already, people ceased their involvement with the party and its activities, sometimes through disgust with the perpetual squabbling, sometimes because the necessary guidelines for activity were not forthcoming. The reports in this sense are frequent. The comment on the fascism of Padua in 1934 highlights all the points listed above: 'The organizations live a meagre life, without enthusiasm; the better people who don't have interests to protect take their distance and Fascism is reduced to pure *esteriorità*'.[89] Again in 1934, an informer wrote from Perugia that '[t]he ranks of the *fasci* of the province of Perugia are dissolving from lack of direction...' The *federale*, it was stated, was doing nothing: 'he neglects the Federation almost continuously, without sorting out anything, causing serious disquiet in all the *fasci di combattimento* of the province'.[90]

Thus, as the 1930s wore on, there seems to have been an increasing sensation in many areas of a party that was stagnating, basing itself on repetitive demonstrations and purely 'external' expressions of its existence—what had been described in Turin as 'excessive convocations and meetings which follow each other with great frequency'.[91] Poor leadership worked together with the Staracean view of the party as an unthinking, disciplined, organism to produce a sense of pointlessness. 'Everything is often reduced to an empty formalism, wordy and irritating, which—particularly in the periphery—is happy with grandiose demonstrations held with the sole aim of satisfying ridiculous personal vanities', wrote one anonymous advisor of the *duce*.[92] For the old hands, the 'essence' of Fascism was missing: 'in these last 7/8 years the party has castrated the fascists, pushing the level downwards', wrote one disgruntled fascist in 1938.[93]

These criticisms of the party were reproduced by several fascist leaders—sometimes at the time, sometimes later in their memoirs. They noted the paradox of the situation in the second half of the 1930s. The party had extended its influence to most aspects of Italian life and yet it was considered to be achieving little. In many respects it was thought to be elephantine and increasingly oppressive, stifling rather than stimulating any positive 'fascistization' of the nation. As early as January 1936 Bottai (predictably) noted in his diary that the PNF 'tends to deform, to suffocate or even to suppress the real workings of organs like the *fascio*, the union, the Corporations...'[94] Galeazzo Ciano referred to the party as 'stultified', observing that, with the policy of 'depersonalizing', the party had never been so dominated by 'personalisms'. Dino Grandi, writing later, called the party 'a kind of huge military

[89] ACS, PNF, SPEP, b. 11, Padua, 11 March 1934.
[90] ACS, PNF, SPEP, b. 25, Perugia, 4 June 1934.
[91] ACS, PNF, SPEP, b. 25, Turin, 6 July 1935.
[92] ACS, MI, DGPS, Polizia Politica, b. 219, June 1940.
[93] ACS, Ibid., anonymous—from 'a modest *gerarca*, long-time fascist' to *duce*, 23 July 1938.
[94] Quoted in Emilio Gentile, *La via italiana al totalitarismo*, Rome, NIS, 1995, 184.

barracks' and condemned the work of Starace in bureaucratizing the party with the phrase '[h]e has been the instrument through which the dictatorship killed Fascism'.[95] Tullio Cianetti—a prominent union leader—was just as cutting, speaking of 'the devastation of the whole patrimony of the Regime' during the secretariat of Starace—'a second lieutenant of a barracks'.[96]

Some of these negative judgements are more than tinged with long-standing anti-Starace sentiment; some of them are simply being wise after the event. Yet it was a fair comment on the condition of the party that the secretaries of the PNF who would follow Starace after November 1939—Muti, Serena—would place great emphasis on the need for a 'streamlining' of the party in order to get it working again after years of expansion that had, paradoxically, produced decline in real capacity to 'fascistize' the population.

This decline, it should be noted, was not always for lack of activity. In fascist terms, it was more the 'quality' of the activity that was in question. We began this chapter by talking about the fascist obsession with numbers and the high level of fascist activities. Much of what was going on seems, however, to have been fairly empty and 'unpolitical' activity that was taken, by the authorities, to be an expression of mass participation in Fascism but was in reality often no more than activity for activity's sake. Socialization and participation did not necessarily mean fascistization. The leisure organization was a case in point. As Victoria De Grazia has argued in her study of the *Dopolavoro*, the ideological content of much of what went on within the buildings of the leisure organization was virtually nil. The absence of ideology was a consequence of the regime's conviction that activity could serve as a substitute for politics—that activity *was* politics, in a way. But, De Grazia writes, 'without politics there could be no real legitimacy;...any thoroughgoing political mobilization risked slipping out of fascist control and was virtually impracticable in any event as a result of the ossification of the party apparatus by the late thirties'.[97]

At the local *Dopolavoro* people danced, played cards, bowled bowls, and drank wine and grappa, very much as they had done in the old socialist *case del popolo* (sometimes, of course, they were the same place, just with the name over the door changed). They enjoyed themselves—too much, according to some. As one disgusted critic put it, recognizing that participation was not the same as politicization, far from being '*fascistizzato*' the *Dopolavoro* was '*alcolizzato*'—the OND had become the ONO, the '*Opera Nazionale delle Osterie*' rather than a serious political institution.[98] The overall consequence of the absence of politics was that the capacity of the OND for indoctrination was atrophied. The 'unpolitical', which had

[95] Quoted in Emilio Gentile, *La via italiana al totalitarismo*, Rome, NIS, 1995, 184.

[96] Tullio Cianetti, *Memorie dal carcere di Verona*, Milan, Rizzoli, 1983, 279.

[97] De Grazia, *Culture of Consent*, 243. The author notes the way in which membership of the OND was always something less than an explicit political statement by the 'joiners'. People would relate to the specific functions and activities of the organization rather than to any broader political inspiration (41–3).

[98] ACS, MI, DGPS, Polizia Politica, b. 219, anonymous—from 'a modest *gerarca*, long-time fascist' to *duce*, 23 July 1938. See also ACS, PNF, SPEP, b. 14, Piacenza, letter from Rome, 2 August 1936: 'The fact that the *fasci* rionali are used only as dance halls attracts a lot of comments'.

been intended to lead to the political, remained obstinately unpolitical; the 'fascist' tug-of-war became nothing more than a banal and normal tug-of-war.

This evolution was to some extent inherent in a regime that did everything it could to discourage the discussion, among ordinary people, of politics and of political alternatives to Fascism. The cult of hierarchy and discipline—'he who says hierarchy, says discipline'[99]—produced passivity among the faithful, fostering conformism and an unimaginative following of orders rather than encouraging more colourful initiatives. The very heavy bureaucratization of the party structure, with its multiple dependent agencies, was characterized by this passivity. It has to be said that, in this respect, Farinacci, certainly not an impartial critic, had correctly read the writing on the wall as early as 1932 when he had written to Mussolini that 'I see our party worn out... destroyed by a bureaucracy inimicable to any initiatives'.[100] A further biting comment on passivity was provided, in 1936, in the pages of *Critica Fascista*, where an irritated fascist described a hypothetical local party meeting: 'Who asks to speak? Nobody. Who puts forward ideas? Nobody. Who criticizes? Nobody. Precisely because there is little that it is permitted to criticize.'[101] Leadership, at the local level, was interpreted as uncritical obedience and this could not but stifle initiative.

To this very undynamic conception of Fascism was added the instability generated by factionalism, by a profound loss of direction among many local fascist leaders, constantly at war with each other. Even where local conflicts had been quietened and some appearance of stability achieved, as was the case in many provinces in the later 1930s, latent tensions discouraged enterprise and Fascism was often more a question of administration than of active and emotive commitment to a cause. Indeed, it may be advanced as a hypothesis that, in those provinces which saw high levels of infighting in the period of consolidation of the regime, any subsequent calm was often achieved as the result of doing only what was strictly necessary to regiment and to organize, and avoiding any important initiatives that risked dividing the local communities once again.

Factionalism, and what underlay it, generated political distance—between leaders, and, perhaps more seriously, between leaders and led—and fundamentally impaired the transmission of fascist ideology between the centre and the periphery. The struggle for personal position assumed greater importance than the communication of ideology. It conditioned the evolution of local fascist movements in the direction of low-level mobilization, excluding divisive themes, encouraging bureaucratization, and generating political immobility. For a party that, according to the 1937 statute, had been assigned the task of 'the political education of Italians', these limitations were more than serious. Because of them the single party became, certainly, the instrument of the 'fascistization' of Italian public life—you could hardly do anything without encountering the party—but, precisely because of its incapacity to express convincing ideological content, in the closing years of

---

[99] The phrase is Mussolini's, quoted in A. Canepa, *L'Organizzazione del PNF*, Palermo, Ciuni, 1939, 111.
[100] ACS, SPD, CR (1922–43), b. 40, 20 January 1932.   [101] Germino, *Fascist Party*, 34–5.

the 1930s the PNF became more an obstacle than an aid to the objective of the 'fascistization' of the Italian masses.

6.5. BEYOND THE PARTY

The party was not the whole story, of course. It was the most visible feature of local fascism and it was a constant point of reference for a large part of the population. But the party was not the state—a fact sufficiently underlined by the institutional settlement between 1925 and 1927. As Mussolini himself said, '[i]f, in Fascism, everything is within the State, even the Party cannot escape this inexorable necessity'.[102] At the provincial level, prefect and police chief were enough to keep this subordination clear in the minds of the *federale*. Yet, to put things in their proper perspective, it is important to remember that the fascist 'State' was not just prefect, police chief, and the *Carabinieri*, but also by the mid-1930s a vast network of institutes and semi-public agencies, largely independent of the PNF and run in parallel with the party. The fascist 'State', pursuing its corporative destiny, not only carried out an impressive reorganization of ministries, but also expanded the public sector enormously, creating a large number of structures that permeated the provinces and provided employment for politically reliable administrators.[103]

These structures were kept, often deliberately, out of the hands of the local leaders of the PNF. The party would have a representative on the board of administration, but this was very different from having a controlling voice. The new bodies were directed by people who were formally fascists, of course, just as the fascist presence within many ministries in Rome was notable, but, in the same way as the Rome ministries attempted almost always to protect their autonomy of action from other ministries and in relation to the party, so the new provincial structures would look to maintain at least a relative independence from the local party. There was no point in being the director of a local technical agency if you had to take your orders from a (probably technically incompetent) *federale*.

To some degree this development reflected a simple division of competencies. The party's role was fundamental to the regime, but that role—as defined by Mussolini—clearly could not cover everything. In part it also reflected the fact that, from early on, the fascist movement had appealed to those who saw the opportunities provided by decisive, authoritarian government for 'technical' solutions to social and economic problems.[104] The possibility for government action on specific questions, neither bridled by the divisive intervention of representative bodies nor

---

[102] Quoted in Aquarone, *L'Organizzazione*, 164.

[103] For a brief analysis of administrative reorganization, see Cassese, *Lo Stato fascista*.

[104] To some extent such people looked to the precedent provided by the foundation of the *Istituto Nazionale Assicurazione* (INA) in 1912. Its director, Francesco Saverio Nitti, was a strong supporter of the idea of government intervention in social affairs through special agencies, supposedly more efficient than the traditional ministerial sections. On the relationship between Nitti and Alberto Beneduce, the foremost financial figure of the regime, see Paolo Frascani, 'Nitti, Beneduce e il problema della regolazione del capitalismo italiano', (2009) 31(123) *Società e storia* 97.

conditioned by local client networks, seemed to open the path for 'experts' to act as they thought best. That embarrassing and ever-recurring gap between decisions and their implementation could thus be eliminated.[105]

A corporativism built on the idea of 'competence' rather than political influence had been one of the planks of early Fascism, and it remained a strong impulse throughout the regime. Mussolini himself seems to have been sympathetic to this way of thinking. His preference for 'technical' solutions to many problems was often very evident, no doubt because it seemed that good technicians knew the answers, did not argue, and got on with the job. This was, of course, any dictator's dream; in Mussolini's case it probably also reflected the fact that with technicians he felt he had a direct relationship and much more room for manoeuvre than he had when the PNF had to be consulted.

The *ente* or public sector agency, separate from the party and with precise responsibilities in a clearly defined area, became one of the characteristic forms of fascist government, therefore. The best known are those related to the reorganization of the financial sector after the 1929 crisis (the state holding institutes of IMI (1931) and IRI (1933)), which imposed relations of close collaboration between business, the world of credit and finance, and government, but in which technical and financial rather than political considerations tended to be paramount. A further, and fundamental, feature of the expansion of government agencies was the creation (up to 1943) of more than 350 *enti pubblici* (public sector agencies) with a myriad of separate responsibilities, many of them expressed at provincial level. These were essentially auxiliary government agencies, taking over specific roles previously assigned to ministries, and, perhaps more than IRI and IMI therefore, responsive to the political objectives of Fascism. The organization and regulation of activity through the various consortia (land reclamation, afforestation, agricultural production) and the proliferation in the 1930s of the corporative 'sector agencies' (agencies dedicated exclusively to overseeing the production of silk, of rice, of sugar beet, and so on) represented a real penetration of government into the field of economic activity.[106]

This labyrinth of new, semi-autonomous, public sector agencies constituted what became known as the *parastato*, present in every provincial centre and asserting its presence with its modernistic fascist buildings, designed to express both power and permanence. Between them, state bureaucracy and the *parastato* exercised an enormous influence on economic activity, controlling flows of credit, decisions regarding industrial concentrations, distribution of government funds for transport, public works, building and urban growth, and so on. In particular, the *Istituto Nazionale Fascista per la Previdenza Sociale* (INFPS), responsible for collecting workers' insurance contributions and distributing pensions, family allowances, unemployment pay, and other subsidies, had a very important role at

---

[105] On the enthusiasm of many who saw in Fascism the opportunity to pursue 'technical' and not 'political' objectives, see Pellizzi, *Rivoluzione mancata*.

[106] Melis, *Storia dell'amministrazione*, 357–68; on these developments, see also Mariuccia Salvati, 'The Long History of Corporativism in Italy: A Question of Culture or Economics?', (2006) 15(2) *Contemporary European History* 227.

provincial level in so far as it represented the organ of government social welfare schemes and was thus an institute that, at one time or another, involved a large part of the population in its activities.[107]

At provincial level, the new administrative structure was often very jealous of its independence from the local party and would resist, when possible, the unrequested intrusions of the *federale*. Collaboration, where possible, was the official policy, rather than subordination to the dictates of the party. Following the general pathology of the fascist regime, the new public sector agencies constructed their own client systems—extremely powerful weapons for generating acquiescence with the regime. By 1943, more than 600,000 people were employed within this structure—the army of 'public servants' and so-called *parastatali* who constituted one of the major social changes of the period.[108] In many areas, the young and upwardly mobile would find a place within this system rather than within the party bureaucracy, often (as already suggested) enjoying better pay and conditions of work than those offered in the various offices of the party itself.[109]

Unsurprisingly, one of the main objectives of many *federali* during the 1930s was precisely to try to get some kind of a foothold in this parallel network of power, which represented a competitor for control within the province. Local party leaders would attempt to secure appointment *ex officio* to non-party administrative boards and would try to ensure the employment of their own people within the various *enti*. But equally, directors of the *enti*, concerned about levels of efficiency on which they would be judged, might well prefer technical competence to political allegiance in their employees and resist such pressures.[110] 'Good relations' between political and administrative structures were always formally encouraged but not always forthcoming. The really important provincial leaders—Balbo in Ferrara, the Ciano family in Livorno, Farinacci in Cremona—managed to control both party and parallel networks within their provinces. Others, particularly those without connections in Rome that went beyond the party, were markedly less successful.

A further limit to the influence of the party was that represented by the links established in the course of the *ventennio* between banks, insurance companies, capitalist farmers, small and big business, and the institutes and ministries responsible for regulating their activities. Banking, insurance, and big business in no way coincided with the fascist state, of course; the 'industrial triangle' of Milan, Turin, and Genoa remained separate from Rome not only geographically but also culturally. Strong, centralized government could have its attractions for industrialists and landowners but it could also pose a threat. In general, as Paolo D'Attorre has argued, the complementary nature of interests prevailed. The answer to the

---

[107] Chiara Giorgi, *La previdenza del regime. Storia dell'Inps durante il fascismo*, Bologna, Il Mulino, 2004.

[108] Melis, *Storia dell'amministrazione*, 329. The figure excludes those in the armed forces, who went from 132,000 in 1923 to 634,000 in 1943.

[109] Ponziani (Introduction to *Prefetti*) confirms this for the South; see also Gagliardi, 'I ministeri economici', 160, Giorgi, *Previdenza*, 205–6, and Salvati, *Impiegati*, 203.

[110] Giorgi, *Previdenza*, 205–10.

potential problem posed by a fascist *dirigisme* was a substantial merging of many economic and managerial interests with fascist administrative and organization structures—sometimes almost a fusion, sometimes a kind of working agreement, mutually beneficial to both sides.[111] Although the *enti* were government-financed, they were also in many cases open to contributions from private sources, which would then be represented on the board of administration. This opened the door to collaboration between the public and the private sectors, even (in some cases) to the conditioning of the first by the second.

In this sense, perhaps, can be understood the manner in which the more prominent captains of Italian industry gradually, one after another, took the party card, usually indicating readiness to collaborate with the regime and to use it, more than any passionate devotion to the cause. Guido Donegani (Montecatini chemicals) joined relatively early, in December 1925, while Giorgio Falck (iron and steel) kept his distance until March 1928. Three of the most important—Giovanni Agnelli of Fiat and the Pirelli brothers (rubber)—joined as late as 1932, finally acknowledging that collaboration with Rome, to some degree on Rome's terms given the financial crisis, was essential for their interests.[112] Even so, the relative autonomy of many major financial and industrial groups remained evident. In some areas in which the presence of economic interests and lobbies was particularly strong—for instance in the developing petro-chemical complex of Ravenna—the party could be reduced to a very secondary role as powerful local interests dealt directly with Rome.[113]

It was in this way that the *ventennio* saw the formation of important new circuits of power in which public and private interests were often intertwined, the state providing financial and administrative structures that influential groups were able both to condition and to exploit. Thus, in the provinces, politics, business, and finance often came together in the shadow of the regime, encouraged by the new administrative structures of the fascist *parastato* to form new aggregations, many of which would be of great importance in the economic developments following the Second World War.[114] To some extent this intertwining of structures served to give a greater flexibility to the regime, in as far as monolithic, state direction of the Soviet kind was avoided, even though the new structures did undoubtedly represent the penetration of a centralizing bureaucratic network into the provinces. At the same time, however, the mixture of public and private interests within many of

---

[111] P.P. D'Attorre, 'Aspetti economici e territoriali del rapporto centro/periferia', (1991) 184 *Italia contemporanea* 405–17.

[112] Musiedlak, *Lo stato fascista*, 179. It should be noted that Beneduce, the director of IRI, joined the PNF only in 1940 and only then at the direct request of Mussolini.

[113] One example of fruitful collaboration between politics and business, and between periphery and centre, is provided by Siena, where the dominant local figure, Alfredo Bruchi, managed to use his friends in Rome in order to keep the local fascist hotheads at bay, and also succeeded, by playing on his close contacts with financial institutions in Rome, in turning the Monte dei Paschi di Siena from a regional into a national bank during the course of the 1930s. See Pasquinucci, 'Classe dirigente', 441–68.

[114] Guido Melis, 'Società senza Stato? Per uno studio delle amministrazioni periferiche tra età liberale e periodo fascista', (1988) 4 *Meridiana* 91.

the agencies did provide a means by which provincial interests could obstruct and oppose decisions made at the centre.[115]

The growth of this kind of network during the 1930s represents one of the more significant developments of the fascist period. In many respects—the best example is probably the growth of INFPS—it represented a real centralization of administrative control because the various agencies functioned on a national rather than a local basis. It is equally significant, however, that the developments took place through channels that either completely side-stepped the party or involved it only marginally. Even where many agencies could boast a high-level fascist as their president, the public sector looked towards government ministries rather than towards the PNF for guidance. Italy, under fascist direction, was moving forward in a process of modernization (although the exact nature and level of that modernization is still contested), but it was achieving this through institutions and mechanisms to which the PNF was hardly central. Certainly there were exchanges between the political and economic worlds and there was a great deal of mediation between the two. People moved between good jobs in business and influential positions in the party structure, and vice versa. A common interchange was for influential businessmen to be elected to the Senate, while important senators would be recruited for boards of administration in important companies. Yet these were essentially the exchanges of personnel in a restricted oligarchy (often exploiting rich pickings), and did not constitute in any way a fusion of party and state.

In fact, in all this, the party as such was a marginal player. Its role bore little relation to what the intransigent Farinacci had thought the party should be doing. Even the more moderate desire of Turati to place 'a blackshirt in every position of command' had been amply thwarted. The alliance between government, administration, and the world of finance and business, and the huge expansion of the public sector, had produced a fascist 'state' which was not directly controlled by the PNF but ran in parallel to it. Nominally everything was 'fascist' but often the leaders of the local fascist federation had little say in what went on in agencies not directly affiliated to the party. 'Who controls?' was a very legitimate question for these party bosses, but the answer they got was rarely to their satisfaction. Fascist criteria certainly operated (usually, if not always) in the workings of this new circuit of power, but they were not by any means the only criteria. Extremely telling in this respect is the fact that it was only in 1933 that public competitions for employment in many areas of the public sector required that the applicants be members of the PNF.[116] Even as late as 1940 public administrations were still unsure about whether long-standing employees, who had entered service before 1933, had to be enrolled in the party if they wanted to be considered for promotion.[117] The regime was surprisingly slow in creating its 'new class' through the party, apparently preferring to trust more traditional methods of selection. Melis writes that 'within the ministries . . . the fact emerges of the jealous control of careers

---

[115] Salvati, 'Corporativism', 232.
[116] See Melis, *Storia dell'amministrazione*, 337–8, also in Melis (ed.), *Lo stato*, 100–101.
[117] Aquarone, *L'Organizzazione*, 258.

(and of access to them) by the top bureaucrats, on the whole still those of the pre-fascist period'.[118] It is instructive that in 1937 in the Ministry of the Corporations—the fascist ministry *par excellence*—all of the thirty directors general or division heads had entered the service before 1916.[119] Party or no party, it seems, the state—even the fascist state—had its own rules and its own imperatives and a badly functioning party was no doubt a further incentive to respect those rules and imperatives.

[118] Melis, in Melis (ed.), *Lo stato*, 102.   [119] Gagliardi, 'I ministeri economici', 160.

PART 2

THE PARTY AND THE PEOPLE
IN THE 1930s

7

Growing Disjunctions: PNF Rule and Popular Reaction

So far we have concentrated primarily on those factors that impeded the efficient functioning of the PNF at provincial level—the factionalism among local fascists, the contests between local party secretary and prefect reflecting the clumsy dualism of parallel administrations, the poor quality of the local leaders. Now, in the second part of this book, it is time to shift our attention from the workings of the party itself to the reactions of the population to what the party was doing. Fascist objectives required that there be an identity of outlook between leaders and led—that all should identify with and find purpose in the strengthening of the nation and the state. It was essential, therefore, that the party should educate the population in order to realize this identification and that the people should react positively to this education. Regimentation could not be avoided—indeed it was part of the process—but something more was required. The regime looked for commitment, for conviction, for enthusiasm even. The reaction of the population to the functioning of the party was an essential element in the equation of fascist rule, therefore. Without the fascistization of the masses, the regime could not realize its ultimate objectives.

The problem of people's reaction to Fascism is complex. Even the definition of 'people' in this context is far from easy. Different social groups would often have different perceptions of the operations of local Fascism, as would people of different ages. Inevitably, reactions might be mixed, with some aspects of the regime finding favour, others not. In the same city the more conservative middle-aged and elderly might welcome fascist 'order' but also deprecate the presumption and the corruption of the regime. While there is ample evidence that many young people resented the discipline of the obligatory youth groups, adolescents might still see a liberating energy and vitality in the other possibilities offered by the party. Shopkeepers would look at the blackshirts and see protection from socialism and the socialist cooperatives, but they might have a different attitude towards fascist attempts to impose price controls. Workers might enjoy the *Dopolavoro* but would (on the whole) be more aware of repression, of wage reductions and new rhythms of work, and of the lack of any effective representation in their relations with the bosses. Moreover, all these perceptions could vary over time. In the course of the *ventennio* there were ups and downs in the relationship between party and population in most provinces. The party changed; people changed. As important in any assessment of the relationship between the party and the people, different regions lived different experiences. Whereas Tuscan Fascism, particularly that of Florence, was relatively stable after the purges following the 1925 *fatti di Firenze* and the ascent to power of Alessandro Pavolini, many of the Po Valley provinces oscillated fairly consistently between superficial order and more or less complete chaos. The southern provinces of Taranto and Reggio Calabria also seem to have had their own particular pattern of evolution, characterized by a slow slide into inactivity as the years passed.[1]

7.1. SOURCES, SPIES, AND SURVEILLANCE

This varied nature of Italians' experience of Fascism makes generalization very difficult. The problem is compounded by the nature of the sources. Individual accounts of 'what people thought about Fascism' do exist—in diaries, in private letters, and in contemporary memoirs—and can throw some light on the issue, although—particularly in the case of memoirs—the material has to be used with some caution. Personal diaries can be a useful guide, even if, unlike the diaries of Soviet revolutionaries, they rarely contain the kind of heavy historical baring of the soul characteristic of the Russian tradition of personal diary writing.[2] Furthermore, the diaries and private letters of non-central figures always pose the problem of representativeness. Whether fascist, anti-fascist, or a-fascist, the exact place of the writers is difficult to assess. Are these figures isolated cases or are they representative of general trends of thought and widespread popular attitudes? It is usually impossible to find out.[3]

Much of the same caution has to be expressed in relation to some of the documents used in this volume. Anonymous letters sent to the PNF secretary general or even directly to Mussolini need to be used carefully. They are usually part of the political battle and constitute an attempt to condition the choices of central government in its intervention in provincial politics (for this reason it is legitimate to see them as a sign of the increased influence of the centre under Fascism). There is obviously the possibility that such letters may be pure invention, bearing almost no relationship to the reality of a local situation—the reader has to be careful and verify from other sources. At the same time, precisely because the letters are anonymous, they may also provide insights an identifiable writer would be frightened to speak about, given the context of fascist violence and repression. In the main, such letters are most useful when they are not denouncing specific people but describing

---

[1] For Calabria see Ferdinando Cordova, *Il fascismo nel Mezzogiorno: le Calabrie*, Soveria Mannelli, Rubbettino, 2003.

[2] For these, see Jochen Hellbeck, *Revolution on my mind. Writing a diary under Stalin*, Cambridge (Mass.), Harvard University Press, 2006.

[3] The National Archive of Diaries at Pieve Santo Stefano (near Arezzo) has an excellent collection of diaries from the fascist period, a few of which are quoted in this volume. Many are very revealing of the reasons for which people accepted, rejected, or remained indifferent to Fascism. The problem of representativeness remains, however. What some of the diaries certainly do manage is to put a personal perspective on events and suggest personal priorities. One short entry for 5 November 1918 says it all: 'The war ended today. The cat is pregnant again'.

in more general terms the condition and mood of local Fascism. Here they may reveal a great deal. Many of the letters sent directly to Mussolini fall into this category, deploring the overall direction of events and attitudes rather than accusing individuals. They refer to general social and political problems which bedevil the politics of the locality and assess, usually in very negative terms, the contribution of the local fascist movement to their solution. In these letters there is always, almost inevitably, the justification of anonymity because of fear of reprisals—a good indication of where the writers stand within local politics.[4]

Generally more useful are the reports by police, PNF, and MVSN informers—the *fiduciari*.[5] But these also present problems. Informers may say what they think their bosses want to hear; they may exaggerate or even invent problems in order to make their services seem indispensable; they may have personal axes to grind which distort their observations. All these possibilities are present and sometimes one or more is very evident in a particular report. It is essential to remember that many of the informers were recruited among men and women who had been, or even still were, active in the fascist movement. Their reports could represent, therefore, attempts to condition the reaction of central government in respect of a particular target. Personal considerations might well come into play at times, therefore. *Federali* would sometimes protest to the Rome authorities that the unknown informers reporting on them and their activities were simply carrying out personal vendettas and were not to be credited. This makes evident the fact that many informers report from 'within' Fascism and are in no sense detached and external observers of the movement—something that becomes evident in the final years of the 1930s, when certain of the informers become so exasperated with the paralysis of provincial Fascism that—as we shall see—they turn themselves into advisers and counsellors of central government, invoking often drastic remedial action that their spying has suggested to them.

As with the anonymous letters, the informers are more credible when describing public mood than when attacking an individual—usually by recounting hearsay. Some of the informers manage to get very close to their sources of information. They report from bars, markets, bus and tram queues, crowded trains. At times they even give the names of people who are clearly part of their own group of close social acquaintances—people unaware of the activities of their friend or colleague. Yet, as Mauro Canali has rightly insisted in his massive work on the *Spies of the Regime*,[6] for an evaluation of the value of informers' reports, it is essential to get away from the idea that the Italian secret services under Fascism were amateurish and inefficient, made up exclusively of middle-aged men in Borsalino hats, listening to unguarded conversations as they hid behind the sports pages at the corner table of the local bar. This idea, in reality, is part of the myth of 'kind-hearted, non-serious Fascism' generated after the Second World War in the more general process

---

[4] See the considerations of Mimmo Franzinelli, *Delatori. Spie e confidenti anonimi: l'arma segreta del regime fascista*, Milan, Mondadori, 2001, Introduction.
[5] On the methodological problems associated with the use of these sources, see Colarizi, *L'Opinione*, 14–29.
[6] Canali, *Le spie del regime*.

of Italian self-absolution for Fascism.[7] Certainly this aspect existed. Many of the reports retained in the party and police archives and in the papers of the Secretariat of the *duce* do come from exactly the kind of source described above. But the informers (and, in turn, their own networks of sub-informers) were far from casual operatives, enthusiastic amateurs playing at surveillance. They were part of a large and, it seems, very efficient information gathering service that, because of its web of intersecting reports, left little space for amateurs, or for invention or falsehood. Over the course of the years, many informers were in fact dropped because of unreliability; a few were even imprisoned for false reporting. The fascist secret police—the *PolPol* and the OVRA—may not have the chilling reputation of the Gestapo, but it would be a mistake to underrate their efficiency because of that. Many of the operations charted by Canali (and by Mimmo Franzinelli[8]) demonstrate a pitiless cynicism—and, occasionally, brutality—towards opponents of the regime that can certainly stand comparison with the Gestapo or the Kripo.

Like other dictatorial regimes, the fascist regime was extremely attentive to public mood. But it faced the problem inherent in all regimes founded on coercion. Dictatorships impose order but, at the same time and by virtue of that imposition, they sever many of the channels that permit communication between government and governed. Free elections and a free press no longer exist; the public sphere is deformed, and civil society ceases to express itself spontaneously. In such regimes, therefore, genuine popular opinion becomes extremely difficult to assess. Paradoxically, given the extent of coercive control, this difficulty generates great uncertainty on the part of the authorities; the dictator knows he cannot really trust the cheering crowd. For this reason dictatorships are noted for their obsession with discovering what people are really thinking. Fascist Italy was no exception to this. The importance of the task required that the spies knew their job, therefore. Moreover, they knew that they were themselves subject to close scrutiny by attentive central agencies and bureaucracies.

The spies themselves came from all walks of life and from all social classes. Both men and women were used. Journalists and lawyers were prominent among the professions in which spies were recruited, but there were also union officials, soldiers, academics, writers, shopkeepers—and priests.[9] At the national level (*PolPol* and OVRA) some spies would be recruited because of known loyalty to the regime

---

[7] Filippo Focardi, 'La memoria della guerra e il mito del "bravo italiano". Origine e affermazione di un autoritratto collettivo', (2000) 220–21 *Italia contemporanea* September–December 393; also Ibid., 'L'ombra del passato. I tedeschi e il nazismo nel giudizio italiano dal 1945 a oggi', (2000) 3 *Novecento* 67.

[8] Mimmo Franzinelli, *I tentacoli dell'OVRA: agenti, collaboratori e vittimi cella polizia politica fascista*, Turin, Bollati Boringhieri, 1999; also Michael Ebner, 'The political police and denunciation during Fascism: a review of recent historical literature', (2006) 11 (2) *Journal of Modern Italian Studies* 209.

[9] Canali lists the names of some 650 informers, many of whom would have large networks of sub-informers. Not all were active for the whole period of the regime; some seem to have sent in reports only for a few years. See Canali, *Le spie*, Appendix. The number may be compared, with due adjustment for the size of populations, with the 3,000 full-time informers of the SD in Nazi Germany (in 1939) and their 50,000 part-time agents. See Jeremy Noakes and Geoffrey Pridham, *Nazism 1919–1945*, vol. 2, *State, Economy and Society*, Exeter, Exeter University Press, 1984, 569.

and because their personal position gave them access to social and political groups of interest to the police. Others would be enrolled through a whole series of stratagems—blackmail relating to family questions (infidelities could be exploited profitably), because the prospective spies had severe economic difficulties, or because they were threatened with long prison sentences—but always because of their access to specific sources of information. A further source of recruits was constituted by the opponents of the regime. Communists, socialists, and anarchists were often 'turned' after capture and sent back to report on their friends. The information these spies provided was central to the defeat of the anti-fascist organizations both within Italy and abroad. More locally, the police department could utilize its position of strength to effect on people who, for one reason or another, depended on the goodwill of the police. Hotel keepers, people who rented out rooms, owners of bars and small *trattorie*, street traders (in fact almost anyone who required a licence for their activity)—all might be encouraged to cooperate with the authorities and to repay the consenting or the blind eye of the police to some irregularity with a little information.

However, the majority of the 'professional' informers were sympathetic to Fascism and were recruited because their political orientation served as some guarantee of the credibility of their reports. Many were recruited from within the PNF itself, which permitted Bocchini (and Mussolini) to know what was going on inside the party, and many came also from areas of dissident Fascism.[10] Often these last were, at least into the early 1930s, representatives of the early period of Fascism—'movement' rather than 'regime' fascists—who had been expelled or otherwise side-lined from the local party, but were still sufficiently on terms with the in-group to be able to report on what was happening in their locality. With the passage of time, these figures become less prominent, and their places are taken by more middle-of-the-road fascists. Some informers—for example informer number 40 (Virginio Troiani)—managed, because of their ability to construct networks of sub-informers and deliver reliable information, to work undiscovered for the whole period of the regime.

Although most of the information used in this study comes from fascist sources, it is important to stress that these are different sources, representing different viewpoints. This difference permits the historian some possibility of control. Are the sources saying roughly the same things? Comparison of viewpoints is possible. The reports of police informers can be tested against those coming from other directions. The local police chief, the prefect, the *federale* would all

---

[10] Surveillance involved not only the population at large. Spying and the compilation of dossiers on rivals was an integral part of the fascist system of personal relations. As Farinacci wrote in 1932, '[t]here is not a Minister, nor a *gerarca*, nor any prominent fascist, who is not the object of surveillance and control in his every word and action...Every *gerarca* creates his own nucleus of informers against his own personal enemies', thus contructing a world of suspicion 'which destroys the energies of the party': ACS, SPD, CR (1922–43), b. 40, 20 January 1932. Emblematic is the exchange between Turati and Farinacci in mid-1926, when Turati, only recently installed as party secretary, asked Farinacci for a copy of a letter sent by a Signora Cuppini to Balbo (Farinacci's enemy). Farinacci, playing the honest citizen, refused to cooperate (and kept the evidently compromising letter for himself): ACS, Ibid., 20 August 1926.

make frequent reports to the relevant Ministries and to the PNF headquarters in Rome and these can be cross-checked with each other and with those coming from the undercover agents. Even here, however, there are obvious problems of credibility. The local figures of authority would inevitably tend to defend their activity against expected criticism. Thus the police chief would be inclined to insist on successes rather than on continuing problems, the prefect on the perfect public order in his province, and the *federale* on the more positive aspects of provincial Fascism. Yet these reports, even when they do clearly demonstrate this tendency, remain valuable, often because any difficulties encountered will be blamed on one of the others responsible for provincial administration. Thus the prefect will recount the deficiencies of the *federale*, and vice versa, as an explanation of any less-than-perfect administration or the persistence of particular problems, and the police chief will indicate the poor functioning of the local party machine or the misdeeds of the local militiamen if this helps him to explain public order problems for which he is responsible. Checked against the spies' reports, these documents help to build up a fairly reliable picture of certain popular attitudes at certain moments. The historian is still on shaky ground, but some firm stepping stones do begin to appear.

Going beyond the question of the reliability of the sources, it is also necessary to recognize that what ordinary people thought about Fascism was not necessarily or exclusively a consequence of their direct experience of the local party organization. People experienced Fascism in many different ways. Economic hardship or well-being might play a large part in determining relations with the regime. As already suggested, for many workers the fascist union would be the main source of contact with the regime, backed up by possible visits to the *Dopolavoro*. For others, the regime might seem most present in the various agencies responsible for health care; young women's experience of the antenatal clinics of the ONMI is an obvious example. For most young people, the youth, educational, and sporting organizations would be the principal point of contact with the regime, but there would be a radical difference between the experiences of those who left school at thirteen or fourteen (the vast majority) and those who carried on to higher levels. Some people might be influenced mainly by propaganda, by what they read in the newspapers, heard on the radio, and saw at the cinema, or by more sophisticated cultural factors, others by apparent foreign policy successes and by a new respect they thought ascribed to Italy on the world stage. And always, looming over everything else, there was the figure of the *duce*, provoking, as we shall see, often very contradictory attitudes among the people towards Fascism. Most Italians would experience Fascism through a combination of several of the above factors.

What they might say and think about the Fascism they experienced was, of course, much conditioned by the fact that they were in some way dependent on the regime or feared the reaction of the regime to their comments. Here violence played its part. It is an error to imagine that the violence of Fascism, greatly under-emphasized in much of the more recent writing on the regime, was restricted to the first phase of the seizure of power: in fact it remained a constant, if, in later years, unsystematic, element of control throughout the *ventennio*.[11] Party documents show again and again that the person who was judged to be in some way critical of the regime was often the object of a beating. Fascists were particularly sensitive to behaviour that seemed to be dismissive of Fascism, or did not concede the movement its full importance; even more to attitudes that suggested derision. Even before *squadrismo* was given its official second wind in the late 1930s following the blackshirts' 'voluntary' participation in the Spanish Civil War, *federali* made no secret of the fact that they used violent methods against opponents. Indeed, some were clearly proud to declare that they sorted out problems with direct and informal methods. *Federale* Bofondi of Reggio Emilia wrote to Starace in 1934 stating that a presumed 'subversive' had died after throwing himself out of a third-floor window in order to avoid arrest (this was the usual story). Other suspects, on whose account it was not possible to prove anything, would be 'dealt with *in our fashion*' within the four walls of the fascist headquarters.[12] A handwritten letter from a fascist in Padua to Starace in late 1935 recounted that 'someone was beaten up because he asked for a foreign newspaper'.[13] The *federale* of Turin boasted with pleasure in September 1935 of 'a careful and intelligent vigilance which, from time to time, allows us to cudgel someone...'[14] Simply failing to take off your hat as a fascist procession passed by could earn you a thrashing, and age was no protection. In Padua in 1937, during a ceremonial march of the soldiers returning from Africa, 'two old men were beaten up because, inadvertently, they failed to take their hats off when the marchers passed by them'. The same account finished with the statement, not linked to anything in particular, 'at midnight two foreigners were beaten up'.[15] This was evidently just part of a normal day's work. Later, in September 1939, when Mussolini invited his followers to 'clean out the corners'—an invitation to act against all critics of Fascism—informers reported consternation among some of the public because of a fear that this would encourage a recrudescence of the violence of the hothead *squadristi*.

But if it is clear that the open violence of Fascism did not finish with the March on Rome but continued throughout the twenty years of the regime, people probably feared the fascist cudgel less than they feared other reprisals.[16] Fear would inevitably condition expression of opinion. Even in the second half of the 1920s, therefore, fascist informers were not observing daily life on a level playing field, much less so in the 1930s. What informers saw and heard was already a result and a reaction to an explicit and implicit conditioning by the regime. People depended on the party for a whole series of things—principally for work and for promotion, but also for welfare, for subsidies, for a pension, and for other forms of assistance, even in some cases for housing. Control of labour and of the allocation of essential resources was a fundamental element of fascist control of the population, as

---

[11] See Ebner, *Ordinary violence*, Introduction.
[12] ACS, PNF, SPEP, b. 18, Reggio Emilia, 13 September 1934, emphasis in original text.
[13] ACS, PNF, SPEP, b. 11. Padua, Baseggio to Starace, 21 October 1935.
[14] ACS, PNF, SPEP, b. 25, Turin, 26 September 1935.
[15] ACS, PNF, SPEP, b. 11, Padua, 18 May 1937.
[16] On this type of conditioning, see Corner, 'Italian Fascism'.

document after document makes clear. A report of April 1938 coming from Padua revealed that 'employers have been made to identify all their workers who have refused to enrol in the Party'.[17] There can be few doubts about what was going to happen to those who continued in their refusal. In both Naples and Reggio Calabria reports indicated that people could not speak out because they feared for their jobs. The withdrawal of the union card or the *libretto del lavoro* (work permit) could have disastrous consequences for the whole family. Other kinds of reprisal were possible. When, in 1937, the *federale* of Padua visited a poor area of the city to watch the distribution of food by the fascist authorities, he was unwise enough to ask an elderly woman what she thought of the quantity and the quality of the produce distributed. 'She had the courage to tell the truth about the quality and the quantity, both inadequate'. The next day the woman had her *libretto di assistenza* (welfare book) withdrawn.[18]

While this kind of dependence on the fascist authorities might produce positive reactions among beneficiaries, grateful for the protection of the party when it was forthcoming, it most certainly discouraged people from expressing displeasure, unless convinced that no one hostile was listening. 'If the population keeps calm it is only because they are afraid', wrote one *fiduciario* in 1937.[19] 'People keep quiet because they are afraid', reported another in 1939.[20] Men and women were convinced that there were ears listening everywhere. Talk hostile to the regime *was* risky if you could not trust the person next to you in the bus queue. Moreover (and this was an important factor in generating the kind of self-surveillance among the population characteristic of totalitarian regimes)[21] those present when others were expressing doubts about the regime or making direct criticisms of the *duce* were themselves liable to be punished if they had done nothing to counter the affirmations made in the conversation or had failed to denounce the offensive remarks to the authorities. The police files are full of reports from agents who had overheard comments critical of Fascism during casual conversations in train compartments, during which someone present would invariably ask the others to shut up, because, in one way or another, *all* risked unpleasant consequences. Potentially everyone was a spy. This danger inevitably made people cautious in what they said in public. As Canali writes, almost as a conclusion of his work on surveillance under Fascism, 'the ordinary citizen learned quickly what enormous power was in the hands of the political police and the confidents of the OVRA—and the degree to which their hostility could represent a real disaster if you incurred it'—a power which, if turned against you, probably meant 'personal ruin'.[22]

---

[17] ACS, PNF, SPEP, b. 11, Padua, informer's report to Starace, 23 April 1938.
[18] ACS, Ibid., 17 February 1937.
[19] ACS, MI, DGPS, Polizia Politica, Materia (1927–44), b. 220, Florence, 17 March 1939.
[20] ACS, PNF, SPEP, b. 11, Padua, 10 January 1937.
[21] For the concept of 'surveillance societies' see Robert Gellately, *Backing Hitler. Consent and Coercion in Nazi Germany*, Oxford, Oxford University Press, 2001, 256. The atmosphere of mutual suspicion between ordinary people in Nazi Germany is well conveyed in Hans Fallada, *Everyone dies alone*, Melville, New York, 2009 (original German 1946).
[22] Canali, *Le spie*, 201.

Because of people's reticence, information gathered by the police often depended on eccentric or drunken behaviour or on the results of denunciation. An example of the former—the eccentric—was the ingenuous farmer who named his pig after the *duce* in order to have the pleasure of going into the field every morning and shouting (with impunity, he thought) 'Mussolini Pig' at the top of his voice (he got five years of *confino*).[23] The drunken can be illustrated from the spirited but improbable defence of a newly sober man from Como province: 'When I hit the bust of Mussolini with the chair I had no intention of offending the head of Government.'[24] In another case it was the latter—the denunciation—which prompted the report. Here an artisan, betrayed by an acquaintance, was accused of recounting to his friends that 'Franco's widow had had to go to the Pope's successor to tell him that Hitler had been killed at Mussolini's funeral', adding that Italians would only be happy when all four were dead. The artisan defended himself in the usual way, saying that he was only repeating what someone else had told him, and that he was repeating it in order to deprecate the sentiment expressed. His friends denied any intention to denigrate the figures mentioned. Very understandably in the circumstances, all protested their undying loyalty to the regime.[25]

The declaration of loyalty of the accused in this last incident indicates a further problem with assessing opinion—a problem present in all totalitarian or would-be totalitarian regimes. This is the question of dissimulation, one of the features of such regimes that makes assessment of popular opinion particularly difficult. Totalitarian regimes spend a lot of time and energy attempting to create the appearance of popular unanimity. Inevitably the people have to cooperate in this operation.[26] Thus, like the artisans described above, when necessary people in Italy behaved and spoke *as if* they were loyal fascists, even if they were not.[27] It was usually in their interests to do so. Such behaviour was normal practice; it represented a mode of conduct that everyone understood, and it is a topic to which we will return. Here it is sufficient to note that declarations of fascist 'faith' were not always what they seemed. It is worth reminding ourselves that a considerable number of

---

[23] He seems to have had a more general problem with authority. His other two pigs were called Vittorio Emanuele (the king) and Principe Amedeo (the crown prince): Pierluigi Orsi, 'Una fonte seriale: i rapporti prefettizi sull'antifascismo non militante', (1990) 2 *Rivista di storia contemporanea* 280.

[24] ACS, MI, DGPS, AGR, PS 1935, b. 10, 16 October 1935. A further, colourful, example is provided in Richard Bosworth, *Mussolini's Italy. Life under the Dictatorship 1915–1945*, London, Allen Lane, 2005, 333–7.

[25] ACS, PNF, SPEP, b. 11, Pavia, 10 June 1939. According to one of the interviewed, another version of the joke related Mussolini's death to his excessive pleasure at hearing of the death of Stalin.

[26] On the force and importance of *apparent* unanimity in totalitarian regimes, see Martin Sabrow, 'Consent in the Communist GDR or How to Interpret Lion Feuchtwanger's Blindness in *Moscow 1937*', in Corner (ed.), *Popular Opinion*, Chapter 10.

[27] On the 'as if' factor in totalitarian regimes, see Vaclav Havel, 'individuals need not believe all these mystifications [of the regime], but they must behave as though they did...'; 'The Power of the Powerless', in *Open Letters*, New York, Random House, 1992, 136. For totalitarian regimes, the topic is huge. See, in particular, Alf Lüdtke (ed.), *The History of Everyday Life. Reconstructing Historical Experiences and Ways of Life*, Princeton (NJ), Princeton University Press, 1995, and Sheila Fitzpatrick, *Everyday Stalinism. Ordinary Life in Extraordinary Times: Soviet Russia in the 1930s*, Oxford, Oxford University Press, 1999.

Italians—the problem is to know how many—never accepted the legitimacy of a regime that had achieved power through violence and had maintained it through continued intimidation. The refusal to accept meant, particularly for the working class, that belonging to the fascist union or even to the party was often no more than an unavoidable means of survival—something that had been true since the early 1920s in those areas where the fascist movement had succeeded in destroying the socialist and Catholic unions and achieving an effective monopoly of the control of employment. Opinion expressed by some could be the opposite of that implied by the colour of their shirts, therefore. As one report from Reggio Emilia put it, even as late as 1938, '...there is a large number of workers who, even if they wear the black shirt in order to get work (as they themselves admit), are still socialists in their hearts and minds'. The remark of Francesco Bacci, a leather worker at Certaldo (Florence), is eloquent of this condition: 'The majority came to terms with the situation. They went to the fascist demonstrations because, they said "At least, I get to work and to eat." They knew how to lie'.[28] Here PNF did very clearly stand for *Per Necessità Familiare*.

7.2. PARTY AND PEOPLE: GROWING APART

It was probably the difficulty of assessing public mood through what people were saying that led informers to speak very often about what people were *doing* or, usually more significantly, not doing. In this respect—action and inaction—they invariably place the role of the local party machine at the centre of their attention. They do this for both good and ill, whether relating opinion supportive of the regime or recounting negative attitudes, and by so doing they do indicate that so many of the activities of the regime at local level did depend in one way or another on an authoritative lead from the party. If this were missing, capillary agencies, dependent formations and affiliate organizations tended to run down. As a consequence of Mussolini's decisions following the Matteotti crisis, the party had been allocated the job of being essentially an educational, organizational, and administrative transmission belt, responsible at provincial level for bringing the masses under the regimented control of the regime. Its role in the great transformation of Italy was crucial, therefore. In the view of the informers, and it could hardly have been otherwise, the standing of Fascism in the local public eye did depend on the smooth working of the local PNF. If the party were paralysed by factional struggles, there was a strong risk that welfare, youth, and leisure organizations would feel the consequences. As suggested in the last chapter, there was a limit to the extent to which such organizations could withstand the pressures created by constant instability. Even the fascist unions, which did come to assume some kind of existence autonomous of the party during the 1930s, found it difficult to operate effectively in areas where the party was not fulfilling its required role. The *federale*

[28] Quoted in Francesco Rossi (ed.), *Certaldo negli anni del fascismo; un comune toscano fra le due guerre (1919–1940)*, Milan, La Pietra, 1986, 213; my emphasis.

was, after all, the head of the *comitato intersindacale* (until 1937) and had to be up to carrying out his functions of mediating and guiding political and economic organizations.

That the party was not the well-oiled motor it was meant to be inevitably had repercussions for all aspects of activity and, where this happened, popular attitudes towards the regime reflected this malfunctioning. In fact, in report after report sent in to the central authorities by the informers—but also by disgruntled *federali* or officious prefects—the consequences of a badly functioning party are the central theme of the communication. In many areas popular discontent with the party took time to develop, however. That disjunction between the party and the people which was to be a characteristic of the 1930s—particularly, but not exclusively, the later 1930s—became apparent only gradually.

In the mid- and late 1920s, police informers speak relatively little of popular mood and concentrate their attentions on the squabbles within the party, thus conveying the impression of a largely quiescent population waiting on events. No doubt many non-fascists were still attempting to absorb political defeat or, more simply, still trying to work out exactly how the advent of Fascism would affect their lives, and were little troubled by tensions within the party. These were the years of the launching of the great 'battles'—for autonomy in grain supplies (the battle for wheat), for the stabilization and revaluation of the lira ('Quota 90'), and for the eradication of tuberculosis and malaria. Local party organizations would be much involved with the population in the propagation of these campaigns, which had considerable propaganda force. As popular mobilizing exercises they undoubtedly had their impact, giving the impression of a new vitality and a new direction in government after the dark years during and after the war. The powerful image of 'Italy on the move' belongs to this period, and Italy's young and assertive leader was part of this positive image.[29] It is only from 1927 that a different tone appears in reports, when one of the tasks of the provincial party organizations was to impose, through the unions, the across-the-board wage reductions determined by revaluation and consequent deflation. This manoeuvre did create tension; predictable murmurs of protest were heard in many areas. Even party secretary Turati was forced to confess that the cuts were greater than was justified by the reduction in the cost of living.[30]

More significant indicators of opinion came with the popular response to the Concordat, with the plebiscite of March 1929 (a legitimating exercise, designed to coincide with the tenth anniversary of the founding of the fascist movement), and—perhaps most important—with the advent of the world economic crisis. These were significant in the sense that they represented moments in which the party, in the process of consolidation, was able to relate closely to the population and in which the terms of the relationship were to become more explicit.

That the Concordat was an enormous propaganda success for Mussolini and for the fascist movement cannot be doubted. The agreement represented a powerful

[29] Gioacchino Volpe, *L'Italia in cammino: l'ultimo cinquantennio*, Milan, Treves, 1928.
[30] Agusto Turati, *Un popolo, un'idea, un uomo*, Milan, Istituto fascista di cultura, 1927, 185.

endorsement of Fascism which few could fail to recognize and as such was unquestionably a diplomatic triumph. It permitted the *duce* to parade himself as the politician who had finally solved the historic division between Church and Italian state—the 'man of providence', a title easily extendible to other spheres of activity.[31] It put propagandists for the regime in almost every pulpit in Italy and at last priest, *federale*, and *podestà* could appear officially on the same platform or in the same procession.[32] In small towns and in rural areas the apparent unity of secular and spiritual authority carried a great deal of weight and certainly bolstered the fascist cause. Endorsement of Fascism by the Church helped to alter the perception of the movement, previously too much associated with violence, among many in the population. The revision of opinion may have affected women in particular, more inclined than men, it has been suggested, to defer to the priest.[33] But, triumph as it was, it was in some respects a fairly generic triumph; a priest benevolent towards Fascism did not create jobs or reduce the price of bread.

Nor did the Concordat greatly involve the party at local level. Here the impact of the 1929 plebiscite was more immediate. Although the 'campaign' was short (only three weeks) and the choice limited to a straightforward 'yes' or 'no' to the list of candidates proposed for the new fascist parliament, the degree of regimentation involved in the 'plebiscitary election' (as it was called) was evident to all.[34] Local *fasci* were advised that the voters should be escorted to the polling stations 'perfectly regimented' (by the *fasci*), that they should sing as they went, and that efforts should be made to identify those who were thought likely to abstain in order that pressure could be exerted on them: 'Even the smallest internal dissent must be silenced'.[35] Inside the polling booths, voters were presented with two differently coloured voting slips—one for 'yes' and one for 'no'—and had to place the selected voting slip in one of two urns—again, one for 'yes' and one for 'no'—under the watchful gaze of fascist officials. A 'no' vote was immediately identifiable,

---

[31] Pius XI's phrase was, in reality, much more neutral: it carried the sense of 'if this is the man providence has sent, then we must do business with him'. Even Catholic newspapers embraced the contracted, pro-fascist, form of the phrase, however.

[32] Despite the Concordat, the relations between church and state would remain unstable for much of the 1930s. See, among a growing literature, Renato Moro, 'Religione del transcendente e religioni politiche: il cattolicesimo italiano di fronte alla sacralizzazione fascista della politica', (2005) 1 *Mondo contemporaneo* 9; Emilio Gentile, 'New Idols: Catholicism in the face of fascist Totalitarianism', (2006) 11(2) *Journal of Modern Italian Studies* 143; and, more recently, for an analysis which emphasizes the extent of 'negotiation' and 'accommodation' between the regime and the Church during the 1930s, see Jan Nelis, 'The Clerical Response to a Totalitarian Political Religion: la Civiltà Cattolica and Italian Fascism', (2011) 46(2) *Journal of Contemporary History* 245.

[33] Willson, *Peasant Women*, 186.

[34] The 1929 plebiscite asked a significant proportion of the male population to reply 'Yes' or 'No' to the question 'Do you approve the list of parliamentary deputies drawn up by the national Grand Council?' But, since it was readily apparent to everyone, fascists included, that parliament had ceased to count for anything, the vote was seen everywhere as a request for approval of fascist government. On the 1929 and 1934 plebiscites see Enzo Fimiani (ed.), *Vox Populi? Pratiche plebiscitarie in Francia, Italia, Germania (secoli XVIII–XX)*, Bologna, Clueb, 2010, Ferdinando Cordova, *Il consenso imperfetto*, Soveria Mannelli, Rubettino, 2010, Chapter 2; Paul Corner, 'The Plebiscites in fascist Italy: national unity and the importance of the appearance of unity', in Ralph Jessen and Hedwig Richter (eds), *Elections in Twentieth Century Dictatorships*, Chicago, Chicago University Press, 2011.

[35] See Turati's instructions to organizers: ACS, SPD, MDRF, b. 52, 5 and 13 March 1929.

therefore.[36] If anyone still had doubts about the meticulous controlling function of the local party, the plebiscite must have dispelled them. In fact, the result was a foregone conclusion, and testifies principally to the extent of fascist control in the provinces. In the southern province of Cosenza, for example, the 'no' votes were 37 in a total of 157,200—a good measure of the domination of the party or of influential people who supported the party. In the province of Matera, in a total vote of nearly 30,000 there were no opposing votes cast at all.[37] This was entirely predictable. Indeed, almost a year before, when the plebiscite had just been announced, one state employee from Florence, 'forced to his shame to wear the fascist badge' as he wrote, had even hazarded a guess at the result of the coming plebiscite, showing that he had understood the mechanisms of dictatorship very well: 'Registered to vote 12 million; votes cast 13 million; "yes" votes 14 million; "no" votes none'.[38] In the event he was not so far wrong.

With the Concordat signed and the plebiscite concluded Mussolini appeared to have got both God and the people on his side in the space of a few short weeks. This success created a public image invaluable in terms of his international reputation and undoubtedly greatly reinforced his position at home. For many, the alliance of church and state must have removed lingering doubts about the regime, while for others the semblance of national unity, as expressed through the plebiscite, made it much more difficult to sing out of tune. Indeed, from certain points of view, it is tempting to suggest that this moment in 1929, and not 1936 after victory in Ethiopia, was the high point of the regime. Many problems had been resolved after 1925–6; others had not yet shown themselves to the full. At the same time, however, and despite Mussolini's successes, it becomes possible around 1929–30 to begin to sense a developing disjunction between the official image of the regime and the reality of popular sentiment towards it. And this is most readily seen at the local level and in relation to attitudes towards the local party, where the successes of the regime at national level were not always faithfully reproduced in exactly the same terms. Often the economic crisis was at the centre of this growing disjunction.

The crisis, which had been developing in Italy since the manoeuvres revolving around the revaluation of the lira in 1926–7 and which had inevitably worsened with the international economic implosion of 1929, probably reached its peak in 1932.[39] The crisis represented both an opportunity and a test for the regime. People expected something from the party; total control implied total responsibility. Where the party worked well, the crisis offered the possibility to 'reach out to the people' through the organization of assistance for the unemployed and the needy,

---

[36] Turati ordered that those fascists or state employees who had handed in a blank voting slip were to be expelled from the party: Ibid., 3 April 1929.

[37] Results published in *Corriere della sera*, 26 March 1929.

[38] ACS, SPD, b. 94, 'Starace', 18 March 1928.

[39] For more information on the nature of the crisis, and on economic conditions in general during the fascist period, Gianni Toniolo, *L'economia dell'Italia fascista*, Rome & Bari, Laterza, 1980; Vera Zamagni, *Dalla periferia al centro. La seconda rinascita economica dell'Italia*, Bologna, Il Mulino, 1993; also Paul Corner, 'L'economia italiana fra le due guerre', in Giovanni Sabbatucci and Vittorio Vidotto, *Storia d'Italia*, vol. IV, *Guerre e fascismo*, Rome & Bari, Laterza, 1997.

in this way demonstrating the paternalist face of an apparently caring fascism. But where the local party was not functioning properly, often for the reasons seen in the previous chapters, the consequences for popular sentiment were less favourable. Party and population no longer got on together. Informers' reports suggest that this second circumstance was common. Thus, in the province of Reggio Emilia by 1929, the internal squabbles of the local party organization had left the party in a condition of 'deep crisis of depression and loss of direction' and the informer reported that disorganization in the fascist camp had provoked a total loss of contact with the population who, while putting up with the critical economic and social conditions provoked by the crisis, no longer had the 'stimulus of the party' to help them. He concluded that the party was not doing anything to ease unemployment and prevent an impression of abandon among the masses.[40]

Similar situations developed in many other provinces. In Savona where, as we have seen, the battle between Lessona and Dupanloup dominated almost the entire period from 1926 onwards, the paralysis of the party was reflected in public mood. In October 1931, an informer indicated that provincial Fascism still had a long way to go to regain 'its full moral and material efficiency'.[41] According to a report of January 1932, the squabbles had 'driven the masses away and made them almost suspicious',[42] while in 1933 a further alarmed report noted 'the impression—certainly not favourable—that the people are getting' when faced by repeated struggles within the party.[43] Further west, the province of Padua was so disrupted by fighting between groups in the early 1930s that informers found little time to speak of how the population was reacting, although in early 1931 a report did denounce the fact that 'the workers keep their distance, disgusted, and the subversives take advantage of this'.[44] Another stated that there was 'general apathy...specific interests dominate. Little passion in the faith'.[45] As already noted, the *fascio* of Padua reported to Rome in 1934 that the only activity it was able to carry out was that of assistance and relieving misery, but even this it was doing badly because of lack of funds.

In the South many areas saw the same problems. At the end of October 1931 Mussolini paid a visit to Naples. The crowds welcomed him, but reserved a chilly silence—'not a single cheer'—for all the other local dignitaries. 'Apathy and absenteeism' were recorded as the predominant sentiments of the day.[46] The silence suggests that the opportunities offered to Fascism by the crisis—the possibilities of gaining support through the use of public assistance—had not been exploited. A subsequent report seems to confirm this. A signed letter to Starace of March 1934 protested about the fact that, at Vico Equense near Naples, 'women

[40] ACS, PNF, SPEP, b. 18, Reggio Emilia, report on the political situation in Reggio Emilia, undated, but early 1929.

[41] ACS, PNF, SPEP, b. 20, Savona, informer, report of October 1931.

[42] ACS, Ibid., informer, report of January 1932.

[43] ACS, Ibid., undated report, but 1933.

[44] ACS, PNF, SPEP, b. 11, Padua, informer, 8 February 1931.

[45] ACS, Ibid., PNF report on situation in Padua, 27 March 1931.

[46] ACS, PNF, SPEP, Naples, informer, 20 March 1934.

are dying before the eyes of the Political Secretary because medicine is being denied to the poor'.[47]

The two crises—that is, the economic crisis and the crisis of confidence in Fascism—hit Reggio Calabria hard as well. Again, the party had failed to rise to the occasion. The *federale* was forced to admit, in September 1931, that the *podestà* of nearby Riace had done nothing for his citizens and that, as a consequence, Fascism was 'slowly wasting away'. 'Fascism is still a long way away from Riace, because those who believed in the new creed at the beginning are now asking if the mission that the Party should have carried out in the town has not failed...'[48] The *federale* did not fare much better himself, being indicted, in a long and detailed informer's report about the woes of provincial Fascism over previous years, as the principal culprit. In concluding the informer stated that the weakness of the *federale* ('a real nobody'), together with the economic crisis, had produced a *marasma* which saw provincial Fascism tearing itself apart, leaving 'the *fasci* abandoned, closed now for months' and 'the masses without any confidence, disillusioned, obstructed in their everyday life, offended'.[49]

Turin presents an interesting contrast with all those provinces in which, as far as it is possible to make out from the documents, the local fascists had never managed to get their act together for any period of time and in which the economic crisis had not met with any positive response from the party. The history of the fascist movement in Turin in the 1930s demonstrates the ways in which the party could both work and not work in different periods, and also the variations in popular reaction to the party's performance. There is separation between party and people at times, but there is also some successful involvement of the population. That it is, in the end, a decline in the capacity of the party to attract support lends weight to the thesis that the dysfunctional factors within the local party federations tended, in most cases, to find their way to the surface.

The situation of confusion in Turin in 1930 and 1931 was very similar to those of the provinces described above. It was a confusion which had historical roots. Throughout the 1920s Turin had shown itself fairly resistant to Fascism. The Piedmontese tradition, strongly monarchical, argued against the pretensions of the regime among the local elite and induced an almost palpable diffidence, often bordering on disdain, for the fascist newcomers. This suspicion was a constant source of difficulty for local Fascism. The regime attempted to use aristocratic supporters in the hope of bridging the divide, but with little success. At the end of 1930 the local commander of the MVSN attributed 'a sense of laziness in the fascist masses' to the fact that local fascist leaders had been chosen from titled people 'incapable of going down to the piazza and carrying out, in contact with the masses, the programme of the Fascist Revolution'.[50] A memo of 1934 summed up the question very well: 'The Fascist Revolution has attracted little support from the Piedmontese professional classes, apart from a few young enthusiasts; the majority,

---

[47] ACS, Ibid., 2 March 1934.　　　[48] ACS, PNF, SPEP, b. 18, 7 September 1931.
[49] ACS, Ibid., informer, undated, but 1931.
[50] ACS, PNF, SPEP, b. 25, Turin, 22 December 1930.

which remains faithful to the old doctrines of liberalism and linked to the old political personalities of Piedmont, has greeted the new national politics with a certain reserve'.[51] Persisting socialist and communist allegiances among the working class—the largest in Italy—represented further obstacles to fascist penetration. Testimony to this last was Mussolini's visit to the Fiat works in 1930—a famous flop, with the *duce* leaving the platform visibly irritated by the stony silence with which the workers had listened to him. Evidently they saw little in Fascism. There was, after all, no equivalent in Italy to the Nazi 'Beauty of Labour' organization, designed to give workers a greater degree of self-respect and to promote sympathy for the regime. Moreover, Fiat had its own *Dopolavoro*, to all effects independent of the regime.[52]

Few of the detailed reports of either 1930 or early 1931 leave any question about the feelings of most Turin workers. The crisis hit the city severely from the autumn of 1930. By 1931 informers were writing to Rome relating the difficulties being faced by almost everyone. Fiat was sacking a substantial part of its workforce because of a decline in demand; across 1930–31 around 15,000 car workers lost their jobs. Small businesses and artisans in particular had been badly affected by a reduction in orders, sometimes by as much as 70 per cent in 1930, and were laying off workers in large numbers. The local textile industry was feeling the full brunt of low-cost Japanese competition. As serious for the regime was the fact that many office staff were also being sacked and their functions assumed directly by the owners themselves or their families.

People lost no time in blaming the regime for their troubles. Some criticism was fairly generic: 'There's a build-up of falsehoods and criticisms of all kinds about the regime. People take pleasure in saying that the Government requires economies of everyone... but does not carry them out itself. They criticize the armament policy, the manoeuvres, the mass demonstrations, the cost of the Militia, the desire to fight a war, etc, etc'.[53] Much of the criticism was related to the local situation, however. Employers in Turin complained that they were hampered in dealing with the crisis by a maze of bureaucratic structures relating to employment and welfare and that the party was doing nothing to help them. Workers protested about the low level of public assistance, feeling that they had little or no protection in time of crisis. The reports of the informers note that, by 1931, the anxiety among many of the industrial workers, already evident in 1930, had become a kind of desperation. 'In a large part of the public a real fear of next winter is growing and many are predicting serious problems...' People were worried and tired. They had lost any confidence in the future. There was a generalized sense of 'resignation best seen in the phrase currently in vogue: "Let what's going to happen happen, by now I couldn't care less"'.[54] From the hinterland one *fiduciario* spoke of 'a certain ostentatious disinterest for every initiative of the Regime'.[55]

[51] ACS, PNF, SPEP, b. 25, Turin, 7 May 1934.
[52] De Grazia, *Culture of Consent*, 68, note 29.
[53] ACS, PNF, SPEP, b. 25, Turin, 20 July 1931.
[54] ACS, Ibid.
[55] ACS, Ibid., report for the month of July 1931.

What was the party doing to meet the situation? Very little, it would seem. In June 1931 the monthly report of a police spy expressed the opinion that

Turin Fascism needs to be stimulated and reconstructed, because for some time there has been a growing indifference for matters concerning the Party. Even those people who, as inspectors of the federation, are in charge, adopt such a relaxed attitude that it provokes a worsening of the situation. These are young people and politically little prepared for the responsible positions they have been given.[56]

Many of the problems in Turin arose, as always, from internal bickering within the *fascio*. The new party directorate, created in early 1931 and including titled figures, had little following in the city and the hinterland (or even among the local fascists). Prominent names among the city fascists had been excluded from the directorate and—across the whole province—many people had had their application for a renewal of the party card refused 'often because of local disputes of little importance and certainly not justifying exclusion'. As a result many of the *fasci* in the centres surrounding Turin stopped any activity; 'the majority of the *fasci* are neglected by their leaders and it can be said that they exist more in name than in fact'. Typically, as a consequence of internal squabbles, people had abandoned the fascist organizations; 'a lot of the people who had the ability and could have worked profitably for the Party have completely abandoned everything that smacks of local politics, to the extent that it is becoming quite difficult to replace both leaders and led'. When substitutes were found, they were 'not always of sufficient experience and political sensitivity'.[57] Understatement is to be suspected in this last, guarded, judgement.

The condition of disarray produced an almost inevitable loss of confidence even among convinced fascists, further demonstrated by the fact that, not only had many ceased to work for the party, but others were trying to hide the fact that they were fascists. The party was doing so little that, among fascists who wore the party button-hole badge, 'some of them take it out, saying that it makes them uneasy'. As a result '…a good number of those fascists who for professional reasons are obliged to work with the public hide their political position'. These would keep the badge in their pocket and bring it out when necessary 'saying that despite their beliefs, they feel uncomfortable because of a very clear form of diffidence directed towards them'. They felt this because, when in public, 'everyone around us goes quiet', as people blamed the regime for the crisis.[58]

Even the *fascio femminile* was not spared criticism. Directed by Countess Barattieri (note the title), it was characterized by the 'intrusive manoeuvres by some people who further their own ambition rather than the party'. Here the women's *fascio* would appear to have had some of the same problems as the men's movement. The women were also criticized for a certain lack of tact. Some of them, when handing out food parcels to the poor, 'like to visit the poor wearing such a show of unnecessary ornamental objects that they provoke bitter comments'. For

---

[56] ACS, Ibid., report for month of June 1931.   [57] Ibid.
[58] ACS, Ibid., Turin, 20 July 1931.

many unemployed this was the last straw. 'The poverty of many workers' families does not find any comfort in the strident contrast which is created by the meeting of misery and riches'.[59]

Popular opinion seems to have changed to some extent during late 1932 and 1933. This was a result of a slow climb out of economic crisis, which saw many local industries—Fiat included—beginning to take on workers again and, most important, not shedding them with the arrival of winter 1933. But fascist informers also attributed the turn-around to a changed situation within the party. A new *federale*, Gastaldi, had been appointed in late 1931 and had immediately set to work to redeem the disastrous condition of the local federation. His actions had been concentrated on two fronts—the first, persuading central government to intervene to avoid closures and to prevent local industries from moving away from Turin; the second, reinforcing the efforts of the party designed to soften the impact of crisis through public assistance. Thus, according to reports, the population had modified its hostility to the regime, seeing the local fascist organizations attempting to work in its favour. One informer had no reservations in attributing the credit to the new *federale*: 'I formed the impression that the actions and the activities of the Federal Secretary are widely approved; on this everyone agrees—if the situation in Turin has changed it is down to his actions and his temperament'. In particular, it was his capacity to raise money for assistance that attracted praise; 'the funds raised by the *Segretario federale* for the Welfare Association are notable and ever increasing'. This, in turn, was attributed to the fact that he had put the local federation back together again: 'the citizens now believe very widely that all the major office holders get along with each other, thus avoiding those attitudes and interferences that damaged the life of the city'. He was on good terms with the *podestà*, who was also working hard in defence of local industries, and with the prefect, with whom it had been possible 'to overcome the disagreements that had developed previously between the Prefecture and the *Segreteria federale*'.[60]

This picture of moonlight and roses was no doubt somewhat exaggerated, but it does contain some important points. Popular opinion about local Fascism was, very obviously, related to what the party was doing; in the context of the economic crisis, judgement was linked to the ability of the party to operate in a way that was seen to be favourable to the population at a time of great difficulty. In Turin, the *Opera Assistenziale* did produce results in terms of increased appreciation for the regime. In fact Mussolini, who visited the city again in 1933, got a much warmer reception than he had received in 1930. The capacity of the regime to control and to direct resources was a potent weapon, if used properly, and the poor, the unemployed, and the aged would inevitably respond to a movement which proffered help. They would do so, of course, less for any ideological motive than through simple necessity. Fascism was a resource to be utilized when it offered benefits and many were in no position to bite the hand that—literally—offered to feed them. One report noted precisely this, distinguishing between ideological commitment and utilization of facilities provided by the regime. While 'many workers and

---

[59] ACS, Ibid., report for month of June 1931.   [60] ACS, Ibid., 29 November 1933.

ordinary people' displayed 'sentiments which are unfavourable to the Regime', there was, nonetheless, 'a greater disposition to frequent the leisure organizations of the Regime...'[61] Even so, there was no hiding the fact that this was, in a sense, conditional acquiescence with Fascism, based on fulfilment of interest. If the condition—the requirement for and the provision of resources—were to disappear or to weaken, the acquiescence was likely to disappear as well.

The further point that emerges from the example of Turin in crisis is the importance of a party leader able to unite the party and to work with the other authorities. As the informers noted, this was the basis of Gastaldi's success, because it meant that internal divisions were no longer producing paralysis. The *federale* was able, therefore, to 'sell' himself and the party to the population in much more convincing form, permitting him to operate along those lines which accentuated themes of community and common interest. If, by November 1933, there was 'a sentiment of gratitude towards the authorities', this was because the party had been successful in presenting itself as an organization with the interests of the population at heart and not simply as a group of squabbling and ambitious politicians, intent on furthering their own interests. Facing up to crisis had galvanized local Fascism and provided a motivating and a mobilizing objective, rather as the provision of Winter Aid did for provincial Nazi groups during the 1930s. Presumably, from the tone of the reports, by the end of 1933 people in Turin were no longer hiding the fact that they were fascists.

As in so many other provinces, however, successes would prove to be fragile. Despite the praises heaped upon him from some quarters, in the course of 1934 the usual criticisms of the *federale* began to be heard again among the local fascists. Gastaldi was judged to be a good propagandist and to have been successful in persuading the population to look more benevolently on Fascism, but was accused at the same time of putting himself at the centre of everything (he appears to have been guilty of *personalismo* on a grand scale) and of paying scant attention to the needs of the old *squadristi*, whom he had described as 'all delinquents', or the emerging younger fascists ('fanatics and dreamers').[62] The PNF national secretary, Starace, gave credence to these accusations and Gastaldi was replaced, but not totally removed, in as far as the new man, the 'Staracean' Piero Gazzotti, was generally considered to be a creature of the former *federale*. Almost immediately following these manoeuvres, infighting began again and local initiatives began to falter. There was a report in May 1934 that the youth movement was 'not looked after';[63] in April 1935 an informer noted 'serious absenteeism' of local fascists, 'cold and absent', who had ceased to take part in any activities, 'not turning up for demonstrations, lectures and roll calls' and failing to show up at the commemoration of the founding of the fascist movement on 23 March.[64] A further report of the same period pointed to the fact that people were fed up with useless meetings and continual call-outs for senseless demonstrations and had begun to abandon the movement again. 'Lack of interest and tiredness' were the keywords of the period so far

---

[61] ACS, Ibid., 8 August 1931.   [62] ACS, Ibid., 23 June 1934.
[63] ACS, Ibid., 10 May 1934.   [64] ACS, Ibid., 15 April 1935.

as local fascists, among whom there were 'many absentees', were concerned.[65] Public assistance, less necessary because of the economic revival in the city, had declined, and, as a consequence, people felt less beholden to the fascist party than they had done in 1933. Thus, by March 1936 (in full Ethiopian campaign, therefore) a report from Turin stated, again with some understatement it would seem, that 'there are notable levels of public opinion, confined to the working class and the industrial categories who secretly conserve attitudes not entirely favourable to the Regime'. The same informer went on to illustrate his point, this time being far more explicit (and at the same time revealing the close contact—probably of his sub-informer—with the people he was talking about).

> The great majority of the metalworkers who depend on Fiat, although apparently members of the fascist union organization, and although enrolled in the party, have stayed where they were, that is, they are convinced socialists and communists. In the reunions of these workers, anti-fascist 'murmurs' always appear along with criticisms of the *gerarchi*, etc.[66]

The regime, used by the workers as a resource in time of need, had evidently failed to engineer conversion.

In Turin, after the passage of the worst years of the crisis, it was largely a matter of going back to square one. The position the party had built up in the later years of the crisis had been squandered. An anonymous letter to Starace at the end of 1936 repeated the usual story:

> almost the totality of the Turin *gerarchi* are so full of ambition that they think they are omnipotent, not only where the fascist followers are concerned, but also with the peaceful citizens... Their main activity is to compete among themselves for the most important jobs and, thereafter, for the honorary titles. The Piedmontese people... cannot tolerate the cheek and the cheating of so many rogues.[67]

The level and the methods of public assistance came in for criticism, again in terms that had been heard before: 'during the winter, welfare is carried out a couple of days a week by the Fascist Ladies and by a few other arrogant figures. The Fascist Ladies deck themselves out very elegantly, with very valuable jewels, and it is not unusual for them to receive the needy poor with a cigarette hanging from their lips'. Where house visits were made, the women visitors were said to be more amenable, but had little to offer. One complainant spoke of getting for a fortnight enough food for three days. Another complained that it was very much a case of one piece of used clothing for the whole family, one jar of jam, a couple of vouchers for 1 lira to last a fortnight and 'a word of encouragement and that's it'.[68] Enthusiasm had long since passed, and respect for the party with it. By 1940 it was possible for an informer to write, 'one has the sensation of being in a city which is not fascist'.[69]

Interestingly, an attempt in 1935 to increase activity in Turin through the compulsory enrolment in the *fascio femminile* of all the women in the families of the

---

[65] ACS, Ibid., 6 July 1935.   [66] ACS, Ibid., 17 March 1936.
[67] ACS, Ibid., undated, bears office stamp 15 December 1936.
[68] ACS, Ibid.   [69] ACS, Ibid., 23 January 1940.

1,500 local fascist organizers met with strong opposition from the organizers themselves, who judged the initiative an invasion of the privacy of the family. Some said they would agree to enrol the women of their households, but that there was no question of them participating actively in events. Others seem to have been unsure that their wives thought as they did and objected that 'this business is creating arguments at home', while others—'above all those who are husbands, show themselves to be irritated, arguing that, for various reasons, the presence of their wives would be inopportune'. All in all, the request was resisted because 'for some it seems that [the issue] is generating difficulties within the family'.[70] Whatever Fascism was to these male organizers, family—and their role within the family— was clearly of greater importance.

The period we have been looking at here—from broadly 1929–30 until the declaration of war on Ethiopia in 1935—corresponds of course to Renzo De Felice's 'years of consensus'.[71] In the sense that the regime was not faced with problems that in any way threatened its existence, it is possible to go along with this judgement. But if the nature of this consensus is called into question, the judgement requires a great deal of qualification. A popular consensus for the fascist movement would seem to imply a favourable attitude to the local party, seen to be working on the population's behalf. Instead, in province after province, the opposite picture emerges. The party was simply not doing its job and the people responded accordingly. Turin is by no means typical of Italy, of course. As a major industrial city with a large working class, it differed strikingly from many of the smaller provincial centres of the North and even more from those of the Centre and the South. Even so, the words and phrases describing sentiment in Turin in this phase are fairly typical of those encountered in the reports of police and party spies in other areas, as we shall see in the course of the following chapters. The characteristic of public mood in Turin, apart from the brief interlude of 1933–4, seems to have been apathy and resignation. Apathy, in particular, is the word reproduced constantly in the reports, referring both to the spirit within the fascist movement and to that outside it. The change of heart in Turin in 1933 was no more than temporary, therefore, with workers and unemployed returning to a default position of criticism and diffidence as the crisis lifted and the local party fell apart once again. The generalized conviction was that things were not going to change for the better and that there was little to be done about it. Lack of alternatives made any other response impossible.

This *was* consensus of a kind—perhaps better described as reluctant acceptance and resigned acquiescence in a situation in which there was little prospect of change and where all the cards were in the hands of local party and fascist unions. There was little enthusiasm around—in Turin or anywhere else, as far as one can see— precisely because the party failed to make use of its cards. If this—enthusiasm—is what is intended by consensus, then to speak of a 'mass consensus' for Fascism would be to go well beyond what the terms used by police and party informers

---

[70] ACS, Ibid., 6 July 1935.
[71] De Felice, *Mussolini il duce*, vol. 1, *Gli anni del consenso 1929–36.*

permit. It would, in any case, be to run the risk of divorcing popular sentiment from the coercive context in which it was formed. Even after the worst of the crisis had passed, times remained very hard. Coercive mechanisms, both active and passive, reminded people that such times had to be endured in relative silence.

7.3. ETHIOPIA AND ENTHUSIASM

If it is enthusiasm that we are looking for—even totalitarian regime-type mass enthusiasm—then the fascist conquest of Ethiopia between October 1935 and May 1936 would seem to be the right place to look. Usually considered to be the high point of the regime, in the sense of representing the moment that saw the greatest spirit of unity between the regime and the population, the Ethiopian war moved fascist Italy into another dimension—the international dimension—in a way fascist diplomacy had not achieved up to that point. For a brief period, Italy became the centre of international attention. The crisis surrounding the Italian aggression could not but stimulate popular opinion and at least to some extent shake it out of the apathy we have seen in the previous section.

The Ethiopian crisis and the military campaign need to be seen in the context of the situation described above. The condition of relative stall of the fascist movement in the first half of the 1930s was widely recognized. The party had been emasculated to a great degree and reduced in its functions; other fascist organizations often worked with only partial efficiency. If bank salvages and the creation of IRI marked a distinctively original response to the crisis at governmental level, the corporative state continued to fail to take off and its propositions were felt little or nothing at popular level. As we have noted, numbers enrolled in fascist organizations were often high; the problem was that conviction was low. It was not that the fascists risked losing control—there was no danger of that—but rather that they found it very difficult to communicate any kind of dynamic message to the population in order to stimulate a genuinely enthusiastic participation in the movement. Mussolini had evidently got wind of this when, in July 1934, he warned, '[i]t is essential that the whole Party come together in a less formal, more responsive, discipline, less given to those "exterior" forms which, when repeated, tire and become conventional'.[72] He, like Starace, had read the reports that spoke of apathy, apathy, and apathy again. These were hardly the emotive conditions in which the virile, energetic, and war-loving New Fascist Man would be formed. Moreover, the contrast with what was happening in Germany at the same time was there for all to see.

The decision to launch the Ethiopian campaign in October 1935 has often been seen as a response to this situation. Prompted no doubt by the historical memory of defeat at Adua in 1896 and by the immediate awareness of Hitler's determination to penetrate the areas of South-East Europe in which Italy had hoped to secure at least economic dominance, Mussolini was also conscious of the possible

---

[72] From Canepa, *PNF*, 95 note 27.

effects of war on the home front. As always (but in this case with more than ample justification), it was assumed that the war would be victorious; the fruits of victory—in the form of colonies—could then be exploited to the full in propaganda terms. But it was also clear that the campaign itself, in the circumstances of a generalized condemnation by world opinion, could serve as a powerful weapon in uniting the nation and mobilizing Italians behind Fascism. It could serve to give the regime that fillip it so badly needed.

Whatever its origins, the Ethiopian war provides a further viewpoint from which to assess popular opinion in respect of the regime. Few would question that, in certain moments and particularly, of course, at its victorious end, the war was seen with enthusiasm by large segments of the population. Both as a military operation and as an exercise in international diplomacy, the war seemed to represent a notable success which, in the short if not in the long-term, penetrated popular thinking. Successful national affirmation was gratifying to most; further, the mirage of land and work offered by the realization of empire was understandably attractive to those who, at home, had neither.

Even so, the Ethiopian war should be treated with some caution so far as popular opinion is concerned, precisely because Italian opinion was itself part of the diplomatic game. The picture of an offended Italy, denied its rights, was a card Mussolini intended to play for all it was worth. Although popular opinion had little real chance of influencing the decisions taken by the fascist regime, it remained very important for the image of Fascism which the regime presented to the outside world. The importance of the image of unity was crucial in the months of late summer and early autumn 1935 when the Ethiopian crisis was at its height. Mussolini was very determined to demonstrate to the European powers that he had the backing of the Italian nation, that war, if it should come, was a war 'wanted by the people'.[73]

Even a brief survey of the principal Italian newspapers in the period leading up to the declaration of war shows the degree to which the regime attempted to secure this support by manufacturing opinion. Italy's 'civilizing mission' in the face of a backward, slave-dependent society, the rights of a demographically exploding Italy to her place in the colonial sun, the hypocrisy of the French and the British—these were all themes hammered out day after day with the intent of producing a unity of national purpose.[74] Popular opinion, and not only the thinking of government, it was suggested, was 'exasperated' by the negative attitude of Italy's opponents and was on the point of 'losing patience'.

---

[73] Mussolini summed up his position very well in the frontispiece to the first issue of the fascist journal *Gerarchia* for 1936:

The war we have begun on African soil is a war of civilization and liberation. It is the war of the People. The Italian People feels that it is theirs. It is the war of the poor, of the dispossessed, of the proletarians. In fact against us have lined up the representatives of conservation, of egoism and of hypocrisy...Certain of this unanimous and profound consensus of all the Italian People...the Regime will forge ahead.

[74] See Nicola Labanca, who observes that the propaganda effort was more suited to a world war than a colonial adventure: *Una guerra per l'impero. Memorie della campagna d'Etiopia 1935–6*, Bologna, Il Mulino, 2005, 45–51.

It is important to keep in mind this aspect of the politics of the regime when attempting an assessment of popular attitudes towards the war. For external propaganda purposes—to put pressure on the European powers—the fascist government required the enthusiastic participation of the population in the crisis, did everything it could to realize that participation, and—and this is the important point—in any case stopped at nothing in order to make it look as though that participation really did exist. This means that the picture we are fed by official sources of an Italian people inebriated by patriotic fervour constitutes *part* of the regime's programme and is not exclusively a *consequence* of that programme. Genuine enthusiasm there most certainly was, but, because of the requirements of government presentation, on occasions it becomes difficult to identify what is genuine and what is not.

The key moment in which popular support for the regime was to be shown was in the *adunata generale* of the nation—a nation-wide public demonstration, called on 2 October 1935, in which national unity was to be demonstrated to the world in all the principal cities of Italy. Far from being a last-minute operation, the projected demonstration was announced in the *foglio d'ordine* n. 141 of 10 September 1935 (distributed to all fascist officials, therefore, and published in the national press), but without a firm date. It was stated that the exact moment would be communicated with the sounding of sirens and the ringing of church bells, at which point the people were to go to the town square the local fascist authorities had indicated. The very precise instructions show that the authorities were aware that organization *was* necessary in order to guarantee the outcome. In fact, prefects and party officials had been reporting for some time that public opinion was anything but convinced of the need for war.[75] People were said to be doubtful about the 'civilizing mission' of Italy. Phrases such as 'the Africans are more civilized than we are' and 'we are the barbarians' appear in police summaries of conversations.[76] There were doubts about the real extent of the resources a conquest of Ethiopia would bring to Italy—one man observing cynically that, if the country were really so rich, the English would have moved in long ago.[77] But above all there was a fairly generalized perception of an expensive and unjustified aggression, based on flimsy pretexts, that carried with it great risks of provoking a wider European conflict. The fascist informers were forced to write on many occasions that, at least prior to its declaration, the war was 'not wanted' emotively by the population, which had other, and much more pressing, problems nearer home.

---

[75] In June 1935 a fascist informer had written

there are numerous exceptions constituted by those who think and hope they have something to gain, but in general one can say that public opinion is not favourable to the government in this case. There is the precise sensation that, in the final analysis, it is a question of a bellicose expedition of conquest on our part, and there is a tendency to accept rather than to reject the criticisms made in the foreign press and reported in our newspapers...

ACS, MI., DGPS, AGR (1920–45), C1, fasc. 'Mobilitazione classe 1911', 20 June 1935. A fuller version of the document is reproduced in De Felice, *Mussolini il duce*, vol. 1, 620–21.

[76] 'We are the bad guys who are going to disturb Abyssinia and take their stuff. The Abyssinians are not bad, therefore. They say that the Abyssinians cut off the b...of our prisoners, I would cut them off Mussolini'. ACS, MI., DGPS, AGR, C1, Conflitto Italo-Etiopico, b. 3, 7 April 1936. The man who said this got five years *confino* because of his offence to Mussolini.

[77] ACS, Ibid., 15 April 1936.

Even students, it seems, had their reservations. An informer's report from Milan on 25 May 1935 spoke of the 'coolness of the young people towards the imminent African campaign',[78] while another, from Venice, on 5 October, asserted 'I've heard university students in Padua complain like those in Milan about the Fascist Government...and I repeat that among them there is no enthusiasm for the war. They say that many young people have rushed to enrol in university (in Venice, at Ca' Foscari) in the hope of avoiding being called up'.[79] Tullio Cianetti, in his Memoirs, recalls that in 1935 'young people responded little', considering this 'an alarm bell' of which the PNF did not take notice.[80]

It should be noted at this point that, in 1935, Italy was already at war, and had been for a long time. The war in Libya, conquered in 1911–12 but never really pacified, was still going on in the early 1930s and the situation in Eritrea remained precarious. People in Italy may already have had some wind of the difficulties involved in foreign conquest and of the hardships determined by the efforts to develop colonies. Soldiers and workers involved in the North African operations did not keep quiet either abroad or on their return. Particularly striking is an informer's report about the 'impressions given to travellers in the station of Bologna by a group of sick labourers, returning from Massawa' in which he describes the conditions of the workers, dirty, without shoes, with their clothes in tatters—'a sorry picture of disorder and misery'—and quotes the stories which the workers told the other travellers. 'They gave a picture of a woeful situation of disorder and exploitation in Africa, where they were subjected to all kinds of hardships and torments by the employers—badly fed, cheated of the water ration allocated to them, forced to buy food and other small pleasures at prohibitive prices'.[81] In similar vein was the letter home from Eritrea of a young soldier:

> you should know that in the 20 days I've been in this place around 150 of the 300 [workers] have fallen ill...what did we do on this earth to be so tortured by God? and those irresponsible people who made us come? promising to give us the mountains and the sea? yes, they have given us mountains—to break up with our pick-axes, nothing else. So, please, if anyone else wants to come, if he isn't a real delinquent, don't let him come...[82]

To combat these stories and these reservations—and to contain them as much as possible—the *adunata generale nazionale* of 2 October was organized down to every last detail. In fact there were complaints in Milan on the day before the demonstration about the 'exaggerated organizational effort which in some cases has assumed the characteristics of an authentic enforced recruitment'.[83] Certain of the

---

[78] ACS, MI, DGPS, Polizia Politica, b. 219.

[79] ACS, MI, DGPS, Polizia Politica, b. 109. The university population does see a rise of some 15 per cent between 1934 and 1936 (from 62,020 to 71,512).

[80] Cianetti, *Memorie*, 283.

[81] ACS, MI, DGPS, AGR, C1, 'Conflitto Italo-Etiopico', b. 14, Milan, 20 June 1935. Frontini Luigi to his father, 8 June 1935.

[82] ACS, MI, DGPS, AGR, C1, 'Conflitto Italo-Etiopico', b. 17.

[83] ACS, MI, DGPS, Polizia Politica, b. 219, *relazione fiduciaria*, Milan, 1 October 1935. The informer explained that these methods were adopted because 'the leaders fear that what usually happens is repeated, that is absenteeism from the demonstrations not only of the population but also of those enrolled in the Party'.

methods of organization were already well known. Even before 1935, attendance at important demonstrations had never been exactly voluntary.[84] At the given signal, people in all types of fascist organization, workers in factories, those in public sector offices and in the central administration, were to leave what they were doing and file down in military formation to their allotted places in the local piazza. Ministries in Rome were invited to draw up lists of those considered essential for the continuation of the functioning of the ministry, who were to be exonerated from attendance, while all other functionaries were to be forced to attend. To guarantee obedience to the order of assembly, all those in fascist-related organizations were given a *cartolina precetto* (notification of convocation), bearing their name and the number of their party or fascist union card, and also carrying warnings of 'fines', 'disciplinary proceedings', and 'serious sanctions' for those who failed to respect the convocation.[85] The fascist neighbourhood groups were particularly active in distributing these cards to those for whom they had responsibility.[86]

The procedure envisaged that on the day of the demonstration the cards would be handed in to fascist officials sitting at specially designated tables at the entrances to the piazza, who held registers of those to whom the cards had been distributed. In other words, those present were counted, those absent were noted. This close control explains the desperate attempts of those, away from their town of residence for reasons of work on 2 October, to hand in their postcards to the local officials or to telegraph their home organization in order to explain their absence. It also explains the serious worries of many about the fact that, for some reason, the counting tables had not been set up at certain of the entrances to Piazza Venezia in Rome, preventing people from leaving their cards and thus exposing them to the risk of sanctions.[87]

Mussolini would later refer to three '*adunate improvvise*' [spontaneous demonstrations] relating to the Ethiopian war, of which 2 October was the first. That it was not exactly spontaneous and unexpected was clear to many foreign observers.[88] Many expressed their reservations about the event. For example, when asked his impressions of the demonstration the correspondent of the *New York Sun* observed '[c]ertainly it was a well prepared demonstration of an obligatory nature—but was it sincere? In a totalitarian regime, where discordant opinions are not permitted, where there are only fascist newspapers, where it is not possible to express publicly your opinions, the historic *adunata* must leave the neutral observer with severe doubts'.[89]

---

[84] See the testimony of Danilo Scarselli, a worker at Certaldo, near Siena. Referring to 1938, he recounts: 'They [the *fascisti*] forced me to go to Florence when Hitler came. I had never taken part when they did their festivities. I told him that I wasn't going to Florence. The secretary of the *fascio*, Vichi, said to me, "If you don't come to Florence I'll arrest your father and your mother." I got my clothes together to go to Florence'. Quoted in Rossi (ed.), *Certaldo negli anni del fascismo*, 279.

[85] ACS, MI, DGPS, carte Capo Polizia, cat IV, 20 September 1935.

[86] According to one critic, 'the great *adunata* of the forces of the Regime was enforced by the . . . Circoli Rionali': ACS, MI, DGPS, AGR, C1, 'Conflitto Italo-Etiopico', b. 3, 6 November 1935.

[87] ACS, MI, DGPS, Polizia Politica, b. 219, Rome, 4 October 1935.

[88] The difficulty of distinguishing between obligatory and genuine enthusiasm was noted by fascist officials. One commented that the demonstration was 'something prearranged and obligatory, which lost its spontaneity and therefore its meaning and its value': ACS, Ibid.,12 October 1935.

[89] ACS, Ibid., 3 October 1935.

Formally the *adunata nazionale* was a great success. Estimates of those present in all the town squares of Italy varied from 10 to 20 million, but there was no question about the scale of the event. Fascist sources hailed the 'totalitarian' participation of the population. The message that the Italian people was behind its *duce* was broadcast to the world and foreign resistance to fascist pretensions was portrayed as an affront to the whole nation. Many of the reports from both Rome and the provinces, written by fascist informers, did stress the 'spontaneous' enthusiasm of the crowds as they flowed through the streets down into the piazza and as they listened to Mussolini's words either directly or through loudspeakers.[90] Others showed more caution, though. Particularly interesting is the report of a conversation among a group of fascists in the crowd in Piazza Venezia in Rome. The writer notes

> I listened to a lot of participants at the *adunata*, among whom [here he gives a list of names][91] ..., who commented that they were there in observance of party discipline, and certainly not because of adherence to the policies of the Regime, because anyone who has already fought one war certainly could not want another. The same people expressed the opinion that many others thought as they did, and that unfortunately their respect for discipline could be mistaken for—and presented as—an intention that was not there. [The same *fiduciario* noted that] the crowd at the edges of Piazza Venezia, and beyond, did not show signs of enthusiasm and approval during Mussolini's speech, but listened to it in a composed manner and in silence, almost as if it represented a nightmare rather than an incitement to action. In fact a lot of people had this impression; ... yesterday's demonstration and the unusual activity that followed it were not the fruit of enthusiasm but rather of a state of worry and preoccupation. [Another informer wrote of a similar impression, again referred to the Rome demonstration] It was good to see the groups of workers from the small building companies and from the small workshops, drawn up as they were alongside the industrial workers. The enthusiasm of these people was limited, however ...[92]

An observer inside the Vatican also reported reservations about the *adunata*: 'In Catholic circles they were commenting on yesterday's demonstration, saying that it lacked organization and that it was something imposed on everyone by force, in as far as the people and the single individuals took part because they were compelled to do so, because otherwise they would not have gone at all'.[93] In a further report, informer no. 40 also signalled his doubts about the Roman crowd, concluding very significantly 'the country obeys, but I think it useful to reconfirm my opinion that the spirit of the population is not what it seems nor that which applauds'.[94]

---

[90] Some of these reports are so similar—and rhetorical—in their wording that one suspects some kind of ministerial or party template being adopted.

[91] The provision of names suggests that the *fiduciario* considered it worthwhile identifying people specifically, possibly in order that action could be taken against them. It also indicates, of course, that the informer was a fairly close contact of the people on whom he was reporting.

[92] ACS, MI, DGPS, Polizia Politica, b. 219, Rome, 3 October 1935.

[93] ACS, Ibid., b. 219, Città del Vaticano, 4 October 1935. Doubts about the justice and the wisdom of the campaign were strong within the Vatican; see Lucia Ceci, '"Il fascismo manda l'Italia in Rovina," Le note inedite di Monsignor Domenico Tardini (23 settembre–13 dicembre 1935)', (2008) 120(1) *Rivista storica italiana* 294.

[94] ACS, MI, DGPS, Polizia Politica, b. 219, Città del Vaticano, 4 October 1935, also cited in Colarizi, *L'Opinione* (2009 edn, 194).

Similar observations, suggesting reticence and reluctance, can be found in the reports on the demonstration coming from other regions of Italy.[95] Along with a large number of—usually very rhetorical—accounts of the 'totalitarian participation' of the people, there are also many that describe a different picture. In Milan one report spoke of 'some coldness in the piazza',[96] while another described 'the extreme calm that pertained during the *adunata*; even the expressions of hosanna and jubilation were very limited. In general I noted a sense of resignation and of dejection.... The spirit of the crowd is tired'.[97] A third informer attempted an explanation of the low spirits of the crowd: 'The majority [of those present] turned up because the were afraid of reprisals, as had been threatened previously; they turned up regimented and, I would say, "silent"'.[98] This was confirmed in another report: 'Enthusiasm shown? None'.[99] In Brescia a fascist engineer remarked on the 'substantial coldness among those citizens drawn up in the principal square to listen to the speech of the *duce*',[100] and one anonymous observer in Cremona wrote directly to Mussolini to tell him that 'people came to the demonstration because they were frightened of beatings or reprisals; they shouted not from enthusiasm but because they were fed up with waiting'.[101] All too often, it seems, the loudspeakers set up in the square to relay the speech of the *duce* did not work, leaving the crowd with nothing to do.[102] This last point—the tedious nature of the exercise—comes across in several other reports. From Florence an informer spoke of a general impression of a 'pointless and disturbing' demonstration.[103] The irritation of many participants, obliged to make 'long and pointless marches' across town finds expression.[104] One Roman made his position crystal-clear in characteristic Roman fashion: 'next time...I'm not coming; I'll spare myself the effort'.[105]

Very revealing are the comments of a schoolteacher, Augusta Cocchi, enrolled in the *fascio* of Granarola (Bologna) and head of the fascist association in her school, who was heard saying 'the demonstration of the forces of the Regime was an obligatory demonstration just like the elections, when the electors were compelled to vote under threat of being beaten up'. She added that she had little faith in fascist propaganda about enthusiasm for the war; 'as far as that is concerned, those who live in the midst of the people know very well that there is no enthusiasm on the part of mothers who have sons in danger'.[106]

---

[95] Given these reports, it is difficult to accept the judgement of Colarizi (*L'Opinione*, 2009 edn, 192) on the enthusiasm shown in the demonstration: 'There is not one discordant report in the communications that arrive from all over Italy'.

[96] ACS, MI, DGPS, Polizia Politica, b. 109, Milan, 20 October 1935.

[97] ACS, Ibid., b. 219, Milan, 4 October 1935.

[98] Ibid.

[99] Ibid., Milan, 3 October 1935.

[100] ACS, MI, DGPS, AGR, C1, 'Conflitto Italo-Etiopico', b. 3, 19 November 1935.

[101] ACS, Ibid., handwritten letter of 2 October 1935.

[102] ACS, Ibid., Florence, 3 October 1935; Turin, 3 October 1935; Rome, 3 October 1935.

[103] ACS, MI, DGPS, Polizia Politica, b. 219, 3 October 1935.

[104] ACS, Ibid., Vatican City, 4 October 1935.

[105] ACS, Ibid., Rome, 4 October 1935.

[106] ACS, MI, DGPS, AGR, C1, 'Conflitto Italo-Etiopico', b. 3, Prefect of Bologna, 30 November 1935.

That there were faint-hearted among the faithful was further demonstrated little more than two months later. The *Giornata della fede* of 18 December 1935 seemed to find fascist Italy once more in the throes of patriotic convulsions as women queued up to hand over their wedding rings.[107] As a propaganda exercise the event was very successful, possibly because it involved more than just listening to boring speeches in a city square and waiting to applaud at the given moment. Giving your wedding ring meant conscious participation at a direct personal cost and inevitably induced reflection on those forced to make the sacrifice. The newsreels showing austere matrons scaling the ramps of steps of the *Altare della Patria* in Rome in order to throw their rings into the vast urn set up to receive them had an undoubted force to them. Prefects and informers throughout Italy insisted that the sense of patriotism and the spirit of sacrifice had never been higher, and, following the imposition of sanctions, there had clearly been some rallying to the flag.

At the same time, it is instructive that the same prefects and *fiduciari* had been obliged, in the days before 18 December, to report on a whole series of tricks designed to help women avoid giving their rings. It seems that from early December—but the phenomenon would continue well into the first months of 1936—a flourishing market had developed in the production and sale of iron rings, similar to those promised and then given by fascist officials to women in return for their wedding rings.[108] This iron ring was, in effect, a receipt for a gold ring sacrificed to the cause. It is obvious that those who bought the imitation iron rings could avoid giving their real gold rings—they already had the receipt displayed prominently on their finger. Women would also try to find an alternative gold ring, usually of inferior quality, in order to be able to keep an item of notable sentimental value. A further trick was to take the wedding ring to a jeweller and to substitute it for a ring of inferior quality, sometimes by having the original melted down with only a minimal part of the gold re-used in the new ring. After payment, the owner would pocket the difference. This practice was so common that the government was forced to issue an ordinance forbidding jewellers to melt down rings and obliging them to keep a register of all activities involving gold. The number of denunciations for breaches of these ordinances during the first months of 1936 suggests that they had little effect.[109]

That there were limits to obedience is indicated by the incident involving one Martino Leva, an usher at the *comune* of Prà near Genoa, enrolled in the party, who was reported as saying to a tram driver: 'If my wife were to give her ring to the *fascio* I would throw her out of the house. Let the *duce* give money to the fatherland; he is rich with millions, although I knew him [when he was] poor'. Leva admitted the phrase, but pointed out that he had handed over a pair of gold earrings and other pieces of metal a few days before. Evidently the earrings were one thing, the wedding ring another—and as such merited protection.[110]

---

[107] On the *Giornata* see Petra Terhoeven, *Oro per la patria*, Bologna, Il Mulino, 2006.

[108] ACS, MI, DGPS, AGR, C1, 'Conflitto Italo-Etiopico', b. 14, Trieste, 13 December 1935; Parma, 31 December 1935.

[109] Terhoeven, while noting the various methods women used to avoid handing over their wedding rings, argues convincingly that the propaganda value of the operation was of much greater importance to Fascism than the actual value of the rings themselves.

[110] ACS, MI, DGPS, AGR, PS 1935, 27 December 1935.

Popular reactions to the possible price of patriotism can also be seen in December 1935 in the rush, reported in many towns, to reclaim items left at the local *Monti di pietà* (pawn shops), following a rumour that the government was planning to requisition all gold items and other objects of value deposited in the *Monti*.[111] And, while the government's invitation to the public, in early 1936, to donate all gold objects to the national cause, did have a certain success, in the sense that around 35,000 kilos of gold were collected, it is worth noting that many people, who could choose between giving the gold and selling it to the Bank of Italy, often chose this second path. Around 45 per cent of the gold gathered in came through private sales to the Bank.[112]

Even this might seem a good result. After all, it meant that around 55 per cent had been donated. But the real nature of the 'voluntary donation' has to be assessed. Fascist pressures for such donations were already well known to prosperous members of the community, often obliged to support fascist initiatives at what was little short of the point of a gun. Revealing in this respect is the ministerial circular, sent by the head of the police to all prefects, in which the invitation to collect all available gold and silver from the office staff was repeated. The circular required that all precious metals and other objects collected should be sent in to the Ministry, together with two copies of a list which indicated 'for each functionary, employee, and policeman' the nature and the size of the contribution made 'by each individual person'. The same circular stressed that the donations should be 'absolutely spontaneous', but added that it was the job of each section chief to make sure that 'all the personnel, with no exceptions... contribute with donations of gold and silver'.[113]

This was the fascist conception of 'spontaneity' in a nutshell. It was a conception which imposed obligation, and then masked that obligation with words that had become meaningless. But the requirement to donate spontaneously was more than just an oxymoron; it was a further example of that *esteriorità* that had come to characterize the movement in the 1930s. Actions no longer had to correspond to sentiments. It was almost as if the action had substituted for the sentiment behind it. The doubts and reservations expressed about the Ethiopian war suggest that the two—action and sentiment—had become divorced for a part of the population, regimented rather than convinced, and deprived of other options. That disjunction between the party and the people that we have noted in the course of this chapter was not closed by the Ethiopian campaign, therefore, despite the massive demonstrations; so much of the shouting was obligatory shouting, produced on tap for propaganda purposes. What the campaign did do was reveal the continuing need for regimentation and coercion in moving the Italian public to express its support for Fascism. The English journalist had not been much off the mark when, in November 1935, he had described the Italian people acutely as 'a nation of prisoners, condemned to enthusiasm'.[114]

---

[111] See, for the zone of San Lorenzo in Rome, Piccioni, *San Lorenzo*, 103.

[112] De Felice, *Mussolini il duce*, vol. 1, *Gli anni del consenso 1929–36*, Turin, 1974, 627; also Terhoeven, *Oro*, Chapter 8.

[113] ACS, MI, DGPS, AGR, C1, 'Conflitto Italo-Etiopico', b. 14, 3 November 1935.

[114] ACS, Ibid.

8

Perceptions of the Party

Mussolini's announcement of the conquest of Abbis Ababa, made from the balcony of Palazzo Venezia in Rome on 9 May 1936 to a hastily assembled crowd from local schools, offices, and shops (all closed for the occasion), was received with understandable enthusiasm. 'Italy has her Empire' was a heady phrase, even allowing for justified perplexities about what Libya and Eritrea had represented in previous years. The enthusiasm appears to have been short-lived, however. When reading the informers' reports on popular mood, there is no sense of discontinuity between the period before the Ethiopian war and that following it. What is really surprising about the aftermath of the war is the speed with which the old pattern of complaints, grievances, and resentments reappeared among the population. This continuity is more than anything an indication that the Ethiopian war had not served to change the realities of provincial Fascism but had, in a sense, been superimposed upon the movement without provoking any real structural or behavioural changes. What new stimulus and dynamism there was lasted only as long as the war itself. As the moment of triumph receded, the old problems reasserted themselves. Many Italians may well have been proud to see that Italy had an empire—there can be little doubt that Mussolini's reputation rose fairly dramatically as the result of his success—but provincial Fascism continued to be a story of petty rivalries, nepotism, and clientelism, corruption and injustice. Empire did not change this. What it did do was raise expectations that could not be fulfilled and, more immediately, push up prices for basic foodstuffs. In this sense, war made Fascism in the provinces less rather than more bearable. As Renzo De Felice has observed, the Ethiopian conflict essentially destabilized the regime, despite appearances to the contrary.[1]

8.1. DISCONTENT, DISAFFECTION, DISGUST

News filtering through from soldiers and workers in Ethiopia may also have served to dampen enthusiasms. Conditions were often harsh, illness frequent, and letters home expressed reservations about the physical characteristics of the new paradise and contained references to the same kinds of injustice as experienced in Italy. Illuminating in this last respect is a letter sent from Abbis Ababa in October 1936

---

[1] Renzo De Felice, *Mussolini il duce*, vol. 1, *Gli anni del consenso*, 775–88.

in which a young worker, in hospital, described what was going on in Ethiopia to his brother:

> Here, dear Ariosto, it's all over; that is, for the *signori* it's the best time, they are OK, beautiful houses—a licence to steal—etc, etc. If you could see the stuff—recently they set up a company, the so-called CITAO, with Teruzzi (Minister for Italian Africa) as president—you should see the stuff—and consider that CITAO, which stands for *Compagnia italiana trasporti Africa orientale*, they call *Compagnia italiana truffatori abilmente organizzati* [Italian company of well-organized fraudsters]... the locals are all dumbstruck.

The writer moved on to explain his personal position and the reasons why he hoped to leave Ethiopia in order to join his emigrant brother in France. 'I can't carry on here,' he wrote, because of the cost of his cure from malaria: 'if you don't give the doctor 50 lire he doesn't give you the injection and if you don't have 50 lire you die'. He risked being ejected from the hospital because his money had run out: 'they told me to pay up or get out'. His conclusions, after this tale of woe, are interesting: 'now you can see that it is pointless for them [the fascists] to talk to us about social policy, etc'.[2] If letters like this were doing the rounds, it was small wonder that the Ethiopian victory did little to change at least some attitudes towards the regime.

What certainly did remain a constant of the period before the Ethiopian war and of that following it was the poor reputation of the local party among the population. Never high in the first half of the 1930s, between the moment of victory in 1936 and Italy's entry into the Second World War in June 1940 that reputation appears only to have declined further. The many criticisms and accusations levelled at *federali* and, to a much lesser extent, at *podestà* (which we described in Chapter 6) denounced behaviour which continued to attract the attention of the population and influence popular opinion in a negative sense. Despite victory and the establishment of empire, the authority of the party had not increased. A report of a *fiduciario* of September 1936 is especially telling in what it reveals about the 'flavour' of provincial Fascism. Without mincing his words, the writer spelled out one aspect of the difficulties experienced in the provinces, which he considered emblematic of the party's decline—the fact that local Fascism was often making itself ridiculous in the eyes of the population. He identified the same defects we have already had occasion to comment on. Servility towards the *gerarchetti*—the little Mussolinis, too often absurdly over-praised by the local press—produced ridiculous exercises of sycophantic hyperbole: 'The little provincial news-sheets...are full of boundless praise in respect of this or that local chief. Praise which, if you talk to people who live in the area, has no justification and derives from some favour already conceded or which someone hopes to get in the future'. But, the informer observed, as soon as the particular figure was removed, he was totally forgotten and his successor became the object of the same kind of fawning attention. This excessive praise had unfortunate consequences: servility 'has become a real illness, and, like all illnesses, it does harm and leaves traces'.

---

[2] ACS, MI, PS 1939, b. 24, 18 October 1936.

The writer returned to the issue of the absurd exhibitionism of the *gerarchetti*—one of the characteristics of provincial Fascism to be criticized again and again by informers, but to little effect. Here the informer was even more scathing, illustrating the way people reacted to the behaviour of the leaders and their underlings. The tone of the comments is worth noting; he was clearly unafraid of telling it like it was:

> As far as exhibitionism is concerned, the sickness has very deep roots even in the big cities and we have to have the courage to say that very often it generates an unbearable irritation. And with irritation, hostile criticisms and discontent. Many *federali* are far from immune from this contagion [of exhibitionism], just as their dependents of whatever category are not immune either. On the contrary, I have to add that the employees in certain fascist federations, even if they have very unimportant positions, give themselves airs and treat people with a condescension which we could happily do without. In this respect it is enough to go to visit the *Federazione dell'Urbe* [Rome].

In conclusion, in an apparent effort to moderate the force of his criticisms, which went very close to the bone, the *fiduciario* conceded that not everyone behaved like this. Even so, he found himself returning to the fact that the effect of those who did was so devastating that it obliterated the efforts of the honest and sensible fascist workers: '. . . this illness affects only a few but it is so blatant that it makes us forget the splendid behaviour of all the others'. Instead such behaviour did nothing other than provoke 'mocking laughter and insolent jokes from the ordinary people and not only from them', destroying any authority the party might claim to have.[3]

Absurd behaviour was accompanied by a feature we noted in Chapter 6—a sense, on the part of the *gerarchi*, of omnipotence that produced abuse of position. In many provinces there appears to have been a fairly generalized resentment at the abuse of power by the local fascist officials from the second half of the 1920s—almost from the outset of the regime, that is. This sense was determined by the reluctance of the officials in question to recognize any kind of control to their actions beyond the authority of Mussolini. Having subverted the authority of the liberal state so successfully, they had great difficulty in adjusting to the new realities of Italy after 1925, assuming that they could do much as they liked.

In this context, something already noted briefly in Chapter 3 should be repeated. Many of the documents referring to disciplinary measures taken against rank-and-file fascists by the party itself or by the police make clear the presence within the early fascist movement of a fair number of people with criminal records or criminal tendencies. As had become obvious during the enquiries into the *fatti di Firenze* of 1925, the apparent impunity provided by membership of the party had stimulated illegality on a large scale. Purges were carried out by the central party authorities from 1925 onwards; both Farinacci and Turati made efforts to face up to the problem. There can be little doubt, however, that the purges were only partially successful and that, together with those blackshirts who assumed that the fascist victory

---

[3] ACS, MI, DGPS, Polizia Politica, b. 109, informer, 16 September 1936.

meant they could do just what they wanted, there also remained those accustomed to use illegal means to realize their ends. Anonymous letters make frequent references to the criminal backgrounds of the local leaders they are denouncing. As late as 1935 the federation in Perugia was defined as a 'den of thieves' (in an official letter, which listed the criminal records of the administrators). It was reported that young people were deterred from adhering to the federation because the leaders, 'on whose behalf the criminal records testify eloquently', were not 'morally qualified'.[4]

Abuse of power had many manifestations, some less serious than others. As we have seen, a constant source of popular comment and irritation throughout the regime was the life style adopted by many of the local *gerarchi*. In the same way as rivals for power within the fascist movement would denounce the extravagant behaviour of their opponents, people less involved with the movement—often, in a sense, the onlookers—would rail against the excesses of the local *duce* and his followers. Here they had a fairly easy job. The standards the fascists set themselves were clear and widely proclaimed; the qualities of the true fascist were to be shown in 'self-control, disdain for the comfortable life, sacrifice of all ambition, all vanity and all scheming, in the renunciation of all happiness, and in living dangerously'.[5] To judge by many reports, most *gerarchi* failed on all counts. Letters and anonymous denunciations produced a fairly standard list of abuses—the restaurants, cars, holidays, and women of dubious reputation we have already noted—but also and perhaps more seriously, administrative incompetence, laziness, arrogance, and threatening behaviour. An informer in Taranto in 1931 summed up as follows the causes of a long local crisis that had provoked the sending of a party inspector from Rome, reporting what people were saying:

> The accusations that they level at the *federale* are well known and can be summed up thus: bad habits in dealing with the public in general, fascists not excluded; arrogance in his behaviour; authoritarian attitudes; excessive claims when asking for voluntary contributions for the fascist provincial federation; no confidentiality; changeable in his intentions, bad administration. These accusations are in large part justified and it should not be too difficult for the Party Inspector to establish the degree to which they correspond to the truth.

The examples we noted in Chapter 6 of 'Napoleonic' behaviour on the part of local party secretaries make it difficult to doubt the veracity of this *fiduciario's* report. Others spoke of 'gladiatorial poses'.

People also reacted against the *cost* of the fascist organizations, which seemed unjustified at a time of great economic difficulties for the mass of the population. Newly wealthy fascist leaders served only to add insult to injury. As already seen, the accumulation of positions—the taking on, by the *federale* and by other leading fascists, of a whole series of appointments, very often purely non-executive posts, which carried with them significant salaries—attracted considerable popular

---

[4] ACS, PNF, SPEP, b. 13, Perugia, Comando fasci Giovanili di Combattimento to Starace, 25 April 1935.

[5] Canepa, *PNF*, 97.

protest. The injustice of the 'accumulations' was all too obvious. The regime might preach 'social justice', as it did, but the reality of what was going on was lost on nobody. Many people had no job; a few had too many, and very well paid ones at that.[6] Resentment increased as government directives against this kind of exploitation of position had no effect at all.

There is still no good and comprehensive study of the finances of the fascist movement, particularly at local level.[7] Some information does emerge from the party documents, however—usually when an inspector has been sent to look into a crisis within a provincial movement. What does become clear is that, after the attempts of the national party organization to control and centralize the finances of the movement—attempts made repeatedly in the course of the early 1920s—by the end of that decade the local federations had once again achieved some autonomy in their financial affairs. We have already noted the way in which, in Piacenza, the local party organizers had been found to be paying ill-defined 'subsidies' to themselves and to others whose merits or needs remained unclear. The 1941 inspection of the federation of Pisa, already cited, condemned exactly the same kind of practice. In Pisa the subsidies did attract the attention of the inspectors, aware that some provincial federations had become a gravy train for those who controlled them. Few doubted who was really paying for the boxes at the theatre, the expensive restaurants, the big cars and the petrol needed to run them, or the entertainment offered to the ladies 'of easy ways' so often mentioned in letters of complaint.

Federations were financed in part by the subscriptions paid by those enrolled in the party. The renewal of the party card each year envisaged the payment of a small sum to the local federation. Where the party worked well, this system functioned up to a point; some income was guaranteed, even though the amount coming into the coffers was unlikely to cover the expenses of the federation. Many local federations did not work well, however. As we have seen, conflicts within the federations produced administrative confusion, with the consequence that fascists decided in some cases to have nothing more to do with the movement and in others to limit their activity. In the early 1930s many federations reported that the enrolled were not renewing the *tessera*. These were not usually declaring their aversion to the movement; rather, they were remaining formally fascist supporters, but simply not bothering to do what was required of them at the administrative level. They continued to figure as members, but behind in their payments. In some cases the *federale* would report that, in a time of economic crisis, people were reluctant or unable to make the necessary payment for the issue of a new party card.

---

[6] Studies indicate (rather unsurprisingly) that distribution of wealth became more unequal under the regime, with a restricted oligarchy of politicians and businessmen receiving large remuneration from their various appointments. The fact was sufficiently obvious—and sufficiently unpopular—to provoke an official enquiry in 1942 into the 'plutocratic drift' within fascist institutions. See Musiedlak, *Lo stato*, 197–205; also, for more general comments in a longer perspective, Pierluigi Ciocca, *Ricchi per sempre?*, Turin, Bollati Boringhieri. 2009.

[7] One aspect of the question, worth noting here, is that there is a great deal of evidence in the provincial documentation to suggest that local *fasci* were often short of funds and that this prevented the realization of what were sometimes very grandiose projects.

Whatever the reasons, there is evidence that many federations had financial problems by the early 1930s. Indeed, when enrolment to the party was once again opened in October 1932, observers were unimpressed by the official explanations of the reopening and interpreted the move simply as a means of raising much-needed funds through the sale of party cards to the newcomers. The fact was that Fascism was expensive; large-scale public works, a *casa del fascio* (local fascist head-quarters, usually newly built) in every town, the programmes of public assistance, the party bureaucracy, armaments and wars—all cost money.[8] Money coming from central government was limited in a time of crisis and provincial revenues could not fill the gap. As it was, *comuni* often found that they had to increase local taxes considerably, provoking popular protest against the *podestà*, and provincial federations would become involved in the conflicts.[9]

The scale of the problem was such that the federations could not rely on official sources of funds and had in many cases to adopt other, independent, ways of raising money. Local fascists—those in influential positions—were repeatedly accused of using their position to extract money from those who depended on them in some way. Veiled—and sometimes not-so-veiled—references to extortion are not uncommon. For example, the inspector's report from Taranto in 1931, quoted above, detailed the way in which 'voluntary contributions' to the cause had been exacted by the local federation. Obligatory, and very expensive, advertisements in the local fascist newspaper were one of the favourite ways of taxing local professional people and shopkeepers, payment being made by these people in order not to have the party card withdrawn. In Taranto, in the case reported by the inspector, the lawyer being pressured actually refused to place an advertisement, on the grounds that advertising in newspapers was not appropriate to his profession. He did agree, however, to make a sizeable 'voluntary contribution' to the federation.[10] In much the same way, it was rumoured that the President of the province of Taranto, in receipt of a one-off payment of L.350,000 as a consequence of the liquidation of the local workers' bank, had been 'invited' to contribute L.100,000 to the *fascio* on pain of losing his fascist card.[11]

The 'voluntary contribution', made to keep in with the party if you were already a member or to avoid its wrath if you were not, was a device which inevitably created resentment. This was particularly so when those who could scarcely afford

---

[8] Incredibly wasteful projects and programmes also ate up funds. One aspect of the local crisis in Modena was the massive debt of the federation, caused by an excessively long payroll of hangers-on, by uncontrolled car expenses, and by the purchase and maintenance of 'a complex machine for the interception of telephone calls, by which . . . they listened to all the conversations that took place in the Littorio building [the local fascist headquarters] between the various offices and between these offices and the telephones of the headquarters of the province': ACS, PNF, SPEP, b. 8, Modena, report on situation in province, March 1931.

[9] Vittorio Cappelli (*Il Fascismo in periferia. Il caso della Calabria*, Rome, Riuniti, 1992, 70) cites the example of Carfizzi in Calabria where the people burned down the house of the *podestà* as a protest against an increase in communal taxation. See also, for numerous examples of popular protest in the South, Piero Bevilacqua, *Le campagne del mezzogiorno tra Fascismo e dopoguerra. Il caso della Calabria*, Turin, Einaudi, 1980, in particular 122–49.

[10] ACS, PNF, SPEP, b. 23, Taranto, report for month of February 1931.

[11] Ibid.

such contributions could see the ways in which their money was being spent. The expensive life styles of some *federali* contrasted badly with the generally recognized poor quality of the public assistance the party organized to help the needy. For this reason the local fascist movements often generated a serious credibility gap, with people seeing through the rhetoric of collective responsibility and recognizing the reality of private and personal advantage. Thus, in Reggio Calabria in 1938, 'Several Unfortunate Fascists' wrote directly to party secretary Starace to protest that 'the bosses go round by car, they couldn't give a damn about anyone and are only good for getting money out of you with threats'. The federation, according to these correspondents, was known to everyone as the 'federation of the bloodsuckers'.[12]

It was symptomatic of the situation in the provinces that almost immediately after the end of the Ethiopian war rumours began to circulate about the destination of some of the gold and other precious metals gathered in by the party to help pay for the conflict. Newly rich fascist officials found accusatory fingers being pointed at them, as people suspected that the wedding rings donated had not exactly gone directly to help the national cause. In Modena, for example, it was said that one of the leading members of the provincial federation—the person who had been responsible for collecting the gold rings—was living 'with the fear that you may get to know how much he gained personally from the collection of gold carried out by his group'.[13] When, in 1940, the government announced that a register was to be drawn up of all copper objects in the country, reaction was immediate: 'They say that the register of copper will soon be transformed into requisition, so, with one pretext or another, the same thing will happen which happened with the wedding rings—requested for the fatherland, but much of that precious metal changed direction, thanks to many high-up fascists for whom any real control is impossible'.[14] It was, of course, impossible to verify the suspicions; face-to-face challenges to those in authority invited a bad end, and the fascist movement was not going to press charges openly against anyone thought guilty of such malpractice for fear of a serious loss of face.

Whether money extorted with threats, open or implied, was going to the public purse, so to speak, or into private pockets is not always easy to tell, nor is it always easy to make the distinction. In this respect at least, totalitarianism—in the form of the local fascist movement—had often effectively destroyed the distinction between public and private.[15] The problem was that the distinction had been destroyed in favour of the private, in the sense that, often, people suspected a private destination for their contributions. Many paid up, in order to have the party card, but they had no idea at all where their money went: '... everyone knows that the majority of those enrolled in the party pay not inconsiderable sums every year [to the local federation], which add up to many hundred lire, whereas only 3 lire per person enrolled are paid into the [central] Party funds. Everybody is asking

---

[12] ACS, PNF, SPEP, b. 17, Reggio Calabria, 23 March 1938.
[13] ACS, Ibid., b. 8, Modena, Guido C. to unnamed Camerata, 27 March 1938.
[14] ACS, Ibid., b. 9, Naples, 25 January 1940.
[15] Symptomatic is a joke that circulated widely: Two fascist militiamen pass in front of a crowded bar. One says to the other, 'Shall we take something?' The other replies, 'Yes, but from whom?'

where the money paid by the Fascists ends up and nobody knows why an account sheet is never drawn up...'[16] This suspicion was an aspect of a more generalized sensation that fascist officials were making money through abuse of authority. As one arrested man had said, there was a popular conviction that 'the quality necessary for high political or administrative office is that of refined delinquency'.[17] The sentiment was echoed by a housewife from Como, who considered that 'the district leaders of Fascism are all exploiters and profiteers'.[18]

Inevitably this kind of abuse of office—sometimes effected through the application of pressure, sometimes through more clearly illegal practices—invited popular cynicism and disgust. People talked, and very quickly even the smallest rumour of malpractice became a fact, inflated beyond all measure. This disposition to believe is itself indicative of the general climate of opinion. Thus, in Modena, for example, where party secretary Feltri had been facing the accusations recounted in Chapter 5, the prefect lamented the fact that the local party was in total disrepute: 'They have generated lack of confidence. Bread with marble flour, oil, petrol, *gerarchi*, Fascism—all mixed into a minestrone of men and deeds, served up on every table, to the damage of certain people, but above all, to the damage of the Party'.[19] A fascist of 1919 from Vicenza wrote, at the end of 1938, that 'I am bound to tell you...that the party is slowly becoming a dead weight...In particular nepotism and the system of favours is much criticized and creates general bad feeling'.[20] At Pomigliano d'Arco in 1940 there were riots among the workers, which some attributed to the bad working of the labour exchange. The anonymous report on the events connected the problems instead to the way in which the *federale* was selling jobs to the unemployed: 'the primary reason for discontent among the workers is to be found in the systematic money-making of the local *gerarchi*...'[21]

Much of this may have been no more than malicious gossip. Nonetheless it is significant that such suspicions were common currency; the probity of fascist officials was far from being taken for granted. On the contrary, the assumption seems to have been that, as a fascist official in a small provincial town or even in a larger city, you were on the make unless proved otherwise. The assumption can be linked to the infighting within the *fasci* that we described in Chapter 5 and the accusations made between fascist rivals in the course of the various internal party struggles. Many of the accusations made between fascists—those of arrogant and bullying behaviour, of personal enrichment, of clientelism and the abuse of public position for private interest—were precisely the same accusations made by people less close to the federations, in many cases not even enrolled in the movement. The politics of defamation utilized within the provincial movements found its mirror in the population at large, therefore. Nor could it have been otherwise. If the local fascists spent so much of their time speaking ill of each other, it was small wonder

[16] ACS, MI, DGPS, Polizia Politica, b. 109, 3 January 1936.
[17] ACS, MI, DGPS, AGR, PS 1935, 'Offese al Duce', Prefecture of Foggia, 19 August 1935.
[18] ACS, Ibid., Prefecture of Como, 10 August 1935.
[19] ACS, PNF, SPEP, b. 8, Modena, report of inspectors, January 1940.
[20] ACS, Ibid., b. 11, Padua, 'Vicenza: Spirito Pubblico', 21 December 1938.
[21] ACS, Ibid., b. 9, Naples, 18 July 1940.

that others would take up the same themes, at times, no doubt, exaggerating, inventing, distorting, but always working within a culture of scepticism and suspicion in which it was often hard to distinguish truth from falsehood. Factionalism not only risked paralysing the party, therefore; it also brought it into bad repute.

As already suggested, people found it almost impossible to act against the abuse of power by fascist *gerarchi*. In a very illuminating report of January 1937, informer number 52 (code-name 'San Marco', one of the most reliable and accurate) wrote from Milan that rumours about the transformation of the party (in reality, about the suppression of the party) had been greeted with 'general understanding and consensus, because people expect much less abuse [of power], particularly in the periphery—abuse deplored by the great majority of citizens'. He went on to explain that people did not denounce the abuses because of fear: 'with the present system of partisan control, inspired by the principle "We must not create scandals", not only would you not get very far, but a person who decided to let the authorities know about the abuses would risk paying a high price'. In turn, he explained, this reflected a total lack of confidence in the fascist system of justice. Those wronged did not denounce injustices 'because denunciations are usually considered to be inspired by vendetta and the denouncer, perhaps an old fascist *squadrista*, would be called an anti-fascist—very useful in order to better punish him through some summary procedure of the Federal disciplinary commission, the workings of which enjoy no confidence, not only among those outside [the party] but among fascists as well'.[22] Evidently, where denunciations of abuse of power were concerned, you were damned if you did and damned if you did not.

As a consequence of so much resentment against the party, the provincial federations lost contact with the people they controlled. As we have seen, this tendency had been evident in some areas from the beginnings of the economic crisis. Loss of contact occurred in provinces where there were particularly marked contrasts between the *gerarchi,* in those where fascist energies were put almost entirely into conducting internal intrigues, and in those where abuse of position was obvious. As early as 1929 a report from Reggio Emilia made the point very forcibly: 'Depression and disorganization in the fascist camp increase the moral unease of the masses, who, in putting up with the critical economic and social conditions, no longer have the encouraging stimulus of the party'. The informer went on to announce that the 'spirit of Bolshevik revolt' had broken loose again; even worse, 'in Bibbiana we were forced to watch as the [fascist] hymn "Giovinezza", sung by the children from the elementary school, was greeted with jeers, as was the appearance in a film of His Excellency the Honourable Turati'. In the provincial capital people had turned against Fascism. The informer had been horrified to see that 'even in the city of Reggio Emilia the showing of films of fascist official ceremonies was received, not with applause, but with silence or with brief phrases of insufferance'. He concluded that it was the party which was simply not doing

[22] ACS, MI, DGPS, Polizia Politica, b. 109, 'Voci di trasformazione del Partito', Milan, 11 January 1937.

anything 'to ease unemployment and prevent this state of disgust and depression in the masses'.[23]

Throughout the 1930s informers and others sent in reports that testified to the problems provincial Fascism faced. Thus in Padua, which went through a serious crisis in early 1931, a special commissioner noted among the population '[g]eneral apathy about public affairs…Little passion in the faith—total disorganization'.[24] Intervention from Rome and a prompt rotation of officials would often restore the situation, at least for the time it took for factions to reorganize and re-emerge. This was what happened in Padua, but by 1934 it was again reported that '[t]he organizations are having a miserable time, with no enthusiasm; the better people—those who don't have particular interests to protect—take their distance and Fascism becomes simply an outward show'.[25] In Modena the *Cassa Provinciale di Assistenza Fascista*—the local body responsible for helping the poor and the unemployed—had debts of L.1,400,000, in part because L.500,000 had been spent on office furniture for the *fascio* and charged to the account of the *Cassa*. Unsurprisingly, morale was very low. The *fiduciario* wrote that 'it is necessary to restore the faith and the conviction of the enrolled, who have been shaken by the exhibitionism and self-interest of a few'.[26]

In Naples, in March 1934, a speech by Mussolini was broadcast through loud-speakers in various points of the city but found few listeners. In the magnificent main arcade, Galleria Umberto 1, there were gathered 'around a hundred apathetic and curious people, much the same in front of the *palazzo del Governo* in Piazza Plebiscito'. The informer was clear about the cause of the apathy and about its extent:

> As I am bound to do, I bring to your attention this worrying phenomenon of apathy and absenteeism on the part of the population when faced with the most brilliant and imposing expressions of the Regime. The absenteeism is all the more dangerous and worthy of the serious attention of the responsible authorities if you consider that not even the commanding phrases of the *duce* shake the people, galvanizing them heart and soul as in the past. I have the precise and frightening impression that the depression of the people faced with dramatic material difficulties has reached a critical level, reducing any capacity for resistance or reaction and producing, in the passionate and extremely sensitive Neapolitan, a spiritual attitude of cold Muslim fatalism—hostile and suspicious.[27]

In later years, as the 1930s progressed, the reports of public disillusion rose. Economic hardship and high levels of unemployment in many places increased the expectations placed on local officials and made the corruption, inefficiency, and factionalism of the provincial federations all the more intolerable. Even at the time of the Ethiopian war, popular attention seemed to be directed more towards local

---

[23] ACS, PNF, SPEP, b. 18, Reggio Emilia, report on the political situation in Reggio Emilia, undated, but early 1929.

[24] ACS, Ibid., 'PNF Padua. Rapporto sulla situazione fascista in Padova', 27 March 1931.

[25] Ibid., 11 March 1934.

[26] ACS, PNF, SPEP, b. 8, Modena, report on situation in province, March 1931.

[27] ACS, Ibid., b. 9, Naples, informer, 20 March 1934.

questions, in particular unemployment and high prices, than to those related to the acquisition of empire. The most common reference to the conflict relates to the problems of choosing those who were to go to work as labourers in Africa from among the mass of unemployed.[28] From Naples in September 1936 (shortly after the victory) it was said that 'people often talk about hunger, about unemployment, about the unfair distribution of welfare. This population openly attacks the institutions and the leaders'.[29] A report from Modena for the same month complained that 'the population of the province of Modena, and in particular that of the provincial capital, went in very small numbers to the public squares to hear the broadcast of the speech of the *duce* in Avellino'.[30] The same lack of enthusiasm was reported from Padua in 1937: 'On the occasion of the speech of the *duce* at Tripoli loudspeakers were installed in the squares of the fruit and vegetable markets, but— as usual—they spoke to the wind'.[31] Again from Padua a local fascist (whom we have met before), the ex-*squadrista* and former night-watchman Ferdinando Baseggio, wrote to Starace to tell him that '[t]he masses are desperate because of hardships... and they assign all the blame for the present situation in the province to the local *gerarchi*'.[32]

Soldiers who returned from Africa to face further unemployment constituted a common difficulty in the later 1930s. The demobilized from Spain only added to the problem. 'They only remember us when they need cannon fodder,' complained one group of returnees to Piacenza, continuing, 'when Africa finished we interrupted misery and unemployment with the story of Spain... all for a stale crust of bread'.[33] In Naples the soldiers argued that the priorities of the fascist movement should be directed towards poor Italians rather than towards 'civilizing' the Ethiopians: 'First redeem the Neapolitans, then the blacks. Naples is below the Negroes, the Chinese, the whole world'.[34]

A further factor in determining popular disaffection with the regime was the way in which fascist officials treated ordinary people. The extension of the state and *parastato* bureaucracy under the regime ensured that most people found that they had to visit offices and talk to officials, fill in forms, make applications, and so on. From many reports it appears that fascist bureaucracy was anything but user-friendly. People complained that they had to sit in waiting rooms for interminable periods while they watched the friends, girlfriends, and supporters of the particular

---

[28] Even here there were accusations of corruption. The *federale* of Pescara was accused in an anonymous letter of asking for payment from the unemployed workers who were selected: 'In the Ethiopian war he sent to Africa those who paid him'. ACS, Ibid., b. 14, Pescara, undated to party secretary Muti.

[29] ACS, Ibid., b. 9, Naples, 1 September 1936.

[30] ACS, Ibid., b. 8, Modena, 15 September 1936. One of Starace's injunctions was that it was obligatory to write the word '*duce*' in capital letters. Pronouns referring to HIM also had to be capitalized.

[31] ACS, Ibid., b. 11, Padua, 20 March 1937.

[32] ACS, Ibid., Baseggio to Starace, 2 June 1938, in which he advises the PNF leader against organizing a visit by Mussolini to Padua: 'it would mean HE would appear in a bad light'.

[33] ACS, PNF, SPEP, b. 14, Piacenza, 13 September 1937.

[34] ACS, Ibid., b. 9, Naples, letter from 'a numerous group of soldiers returned from Africa', August 1941.

official jump the queue and pass in front of them. Often they were treated with disdain: 'for example, anyone who has to go the *Federazione dell'Urbe* [Rome] or to certain local district offices gets the precise sensation of being a total nobody in comparison with the first usher he meets...A better way of alienating people would be difficult to find. The lower the level of the clerks, the ruder they are and the more they give themselves airs'. The informer who wrote this repeated that these attitudes were 'not a good way to get the sympathy of the people'. The exaggerated hostility of the bureaucrats always seemed to presage a bad outcome: 'God help you if you say a word more than is necessary. You are immediately classified as an enemy of the Fatherland by threatening eyes which assure you...of disastrous consequences'. In the opinion of the informer, educated people might support such behaviour, but others could not but be adversely impressed—particularly (and this was a revealing phrase) 'the great mass of ordinary people who unfortunately live largely or almost exclusively in terms of what affects and interests them immediately'.[35]

There was confirmation of this picture later, in a report of August 1939, in which an informer writing from Genoa recounted what ordinary people were saying about fascist officials:

> The Regime—Fascism—has a high percentage of people employed in the ministries, in the unions, in the federations, who, for their very obvious lack of education, do not do their jobs, provoking a great variety of criticisms, complaints and unfavourable comments even among the most humble and modest citizens who have to—unfortunately—come into contact with them in order to protect their interests. The lamentable example provided leaves a lot of people cold and unreceptive towards the Regime and fascist support is weakened and begins to collapse.[36]

In a personal diary a veteran militiaman gave an even more dramatic description of the division between people and officialdom, asserting that 'the Party at present is behaving like the foreign conquerors used to behave towards the Italian people'.[37]

A particular place of honour in this tale of disaffection has to be reserved for the fascist militia—the MVSN. People often failed to react to fascist arrogance because of the fear of beatings and the local perpetrators of violence were frequently members of the militia. Set up, as we have seen, in 1923 in the attempt to channel the violence and intemperance of the blackshirt squads into a formal and disciplined military organization, the MVSN seems to have distinguished itself throughout the *ventennio* for indiscipline and petty abuses of authority. Ordinary people were unsure about what the precise powers of the *militi* really were, a fact that opened the door to invention. Prefects were compelled to report on situations in which former blackshirts had taken advantage of their militia uniforms to extort money from people, demand privileged treatment (non-payment of bills in restaurants was a favourite), or threaten reprisals for any hint of opposition. Allegations, often substantiated by subsequent investi-

---

[35] ACS, MI, DGPS, Polizia Politica, b. 109, 8 January 1937.
[36] ACS, DGPS, Polizia Politica, Materia (1927–44), b. 220, 12 August 1939.
[37] ADN, Paolino Ferrari, DG/89, end-December 1938.

gation, spoke of gratuitous violence, drunkenness, rowdy behaviour, theft, extortion, confidence tricks, and occasional cases of murder and rape. Much of this illegal activity reflected the unhappy situation of parallel competencies of state and party. Militia abuses sprang from a presumed right on the part of those who had 'made the revolution' in 1922 to continue to command and to refuse recognition to the ultimate authority of the state. In report after report prefects pointed out that the activities of the MVSN were extremely vexatious for the local population, who were always terribly aware that the fascist militiamen considered themselves beyond the law and acted in the expectation of impunity.[38] People had little faith in the capacity or the will of the state to control such behaviour.

By the end of the 1930s and before Italy joined the European war, the reports of disaffection become ever more common. Unemployment remained high and the complaints about shortages, rising prices, and new taxes increased continually. A generalized atmosphere of depression seems to have pertained. That 'Muslim fatalism' noted in Naples in 1934 seems to have become widespread. Thus a *fiduciario* in Padua wrote in 1937 about the arrival home of a group of soldiers from Africa: 'the company marched through the town amid general indifference', while a month later he reported that 'the demonstration for 23 March took place amid general indifference, without any enthusiasm. The procession seemed like a funeral'.[39] A note from Vicenza in 1938 spoke of a Fascism which had exhausted its energies. 'The general impression is that the population is tired, that it is afraid of war and of economic collapse... The fascists are tired of the formalities of uniforms, of the continous roll-calls, which they see as impositions'.[40] Bodies were on the parade ground, but minds were elsewhere.

On 21 April 1938 came the news that 'in Padua the demonstrations took place among generalized indifference—as usual'.[41] In Piacenza an informer observed, in October 1939, that 'a critical attitude towards the Regime is more than ever evident' and that 'recently the button-hole badge of the PNF has disappeared from the lapels of many members',[42] while by November 1939 it was said that 'there is little enthusiasm in the ranks of the old Blackshirts or of the squads; they make criticisms and begin arguments which are certainly not beneficial to the prestige of the party'.[43] From Pavia in late 1939 came the news that 'to talk of enthusiasm today is a nonsense', with there being little chance of regaining lost ground because party and people could no longer speak to each other: 'one has the impression that between speakers and masses there is no longer even the link of a common language'.[44] A fascist inspector sent to examine the situation in Modena in early 1940 found that '[t]he dominant aspect of the fascist situation in Modena and province is that of a diffuse sense of unease and coolness and, in some quarters, a real hostility

---

[38] Numerous references to criminal activity are to be found in ACS, MI, DGPS, AGR, PS, b. 379, 1930–31.

[39] ACS, PNF, SPEP, b. 11, Padua, 17 February 1937 and 25 March 1937.

[40] ACS, Ibid., 'Vicenza: Spirito Pubblico', 21 December 1938.

[41] Ibid., 23 April 1938.   [42] ACS, PNF, SPEP, b. 14, Piacenza, 18 October 1939.

[43] ACS, Ibid., 22 November 1939.   [44] ACS, Ibid., b. 13, 20 December 1939.

and lack of confidence in the current leaders'.[45] A further report spoke of 'the complete absenteeism of the population'.[46] Similarly, in April 1940 an informant in Trento deplored the fact that the various local commemorations of the foundation of Fascism had been marked by 'complete absenteeism' and 'absolute indifference' of both fascists and population. In Reggio Calabria in 1940 a fascist inspector complained that '[t]he great mass of the inhabitants are a long way away from the party'.[47] The view from Rome provided by one informer in January 1940 summed it all up: 'Unfortunately in the periphery…the misdeeds of this or that *gerarca* have had a profound influence on the moral unease that weighs on the fascist masses'.[48]

All in all, the impression that emerges from a study of the local federations in the late 1930s and in 1940–41 is not exactly that of perfectly functioning organizations, efficiently carrying out at a local level the orders of central government, creating and cultivating consensus, and directing the next generation towards the future fascist paradise of the new Italy. This is not to deny that the party was undoubtedly extremely active in many places; the capillary organizations were involving a lot of people and, in one way or another, the regime had entered into the lives of ordinary people in a very novel way. But expansion of activity does not seem to have been matched by an increase in popular enthusiasm for the regime nor by a popular understanding and appreciation of the objectives of the regime. On the contrary, the continuous reports of apathy, indifference, and exhaustion among the population suggest that, in as far as any genuine mobilization of the population was concerned, the federations were failing in their principal task. What was happening was not, on the whole, related to a recrudescence of anti-fascism; it was much more a question of simple popular apathy. The public image of the local *gerarchi* was such that people found little to stimulate them and much to repel them. In the absence of any prospect of change, a widespread reaction seems to have been simply to go through the motions, as required, and then to turn off.

This picture of rejection of the message of the party is confirmed by Renzo De Felice, who identified a (much qualified) mass consensus for Fascism in the early 1930s, but had no difficulty in writing of a 'pyschological detachment from the Regime' in relation to the later 1930s. Such detachment, he wrote, worked to produce the state of apathy noted by all, 'an almost general repugnance for politics as such', in no way confined exclusively to the popular classes.[49] It was the revulsion of the worker, never a friend of Fascism, and ever less so in a period of rising prices and increased taxes, but it was also 'a strong and widely diffused decline in consensus' among the urban bourgeoisie.[50] De Felice highlighted the 'uneasiness and discontent of the productive bourgeoisie' and the 'black pessimism' of the financial

[45] ACS, Ibid., b. 8, Modena, report of inspectors, undated but January 1940.
[46] ACS, Ibid., 'Situazione politica della provincia di Modena', 16 January 1940.
[47] ACS, PNF, SPEP, b. 17, Reggio Calabria, 27 May 1940.
[48] ACS, MI, DGPS, Polizia Politica, Materia, b. 219, 12 January 1940.
[49] De Felice, *Mussolini il duce*, vol. 2, *Lo stato totalitario*, Turin, Einaudi, 1981, 221.
[50] Ibid., 187.

circles of Milan, Turin, Genoa, and Florence as they struggled to deal with the consequences of party bureaucracy.[51]

Such a situation—'a general repugnance for politics as such'—was little short of disastrous for a movement which aimed at creating a substantial sense of identity between population and regime, in which the population would recognize itself in the objectives of the regime and identify with the equation of Fascism and the nation.

8.2. A SECOND GENERATION?

It is important to note that this disaffection even involved the young. Youth was one of the keywords of Fascism; the projection of the young towards the fascist future constituted one of the main themes of fascist propaganda. Emphasis on sport and on physical fitness reiterated this theme in continuation, as did the introduction in 1934 of the annual fascist *Littoriali*, where promising students from across the nation met to discuss fascist doctrine, compete in their expositions of literary and philosophical themes, and win prizes for their efforts. The privileged position accorded to some young people reflected the fact that it was especially important for the regime to generate a second generation of convinced young fascists, willing and able to inherit power from those of the 'first hour' when the moment for succession arrived.[52] Those born between 1910 and 1920 were the principal target here. They formed a generation that, because it had grown up under Fascism and had no direct experience of alternative forms of politics, should in theory have been most readily convinced by fascist indoctrination.[53]

Many undoubtedly were so convinced. They took the world as they found it and Fascism seemed part of the natural order of things. Some would move fairly automatically through the *Balilla* and the *Avanguardisti* organizations to the fascist *leva* without asking too many questions. However, there is evidence to suggest that the conversion of this generation was not total. And here again the party had its share of responsibility. In October 1937 all youth organizations (including the ONB, removed from the control of the Ministry of Education) had been placed under the direction of the PNF, creating the *Gioventù italiana del Littorio* (GIL). Only the GUF remained autonomous of the GIL, although also under the control of the party. The intention was without doubt that of permitting the party—the 'Great Pedagogue'—to better concentrate its attention on the kind of indoctrination that would produce a new generation of committed fascists. This role was made explicit

[51] Ibid., 188, quoting an informer.

[52] Patrizia Dogliani, *Storia dei giovani*, Milan, Bruno Mondadori, 2003, Chapter 4. It was, of course, significant that the new cohort of young people had not been formed around the experience of *squadrismo*.

[53] On school and university education under Fascism, see Gabriele Turi and Simonetta Soldani (eds), *Fare gli italiani. Scuola e cultura nell'Italia contemporanea*, Bologna, Il Mulino, 1993; Nemo Villeggia, *La scuola per la classe dirigente. Vita quotidiana e prassi educative nei licei durante il Fascismo*, Milan, Unicopli, 2007.

in Article 3 of the new 1938 party Statute, which stated that the function of the party was above all 'the political education of the Italians'.[54]

Membership of the GIL became obligatory for all young people in education in February 1939 and, in terms of numbers, the organization was very impressive. It was also massively financed. But the degree to which the reorganization of the youth movements saw any new stimulus to Fascism is to be doubted. Depending very much on social class, which determined the age at which they left school and, therefore, critically, the amount of time they were exposed to fascist education, most young people seem to have had only limited interest in the fascist movement or to have had an attitude determined by either conformism or opportunism. An intercepted telephone conversation in October 1937 revealed a dramatic situation in Turin: 'The young fascists are not going to the assemblies. Yesterday evening there was only one person from your Centurion and, together with the Commander, that made two. There were twelve from my Centurion. It's just the lists that are full of people enrolled, but the truth is that the young people don't go any longer to the Groups'.[55] In June of the same year a report from Turin had suggested a state of affairs such as to justify a large '*Attenzione!*' scrawled across the page by Starace:

> In student circles scepticism and cynicism are common among the young people, together with a criticism destructive of moral and social values and a very marked form of aversion for Fascism. I had confirmation of this talking to recent graduates, among whom the mood is more widespread than one would think, and it is difficult to explain the origin of this state of mind—absolutely inexplicable in young people brought up totally under the fascist regime and in an atmosphere which ought to be permeated by very different ideas and principles.[56]

In July 1937 an obviously attentive informer in Genoa wrote a lengthy analysis of the problem. Reporting the words of an acquaintance—an educated man in his late twenties—on the question of the formation of a fascist mentality among the young, the informer relayed a pessimistic message: 'I have the impression that young people today (not excluding myself) are not very serious and that the principles they profess are more for opportunism than for anything else. I don't discern deep and rooted convictions and that is reflected in the area of politics'. The agent felt obliged to add his own gloss on the situation, confirming the opinion of his acquaintance: 'We are talking about young people brought up, growing up, educated in full Fascist Regime. The baggage of demo-liberal idealism (not to say worse) that these young people carry around with them is incredible'.[57]

Little more than a year later, another informer, writing from *fascistissima* Florence, commented on the same phenomenon:

---

[54] Canepa, *PNF*, 119. According to Bottai (*Vent'anni e un giorno*, 129) Mussolini had decided on this role for the PNF at least from late 1936: 'The party is trying to do too much. The party should only look after the political education of the Italian people'.

[55] ACS, PNF, SPEP, b. 25, Turin, 2 October 1937.

[56] ACS, Ibid., 22 June 1937.

[57] ACS, MI, DGPS, Polizia Politica, b. 109, 29 July 1937.

…what do modern young people think about Fascism? It would not make sense to maintain that today's youth remains totally extraneous to a system that goes from public education to the facts of everyday life. Yet it remains undeniable that a good part of these young people, as soon as they grow up, are no longer fascist, in the sense that they betray ideas, intentions, critical positions, etc that are not exactly in harmony with the principles and dictates of Fascism.[58]

The causes of this disaffection he found in the fact that the young people had no respect at all for eminent fascist leaders: 'they are all illustrious nobodies, for whom they have no respect. As far as the local leaders are concerned, they are all "turnip heads", at whom discontent is directed and on whom they can put all the blame'. This was a clear statement of cause and effect; where the party was not working well, the GIL would not work well. Another informer's report—this time for 1939—repeated the picture of disaffection: '…in Florence a large part of the young people are very cool towards Fascism, which testifies in turn to the mood that exists within the families'.[59] Despite the fact that, at the formal level, all young people had to enrol in the GIL, a survey carried out by the PNF in May 1939 discovered that about half of the youth of Italy had managed to remain outside the ranks of any fascist organization.[60]

In respect of the young, pessimism was the order of the day for informers. An agent complained that the student demonstrations organized by the party in Vicenza, Venice, and Padua in late 1938 to protest against French diplomatic moves had been marred by infantile behaviour. The demonstrations 'were characterized more by the usual student attitude (on the best hypothesis) than by the recognition of our arguments against France'.[61] In late 1940 it was reported from Reggio Emilia that 'the GIL…today has almost hit rock bottom',[62] while a memo of the same period related that:

[a] very worrying situation, from the point of view of the Party, has been noted in the province of Modena and particularly in the city. A complete detachment between the life of the city and the province and all that concerns the life of the party. The leaders work in a vacuum, they don't find any longer (or almost any longer) the support of the masses; even the mass of young people in Modena live detached from the Party, full of scepticism and indifference.[63]

At Schio (near Vicenza), in 1940, almost no one turned up to commemorate 23 March. The youth groups, who were 'forced to participate', disrupted the whole proceedings. They 'kept on disturbing the speaker with laughter, smoking and getting up to other things, all a clear indication of their total spiritual absence'.[64] The *federale* of Reggio Calabria wrote of the 'complete disorientation of the student masses'.[65] If any-

---

[58] ACS, ibid., 'La gioventù e il Fascismo', 17 November 1938.
[59] ACS, DGPS, Polizia Politica, Materia (1927–44), b. 220, 22 May 1939.
[60] Survey quoted in Germino, *Fascist Party*, 73.
[61] ACS, PNF, SPEP, b. 11, Padua, 21 December 1938.
[62] ACS, Ibid., b. 18, Reggio Emilia, Report signed Mancini, 12 December 1940.
[63] ACS, Ibid., b. 8, Modena, Pro-memoria, undated but either 1939 or 1940.
[64] ACS, MI, DGPS, Polizia Politica, Materia, b. 219, 1 May 1940.
[65] ACS, PNF, SPEP, b. 17, Reggio Calabria, Quarantotto to Muti, 27 May 1940.

thing, matters in Piacenza seem to have been even worse. A report of May 1940 on 'Premilitary Instruction', which all young people had to undergo, informed Rome that:

> [i]nstruction is carried out in the context of complete moral and political disorienta-
> tion, both on the part of the federal command and on that of the recruits... the lack
> of discipline of the recruits is shown by the fact that they turn up every Saturday for
> instruction either because they have been threatened with disciplinary measures or
> because of a resigned acceptance of the fact that, if they didn't, they would be
> denounced to the Military Authorities for habitual and unjustified absence. The young
> people show themselves to be without enthusiasm and unprepared for the duties and
> responsibilities that premilitary training requires of them. They don't even know the
> moral reasons that justify the organization of armed preparation of the *Gioventù del
> Littorio*.[66]

Tracy Koon, who pioneered the study of the second generation during the 1980s, had few doubts about the results of fascist efforts. She wrote: 'After twenty years a new political elite trained under Fascism to assume the responsibilities of command should have been stepping onto center stage. But that second generation never materialized. The Fascist regime failed to produce an army of young Italians loyal to, and prepared to fight for, the *duce* and the Party.'[67] In support of this affirmation can be adduced the fact that Adelchi Serena, when general secretary of the PNF in 1941, directed much of his attention towards young people, convinced—as many before him—that the young constituted the leaders of the future, but also aware that it was necessary, as Emilio Gentile has put it, to combat 'the tendency, which appeared ever more diffused among the majority of the young people, to lose interest in the life of the party and abandon its activities'.[68] An interesting insight into this situation is provided by the diary of a 16-year-old girl, at school in Siena in 1940, when she writes, reflecting on her education, '...the ideals with which they have filled our heads in these years are only smoke. In school they teach fascist culture as if it were a religion and we recognize the total falsity of this identification'.[69]

A partial exception to this picture is provided by the *guffini*—the members of the fascist university organization, the GUF, and, clearly, a small, if influential, minority among Italian youth. Recent studies have rightly stressed the degree to which fascist ideology influenced these young people. Many of the members of the GUF would have come from the urban *licei*, where fascist ideals and values do seem to have been communicated effectively to a relatively

---

[66] ACS, Ibid., b. 14, Piacenza, 1 May 1940.

[67] Tracy Koon, *Believe, Obey, Fight. Political Socialization of Youth in Fascist Italy 1922–43*, Chapel Hill, University of North Carolina, 1985, 250.

[68] Gentile, *La via italiana*, 248. The problem was not new. It is worth recording, in this context, the report of the general secretary of the GUF, Carlo Sforza, on the 'fascistization' of the young, presented to Mussolini in July 1931. Sforza wrote that university students demonstrated 'a lively sense of independence in respect of the Party, and an even more lively impatience with hierarchical and disciplinary controls': Aquarone, *L'Organizzazione*, Appendix 49, 516.

[69] ADN, Bruna Talluri, DP/Adn2, 2 March 1940.

privileged bourgeois elite among Italian youth.[70] The regime had 'myths' and ideals that seemed to give identity and purpose in life to many of them.[71] The *guffini*, as middle class students, were less exposed than others to economic crisis, but even so, there were advantages to be gained from joining the groups. Membership of the GUF offered benefits in both the long and the short term— cheap cinema tickets, the possibility of foreign travel, a reduction in the period of military conscription being among the latter, and, of course, in pride of place among the former, the prospect of a career in one of the many fascist organizations.[72]

Although critics have rightly questioned the proposition put forward after the war by certain of the protagonists themselves, that their activities, often implicitly critical of the regime, really constituted a form of hidden anti-fascism,[73] there is no question that these young people distinguished themselves during the closing years of the 1930s by their calls for a better, reformed Fascism—a position that was, in itself, a very powerful indictment of 'real existing Fascism'.[74] For many of these students it would be the war rather than the problems of the late 1930s that would provoke, first, doubts about Fascism and then rejection of the movement.[75] It has to be said, however, that before this separation occurred those *guffini* who did find jobs within the party administrative structure during the later 1930s and during the war itself do not seem to have left a significant mark on the functioning of the PNF. Following the logic of the regime, they had been trained as administrators rather than politicians and, in the main, they appear to have behaved as just that, often falling foul of the various traps which provincial Fascism set for them.[76]

---

[70] Testimonies to this effect are numerous. See, for example, Eugenio Scalfari, *L' uomo che non credeva in Dio*, Turin, Einaudi, 2010.

[71] Luca La Rovere, *Storia dei GUF*, Turin, Bollati Boringhieri, 2003; Simone Duranti, *Lo spirito gregario*, Rome, Donzelli, 2008. See also Simona Salustri, *La nuova guardia. Gli universitari bolognesi fra le due guerre (1919–1943)*, Bologna, Clueb, 2009.

[72] Bosworth, *Mussolini's Italy*, 435.

[73] Ruggiero Zangrandi, *Il lungo viaggio attraverso il Fascismo. Contributo alla storia di una generazione*, Milan, Feltrinelli, 1962.

[74] Note the testimony of Vito Panunzio, son of the prominent pro-fascist journalist Sergio, who was a young man in 1940 and very active in the GUF. He confirms that many of the *guffini* worked for the realization of a 'true' Fascism, rather than for the overthrow of the regime, but warns against 'a major error of perspective: university students at that time, in Italy, were only a few thousand...For this reason, to identify the youth of Italy in this period and try to understand them on the basis of the students of the GUF and the *Littoriali* would be absolutely mistaken, as well as improper': V. Panunzio, *Il 'secondo Fascismo' 1936–1943. La reazione della giovane generazione alla crisi del movimento e del regime*, Milan, Mursia, 1988, 165.

[75] Two examples of this separation from Fascism are provided by the figures of Luigi Meneghello, who describes his experience in *I piccoli maestri* (Milan, Rizzoli, 1976) and Giaime Pintor, who explains his change of heart to his brother, Luigi, in his last letter, written before his death in September 1943 while seeking to cross the German lines to join the partisans (*Il sangue d'Europa*, ed. V. Gerratana, Turin, Einaudi, 1965).

[76] La Rovere speaks of a 'totalitarian conformism' as the prevailing attitude among a part of the *guffini*, by which he means that the students had little disposition to question the fundamental tenets of Fascism but were prepared to put a great deal of passion and energy in propagating their 'faith' in these ideas. Renzo De Felice's affirmation should be noted: 'the failure of Fascism was in its incapacity to give life to a new governing class': (*Intervista sul Fascismo*, 58).

8.3. FRICTION AMONG THE FAITHFUL

As much of the above suggests, the picture of party activity during most of the 1930s was far from what many fascists would have wished for their movement. If ordinary people, not directly involved in political activity or enrolled in the party, found much of what the party was doing questionable, to say the least, so too did many of the fascist faithful. Looking beyond the internal squabbles of the local movements, we can often discern a growing dissatisfaction among the rank and file of Fascism with many of the innovations to party life proposed from the centre.

An initial indication of evident discontent with the party we have already seen with the reports from the late 1920s that former supporters were taking their distance from the local fascist federations, thought to be too permeated by persistent squabbling and by careerism, or too much linked to particular groups and/or to particular economic interests. Many of those who voiced dissatisfaction belonged to the category of the excluded—no doubt unfairly excluded in their own eyes. Their complaints constituted opinion coming from within the immediate sphere of the movement and reflected the problems the fascist party had in consolidating after 1925, transforming itself from the expression of an unruly movement into the instrument of a more disciplined regime. Many early fascists, as we have seen, did not like the change of direction and retired to watch from a safe distance. Equally, it was only at this late stage that others became aware of what the fascist movement really represented and of what their position within the movement really was. In the province of Rovigo, for example, in 1926 fascists were abandoning the party because of the persistence of what was being called 'agrarian slavery' in the treatment of the landless labourers and because of the refusal of the local party sections to bring the landed proprietors and their industrialist allies to order.

The workings of the PNF in the 1930s were dominated by the figure of Achille Starace—a Pugliese who had been decorated for valour during the First World War. Starace's period as party secretary—from 1931 to late 1939—has become almost legendary, in a negative sense, because of measures and proposals that originated with him.[77] The cult of the *duce*, for example, if already developing from the late 1920s, was massively reinforced by Starace during the 1930s. Even Mussolini seems to have found some of the suggestions relating to reverence for the *duce* exaggerated and bordering on the ridiculous.

The cult of the *duce* was just a part of a very much wider attention to ritual that Starace imposed on the movement, often proposing activities and observances that were patently absurd or that seemed to run against the common sense of most of the movement's supporters. To give one example, the requirement made of *gerarchi* to exhibit themselves in gymnastic demonstrations was clearly going to provoke problems among a middle-aged and often very unfit ruling group. Long lunches

---

[77] For a brief summary of Starace's career, see Sandro Setta, 'Achille Starace', in F. Cordova, *Uomini e volte del Fascismo*, Rome, Bulzoni, 1980, 445–72.

had their cost. The sight of paunchy men throwing themselves through flaming hoops was unlikely to impress anyone who had any sense of the ridiculous.

Starace's foolishness rapidly became proverbial and was the source of many jokes.[78] As one party informer reported, 'there are both fascists and non-fascists who, every time the Secretary General of the Party issues a communiqué, amuse each other with their comments and ridicule the decisions announced'.[79] Yet it would be unwise to write him off simply as a pretentious poseur—no more than a servile and obsequious lackey of the fascist dictator.[80] His contribution to the way in which Fascism developed in the 1930s should not be underrated. Starace understood the importance of ritual for a regime based on hierarchy and discipline and was responsible for many of the measures that moved Italy in the direction of a strictly regimented and militarized society. Alongside the ridiculous and the absurd there was also the reinforcement of regimented and ritualized activity, an extremely important aspect of the regime. The 'totalitarian phase' of Fascism, identified by many historians in the period following the Ethiopian war, owed much to him, particularly in the strengthening of the position of the PNF within the institutional structure of the fascist state. Capillary control was extended through a whole series of provisions and serious efforts were exerted to make basic changes in Italian customs and attitudes. If Fascism was about the saturation of space and time with fascist content, Starace was one of the people most responsible for attempting its realization.

A feature of the second half of the 1930s is the apparently growing dissatisfaction within the party itself. To some extent this was related to uncertainty about what the party represented. Perplexity in this regard had been evident even in the early 1930s, when membership had been opened again for a few months in 1932. Many found it difficult to work out whether it was a good idea to apply for membership or whether they could carry on as before, without the party card. Some were frightened of the consequences of a possible refusal. The quandary was increased by persistent rumours, reinforced by wishful thinking, that the party was to be disbanded, having served its purposes. These uncertainties persisted into later years, when membership was again reopened and more and more categories of employee were required to join the party as a condition of their employment. People began to ask what this compulsory membership implied. What was the party? Was it an active political force or was it a catch-all organization with little political content, a meal-ticket in hard times? Lack of adequate definition produced doubt and doubt produced indifference and disaffection.

An indication of a fairly generalized state of mind emerges from a detailed analysis of the situation of the party, made by a police informer from Rome in March 1937. Reacting to the praise that Starace had received from Mussolini in a recent

---

[78] 'Why does Starace's horse have three testicles?' [testicle = *coglione* = idiot] 'Two underneath and one on top.'

[79] ACS, MI, DGPS, Polizia Politica, b. 109, 7 May 1935.

[80] Starace may have been foolish but he was by no means innocuous. Insisting on going to fight in Ethiopia in 1935, he distinguished himself (according to Bottai) by personally shooting prisoners in the groin because he thought that a shot to the heart did not make them suffer enough before dying.

meeting of the *Gran Consiglio*, the informer pointed out that 'the efficiency of today's party, for which Starace has been commended, has become just conventional and should be doubted, in as far as everyone is obliged to join the Party and those who do not accept this condition do not find work'. The list the informer gave of those obliged to join was long and concerned a large number of people: 'All state employees, all those in the public and *parastato* administrations, all of those in the innumerable political and corporative agencies, have been forced to join the Party. Some to keep a job they already had, some to have the possibility of getting one'. It was not surprising, therefore, that enrolment in the party had increased, 'because they are compelled, not for a question of spontaneity'. Nor was an increase in numbers to be mistaken for increased efficiency. On the contrary, '[t]he efficiency of the party is, therefore, ephemeral, only apparent, because we should take into account not only the numbers of enrolled, but also their quality, and this is compromised and doubtful because many of them are there for convenience, for unwelcome expediency, and because they have been forced to join'.[81]

The unnecessary and pointless nature of much of what was required of party members was a constant theme of complaint reported by informers. Starace's decision to make the (itchy and uncomfortable) fascist uniform obligatory for public servants (on certain occasions) raised a sea of protest. The party card was already considered too expensive and an unjustified imposition (by 1938 it cost L.50); the uniform constituted a further vexation (depending on the cloth, it cost in between L.250 and L.400). Informer number 52 wrote in May 1936:

> the requirement of a fascist uniform has generated a great deal of disapproval among many. Unemployed or partially unemployed professional people, who have a monthly salary of around 500 lire, lawyers, engineers, who do not get much more, are worried about the obligation to buy a uniform, which, for their very limited means, represents a considerable expense, and they don't know what to do to put together the money necessary—the more so because they are already a bit short of civilian clothes and should think about these first.[82]

Problems did not end with the uniform, however; indeed, the uniform was only the beginning. A further, and often repeated, source of complaint were the endless parades and roll-calls. Starace's management of the party, in particular his insistence on a high level of activity, often translated itself into what looked to almost everyone like activity for activity's sake. People resented what seemed to them to be a waste of time. A report from Rome, of October 1937, made the point in a very straightforward fashion: 'People complain about the fact that the Party exploits— too freely—the enrolled, without any respect for their work, for their rest, or for their freedom'. The problem, the informer stated, was that '[n]ot a week passes without the fascists, for one reason or another, and often for unimportant reasons, being convoked, assembled or invited to go to the local group'. Warming to his

---

[81] ACS, MI, DGPS, Polizia Politica, b. 109, 13 March 1937.

[82] ACS, Ibid., 5 May 1936; also transcript of intercepted telephone conversation in Turin: 'I would buy one [a uniform] if I had the money, but I can't even afford a civilian suit'; ACS, PNF, SPEP, b. 25, Turin, 13 October 1936.

theme, he went on, 'there have been ten or even more calls in one month, some-thing that annoys and creates bad feeling, because these calls represent a loss of time, often a lot of time, and a loss of freedom. Thus weariness leads in many cases to alienation and absenteeism'.[83] Similar sentiments were reproduced in Vicenza in 1938, where it was reported that 'the fascists are tired of the formality of uniforms, of the continuous roll-calls, which they consider an imposition'.[84] Fascism, with its clear certainties, had been supposed to make life simpler. Instead it was making life far more complicated.

Clearly the charm of novelty, if there had been any, had worn off. Continual requests that could not be refused without serious consequences produced a pres-sure on people that was telling in the long run. Starace seems to have been a master of the minor irritant, intruding on people's time, on their wallets, on their status, in such a way as to create a general climate of popular discontent among the rank and file of the party. Many of his ideas were badly thought-through. For example, his decision, in May 1936, to require all able-bodied fascists to enrol in the MVSN met general resistance. For many it was 'one thing more, unnecessary' and contra-dicted the idea that the MVSN was a voluntary organization.[85] Demobilized sol-diers, especially officers, found the requirement particularly irksome. As an informer noted, putting his finger on a particularly sensitive issue, the army offic-ers had sworn an oath of loyalty to the King, whereas members of the MVSN swore to Mussolini: 'the oath of loyalty is fundamentally different in both form and substance'. It would be difficult for them to work together. Moreover, the informer went on, there was the question of rank, with former army officers risk-ing finding themselves serving in the MVSN as inferiors to those who had no real training. He made his point very directly, perhaps saying more than he should have:

> ...up to the present the Militia has accepted in its ranks people of any morality, of any kind—even non-fascists and those not enrolled in the party—and has not taken into any account their level of education and their military rank but has accorded ranks and commands on the basis of political influence, strength of appetite, and individual ambition—which has seen corporals become Generals...

Experienced soldiers were not going to join an organization run like this, if they could avoid it: 'they have no desire to mix in with the varied elements which go to make up the Militia and therefore have no intention of conforming to the invita-tion of the Directorate of the Party'. Some, however, could not avoid doing so. The informer registered the fact that 'the state and *parastato* employees cannot escape this provision and say that it puts on their shoulders yet another load, new obliga-tions, a new form of slavery, as if those they already have were not enough'.[86] This was the enthusiasm Starace was so proud of having generated.

---

[83] ACS, MI, DGPS, Polizia Politica, b. 109, 13 October 1937.
[84] ACS, PNF, SPEP, b. 11, Padua, 'Vicenza: Spirito Pubblico', 21 December 1938.
[85] Uncertainty about the exact place and role of the MVSN in the scheme of things was still being voiced in 1939; see S. Foderaro, *La Milizia Volontaria e le sue specialità*, Padua, Cedam, 1939.
[86] ACS, MI, DGPS, Polizia Politica, b. 109, 24 May 1936.

Other measures aroused the same kind of opposition. The decision in 1937 to give the doormen of blocks of flats the role of fascist *fiduciari*—in other words, to turn the doormen into fascist spies—generated a great deal of adverse comment. Formally, the *portieri* were to act as the link between the party and the residents but few had any illusions about the real role intended for their doormen and about the fact that they—the residents—were to become in some way subject to the control of such people. Repeating complaints he had heard, one informer wrote that 'fascists are now dependent on their doormen and must obey a doorman. This is the system—a system which hardly raises the tone of the party and very often offends the susceptibilities and the *amour propre* of the members'. As was evident, status was involved; it was almost a class issue. The same informer suggested that perhaps the party could do better: 'The doormen form the capillary network of the spies and informers of the *Fasci di Combattimento*, but above all the network of spies of the Party. It is obvious that, given the political functions of the Party, it could have been possible to choose people of a higher level and a little more elevated.' This kind of measure, he observed, was producing discontent and pushing people away from the party. After all, he concluded, 'no one takes pleasure from receiving orders from his doorman'.[87]

Similar reactions greeted the 1938 directive that required all taxi drivers, horse-drawn carriage drivers, domestic servants, and even street cleaners to kept their eyes and ears open and report anything suspicious to the authorities. Taxi drivers were to change itinerary and drive their clients direct to the nearest fascist headquarters if they overheard careless conversation in the back of the cab. Domestic servants were told to report to the local neighbourhood groups on what went on within their household, while street cleaners, being the first up in the morning, were to erase any anti-fascist slogans written on the walls and collect any leaflets criticizing the regime. These measures provoked generalized revulsion and protest, even among fascists: 'The impression among the public has been enormous. Everyone criticizes [the measures] severely, offended by this continually growing network of spies'.[88]

By the second half of the 1930s, the idea that the party was not fulfilling its intended function was widespread. Resentments were generated by the fact that membership was obligatory for a large number of people, yet membership itself brought more problems than privileges. As we have just seen, state employees—the group that should have been most favourable to Fascism—seem to have been particularly good at whinging but they knew that the party card was necessary in order to work. As one informer put it, '[t]oday, very decidedly, not being enrolled in the Party means not being able to find work'.[89] Another confirmed this, adding the inevitable reference to the family. The public employee who had had his party card withdrawn for disciplinary reasons 'cannot work any longer, he is sacked, and it can happen that he faces the spectre of hunger, especially if he has a family...'[90] As one fascist put it, the withdrawal of the *tessera* meant 'the withdrawal of bread'.[91]

---

[87] ACS, Ibid., 13 October 1937.   [88] ACS, Ibid., 11 February 1938.
[89] ACS, Ibid., 5 March 1938.   [90] ACS, Ibid., 15 October 1937.
[91] ADN, Paolino Ferrari, DG/89, 6 September 1939.

Yet the high cost of the party card and its associated obligations served to make it unattractive.

Even among the party faithful, therefore, there was the feeling that something had gone badly wrong.[92] The expansion in numbers of the party was not accompanied by any qualitative change in party activity. People could be mobilized— 'attendance at the Federation has almost the character of a plebiscite, but it does not represent consensus; attendance depends more on discipline than on persuasion or consensus'.[93] The problem was that all enthusiasm had disappeared: 'among the great majority of party members all "genuine, spontaneous" enthusiasm has vanished; the local clubs, which should serve to bring fascists together, are deserted...'[94] Several reports refer to the fact that people obeyed, but did not believe; the formation of a fascist mentality was simply not taking place. 'You can bet that if you were to ask ten educated Italians what the essence of Fascism is and what are its objectives, at least nine would find themselves in difficulty when replying and would give very different answers.' This situation had serious implications for the future of Fascism: 'when... faith is lacking how can we hope that the doctrine can survive long enough to renew the Nation?'[95] Ageing fascists complained about the decline of the movement: 'among old fascists there are complaints about the profound spiritual decline of the Party which—they say—is content with external manifestations, with assemblies, to which everyone goes complaining and moaning. Among the *gerarchi*, there is the mania of putting themselves on show...'[96]

Again and again informers, showing their concern about a system which was not working, returned to the question of a party based on obligation rather than conviction. 'Why did people go to the fascist events?', one informer asked.

> They go because they have to, because there is a check; the same can be said of the ceremonies, the parades, etc. They go because they are afraid of being suspended, not for the fact in itself, but because it will be reported in the newspaper and, since the reason for the measure will not be specified, it can give rise to serious and mistaken suppositions. This is the only reason for which the majority attend at all cost; if a concrete obligation did not exist, the presence at the public meetings would be limited to those who have medals to show off.

In any case, this particular informer observed, it was difficult to ask for anything more in Genoa, from where he was writing, where the condition of the party more than justified all the attitudes he had just cited. The *federale* was weak and ineffective and the *vice-federale*, 'crassly ignorant and... blown up and ridiculous as a turkey', was a despised 'semi-illiterate'. The cure the writer advocated was harsh, but he knew what it should be: 'A purge that begins with the *gerarchi* and proceeds

---

[92] See on this Colarizi, *L'Opinione*, 274–82.
[93] ACS, MI, DGPS, Polizia Politica, b. 109, 24 May 1936.
[94] Ibid.
[95] ACS, Ibid., 'Fascismo e Nazione', 27 July 1937.
[96] ACS, Ibid., 28 February 1938.

inexorably down to the last supporter is considered indispensable and unavoidable in order to ensure the vitality of the party...'[97]

This informer was not alone in his drastic proposals for reform. Other fascists thought that the real solution to problems was nothing less than the dissolution of the party, with local power reverting entirely to prefect and police, resolving in this way—hardly a fascist way—what many people thought was a pointless and damaging duplication of structures. Significantly, in respect of duplication, no one— inside the party or outside of it—any longer suggested that it was the prefect who should be suppressed in favour of the *federale*.

[97] ACS, Ibid., 14 November 1938.

9

The Crisis of the late 1930s and the 'Totalitarian Phase' of Fascism

The party was not unaware of the difficulties it was facing in the closing years of the 1930s. At the provincial level there was ample evidence of a rapidly growing popular impatience with the local federations and their leaders. Indeed, impatience is far too weak a word for what people were saying and thinking. How did the party react to discontent—and is there any evidence that it succeeded in regaining lost ground? The so-called 'totalitarian phase' of the regime—the years between the Ethiopian victory and the decision to enter the Second World War in June 1940—was, certainly, a response to disaffection, but it was also something more. It was an attempt to give greater definition to fascist objectives and to propel the nation more resolutely in the direction of the totalitarian state. The new urgency in implementation of policies carried with it a risk, however. It might possibly redress the situation and revive lost enthusiasms, but it might also have the reverse effect of accentuating problems already sufficiently serious.

9.1. POPULAR UNREST IN THE PRE-WAR YEARS

As was inevitable, the late 1930s were dominated by growing international tensions. Within Italy, Mussolini had exploited very ably the sanctions imposed by the League of Nations after the fascist aggression against Ethiopia, calling for greater efforts in the attempt to realize economic autarky. Levels of mobilizing rhetoric remained high. 'Dio stramaledica gli inglesi!' ['God extra-curse the English!'] was a catch-phrase that enjoyed a certain success in petit bourgeois circles.

Increased tensions were reflected in moves, after 1936, to generate a new dynamism among the fascists. The participation of an Italian contingent of 'volunteers' in the Spanish Civil War permitted a renewed insistence on anti-Bolshevik propaganda and measures such as the anti-bourgeois campaign and the introduction of the *passo romano* for the military (effectively, the goose step) were intended to stimulate a fresh sense of purpose among the fascist rank and file. The 1938 Racial Laws, by identifying the existence of an 'internal enemy' in the form of the Jews, are part of the same picture. And legislation concerning the corporations, the structure of the fascist unions, and the welfare and youth organizations were designed to increase the hold of Fascism on institutions and bring the population ever more tightly within the fascist net.

This 'totalitarian phase' of the regime undoubtedly injected a new sense of determination into the public image of the fascist movement. The increasing militarization of the population—particularly the urban population—gave a fresh impetus to fascist activity, now centred around empire and the prospect of European war. Whether this new phase really served to reinforce the regime is another question. The numbers enrolled in the many fascist organizations continued to rise, often to surprising heights, but, looking beyond simple numbers, the new impetus made further requirements of the party and new initiatives brought unanticipated problems with them. As we have already seen, the difficulty of finding jobs for the soldiers returning from both Ethiopia and Spain was a major preoccupation of the local federations of these years, in no way eased by the worsening economic situation. Basing themselves on recruitment promises, many of the demobilized men demanded not only the fascist card but also a secure job in the state bureaucracy—jobs for which many of them were totally unfitted.[1] Throughout this period, *federali* were repeatedly writing in to the central party administration explaining how many soldiers they had found jobs for and how many remained unemployed. The letters make it obvious that, in many cases, *federali* were exercising pressure on local employers in order to try to find a solution to the problem.

Other difficulties were centred around aspects of the so-called 'anti-bourgeois' campaign of the late 1930s—the attempt made to revive a sedentary regime through campaigns designed to change Italian habits and undermine traditional 'bourgeois' ways of thinking.[2] The comfortable people were to have life made less comfortable—the 'slipper wearers' were to be unslippered.[3] The 'unhygienic' handshake was to be replaced by the Roman salute. The introduction of the 'Voi' form of address in place of the traditional 'Lei' is a further case in point; the PNF became the vehicle for the transformation of something as fundamental as everyday language. This particular campaign seems, however, to have suffered the same fate as the *passo romano* in the public eye. The Roman salute and the goose step were considered absurd imitations of the Nazis,[4] and the 'Voi' a ridiculous and historically unjustified 'gallicism', which contributed nothing to the fascist cause. In Florence the 'Voi' was reported to be the subject of 'jokes, insults and irony' (students were referring to Galileo Galilei as Gal iVoi) and the informer—clearly himself opposed to the change—noted that 'when you hear two people use the "Voi" in public, you can be sure that, with only rare exceptions, they do it for a joke, with the intention of making the measure look

---

[1] One desperate *federale* wrote that, in his province, recruitment to the army had been carried out initially among criminal elements. As a consequence, on their return from Ethiopia, he was obliged to let these former criminals into the *fascio*, of which they now constituted around 50 per cent: ACS, MI, DGPS, Polizia Politica, b. 109, 28 February 1937.

[2] The campaign had little impact. At the popular level, many identified the 'bourgeoisie' with the fascist nomenclature: 'The present bourgeoisie is formed precisely by the fascist *Gerarchi* [who] love a comfortable, luxurious, and amorous life': ACS, PNF, SPEP, b. 25, 6 February 1940. See, besides the considerations of Renzo De Felice (*Mussolini il duce*, vol. 2, 93–100), Thomas Buzzegoli, *La polemica antiborghese nel fascismo (1937–1939)*, Rome, Aracne, 2007.

[3] One of the problems was that even fascists could not identify the target of the campaign. See the fascist journal *Gerarchia*, (1939, 17, 1), 51: 'Make it clear. Make it clear. Who is it that you want to attack? This is an objection you can hear repeated with regularity'.

[4] ACS, MI, DGPS, Polizia Politica, b. 109, 22 June 1938.

ridiculous. It's enough to listen to the way they emphasize the "Voi" to understand what they are doing'.[5] In Venice a fascist agent asked the gondoliers what they thought of the measure, receiving the answer, 'it's for the gentlemen, for the educated; the only language we use is the language our mothers taught us'.[6] More seriously from the point of view of the regime, a note from Genoa acknowledged that the 'Voi' was being used by the employees in public offices where it was obligatory 'but in private circles, and in private contacts, it is not observed'. Many were saying that they would never use it with such vehemence that—in the eyes of the informer—it represented a form of rebellion, 'a form of "I'm not obeying," apparently harmless, but worth watching'.[7] The party was much involved in all these campaigns—as a controlling mechanism of observance, but often also as the instigator of the proposed changes.

The Racial Laws provoked a more measured public response, at least to judge from the reports of the informers, who are largely silent on the issue. This relative silence, which presumably reflected the silence of those being watched by the informers, may have been determined by popular perplexity at the measures. People found themselves torn between the Church and the requirements of the regime—a regime perfectly capable of rewarding criticism with the use of one or more of the many repressive weapons it possessed.[8] Informers did note that, at the provincial level, priests were speaking out against the injustice of the laws: 'the clergy and the practising Catholics make clear that they deplore, as persecution, the measures aimed at the Jews...'[9] Many of the informers showed through their mode of expression that they were themselves anti-semitic, but they were forced to concede that where they had detected public reaction to the laws, it was, on the whole, negative. In Turin there were 'demonstrations of solidarity with those affected', indicating the population's rejection of the 'disgusting persecutions'.[10] Rome, which had a large Jewish population, was said to be generally and regrettably 'conditioned by an unrelenting compassion' for the Jews, with the Romans showing sympathy to those who had no fault except to be born Jewish and were, nonetheless, still 'children of God'.[11] Romans were quoted as saying that the Jews

[5] ACS, MI, DGPS, Polizia Politica, Materia (1927–44), b. 220, Florence, 8 July 1939.

[6] ACS, Ibid., b. 219, Venice, 3 November 1939.

[7] ACS, Ibid., b. 220, Genoa, 9 August 1939.

[8] For a comprehensive treatment of the issue, see Michele Sarfatti, *Gli ebrei nell'Italia fascista; vicende, identità, persecuzione,* Turin, Einaudi 2000 (trans. *The Jews in Mussolini's Italy: from Equality to Persecution,* Madison, University of Wisconsin Press, 2006). On the more general question of the penetration of an anti-semitic culture in this period, see Enzo Collotti, *Il fascismo e gli ebrei,* Rome & Bari, Laterza, 2006; also Francesco Germinario, *Fascismo e antisemitismo: Progetto razziale e ideologia totalitaria,* Rome & Bari, Laterza, 2010; Valeria Galimi, in *Storia della Shoah. La crisi europea, lo sterminio degli ebrei e la memoria* (eds Marina Cattaruzza, Marcello Flores, Simon Levis Sullam, Enzo Traverso), Milan, UTET, 2008, vol. 2. A recent contribution, based on a local study, is Carla Antonini, *Piacenza 1938–1945. Le leggi razziali,* Piacenza, ISREC, 2010. For an alternative view, see Alessandro Visani, 'The Jewish enemy. Fascism, the Vatican, and anti-Semitism on the seventieth anniversary of the 1938 race laws', (2009) 14(2) *Journal of Modern Italian Studies* 168.

[9] ACS, MI, DGPS, AGR, b. 7F, 1939, 15 November 1938.

[10] ACS, Ibid., Turin, undated 'Peste-Bruna', but another report from Turin maintained that 'in general people approve these radical solutions, many hope to profit from them...': ACS, PNF, SPEP, b. 25, Turin, 4 September 1938.

[11] ACS, MI, DGPS, Polizia Politica, b. 224, Rome, 21 May 1939.

were a lot better than many Christians and that their commercial acumen and honesty would be missed, particularly by the poor, to whom the Jewish shopkeepers had often given credit.[12] The injustice of the measures against those who had been perfectly acceptable to the regime until a few days before was widely noted. Apart from a few fascist hotheads, who saw the chance for a bit of action and daubed anti-semitic slogans on the walls in the ghetto, the mood in Rome seems to have been fairly unanimous in deprecating the initiative; 'I've heard murmurs in the chemist, in the markets, etc... Everyone said the Government was wrong, everyone said that this nastiness will soon be over.'[13]

Elsewhere there were similar reactions. In Turin students were forbidden to make a present of two books, purchased with a subscription among the students themselves, to Arnaldo Momigliano when he was forced to resign his chair because of the laws (ironically, the books ended up in the library of the GUF).[14] In Modena official anti-semitism provoked dismay even among the *squadristi*, because Duilio Sinigaglia, a Jew and one of the 'martyrs' of Modena *squadrismo*, was the hero and emblem of the local movement and members of his family were still prominent in its ranks.[15] In more general terms, many disliked the laws because they thought they perceived the long arm of Hitler in the background. In Turin wall writings appeared with a caricature of Hitler accompanied by the phrase 'Behold the Führer, *duce* of the *duce*',[16] while in Rome people were saying ironically, 'You know, we were better off under Mussolini'.[17]

Again, like the imposition of the 'Voi', as a mobilizing exercise the measures had little success, creating more perplexity than passion. In part this was due to the nature of the measures themselves, but in part it was also a consequence of the context of serious economic crisis in which the measures were launched. The overriding impression of the period 1937–40 is of a steadily deteriorating economic situation, which slowly but ineluctably became the principal concern of the majority of Italians. Furthermore, it was a mounting concern with an even more threatening backdrop—that of the prospect of war, with its attendant losses, hardships, and shortages. For many it began to look like hunger today and starvation tomorrow. Even the well-off were reported to be expressing their irritation with the government's preoccupation with questions—some of them totally insignificant—that had nothing to do with the major problems Italy was facing.

---

[12] ACS, MI, DGPS, AGR, b. 7F, 1939, Rome, 17 December 1939.

[13] ACS, Ibid., 18 November 1938. There were exceptions to a general rejection of the laws. In December 1938 an informer warned that there were 'insistent rumours' in Rome that Jewish shops were going to be looted and the synagogue burned down: Ibid., 12 December 1938. A further exception was provided by the fascist gymnasts of Rome who, passing the synagogue and seeing people coming out of the door, shouted 'Burn them': Ibid., 1 June 1939. On reactions to the laws see Alessandro Visani, 'Italian reactions to the racial laws of 1938 as seen through the classified files of the Ministry of Popular Culture', in (2006) 11(2) *Journal of Modern Italian Studies* 170.

[14] ACS, MI, DGPS, AGR, b. 7F, 1939, Turin, undated 'Peste-Bruna'. On the experience of another university, see Francesca Pelini and Ilaria Pavan, *La doppia epurazione. L'Università di Pisa e le leggi razziali tra guerra e dopoguerra*, Bologna, Il Mulino, 2009.

[15] ACS, MI, DGPS, AGR, b. 7F, Modena, 18 November 1938.

[16] ACS, Ibid., 1939, Turin, undated 'Peste-Bruna'.

[17] ACS, Ibid., Rome, 17 December 1939.

The wars the fascist regime had already fought—Ethiopia, Spain—had proved extremely expensive and, by 1938, had provoked inflation within the country, hitting wages and savings. At the same time sanctions and the campaign for autarky had disrupted the economy, limiting the availability of imported raw materials and distorting the priorities of production. In agriculture the official requisitioning of crops (the *ammassi*) was increasingly resisted by producers because the guaranteed prices were considered too low—much agricultural produce was being exported below cost to earn foreign exchange. By 1938 shortages of basic foodstuffs were being felt; coffee, sugar, oil were in short supply and the situation would worsen in 1939. Petrol was expensive and difficult to find. In the face of this, people hoarded when they could, but more often made sacrifices, improvised, and went without.[18] Public sector workers in Rome took their lengthy coffee breaks in coffee-less bars.

In some reports to Rome of early 1938, the ordinary people—'*il popolo*' as they were usually referred to, with a mixture of condescension and, increasingly, fear—were said to understand the need for belt-tightening, given the financial difficulties of the nation and the threat increasingly posed by the 'plutocracies', allegedly swimming in gold. Initially, in the first phase of shortages, this may well have been the case. However the mood began to change markedly in the closing months of 1938. In December of that year, an informer in Milan noted that 'it is beginning to get through that Fascism, as a constructive system, has not been a great success and that the gradual impoverishment of the country is not the result of a battle waged from abroad, but the inevitable consequence of a political system'.[19] By spring of 1939 the crisis had become acute. Both industrial workers and white-collar office workers complained that the much-trumpeted 10 per cent wage increases of March 1939 had been totally absorbed by rapidly rising rents and prices. Comments reported by a spy (overheard in a small restaurant in Rome) made the point: 'with what rents are, the cost of living, and everything else, not only is what a worker gets not enough but it would not be enough if they were to give him twice as much'. The question assumed political overtones immediately when the same speakers went on, 'since the world began I don't think any government has starved its own population in the way that is happening to us now with ours'.[20] In a Rome street another conversation included a similar opinion: 'No people in the whole world has been so deceived as ours; they keep on saying that they are giving us things, but this "give," when said by the government, means "take".' His companion agreed, vulgarly: '...if our local leaders say they want to give us something, they do so but always in that place and without spit...'[21] By June 1939, hardship, rather than the fascist campaign to conquer Albania (taking place at the same time), was on everyone's mind.

---

[18] The letter from the *federale* of Reggio Calabria to Starace in February 1939 is very telling: 'It's pointless for me to employ high-sounding phrases when, with the word "misery" I say everything'. Quoted in Cordova, *Calabrie*, 238.

[19] ACS, PNF, SPEP, b. 7, Milan, 20 December 1938; quoted in Colarizi, *L'Opinione*, 273.

[20] ACS, MI, DGPS, Polizia Politica, b. 217, Rome, 7 February 1939.

[21] ACS, Ibid., Rome, 25 May 1939.

A particular cause of anger was the decision to increase, from 1 May 1939, the contributions workers and employees had to make to the various union, welfare, and social insurance agencies—increases that, almost by themselves, cancelled out the pay rises of the previous month. Workers felt cheated—'a typically Italian trick', as they put it[22]—but, in a moment of severe difficulty, they were forced once again to see that they had no protection. 'Who are we supposed to turn to?' one group of unhappy Roman workers asked.[23] Here the lack of confidence in the fascist unions became evident. The unions had been useful to the party for controlling workers and bringing them under the net of Fascism, but had given little in return. Most workers found the unions a waste of time: 'There are innumerable workers who spontaneously give up their rights in order not to have to waste time with the union which, every time it gets to the crucial point, demonstrates that it has those grains of sand in the works which prevent any free and productive movement'. The same source—a fascist source—went on, 'there isn't a worker who doesn't look to the union as a convenient instrument of the employer class, backing up this suspicion from long and varied experience...'[24] The sentiment was echoed in the province of Bari, again from fascist sources: 'seventeen years of Fascism have gone by, fifteen since the creation of the corporative State, and still today there are many, too many [among the employers] who live and work as though nothing had happened'.[25]

This sense of impotence and frustration among workers was heightened by the fact that the final phase of peacetime fascist Italy appears to have been marked by an increase in police surveillance, which made it difficult for people to express their true feelings, even among themselves. The people who made the comments in the Rome *trattoria* cited above were immediately advised by a friend to stop talking in that way if they did not want to risk serious trouble. In Turin, in January 1938, a report commented on the fact that workers were whispering among themselves because they were 'afraid that indiscreet ears were listening'. The informer went on: 'Talking to the workers, you often have the impression that they think they live under a reign of terror and do not open up because they are afraid'.[26] A *relazione informativa* of 17 March 1939, entitled 'Ears are listening', explained the situation in more detail:

> If we want to be honest and objective chroniclers of the differing moods that we note in public opinion, we cannot avoid mentioning one reason for annoyance, disquiet and suspicion. I refer to the general impression of being spied on everywhere and to the mania—indeed the obsession—of thinking that there are ears everywhere, listening carefully.

---

[22] 'Una truffa all'italiana': Ibid., Rome, 29 May 1939.

[23] ACS, Ibid., Rome, 2 June 1939.

[24] ACS, Ibid., Rome, 24 July 1939. For a brief summary of the role of the fascist unions, and of their relationship with the corporative state, after 1934, see Alessio Gagliardi, *Il corporativismo fascista*, Rome & Bari, Laterza, 2010, 125–36.

[25] Francesco Altamura, 'I sindacati fascisti nelle campagne baresi degli anni trenta', (2009) 50(4) *Studi storici* 1065. The quotation is from 1094.

[26] ACS, PNF, SPEP, b. 25, Turin, 6 January 1938.

The writer elaborated on this, saying that he had been watching the evolution of opinion over the years, and that if, in his view, at the beginning of the regime people had accepted surveillance because of a recognized need to combat anti-fascism, there was now the general conviction that 'black lists' were being drawn up by the authorities and that it was all too easy to be put on those lists because of the odd comment, hostile to the regime, overheard here or there. The writer was, perhaps without realizing it, describing the manner in which fascist repressive mechanisms had changed their targets over the years, shifting from the destruction of anti-fascism to a more generalized, and much more thoroughly articulated, con-trol of the population at large. Rather ironically, the same agent complained about this state of affairs because it made his job more difficult. It was, he said, no longer possible to trust what people were saying, particularly when they professed loyalty to the regime. As serious (as far as he was concerned), most people had stopped talking in public. When conversations began to get interesting someone would intervene to curtail the talk, 'because "I don't intend to go to prison"' or because 'there may be ears listening'. Much better, he concluded, to have your enemies out in the open where you could spy on them.[27]

His was not an isolated impression. In June 1939, in Rome, an agent recounted that his friends (who evidently had no suspicions about him) were complaining that 'we all feel that we are being followed, watched and surrounded—all the time and wherever we go—by police'. They—the friends—had noticed that bars and other public places were full of people pretending to read newspapers or apparently 'distractedly lost in their private thoughts', with the consequence that no one wanted to talk any longer. The prevailing culture of suspicion changed people's habits. Groups of friends who had been used to meet together in bars now no longer did so, for fear of compromising themselves in the eyes of the authorities. Everywhere there was in evidence 'an atmosphere of suspicion and control'.[28] Nearby, on the newly reclaimed and immensely publicized Pontine marshes, peas-ants were said to be in revolt: 'they don't want to cultivate the plots of land, because they produce nothing and because they [the peasants] are subject to rigid disci-pline'. But they could not even talk about it among themselves: 'you cannot say anything for fear of *confino*'.[29]

Nonetheless people needed to talk because they had no reliable means of know-ing what was going on and they evidently felt a compulsion to compare their impressions of what was being said at an official level. After the signing of the Pact of Steel in May 1939, an informer from Forlì wrote that popular reaction was extremely sceptical, considering the pact to be as credible as if 'the Devil had formed an alliance with the Eternal Father'. A serious problem was the information available: 'a disillusioned people—like the Italians now, to the point that they don't believe in anything any longer ... do not believe the newspapers any more—you

[27] ACS, MI, DGPS, Polizia Politica, Materia (1927–44), b. 220, 17 March 1939.
[28] ACS, Ibid., Rome, 15 June 1939.
[29] ACS, Ibid., Bari, 17 August 1939. By 1939 many peasants were travelling to nearby Rome to work as building labourers or waiters because the land could not support them and their families.

hear important people say when they are buying the paper "give me six lire of gossip", and others "give me six lire of lies", while the French papers are much sought after. It is because of this that you can deduce that the population in general does not believe anything it is told any more'.[30] Criticism of the sycophantic press was general—'you can't read the papers any more because all they talk about is the *duce*'—with the result that 'the press has the opposite effect to what it intends'.[31] The report found confirmation in a letter from Milan of much the same period, which deplored the state of the local party machine where propaganda was concerned. 'People take what foreign radio stations churn out to be absolute truth and laugh at the articles in our papers, which no one believes any longer. Perhaps the fault is ours in some measure because for some years now there's not even a dog on our side who has any credit...'[32]

The regime was evidently not doing a good job of 'defining reality' for its subjects—a significant failure for a totalitarian regime.[33] It was a failure destined to create an atmosphere in which whispering campaigns multiplied and rumours spread rapidly, only increasing the dominant sense of uncertainty and insecurity. Lack of accurate and credible information opened the door to the wildest fears. Even germ warfare was feared. In Milan people were saying that one of the great powers had at its disposal an enormous number of rats which, at the appropriate moment, would be inoculated with bubonic plague and parachuted into Italian cities.[34] Later, in the face of the Molotov–Ribbentrop pact of August 1939, the press had short shrift from its public: 'People are laughing at the pitiful efforts of the fascist press, which is trying uselessly to say that Italy has always been the friend of Russia...'[35]

It was almost inevitable that, in an atmosphere of such uncertainty, real economic hardship and the sense of an increased presence and pressure of the state would provoke a reaction against that state. One *informatore*, writing from Florence in January 1939, had warned of this likelihood:

> People are saying that this is a system of compression which is getting more and more unbearable. At the moment everyone puts up with it and does not show their opposition openly because they are afraid, but they think that, in the event of a setback that

---

[30] ACS, Ibid., Forlì, 29 May 1939.

[31] ACS, MI, DGPS, Polizia Politica, b. 224, 23 May 1939.

[32] ACS, Ibid., Milan, 8 June 1939.

[33] This failure is all the more surprising if the enormous efforts put by the regime into organizing and controlling information are taken into consideration. It indicates a growing distance between the many very novel ways of broadcasting the fascist message employed by the regime and the reception of the message—a gap which cultural historians of Fascism seem often to neglect. On the media see the classic work by Philip V. Cannistraro, *La fabbrica del consenso: Fascismo e mass media*, Rome & Bari, Laterza, 1975; more recently, Mauro Forno, 'Aspetti dell'esperienza totalitaria fascista. Limiti e contraddizioni nella gestione del "quarto potere"', (2006) 47(3) *Studi storici* 781.

[34] ACS, MI, DGPS, Polizia Politica, b. 224, Milan, 24 July 1939. The fear was not pure imagination. The parachuting of plague-infected rats and fleas into cities was a strategy employed by the Japanese in China during the 1930s. See Giovanni Contini, Filippo Focardi, Marta Petricioli (eds), *Memoria e rimozione. I crimini di guerra del Giappone e dell'Italia*, Rome, Viella, 2011, in particular the chapter by Takao Matsumura on the operation of the infamous Unit 731.

[35] ACS, MI, DGPS, Polizia Politica, b. 224, Milan, 6 September 1939.

shakes the solidity of the regime, there could be a violent reaction to this compression.[36]

The fact that the resentment was unspoken indicated that the people knew who was to blame for their hardships and that they could not complain openly. Indeed, one of the striking features of the informers' reports of 1939 is the way in which the difficulties of which they speak are attributed by the people almost exclusively to fascist policies rather than to international pressures on Italy. By an incontestable logic, totalitarian shortages became totalitarian failures. There is, in the reports of this period, an unmistakable change of emphasis in popular expression. The complaints are not made against the local party federation, or the corrupt *federale*, so much as before, but are now aimed at the *gerarchi* as a class, at the regime as a whole—clearly perceived as a regime which spied, controlled, decided, and therefore bore responsibility for the position in which Italians found themselves.

Many of the reports of spring 1939 suggest a situation of a gravity not seen before by the regime. Faced by crisis, people were taking stock, recognizing that, after years of promises of a glorious future, prospects were in reality bleak and likely to get bleaker. Some were beginning to see Fascism in perspective. A old woman in Rome spoke to a friend on the bus:

> All right, you can't deny it, when the socialists were around we lived badly [because] the trains arrived when they wanted to, the strikes stopped everything, but we ate better and there was no shortage of coffee and the cost of living was lower. Now it's been 17 years in which, rather than living dangerously, we live in anguish, in anxiety and in fear.

The woman would have continued but she stopped when her friend elbowed her to warn her that someone else was listening.[37]

In the Neapolitan countryside people were reported to be saying, 'we work more than before, we eat less, there are shortages of everything, we are in a condition of misery; when there wasn't this mania for greatness we lived better and the ruling class (with rare exceptions) was honest and clean'.[38] Similar comments were heard in Turin in May and the informer who reported them pointed out that the queues formed by people trying to buy coffee provided the perfect opportunity to exchange criticisms of the regime. Those waiting were asking where the money that should have been used to import coffee had gone 'and everyone concludes that someone is stealing'.[39] The discontented would-be coffee buyers were again making a comparison with the past. Another informer listed a whole decalogue of popular grievances:

> They say that before Fascism this didn't happen, that there was coffee, that the bread was made of wheat, that the milk was genuine, that cloth was wool, that you could find everything, that pay was proportionate to the cost of living, that you didn't know what deductions were, that taxes were bearable, that commerce was stable,

---

[36] Quoted in Gentile, *La via italiana*, 197 (from ACS, SPD, CR, b. 41, Florence).
[37] ACS, MI, DGPS, Polizia Politica, Materia (1927–44), b. 220, Rome, 12 April 1939.
[38] ACS, Ibid., Naples, 16 August 1939.   [39] ACS, Ibid., Turin, 29 May 1939.

that work could be found, that people were happier, that you could express your own opinion, that the papers could say freely what was happening at home and abroad...

The report concluded with the observation, 'this shows what a conversation which began with the fact that coffee is short can lead to'.[40] This was an acute observation; the queue was a great vehicle of political discontent. As another agent wrote, 'we have to define the issue of coffee as, from the beginning, a political issue'.[41] The strong protests of the office workers of Rome, faced by the same problem (they threatened 'revolution'), suggests that the absence of one commodity, considered fundamental by most people, finally brought into the open a hostility to the regime repressed up to that point.[42] Shortages and the politics of grandeur did not go well together: 'Mussolini wanted to get Africa. He caused the deaths of many poor mother's boys, threw away millions. We have the empire of misery...'[43] At least in some circles, there were no doubts about the causes of hardship. From Carrara came the judgement, again based on perspective, '[m]any say that this government has done nothing with its policy of autarky other than cause the impoverishment of the nation. They say that after 20 years of Fascism the Italian people was supposed to be in first place while it finds itself in the last instead'.[44]

Other expressions of discomfort were more straightforward and also highly traditional: 'everybody would like at last to have work and bread and peace'.[45] Many were extremely resentful of the fact that the regime appeared to be going ahead as usual with expensive public shows and grandiose plans (the EUR district of Rome was being projected for the proposed 1942 exhibition) while their living conditions continued to worsen. 'The continuous assemblies and demonstrations are criticized';[46] 'Rome is tired, sick, angry with these daily festivities'.[47] The superficial nature of much that the regime was promoting invited criticism. As one report put it (again in May 1939), 'the assemblies for the *ludi juveniles* are looked on badly by the people'. A worker, watching the preparations for the games and seeing a group of girls go by in colourful costumes, expressed his views concisely, 'they'd have done better to leave us with the cup of coffee they've taken away rather than spend money and bring so many tramps to Rome...'[48]

---

[40] ACS, Ibid., Turin, 6 May 1939.

[41] ACS, Ibid., Rome, 19 May 1939.

[42] This was a common occurrence in Soviet bloc satellite states after 1945.

[43] ACS, MI, DGPS, Polizia Politica, Materia (1927–44), b. 220, Rome, 13 May 1939.

[44] ACS, MI, DGPS, Polizia Politica, Materia/Apuania, situazione politica e spirito pubblico 1939–42 cat Q.178–46, b. 234, 22 October 1939.

[45] ACS, MI, DGPS, Polizia Politica, Materia (1927–44), b. 220, 29 April 1939.

[46] ACS, Ibid., Rome, 19 May 1939.

[47] Ibid., Rome, 13 May 1939. Such statements argue strongly against the position of some cultural historians, who see the high level of novel public activities under the regime as a sign of its success in making people feel they 'belonged' to the national community. The position is implicit in Berezin, 'The Festival State'.

[48] ACS, MI, DGPS, Polizia Politica, Materia (1927–44), b. 220, Rome, 19 May 1939.

9.2. THE 'NEW CASTE'

An illuminating *relazione* of early March 1939, based on conversations overheard among journalists and middle class fascists, put its finger on the key point: 'the people who work—the middle and lower classes—feel crushed by a triple weight—expenditure for armaments, expenditure for the ambitious building projects, expenditure for the complex of new organizations of the Regime'. The problem was—the report went on—that, while 'the working people' suffered under this pressure, there were still people who were seen to be doing well: 'on one side there is a closed circle of people who have everything, to whom everything is permitted, on the other the majority, required to make continual sacrifices, deprived of everything, and subjected moreover to an oppressive discipline and a mass of inopportune controls'. The *duce* was doing his job, they agreed, but others were exploiting the situation to their own advantage—'figures who serve the Chief and Fascism only in appearances but who in reality serve their own vanity and their own exclusive interests'. These were people distinguished by the frenetic pursuit of 'their own material enrichment', by 'sudden riches'. They constituted a mafia made up of 'a few cliques, corrupt and satisfied...'[49]

The writer did not have the courage to attack Starace and the *gerarchi* directly (he limited himself to calling for the appointment of a new, 'intelligent', party secretary, who would clean up the movement—the implication was clear enough). But, if anyone had any doubts about his real meaning, dozens of other reports were more specific and spelled out the same message. As always, the *gerarchi*—the provincial potentates—were accused of looking after themselves, their families, and their friends and disregarding the interests of everyone else. Party leaders were condemned for their failure to act against corrupt local leaders: 'Why do they continually squeeze the mass of the workers and employees and permit the new caste created by the regime to make money by the bucket-full, left and right, with all methods and all means?' Specific allegations followed: 'they name the big *gerarchi*, and people like Ciano, Rossoni, Alfieri are not left out'.[50] It was said at popular level that the government had brought the nation to 'a state of penury, while at the same time permitting the amassing of notable riches by a few people—all of them holding high political office'.[51] In June 1939 an informer, writing from Milan, who had evidently been accused of unnecessary alarmism by his superiors, replied that 'the truth, the REAL TRUTH, is even worse than I said because of the public perception of the fascist hierarchy. You could draw up an endless list of fascist administrators and *gerarchi*, known to be unsuitable, dishonest as well as incompetent, generally badly considered, publicly detested and despised'—all well-known, but nothing happened to them. They—the untouchable 'new caste'—stayed in their places.[52]

The chorus of reports was unanimous in underlining 'the ever-widening chasm between the *gerarchi* and the people'. The chasm concerned all social groups: 'In all

---

[49] ACS, Ibid., Rome, 20 March 1939.   [50] ACS, Ibid., Rome, 16 June 1939.
[51] ACS, Ibid., Milan, 6 May 1939.   [52] ACS, Ibid., Milan, 18 June 1939.

social circles... you can hear complaints and bitter protests about the more important *gerarchi*'.[53] As will be evident, the criticisms of the *gerarchi* now went well
beyond those of ridiculous uniforms or personal arrogance. Social justice was the
overriding issue. In the phase of economic crisis that Italy was facing in the first
half of 1939, the most common accusation levelled at the *gerarchi* was of corruption and personal enrichment: 'there is the most barefaced exhibition of appropriation for personal benefit among the more prominent leaders, from the little *gerarca*
of the province to the big one in the city, and from these to the most important
representatives of the Regime'.[54] A repeated suggestion was that officials at all levels
were taking bribes for contracts, concessions, permits, and the like. Offering the
bribes on occasions were those who were called the 'contractors'—the middlemen
who arranged business transactions, fixed deals, and knew their way round government offices—described in one report as 'the dangerous poisoners of those most
prominent in the Regime, but also of many in state and *parastato* offices, from
provincial governments to Ministries'. There seemed to be no stopping them:
'These people go forward buying consciences and disturbing everyone. There are a
thousand indications that their money is working according to the laws of the
greediest egoism'.[55]

The level of corruption made all Mussolini's rhetoric about 'social justice' and
'solidarity' under Fascism totally unacceptable because popular perceptions were
quite the opposite. Indeed, some concerned informers even went so far as to suggest that the fascist regime had set a record and that Italy had never been as corrupt
as it was in 1939: 'never was bourgeois Italy as corrupt as it is today!'[56] 'There is an
atmosphere of corruption around everywhere, from the well-off to those who have
nothing—an atmosphere that is heavy and suffocating; something that suggests a
phenomenon never seen before in Italy'.[57] A convinced fascist made the same comment in his diary, concentrating his attention on the faults of the PNF: 'The Party
has the greatest responsibility for the cruel mortification that is being inflicted on
the Italian people... In all the infinite orders given by the Party there has never
been an invitation to be honest.' Broadening his approach, he went on, '[r]arely
have lies and deceit become part of the habits of a great people in the way they are
currently becoming the habits of the leaders of the Italian people...'[58] More than
one spy overheard people saying that Stalin might have his defects, but at least he
shot the corrupt.

What all these accounts testify to is the resentment, frustration, and—according
to some—the desperation of large sectors of the population. The reports make it
clear that there was, among these sectors, a strong and prevailing 'us' and 'them'
mentality so far as fascists in authority were concerned. The regime's attempts to
create a sense of national collectivity—a community of believers—would appear to
have failed dramatically. Fascist officials at both national and provincial level were

---

[53] ACS, Ibid., Rome, 8 August 1939.   [54] ACS, Ibid., Rome, 16 August 1939.
[55] ACS, MI, DGPS, Polizia Politica, b. 217, 5 August 1939.
[56] ACS, Ibid., b. 220, 20 March 1939.
[57] ACS, Ibid., b. 217, 5 August 1939.
[58] ADN, Paolino Ferrari, DG/89, 'December 1938'.

seen as corrupt, arrogant, and self-serving; ostentatious and unmerited privilege divided the community rather than unite it.

For many ordinary people Fascism was associated with exploitation and injustice. It was, at the same time, in its 'totalitarian' phase, an increasingly repressive regime; people feared the actions of spies and the consequences of denunciation in a way they had not done ten years before. Even where the causes of injustice could be identified, therefore—and people knew where blame lay—there was little they could do about it. This served only to inflame the situation further. The fascist informers, themselves frequently alarmed by the dimensions of the crisis of early 1939, could not avoid pointing out the moral to their superiors. One of them did so in no uncertain terms: 'The working people, beside social justice, are hungry for moral justice...' It was not just a question of wages and coffee, 'more than material sacrifices, what alarms them is injustice, the incredible imbalance between the conditions of a few chosen categories and the poorer classes'.[59] Another repeated the same lament: 'They are saying—Mussolini has already asked for too many sacrifices from the masses to be able to ask for any more. Why does he leave undisturbed the various categories of privileged people who, in these difficult times, lead a life which is an insult to those who work?'[60] The existence of a moral economy, based on the idea of justice, of values rather than interests, was becoming apparent even to committed fascist informers.[61]

How serious was the crisis? There are signs that it was extremely serious—and that it was perceived as such. Various reports make reference to popular revolts— always somewhere different from where the informer is writing. The centres where the revolts were alleged to have taken place are never specified exactly, evidently because the source is popular rumour. It is nonetheless interesting that such stories gained credence. In May 1939 a Rome informer spoke of the concern created in 'all urban circles, fascist not excluded' by the reports of 'the riots and uprisings which for some time have been exploding unexpectedly in one or another part of the kingdom'. Furthermore, he commented on the fact that he had heard that the *Tribunale Speciale* for offences against Fascism was sentencing between twenty and forty people a day—far more than normal—which he read as an index of increasing popular discontent and a sad comment on nearly fifteen years of fascist rule. 'It seems,' he wrote, 'to be a unanimous opinion that the internal situation is extremely serious and may have become impossible'.[62]

Other informers considered the state of affairs within Italy to be explosive and warned of the dangers of public disorder as a consequence of popular anger. There were constant warnings that the limit had been reached and that the economic

[59] ACS, MI, DGPS, Polizia Politica, Materia (1927–44), b. 220, 3 March 1939.

[60] ACS, Ibid., 16 June 1939.

[61] Comparisons can be made with a similar situation in Nazi Germany. The difference seems to have been that corruption among Nazi officials was seen by the population to be the bad side of an otherwise winning regime and tolerated for this reason. In Italy the corruption of the *gerarchi* was viewed in the context of the general stagnation and decline of the regime. When the promise of Fascism disappeared, the privileges of the fascists became intolerable. See, on Nazi Germany, Frank Bajohr, 'La corruzione nel regime nazionalsocialista', (2004) 7(1) *Contemporanea* 69.

[62] ACS, MI, DGPS, Polizia Politica, Materia (1927–44), b. 220, Rome, 9 May 1939.

issue was rapidly becoming a highly charged political question. As we shall see shortly, people began to talk about the future of Fascism largely in relation to the threat of war, but economic hardship also encouraged some to try to look beyond the end of the regime. Lack of coffee seems, paradoxically, to have concentrated minds remarkably. A report from Rome in mid-June 1939 is particularly telling and is worth quoting in full.

> I think it is my duty not to fail to register a fact which is symptomatic of the mood of the country. To have a rough idea of the level that the tide of hatred against the Regime has reached (for reasons I will not go into) it is enough to hear what people are saying everywhere now that the bad weather is (they say) putting in danger the coming harvest. 'Let's hope,' they say, 'that everything goes badly, that we don't harvest anything, that we have a terrible famine, because it is only then, perhaps, that we will get rid of Fascism. Come what may, it is better to get it over with quickly, because we can't stand any more.'
>
> These sentiments—I repeat—do not reflect the ideas of a limited number of people, but are expressed regularly by everyone.[63]

Even, it seems, by many fascists. The crisis was evidently serious within the party as well, because it hit social groups previously committed to the regime. For modest rank-and-file fascists—'food' fascists, with no strong ideological commitment to the regime—the rising tide of discontent was too strong to resist and they were swept along with it. 'Even many fascists curse the actions of the Government,' wrote one informer.[64] During the summer of 1939, as we have seen, people all over Italy were reported to be removing the fascist badges from their button holes and deserting local fascist meetings even more than before.

9.3. THE PROSPECT OF WAR

The backdrop to all this discontent was the prospect of a European war. Reactions to this differed to some extent, largely in relation to social class, but almost all were characterized by alarm and dismay. The party had the thankless task of trying to justify a probable but very unpopular war. Fascist propaganda appears to have made little headway among the population, the critical position assumed by the Church much more. In report after report, Rome was told that 'the popular mood is one of total opposition to a war which is not supported, not wanted, not considered necessary'.[65] Trento and Trieste had been worth fighting for in 1915, but to fight for Danzig in 1939 was absurd, and Tunisia was just not worth the trouble.[66] The deceptive nature of fascist military rhetoric had become evident. The 'battle' against malaria had been one thing, but a battle against France and Great Britain was quite another. As one fascist militiaman recognized, 'there couldn't be

---

[63] ACS, Ibid., 14 June 1939.

[64] ACS, MI, DGPS, Polizia Politica, b. 217, 21 May 1939.

[65] ACS, MI, DGPS, Polizia Politica, Materia (1927–44), b. 220, 17 August 1939.

[66] ACS, Ibid., 28 August 1939.

a more obvious sign of the failure of the verbose and insincere warrior mysticism of the Party'.[67]

At a popular level, war was seen in terms of shortages and sons killed; in other words it was seen in very immediate, personal terms. Again, a report of what people were saying: 'Our Government can only think about arming for war, the needs of the people don't count any more. Here we think that the people need bread—and when I say bread I really mean everything because everything is lacking'.[68] In any case, people had learned their lesson and were doubtful about the benefits of fascist wars. 'As far as the increase in cost of petrol and coffee is concerned, people are saying that, having conquered Ethiopia, the home of coffee, they now have no coffee and its price has gone up, and, having conquered Albania, with all its magnificent oil wells, the cost of petrol has gone up. So they conclude that it would better for Italy not to conquer anything else...'[69] An almost identical sentiment was reported two days earlier from Naples: 'There is discontent with the *duce* who leads the people into repeated wars without the people feeling—after victory—any benefit. Here people are saying that misery and hunger are really the things that have got the upper hand...'[70]

The same kind of criticism of the line being followed by Mussolini was being expressed in Milan. In a revealing passage, an informer identified the principal critics:

> The class that criticizes most is the intellectual class, in particular the lawyers and magistrates who have been, in the main, a pain in the side of Fascism...in the studio of Avv. Borsa the famous [lawyer] Trusolo allowed himself to call Mussolini an idiot and to accuse him of continual idiocies...denigrating the acquisition of Empire from which our principal problems derive. 'If it gave us at least some sign of benefit! Today there isn't even any coffee...'

But, going on, the informer indicated that it was not just lawyers and magistrates who were criticizing the regime. Significantly, many fascists had now joined in: '...what is most damaging is that these bitter comments are made by fascists, and, moreover, by the military'.[71]

Reference was made almost automatically by older people to the harsh experience of the First World War, especially on the home front. People feared the consequences of evident lack of preparation. The existing problem of shortages induced some to make comparison with 1914–15 when, according to (erroneous) memory, the shops had been full to overflowing with goods. Some—in late August—went much further with the comparison:

> Many are remarking on the sharp contrast between the enthusiasm of 1915 at the eve of the entry of Italy in war and the silence of the grave that can be noted in recent days. In 1915 the recruits went to the barracks full of confidence, enthusiasm and pleasure at being called up. Today, as the recruits leave, there are scenes of weeping, of cursing

---

[67] ADN, Paolino Ferrari, DG/89, 26 May 1940.
[68] ACS, MI, DGPS, Polizia Politica, Materia (1927–44), b. 220, 25 May 1939.
[69] ACS, Ibid., 31 August 1939.
[70] ACS, Ibid., Naples, 29 August 1939.   [71] ACS, Ibid., Milan, 30 August 1939.

by the womenfolk, by the recruits themselves, and by the crowd. In 1915 there was a minority which galvanized the people: today there is not even the smallest minority ready to sing the praises of a war alongside Germany![72]

Concern was being expressed about the population's morale, should it come to war. In an interesting gloss on the workings of the regime, one informer wrote in May,

> It is certainly true that totalitarian regimes can adjust public opinion as they like, but war is war, not a choreographed parade. And we might ask, is the morale of the Italian people really as high as is thought? Can a people used to participating in 'spontaneous' regimented demonstrations tomorrow behave like a people whose reactions are motivated solely by enthusiasm?[73]

But, as if the prospect of further and more severe shortages were not enough, opposition to the idea of war was strengthened by the knowledge that the Nazis were the probable allies. There was generalized revulsion at the signing of the Pact of Steel: 'The new pact signed with Germany has been greeted by everyone with real hostility; this disgust is shown not only among the people, but also by authentic fascists and *Sansepolchristi*'.[74] In August the sentiment was the same: 'Among the public there is still a strong hostility to the participation of Italy [in a war] alongside Germany'.[75] At popular level, the Germans were seen as the traditional enemy. Contacts between Italian and German youth groups in the closing years of the 1930s had done little to change the general attitude; indeed, in Padua in 1939, the two sides came to blows. Traditional hostility was increased by dislike and distrust of Hitler. From Turin it was reported that 'in general people are demonstrating a feeling of rebellion against the continuous claims of the Germans...'[76]

In more sophisticated company, the same anti-German feeling was reproduced almost exactly. It was said that, in Genoa, the alliance was judged ill thought-out and premature 'in University, professional, and intellectual circles in general'.[77] At times a greater attention to strategic considerations produced some qualification of this position. Fascist propaganda had succeeded to some extent in creating anti-British and anti-French sentiment among the population. There was a feeling that Italy's 'rights' in the Mediterranean should be recognized and that, in this respect at least, Mussolini had a point. There was much less sympathy, however, for the view that this should be achieved through an alliance with Hitler. Here dislike, distrust, and realism all played their parts. Even before the outbreak of the Second World War (at which point the aggression towards Poland stimulated considerable criticism of the Nazis within Italy),[78] informers related that people were convinced that, even in the case of an Axis victory in a war and despite Hitler's assurances, Italy would inevitably become dominated by and possibly even subject to the Germans.

---

[72] ACS, Ibid., 26 August 1939.
[73] ACS, MI, DGPS, Polizia Politica, b. 224, 25 May 1939.
[74] ACS, MI, DGPS, Polizia Politica, Materia (1927–44), b. 220, 29 May 1939.
[75] ACS, Ibid., 26 August 1939.
[76] ACS, Ibid., Turin, 28 August 1939.
[77] ACS, MI, DGPS, Polizia Politica, b. 224, Genoa, 18 May 1939.
[78] When the Germans invaded Norway in April 1940 there were those in Turin who wanted to go to fight alongside the Norwegians against the Nazis: ACS, PNF, SPEP, b. 25, Turin, 11 April 1940.

In Naples a fascist agent recounted what was being said in the offices of the local newspapers, where pessimism was the order of the day. Defeat was likely, everyone agreed, but 'on the other hand, even if we were to win, we would be destined in the very near future to become the southern edge of Hitler's Reich. This is the certainty here in Naples'.[79] Faced by this prospect, people were inventing a new version of 'O Francia o Spagna...': 'The people are reduced to calculating whether a German hegemony is better than an English one, and a large percentage favour the second'.[80] There were suggestions that, in the event of a German victory, Italy would be reduced to activities relating exclusively to 'hotels and tourism', with little space left even for agriculture.

The crisis was such that, by mid-1939, the question of the survival of the regime was being raised in many quarters. Rumours about Mussolini's health were one sign of this, but there were other more direct indications in what people were saying. Apparently without too many problems, an informer from Florence could write, '[t]his morning we were talking about the fascist revolution and about whether it should continue. This is a question that comes up every now and then...'[81] Among critics of the regime in the Maremma, one agent found that 'the conviction that the regime is collapsing is deeply rooted'.[82] But there were also reports that some people were prepared to give the tottering regime a push. Rumours coming from Naples in mid-August spoke of a possible revolution about to break out among those who had been called up: 'they talk about... the probability of a revolution at the moment of mobilization or when the soldiers have been armed'.[83] A variant on this was heard several days later in Rome, where it was said that '[t]he recruits are not being given arms, not even bayonets—something attributed to the discontent existing among the recruits themselves'.[84] In Milan, employees in the Prefecture, faced by an unexpected event, asked among themselves, 'Has the revolution broken out already?'[85] Again, the importance of these rumours lies less in their accordance with fact than in the situation to which they refer which, because of its incandescent nature, would appear to make them credible to people.

On a slightly different level, but still related to the question of the survival of Fascism, there was no shortage of people hoping for war because it was seen as being the only way of getting rid of the fascists and of overcoming the crisis—the two were now inextricably entwined in many minds. The desperate conditions in Naples are again made apparent in the following report. 'There are those who pray for war as a possible solution, in order to free this population of paupers from a domination that has lasted so long. There are those who say that, if the war comes, it will be the end of Fascism and that therefore it is best that it come quickly'.[86] Certainly there was the common recognition that, with war, the regime was risking

---

[79] ACS, MI, DGPS, Polizia Politica, Materia (1927–44), b. 220, Naples, 12 August 1939.

[80] ACS, Ibid., Naples, 28 August 1939. 'O Francia o Spagna, purché se magna' ('It doesn't matter whether it is France or Spain, as long as we eat') was supposedly the cynical attitude of Italians to foreign conquest in the sixteenth century.

[81] ACS, Ibid., Florence, 17 June 1939.

[82] ACS, Ibid., Grosseto, 14 August 1939.

[83] ACS, Ibid., Naples, 12 August 1939.

[84] ACS, Ibid., Rome, 31 August 1939.

[85] ACS, Ibid., Milan, 28 August 1939.

[86] ACS, Ibid., Naples, 29 August 1939.

everything: 'everywhere people are saying that if Italy goes to war Fascism in Italy will be finished'.[87] Mussolini's apparent reluctance to commit himself was sometimes ascribed to his fear that his fate was linked to a victory of which he could not be certain.

It is important to underline at this point what the informers are saying and, more significant perhaps, what they are not saying. What they are saying should be clear enough from the passages quoted above: life is very difficult for most people and threatens to become more so. Fascist officials at all levels—but the reference is inevitably to provincial officials, the fascists most people came into regular contact with—are generally perceived as being corrupt, arrogant, and inefficient. The difficulties experienced by the population—a population smarting under a profound sense of injustice—are laid squarely at the door of the regime and of fascist policies. Discontent notwithstanding, what the informers seem careful not to say is that the fascist machine is still working imperturbably. This is worthy of note. Familiarity with this kind of source suggests strongly that many of the informers, almost by habit, would snatch at the positive aspects of any situation, usually with the intention of sugaring an otherwise bitter pill of bad news. In earlier years, even when reporting serious problems, they would end the report with florid assurances that, despite the difficulties to which they have referred, the party and other fascist organizations in the province remained strong. This was almost part of a template of a *relazione fiduciaria*. Instead, in the reports of the first eight months of 1939, we find almost no references to the activity of the local party federations, except when accusations of corruption are being reported or when people are said to be deserting those activities, and no reference to the other fascist organizations, except the observations, cited above, about the poor reputation of the fascist unions. There are no references to a rallying of the party faithful in face of the crisis. Inactivity seems to have been the norm; 'no real or effective propaganda work is being carried out. This absence is seen in popular circles as the confirmation of the fact that the fascist leaders, recognizing popular sentiment, avoid discussions and reunions because these would be either unattended or would give rise to incidents'.[88] Absent from the picture provided by the reports are the *Fasci femminili*, the youth organizations, the agencies responsible for welfare. Paramilitary training for young people is mentioned only to say that the young people either do not attend or attend only because of fear of reprisals. It is also interesting to note that, unlike in earlier years, the *relazioni*—although coming from many different provinces of Italy—largely cease to talk about local party problems and local squabbles. It seems evident that what the informers are observing is so generalized that it has ceased to be seen as a problem of a particular area; the crisis has assumed a national dimension. Both in what they say and in what they do not say, the informers communicate the same message. For a population experiencing severe economic hardship and faced by the prospect of war, the fascist regime has lost all credibility.

---

[87] ACS, Ibid., 25 August 1939.   [88] ACS, Ibid., 6 May 1939.

10

The Flight from the Enchanter

The crisis which overtook the regime at the end of the 1930s was serious, if not immediately terminal. Certainly, many Italians must have found themselves confused. Assured for more than a decade and a half that the fascist system represented the solution to Italy's problems, they found themselves in 1939 with shortages, unemployment, and a political class almost universally despised. Accustomed for years to military rhetoric on a grand scale and to the myth of 'living dangerously', they discovered that the prospect of a real war was anything but attractive. Moreover, empire had proved a delusion, bringing none of the benefits it had seemed to promise. Thus, while the past did not make much sense, the future could be viewed only with foreboding. The regime maintained its firm hold and motives for optimism were few. The only element at which people could grasp was that of the *duce*—presumed miracle-worker but, in any case, for many, the last hope in an increasingly desperate situation.

10.1. LOVE THE SINGER, HATE THE SONG

During the crisis of 1939 most informers, clutching at what little was positive, would insist on the fact that loss of faith in Fascism was not the same as loss of faith in Mussolini. Most convinced fascists, even in the dark days of August 1939, still felt that they had the winning card up their sleeve. This was the figure of Mussolini. Like many other dictators, Mussolini managed to avoid being tainted by what was imputed to his higher- and lower-ranking followers. A carefully engineered political construct, the cult of the *duce* erected a dividing wall between Mussolini and the lesser fascists who followed him. If he made mistakes, people assumed that this could only be because he was kept, deliberately, ignorant of the facts or because he was badly advised (this was a further crime that was laid at the door of the *gerarchi*). The well-worn phrase, 'se lo sapesse il *duce*' [if the *duce* only knew...], implied this division, with the fascist leader invoked *against* the realities of provincial Fascism, as if there were no connection between the Fascism of the local *federale* and the politics of Palazzo Venezia. Indeed, it is probable that, at least for a certain period, the more people railed against local fascist leaders, the higher Mussolini's own stock rose.

There can be no doubt at all that the figure and the myth of Mussolini served to carry Fascism forward, even when other aspects of the regime were affected by a prevalent apathy and disaffection. For this reason it is worth examining in some detail the reputation of the fascist leader because it may help to explain why Mussolini's name continued to invoke respect and generate confidence long after the reputation of the fascist movement itself had fallen so low. It may also help to explain where the fascist leader was most vulnerable.

The cult of the *duce* had been launched more or less with the beginnings of the regime, in 1925 and 1926.[1] Turati, when party secretary, had worked hard at magnifying the figure of Mussolini in popular imagination, and his successors continued his work. Starace was the real architect of the more extreme aspects of the cult, stressing the genius of the leader—'*il duce ha sempre ragione*' [the *duce* is always right] was his invention—introducing a kind of fascist catechism for schoolchildren, painting the face of the *duce* and his weightier slogans on the walls of 12,000 houses along the roads of Italy, and sometimes going to lengths to which even the *duce* himself could not go. The objective of the creation of the cult was clear. The national unity sought by the fascist movement required a single authoritative leader to whom all could look up and who was manifestly distinguishable from the rest of the movement. Mussolini's undoubted personal charisma lent itself to this operation; the body language and the staring eyes suggested a person out of the ordinary and, as newsreels testify, Mussolini did all he could to accentuate these aspects.

What people saw in the *duce* is difficult to summarize because perceptions would vary enormously. For some—probably relatively few—he was the ultimate fascist, the man who exemplified the quintessence of fascist being. For people who viewed him in this light he was the strong and decisive national leader, the New Man about to inaugurate a new fascist epoch in Italy—and perhaps in the world. Palingenesis would spring directly from his genius. Some—the Nationalists, for example—would take elements of this picture without necessarily subscribing to the whole fascist liturgy. More conservative supporters, always ready to remember the socialist threat, viewed him principally as the guarantor of order and social discipline. For others, perhaps the majority of his more popular supporters, he represented, on a less ideological and more traditional level, benevolent authority—justice against injustice, order against disorder, a man capable of intervening from above to solve the difficulties of daily life, which he, as a man of the people, could certainly understand. 'If the *duce* only knew' had this sense above all—a sense which had little to do directly with Fascism but a great deal to do with the idea of an external intervention to right wrongs. Here the very strong populist element in Mussolini's relationship with the people made itself felt. People assumed he was on their side against the vexations of authority—even fascist authority—as experienced in day-to-day affairs. Metropolitan legends developed in which this paternal, overseeing function of the *duce* was highlighted. He was, for instance, rumoured to be seen sometimes at night, crossing the Pontine Marshes by motorcycle in order to make sure that all was well with the newly established peasant colonists.

---

[1] See, in general, Angelo Michele Imbriani, *Gli italiani e il duce; il mito e l'immagine di Mussolini negli ultimi anni del fascismo (1938–1943)*, Naples, Liguori, 1992; Luisa Passerini, *Mussolini immaginario*, Rome & Bari, Laterza, 1991.

Unquestionably, much of the language surrounding Mussolini was either directly religious or had religious overtones. In a strongly Catholic country, the paternalist leader was almost inevitably attributed precise qualities deriving from religious experience. He was the 'saviour' or the 'redeemer' of Italy; his alleged apparitions were clearly comparable with those of the saints. In some of the writing referring to him there seems to be almost a fusion of the religious and the political, with Mussolini assuming a semi-divine status. Fascism was, after all, commonly referred to as a 'faith' and Mussolini was the high priest of this faith. Belief in Fascism—and *belief* was the central word for many—necessitated a quasi-religious trust in the *duce*, just as belief in Christianity requires a belief in Jesus Christ. There can be little doubt—and this is borne out by the tone of a large number of the letters to the *duce* conserved in the Archives—that many people, particularly women, considered him to have exceptional powers and to be able to intervene on their behalf, just as a favourite saint or the Madonna might be asked to do. Moreover, the powers deriving from a religious association were enhanced by a further feature. Physical attraction, much stressed by the media's presentation of the *duce*, also played its part. As the letters make evident, many women were much impressed by the fascist leader's oft-vaunted virility. The figure they evoke in their letters is an improbable mixture of a 'generic', all-purpose, saint and a cinema sex symbol—a potent and heady cocktail of Sant'Antonio of Padua and Rudolph Valentino.[2] That a political leader could be physically attractive *was* new—and therefore exciting. As far as we know, few had dreamed of going to bed with Giovanni Giolitti.

The image survived, as we shall see, well into the second half of the 1930s. The same people who wrote reports to Rome that were highly critical of the ways in which provincial Fascism functioned would often insist that the discontents of the provinces were not reflected in any loss of popularity of the *duce*. That informer from Florence, quoted above, who in November 1938 had lamented the lack of any fascist mentality in the young, could write that, nonetheless, '[e]verywhere, high and low, people recognize the superiority of the *duce*, even when they oppose him. His popularity is even surprising'.[3] This enormous popularity was not without its problems, however. Many observers commented on the fact that there existed a 'Mussolinismo' which was quite distinct from Fascism; indeed, in their eyes, it was often 'Mussolinismo' and little more that served to hold the regime together. Even if the young people could not be classified as fascist, according to one informer, they were 'Mussolinian to the roots, but fascists with so many reserves—mental and of principle—that their Fascism emerges deformed and unrecognizable'.[4]

Something of the same could be said of those more conservative fascists—industrialists, landed proprietors, the nationalists—who had never had much time for the PNF and had always placed their faith primarily in the figure of Mussolini. Indeed, the more the party attempted to extend its influence to include almost all areas of life—particularly economic life—the more it became an irritant and a

---

[2] On these themes, see Sergio Luzzatto, *Il corpo del duce*, Turin, Einaudi, 1998.
[3] ACS, MI, DGPS, Polizia Politica, b. 109, 17 November 1938.   [4] Ibid.

potential threat to such people. To some degree Mussolini was seen as the defence against further radicalization of the regime, especially in the corporative and syndicalist fields. The rather disingenuous proposals (in the second half of the 1930s) to disband the party 'since we are all fascists now and the party has no further function' probably originated in this area. For these non-crusading, non-revolutionary fascist supporters, therefore, the *duce* was also very much part of the equation that permitted them to defend their positions and their interests.

The unique position occupied by Mussolini clearly made the fascist movement more fragile in the long term because, as more than one informer noted rather reluctantly (it was something of a taboo subject),[5] it would be very difficult to find a second *duce*. The charismatic leader is a boon for a political movement in the short run, but in the long term he may represent a weakness—because he is mortal. By the end of the 1930s many recognized this.[6] 'Returning to the question of the identification of the regime with the person of its leader, this mentality presents some undeniable dangers for the future. The moral stature of the *duce*, by itself enormous, assumes such dimensions in the eyes of the people that, when compared, anyone else disappears. In these circumstances it is difficult to see a successor appearing on the horizon...'[7]

This was, in one sense, a measure of the success of the cult of the *duce*—a cult that probably reached its height with the declaration of empire in May 1936. Paradoxically, therefore, the increasing resentment directed at the workings of the party that we have seen so far went hand in hand with an increasing respect for the party's leader, at least as far as mid-1936. This divergence of opinion is exemplified by a *relazione fiduciaria* of June 1936—only a few days after the victory speech, that is. A very cautious informer dwelt precisely on this paradox: 'while everyone is unconditionally for the *duce*, there is a certain hostility and an unconcealed popular dislike of certain *gerarchi* and certain political circles'.[8] Intelligent observers noticed this and argued that the profound divide between the popular perception of the party and that of the leader could be lessened by intervening to reform the party. Criticisms of Starace were many and were made with this intention. Few, however, seem to have thought that the other variable—Mussolini's popularity—would or could ever be subject to change.

Nonetheless there are some indications that, following the Ethiopian campaign, Mussolini's star was beginning to shine less brightly in some quarters, even within the party itself. In some respects this was partly a result of the passage of time and the increasing alienation of many older fascists; in others it was a reaction to the attempts made to instil a new dynamism into the fascist movement, which brought

---

[5] In July 1939 Mussolini had forbidden the newspapers to celebrate his birthday, evidently because it implicitly raised the question of his mortality.

[6] Some had seen it earlier. Farinacci had warned Mussolini of his mortality in 1933, reminding the fascist leader that he himself had said that 'Italy cannot have a Duce number 2'. 'Not that I want to shorten your life...', Farinacci added mischievously. In the same letter the Cremona boss summed up the situation as he saw it: 'What is the State today? Confidence in Mussolini. We have still not arrived at the State that gives strength to men. It is one man who gives strength to the State'. See ACS, PNF, SPEP, b. 40, 22 January 1933.

[7] ACS, MI, DGPS, Polizia Politica, b. 109, 29 July 1937.   [8] ACS, Ibid., 25 June 1936.

into question the inept party management of Starace. While many young people continued to worship the *duce* and to hold him up as a role model, Mussolini was more vulnerable in the critical eyes of older fascists. As already noted, discontented former blackshirts constituted a permanent problem for the regime. They would usually argue that the Fascism of the 1930s was not the Fascism they had fought for in the early 1920s (and for this line of argument they had ample justification), but in fact they generally meant that they had not been given the role they imagined was their due. Quite apart from the various purges effected after 1925, 'make way for the young' pushed older people to the side and easily generated rancour. These feelings could create resentment against Mussolini himself, a leader the older fascists had known in other circumstances and at a time when his allegedly miraculous powers had not been so developed as to permit him to dispense with his friends. Thus, in early 1937, it was reported from Vicenza that the '*fascisti-squadristi*' were in revolt.

> Here people are insinuating... that the *duce* carries out business in such a way as to get rid of reminders of the old doctrine... that the *duce* would prefer to sacrifice the old *squadristi* who had embraced the old doctrine. Everyone notices with surprise the way in which the old fascists and *squadristi* have been abandoned, often removed as undesirables by fascists more recently enrolled in the party.[9]

A report from Rome later in the same year spoke of a wider discontent among long-standing supporters—'bourgeoisie, intellectuals... big fish from the Militia... never before today did people shout against the *duce*, everyone has always spoken more or less badly of the people around the *duce*, but today that is no longer so'.[10] Precisely what was going on is not easy to ascertain, but it seems to have been a mixture of frustration over failed ambition, intolerance of party discipline and of the regime imposed by Starace, and rapidly worsening living conditions. From Rome in June 1938 one informer wrote a fairly devastating report.

> In the circles of old fascists you still continue to hear criticisms and comments that are almost totally anti-Mussolinian. It is notable that, while criticisms have always made a precise distinction between Mussolini and his circle, he is now criticized for what he has done. People say that for some time he has been exaggerating with novelties and that if he has not invented them he should at least prevent them. People go back to the *passo romano*, which they call the goose step, and every time—at the cinema—you see parades of soldiers and military formations marching like that, there is no question that, with smiles and half-spoken phrases, people are laughing at this novelty...[11]

There is other evidence that Mussolini's position was suffering erosion by the second half of the 1930s. At popular level, as we have already seen, in some places people did not exactly flock to hear the *duce*'s speeches when broadcast in the piazza. He 'spoke to the wind, *as usual*'.[12] Evidently, there was little point in listening or people were reluctant to hear what they did not want to hear. There is no difficulty in find-

---

[9] ACS, MI, DGPS, Polizia Politica, b. 109, 31 January 1937.
[10] ACS, Ibid., 15 October 1937.
[11] ACS, Ibid., 22 June 1938.
[12] ACS, PNF, SPEP, b. 11, Padua, 20 March 1937.

ing signs of popular antagonism towards the *duce*. Phrases from documents of 1939 are fairly typical: 'If I'm called up I shall go, but the first bullet is for Mussolini';[13] 'I hope both you and Mussolini get cancer';[14] '"M" stands for misery [Mussolini's initial was in evidence everywhere]'.[15] On the same lines, in May 1939, an informer signalled the fact that there had been a worrying increase in the number of jokes going round, many of which 'even mention the Person of the *duce*'.[16] Here, perhaps, little had changed. And when Mussolini returned to Turin in May 1939 his reception by Fiat workers was reported to have been 'glacial', as in 1930.[17]

The crisis of 1939 forced convinced fascists to look hard at the cult of the *duce*. They recognized the strength of the cult, but also its limitations. In June 1939 an informer, writing from Florence, made a very concise summary of the situation as he and his friends saw it, reiterating a sentiment we have already noted above:

> The 'Mussolini' party comprises the authentic majority in Italy and you could say that, although the *duce* persists in talking about Fascism, Italians continue to understand by this word only and exclusively 'Mussolini'. For the overwhelming majority a Fascism without Mussolini is unthinkable, while, perhaps, a Mussolini without Fascism could be understandable.[18]

This was a recognition of the aura of the leader and his hold on the public, but it was also, implicitly, a very strong criticism of the fascist movement, which had evidently failed to root itself as an autonomous force in the country—a fact that was becoming increasingly evident throughout the peninsula. It was, for example, the awareness of this failure which prompted an agent in Florence to observe that 'in Florence we are still a very long way from any deep-seated fascistization', saying that 'a good part of the young people are very lukewarm' and that the middle class, the artisans, and some of the working class were convinced 'that, at the most, Fascism will live and die with the *duce*'.[19]

Inevitably, therefore, convinced fascists were compelled to recognize the extent to which they were dependent on the figure of Mussolini—and he was not, as the cult had tended to suggest, immortal. Speculation about the eventual succession to the fascist leadership sprang from this realization. Loyal fascists, sensing the mood of the country, clearly began to feel themselves to be exposed. Everything depended on one man. The suggestion, circulating widely, that Galeazzo Ciano was the designated successor, seems to have excited no one.

After 1936, when the fascist leader had withdrawn to some extent from the running of internal affairs, he was slightly lost to view among the population.[20] In the

---

[13] ACS, MI, DGPS, PS, 1939, b. 24, Pistoia, 5 June 1939.
[14] ACS, Ibid., Reggio Emilia, 8 September 1939.
[15] ACS, DGPS, PS, 1939, b. 24, 29 September 1939.
[16] ACS, MI, DGPS, Polizia Politica, b. 224, 8 May 1939.
[17] ACS, MI, DGPS, Polizia Politica, Materia (1927–44), b. 220, 3 August 1939.
[18] ACS, Ibid., 17 June 1939.
[19] ACS, Ibid., 22 May 1939.
[20] Bottai suggests in his diary that it was from this time that Mussolini had begun to believe in his own myth. He reports that, in conversations with the duce, he felt that there was already 'a statue' talking to him; Bottai, *Diario 1935–1944*, Milan, Rizzoli, 1982, 78.

short term, this distance may have served to increase the mystique of the fascist leader, now seen to be taken up with events on the international stage, but the gathering war clouds began to put that mystique to a severe test. Mussolini was silent for long periods in 1939. In mid-May he had made a short tour of Piedmont, giving speeches in Turin and Cuneo, and he would reappear, with a major speech to the nation explaining Italian non-belligerency, only in late September. This long silence created a great deal of perplexity—'Mussolini's silence is exasperating everybody', confessed one informer.[21]

Rather predictably, in the late spring and summer, stories began to circulate widely that something had happened and that the *duce's* position was in question. Rumours recounted that he had either already stepped down or was about to do so because of serious illness (sometimes said to be a 'progressive paralysis', sometimes said to be a venereal complaint, sometimes a combination of the two).[22] People were whispering that Mussolini had been deposed and would be allowed to retire to private life; some said that he was already dead. In certain quarters it was suggested that he needed 'mental rest'. There were stories that he had been wounded in an assassination attempt (Caviglia, Baistrocchi, and Badoglio were the variously-named would-be assassins), and even that he had been removed from power by the King and replaced by Balbo (said to be the Vatican's candidate) or (with prophetic vision) by Badoglio or by a military triumvirate. An alleged rupture between the King and the army on one side and Mussolini and the PNF on the other was at the bottom of many of the rumours.[23] In this context, crisis appears to have persuaded people to look towards traditional authority rather than towards the *duce:* 'They say that, if it comes to war, the men who will command in Italy will be the King and Badoglio'.[24] The PNF would be dissolved.[25] Almost as if in confirmation of all this, it was widely reported in September, after the declaration of non-belligerence, that the King was proposing to abdicate in favour of his son, a manoeuvre designed to make it easier for the House of Savoy to dispense with Mussolini and form an anti-German government.[26]

The state of uncertainty and the persistence of rumours provoked reactions from the population, promptly noted by the informers. In respect of the possibility of war, the most common reaction was that implicit in totalitarian dictatorship—notwithstanding uncertainty, or perhaps precisely because of it, people delegated to the leader, assuming that Mussolini knew what he was doing and would produce some miracle at the last minute. He was, after all, an acknowledged genius and 'always right'. He had pulled it off in Munich in 1938, he would pull it off again in 1939. In some ways this was an obligatory reaction for those seeking reas-

---

[21] ACS, MI, DGPS, Polizia Politica, Materia (1927–44), b. 220, 30 August 1939. One informer wrote that people were saying that Mussolini's silences were more frightening than his speeches: Ibid., b. 224, 23 May 1939.

[22] ACS, Ibid., Rome, 3 August 1939.

[23] See, among many, ACS, Ibid., b. 224, 17 and 20 August, 4 and 15 September 1939.

[24] ACS, Ibid., b. 224, 22 June 1939. Badoglio's name appears repeatedly in reports throughout 1940 and 1941 as the probable successor to a Mussolini removed from power and consigned to private life.

[25] ACS, Ibid., b. 219, 8 September 1939.   [26] ACS, Ibid., b. 224, 4 September 1939.

surance. For those who needed to live with hope there was, after all, no alternative
but to suspend disbelief and to trust in the *duce*—he was very much the leader of
last resort. In this sense, moments of intense international crisis, such as August
1939, could play in favour of the fascist leader because even his critics were forced
to realize that, since there was no real possibility of replacing him, he was their only
hope of avoiding war. 'News of the perfect health of the *duce* has provoked an
enormous sigh of relief, given that in all circles—fascist and not—people are convinced that in a moment like this the loss of the *duce* would be a disaster'.[27] The
impression of people whistling the Mussolini tune in order to keep up their spirits
is almost palpable in some of the documents relating to the summer of 1939.

At the same time there was a general sense of apprehension. The continuing
flirtation with Hitler increased doubts about the *duce*'s infallible 'intuition', and
the widespread hostility to the alliance with the Nazis did put Mussolini's judgement in question in many circles. The alliance was, after all, a matter of foreign
policy and could not be put down to the deficiencies of provincial leaders, even
though there was a strong current of opinion that maintained that Mussolini was
being badly advised by top *gerarchi*, who kept him in the dark about many things.
For many, who maintained their confidence in Mussolini, this was the only possible explanation of such a foolish foreign policy. For others, less confident, Mussolini was called directly into play. His character was a source of speculation. People
feared that Mussolini's alleged stubbornness and *amour propre* would make him dig
his heels in.

Even so, in general, his position, if much criticized, was not totally compromised. It depended on the avoidance of war. This condition was present particularly in popular sentiment, in any case already very hostile to Fascism for reasons
we have seen, which posited any remaining respect for Mussolini on his keeping
Italy out of the war. As one informer put it, 'everyone puts their hope in the wisdom of Mussolini, who, if he were not to avoid the disaster, would fall immensely
in popular confidence'.[28] Faith in Mussolini was now heavily qualified, therefore.
It was conditional; opinion would judge him by results, but confidence was far
from total.[29]

Perhaps the clearest indication that the cult of the *duce* was wilting is the com-
motion around the presumed destitution of the fascist leader in the summer of
1939. The persistence of such rumours is itself indicative of a certain state of mind
among the population, generally convinced that the situation in which Italy found
itself was catastrophic. As informer number 40 felt bound to say about the rumours,
'[t]his wide and rapid diffusion [of rumours] could not happen if they did not find
ready and very interested believers, if they did not—that is—find favourable and
ready ground among the public for their divulgence…'.[30] Another experienced
informer—code-named 'Fieramosca', from Florence—explained the disposition to

---

[27] ACS, Ibid., 29 August 1939.   [28] ACS, Ibid., 25 August 1939.
[29] De Felice writes of 'a well-diffused decline…in confidence in Mussolini' among the middle and
lower-middle classes from the early months of 1939: *Mussolini il duce*, II, 187.
[30] ACS, MI, DGPS, Polizia Politica, Materia (1927–44), b. 220, Rome, 26 September 1939.

believe the rumours in another way: 'people are saying that... the *duce* is morally dead, in the sense that there is no longer any confidence in his political acumen' and that the talk of metaphorical death had been interpreted literally by many.[31]

What is surprising is the degree to which these rumours seem to have provoked relatively little surprise or alarm among the population. '*Il popolino*'—the ordinary people—spoke little about the rumours openly 'for fear of beatings or worse',[32] but they were reported to be on everyone's minds. Indeed, it was suggested that the rumours were embraced so readily because they seemed to promise what all hoped for, 'which you can sum up in one phrase: no war alongside the Germans'.[33] If this possibility could be realized, the destitution of Mussolini would be welcome. 'You hear people talk about the near, indeed almost imminent end of the regime with a certainty that makes an impression. You hear people say that it is a pity that Caviglia aimed badly...'[34] Wishful thinking among the population associated the end of the regime with peace. The continued existence of the regime itself was put in question, therefore: 'A kind of trial of the regime is going on, as if it were about to end, and you can hear people say that the King has a second chance to get rid of Fascism, after that of Matteotti'.[35] Here, when combined with a generalized fear for the future, the situation of disaffection, stagnation, and paralysis of the party, felt above all in the provinces, would seem to have undermined even the myth of the infallibility and virtual immortality of the fascist leader himself. Perhaps it was time he should go, it was suggested. In Rome in late August 1939 it was said that 'in all circles people are making spirited comments against the war and levelling accusations at Mussolini and at Fascism. The idea is going round that if Mussolini were to leave government the war might be avoided'.[36] As one informer wrote, again in August 1939, 'that ideal continuity there has always been between the *duce* and his people seems to be finished and broken...'[37]

10.2. NON-BELLIGERENCE 1939–1940

The period of non-belligerence—September 1939 until 10 June 1940—did little to dispel doubts expressed at almost all levels about the direction Mussolini was taking. His speech to the assembled *gerarchi* of Bologna, made in Rome on 23 September, was bellicose but vague and open to almost all interpretations. Most of those who heard it broadcast in the public squares grasped at the phrases that seemed most to indicate that Italy would avoid war. Many fascists had apparently become 'pacifists' by this time, and their mode of reasoning reflected the severity

---

[31] ACS, MI, DGPS, Polizia Politica, b. 224, Florence, 29 September 1939.		[32] Ibid.
[33] ACS, Ibid., 4 September 1939. At the international cycling championships in Milan in late August 1939 the German champion received a hostile reception from the crowd; 'the crowd revolted, throwing cushions, bottles and other similar projectiles at him...': ACS, Ibid., 25 August 1939.
[34] ACS, Ibid., 15 September 1939.
[35] Ibid.
[36] ACS, Ibid., b. 220, Rome, 28 August 1939.
[37] ACS, MI, DGPS, Polizia Politica, Materia (1927–44), b. 220, Milan, 28 August 1939.

of the crisis within the regime. 'Even among many—very many—fascists, opinion is decidedly against [the war]. There are not a few—fascists and not—who believe that if Fascism enters the conflict it will come out badly'.[38] In the event of either victory or defeat, 'the destiny of Fascism would be decided', either gobbled up by the Nazis or compelled to concede to the political systems of the democracies.

Particular attention was paid to that part of the speech in which Mussolini invited his followers to 'clean out the corners' of defeatists and rumour-mongers, generally interpreted at popular level as a licence to the *squadristi* to move into action against presumed enemies—described in one report as 'the Jewish–masonic relics who have manoeuvred the events of recent weeks with the help of all kinds of intellectuals'.[39] In several places renewed blackshirt activity was reported. People were beaten up and castor oil made its appearance once again. In Milan, one agent wrote, '…the actions carried out by the *squadristi* in the various town districts has been effective. Castor oil and cudgels impose justice'.[40] But it is interesting to note that, in more than one city, there was a reaction against the violence of the fascists. The targeted did not always submit passively to a new wave of attacks; 'quietly people mutter dark threats of future vendettas'.[41] The end seemed almost in sight.

The speech of 23 September provided the occasion for a rigorous analysis of the fascist movement by its supporters and provoked a whole series of conclusions—most of them negative. One informer—one of the most experienced—had no illusions about popular opinion, even after Mussolini's 'tranquillizing' speech. His own sub-informants in Rome told him that people had reacted with 'a certain indifference' to the speech and had not rushed to buy the evening paper nor congregated in the bars to hear the radio news, as had sometimes happened in the past after a similar event. The fact was, the informer insisted, 'the people do not identify with and do not want this war'. Positing an interesting difference between the crowds assembled for fascist demonstrations in the past and a kind of unseen silent majority, he warned:

> Even if one day Piazza Venezia will be as full of people as it was on 2 October 1935, the *duce* should not make too many easy inferences about…the demonstration, which will have been organized skilfully by the Secretary of the Party, Achille Starace! The people who do not want the war will not be in Piazza Venezia and they will be the majority!

Quoting an acquaintance, he wrote 'if there had not been a continuing, tough control on the part of the police, the regime—and not from today—would have had some nasty surprises about the "consensus" of the people for the regime'.[42]

A day later, from within the Vatican, the same informer reported that Catholic opinion had found little new in the speech, apart from the threats levelled at a population already very hard hit and unable to face what he described as a new 'turn of the screw': 'particularly in the small centres there is already complete apathy

---

[38] ACS, MI, DGPS, Polizia Politica, b. 224, 26 September 1939.   [39] Ibid.
[40] ACS, Ibid., Milan, 2 October 1939. At the beginning of October 1939 the PNF forbade all political discussion in public places in order to try to quell the 'defeatists' and rumour-mongers.
[41] ACS, Ibid., Rome, 25 September 1939.   [42] ACS, Ibid., Rome, 26 September 1939.

among the population and in several places the peasants are refusing to work the land...; one notes that a kind of "passive resistance" is beginning, which will increase if events move towards war...'[43]

The informer, presenting himself more as counsellor than spy, advised that the regime should look at the causes of discontent and not be satisfied with denouncing and repressing its open manifestations. According to him, the causes were in part generic and in part very specific. At a general level, he noted the popular reaction to Mussolini's affirmation in his speech that the Italians were one of the most intelligent peoples on earth. It had been received with 'some ironic smiles' and then commented with a long list of events and policies in which the people felt themselves to have been deceived and defrauded.

> They talk about social justice, about the idea of reaching out to the people, about the cost of social insurance, about the Austrian episode, about the promised El Dorado of the Ethiopian Empire, about the war in Spain and the friendship with Russia, to get to the conclusion that it is not true that the Italian people has always been treated and considered as an intelligent people. These are just pretty phrases...[44]

This was an impressive list. It included most of the main planks of the regime over the previous decade, and, strikingly, all the ventures of foreign policy. The suspicion was growing among the commentators that—as Bottai would deftly put it later—Mussolini was really more interested in crowds than he was in people.

On a more specific level, the reporter pointed the finger at what were, in his eyes, the main culprits—the party and the *gerarchi*. These were responsible for 'torpedoing' Mussolini's initiatives. Here the informer was joined by others, all convinced that Fascism required more than a 'clean-up of the corners' to regain its prestige and that the place to start was within the party itself. The themes of complaint remained exactly those of the spring and summer but the events of 1 September served to give a new twist to them. A constant of the impressions reported by the informers was that Italy was unprepared to fight a European war, that the armed forces were poorly equipped and badly trained, and—particularly worrying—that there was little or no provision for defence of the civilian population from air attack: 'This impression is confirmed by the officials who come back from the period of call-up and who sum up the situation with a single word—CHAOS!'[45]

Comparison was now made with the evident efficiency of German forces. People asked why Italy was unprepared and where all the money they had paid in taxes had gone. The answer they gave was always the same; the *gerarchi* had stolen the money in order to furnish their lavish life-styles: 'they count the millions stolen by so many people...'[46] Here we return to familiar ground. Even the severity of the crisis did not discourage the *gerarchi* in their malpractices, it was said (from Milan):

> The reasons for discontent are still the same but these are accentuated by the men of the Party, who, with no sense of the moment, even in these times of tension continue to demonstrate that they are only interested in their affairs, showing too well their

---

[43] ACS, Ibid, Rome, 27 September 1939.   [44] Ibid.
[45] ACS, Ibid., Milan, 16 September 1939.   [46] ACS, Ibid., Milan, 6 September 1939.

absolute incompetence... almost everywhere can be seen the sorry spectacle of *gerarchi* who, even in these days,... think exclusively about all the ways they can devise to squeeze money, money, and more money from those who clearly have none...

The informer could only report that, faced by this kind of activity, people were asking why the government did not act against such people and arrest 'the many local leaders who are everywhere pointed to as dishonest and who have enriched themselves committing abuses of every kind'?[47]

Discontent was by no means confined to the towns and big cities. A fascist agent who had personally toured the remoter areas of the provinces of Pavia, Milan, and Cremona and spoken to many 'genuine workers of the land', small leaseholders, and small landowners, found that the rural population thought exactly like the town dwellers he had talked to previously. He found that 'Fascism has not penetrated either superficially or in depth because of the culpable inadequacy and dishonesty of so many *gerarchi*, big and small'. Young men who had been called up were saying, ominously, that a rifle could shoot in many directions (and not just towards France) and making open invitations to desertion: 'don't go, let them go, let Ciano go to fight the war'. Again, the 'them' is very much in evidence.

Significantly, this informer reported that the regime was losing the middle ground in rural areas, among those people who had not previously been opposed to the movement—indeed, in some cases had been part of the fascist rank and file—now shifting towards undisguised hostility towards the regime:

> In the most distant and isolated centres... the masses have remained dangerously subversive, as they have also become where before they were never [subversive], or at any rate very little, and Fascism is discredited, as are discredited the *gerarchi*, against whom they launch insults and make accusations of every kind.

The complaints were then listed and were very similar to those heard in other places: the money spent on the party card was 'a robbery', the 10 lire taken directly from wages every week to pay for the fascist uniform went straight into the pockets of the local fascist leaders, the kilo of fruit that every family had had to give to the *duce* on the occasion of his visit to Predappio had served to 'fatten' the local party secretary. A sense of injustice reared its head again. People were saying that 'too many people are enjoying the good life with the workers' money'. And they were also commenting with great interest on the news of what seemed to them an example of one sort of justice: 'Polish *latifundia* divided among the peasants in the Ukraine'.[48]

Permeating many of the reports of this period is a clear feeling of impotence among the people observed by the informers. Populist paternalism had broken down and people were reduced to asking why someone did not do something about the difficulties they were facing. Should not the state intervene? The reply people gave repeatedly was, in effect, that the state did not exist for the citizens, but for the benefit of the few who were able to take advantage of a position of authority.

---

[47] ACS, MI, DGPS, Polizia Politica, b. 219, Milan, 26 October 1939.
[48] ACS, Ibid., Milan, 28 September 1939.

Criticism was levelled at the fascist bureaucracy, considered not only arrogant and inefficient, but also incorrigibly corrupt. Anyone having contact with a state office, it was alleged, would find that corruption was the order of the day: 'it is precisely among the office workers and the bureaucrats that you find that corruption which so annoys the public'.[49] In respect of the welfare organizations—the flagship of the party—it was rumoured that millions had been stolen: 'people are talking about the discovery of enormous abuse and fraud, they say that only a small part of the many millions the Party gets as welfare contributions ever goes to help the poor'.[50] A vivid summary of what was going on in some offices was provided later, in 1941, by an informer who had evidently lost patience: 'there isn't a company in Italy that is able to get an exchange licence [for purchases abroad], a subcontract, a delivery, an allocation of raw materials if it doesn't agree to pay the usual sum'.[51]

The difference from previous complaints of this nature was that now, in 1939 and 1940, the arrogance, corruption, and nepotism long associated with the local fascist administration was also associated with a situation of danger and insecurity to which people felt themselves exposed. This sense of insecurity helped to sharpen even further their perception of a party *apart* from them, following interests other than theirs.

The main—but certainly not the only—target for criticism was the PNF secretary, Achille Starace. He was widely considered to have exposed the party to ridicule because of many of his almost daily directives, and, as we have seen, he was also resented because of an infinite number of petty rules and regulations introduced in an attempt to change Italian habits and customs. The demand to substitute 'Voi' for 'Lei', which we have seen in Chapter 9, was just one such measure. Non-fascists laughed at him, but many fascists also had little or no time for him, accusing him of superficiality and an excessive attention to appearances. '*Esteriorità*' ['outward appearance'] was a word often used against him, and much bandied about in the late 1930s. The implication was that Fascism had become a mass movement but, because of an excessive attention to outward appearances, it had also become a meaningless one.[52]

Starace had also singled himself out as a committed supporter of the German alliance—a position which attracted further criticism. The strength of feeling against him is shown by an attack made on him by an informer (number 407) in June 1939. The document is itself a good indication of the distance that existed between the organs of the state and those of the PNF. The language used suggests

---

[49] ACS, Ibid., 26 October 1939.   [50] ACS, Ibid., 29 November 1939.

[51] ACS, Ibid., 25 August 1941.

[52] There was a telling reference to '*esteriorità*' in a later document, produced by the governing body of the Scuola di mistica fascista in early 1942. People, they wrote, had simply not understood the Revolution. From this failure derived 'the absence of an intense moral life, which would have permitted the formation of a competent and responsible governing class, and the presence instead of a hierarchy limited to the external aspects of the revolutionary phenomena; from this also the little stimulation to think about ideas and means, the triumph of approximation, intoxicated by the desire for power for power's sake, the fear of criticism and of intelligence, the scorn of personality'. Quoted in Daniela Marchesi, *La scuola dei gerarchi. Mistica fascista: storia, problemi, istituzioni*, Milan, Feltrinelli, 1976, Appendix M.

that the spy must have been sure of finding a sympathetic ear at police headquarters—he was, after all, writing about one of the most powerful men in Italy: 'As long as the *duce* fails to get rid of Starace things will go from bad to worse and overwhelm everything and everybody, because there is no other man who has done and is doing so much harm to the party as this presumptuous illiterate'.[53] Similar sentiments were expressed by another informer in September, when a comparison was made between the *gerarchi* of the Nazi party and those of the fascist movement. Whereas, it was said, the Germans put able and responsible people in positions of command, in Italy 'you hear the names and examples of numerous favouritisms, in particular of people favoured by Starace who are especially targets of dislike, to the point that they are saying that if Mussolini does not discard this ballast he will go the bottom as well…'[54]

Mussolini's reluctant decision to replace Starace with the military hero and former *squadrista*, Ettore Muti, in late November 1939 did nothing to improve matters. The new party secretary had little experience of administration—he was only 37 when appointed—and no aptitude to learn. In the eyes of Renzo De Felice, 'it would have been difficult to make a worse choice'.[55] Although perhaps not quite the genial and muscular numbskull Bottai would make him out to be, Muti maintained the 'Starace system' without any of the energy Starace had employed, imposing himself on others without listening to them, thus producing a further and more rapid decline in the functioning of the PNF. He attempted a wide-ranging rotation of *federali* in the belief that this was the road to salvation for the party, but the effects appear to have been little short of disastrous. According to Tullio Cianetti, with Muti 'we watched a real devastation of the PNF'. Far from representing a radical change in direction, Muti was seen as representing no direction—'we lived from day to day, and the only clear objective was that of destroying the foundations on which the totalitarian regime had been built'.[56]

Neither Mussolini's decision to declare non-belligerency nor a change in party secretary served to restore the fortunes of the fascist movement, therefore. The informers' reports showed little tendency to optimism; living conditions had not improved and people understood that the peace achieved through non-belligerency was probably only temporary. Conversations reproduced in the reports suggest that many people had a strong sense of Italy being drawn inevitably into a conflict that would prove difficult to control and in which Italy would find itself boxing well above its weight. Fascist propaganda had no effect: 'nobody believes it, nobody wants to listen to it'.[57] This was a fair measure of the degree to which the population had 'internalized' the fascist message.

[53] ACS,MI, DGPS, Polizia Politica, b. 217, 9 June 1939. According to Bottai, police chief Bocchini and Starace hated one another, almost coming to blows shortly before Starace's replacement: see De Felice, Mussolini il duce, vol. 2, 705.
[54] ACS, MI, DGPS, Polizia Politica, b. 224, 15 September 1939.
[55] De Felice, Mussolini il duce, vol. 2, 705.
[56] Cianetti, Memorie, 307.
[57] ACS, MI, DGPS, Polizia Politica, b. 219, 26 November 1939.

During the winter of 1939–40 report after report underlined the degree of discontent and disillusion among the population. Coffee returned to Italian tables—officially and, in many areas, only officially—on 1 December but by that time the damage had been done. If Muti was submerged by letters from old *squadristi*, begging him to take his opportunity to 'restore' discipline within Fascism by a recourse to violence, Bocchini's desk must have been covered by informers' reports denouncing the degree to which the PNF was hated by large segments of the population. Increasingly, informers abandoned the caution of the messenger bearing bad news and showed no reticence at all in describing situations of total disarray within the provincial federations and in recounting popular reaction to that disarray. Sometimes the news was threatening: 'You hear all kinds of things... they are saying that the day is not far off when the masses will realize that they possess the strength, and then, finally, we will see the end of those who think they are the controllers of other people's lives'.[58] Another warned, 'I've never before found the workers so depressed and sceptical as they are at the moment... we must listen to the people: the day they lose patience, things will go badly for us!'[59]

There are persistent references to the exhaustion of the population: 'the people are tired';[60] 'the peasants are tired and protest about the regime';[61] 'even the proprietors and those well-off... are showing a palpable tiredness towards the regime, criticizing the policies followed...'[62] For informer number 40 the PNF had now become the 'Trojan horse' of Fascism, the home of 'the dishonest, the exploiters, the opportunists'; it represented nothing less than the 'immediate danger' facing Fascism. Staying with his metaphor, the informer advised that the party was Mussolini's 'Achilles heel', and might pull the fascist leader down with it. He saw the party as the problem in the provinces in particular, where '"*rassismo*" is always protected' and a subject population could stand no more. Muti, it was said, had lost his chance to reform through his defence of the blackshirt squads and his 'obstinate insistence on keeping intact certain political situations [has] accentuated the cancerous process taking place within the party'.[63]

In contrast with the spring of 1939, when the fear of speaking out among the population had attracted the attention of many informers, by early 1940 this fear had largely vanished and people were voicing their grievances openly. The wall of fear had evidently been breached. Several informers were struck by this change and commented on it. It seems that all social groups were involved in what was almost an act of collective denunciation. The account of one agent who had been travelling in the provinces of Milan, Genoa, Cremona, and Parma in late April 1940, noted that the same things were being said in rural and urban areas and among different social groups. 'Without fear of exaggeration you can say that the regime is subject every day to an extremely lively popular reaction, which tries to highlight all those problems that exemplify the conditions of difficulty and economic hardship faced by the Italian people'. There were more rumours of popular risings—

---

[58] ACS, PNF, SPEP, b. 20, Milan, 20 January 1940.   [59] ACS, Ibid., 26 January 1940.
[60] ACS, Ibid., 20 January 1939.   [61] ACS, Ibid., 24 January 1940.
[62] Ibid.   [63] ACS, MI, DGPS, Polizia Politica, b. 219, 12 January 1940.

effectively bread riots: 'In the provinces of Piacenza and Milan people have been talking for days about alleged seditious risings in Parma, following the outbreak of rebellion among the people of that city, given the increasing hardship occasioned by the cost of living'. The stories doing the rounds were claiming several dead and hundreds of arrests, and the rumours were 'in large part considered credible'.[64] Similar rumours of 'attempted uprisings' had been heard earlier, in February, relating to 'certain towns in the Kingdom' and even to some of the poorer areas of Rome.[65]

What informers could not hide was that, in many cases, fascists were prominent among those making the protests. In the case of Piacenza, quoted above, the spy wrote that 'even in fascist families, the substance of the comments is no different from those made generally by the citizens'. The involvement of party members in the process of denunciation had been going on for some time. In late November 1939 an informer in Rome had written the usual pessimistic report, based on visits, 'for obvious reasons', to several small towns around the capital, and had found the usual complaints. 'By now the population is tired of being subjected to continual sacrifices, which have not let up for eighteen years...too much is asked of them, the promised prosperity never arrives, etc'. There was nothing unusual in all this, but what attracted his attention was the fact that fascists were joining in the chorus of protest. 'These statements can be heard in public places, in the communal *Dopolavoro*, and it is worthy of note that those making them are regularly enrolled in the Party, and not recently'.[66] The unease among fascists found confirmation in other reports. A shopkeeper in Rome stated that it was the fascists 'and their wives' who were the most outspoken in their public judgements on the regime.[67] Evidently economic crisis and political uncertainty exacted a price even from the fascist faithful. In part, their loss of confidence was just one aspect of general disaffection, even among the middle classes—what one informer's contact saw taking place in the bourgeoisie, 'fed-up with and tired of the present regime'.[68]

Despite persistent warnings from informers of the likelihood of serious social unrest during the spring and summer of 1939, the party seems, if anything, to have gone from bad to worse in the first six months of 1940. Participation in activities was reported to be at an all-time low and various informers wrote of a total lack of enthusiasm for any initiatives taken by the local party machines. People were abandoning the movement. The discovery that, as we have seen, people 'In the whole of northern Italy' were removing their fascist badges brought the vacillations of the Matteotti crisis back to the mind of one observer. The causes of dissent, he wrote, were to be found in the 'lack of interest in the party among the masses, given that this has lost a great deal of its force in recent times'.[69] Another report claimed that in the hinterland of Milan—Lodi, Casalpusterlengo, Codogno, Abbiategrasso, Magenta—there were 'a lot of people enrolled, but taciturn and silent because

[64] ACS, Ibid., 1 May 1940.   [65] ACS, Ibid., 22 February 1939.
[66] ACS, Ibid., 26 November 1939.   [67] ACS, Ibid., 12 January 1940.
[68] ACS, Ibid., 12 January 1940.   [69] ACS, Ibid., 25 April 1940.

miles and miles away from Fascism'. This distance was attributed to the fact that the union officials had done nothing to defend wage levels and contracts, 'preferring to have a few sealed envelopes at the end of the year' from the employers. Here it was suggested, rotation of *federali* had had no effect at all; leaders had changed but the problems had remained exactly the same.[70] In many cases rotation did no more than leave a vacuum of power in the local federation.

The same negative message is provided by other informers' despatches. For example, it was reported that, in Alessandria, Novara, Vercelli, Cuneo, Torino, 'there is no propaganda activity taking place on the part of the *fascio*'.[71] But the impression of collapse is also reinforced by the tone of the reports themselves. They are no longer the confident *relazioni* of the early or even mid-1930s, recounting events and situations that merit attention but hardly give rise to serious concern. Instead, by 1939–40, the reports are filled with alarm. In many cases, more than reports, they are essays on what has gone wrong and on what should be done to redeem a failing movement. In some it is possible to sense the indignation of committed fascists when faced with what they themselves can see to be the arrogance, dishonesty, and incompetence that characterized the workings of the local federations. From being informers they become advisers and counsellors, issuing warnings which the central authorities will ignore at their peril. There is, at the same time, in some of the reports of this period, a certain distance from the fascist movement established by the informer. The agony of the party is observed, commented on, and criticized, but the reader cannot avoid noting that the reports were being written, in the main, for the police and not for the party, that the two were very far from being the same thing, and that it was the police who really had the upper hand. It was the awareness of this marginalization of the party, perhaps, that persuaded one dedicated fascist to write directly to Mussolini, urging him to disband the MVSN and form a new elite group of militant fascists—'an aristocracy of the specially selected'—clearly on the lines of the Nazi SS. Only in this way, it was suggested, could the movement regain the momentum it had lost.[72]

The celebrations planned on 23 March 1940 to mark the twenty-first anniversary of the foundation of the *fasci di combattimento* were widely ignored by everyone. Descriptions of the ceremonies matched those of 1939 almost exactly. Writing from Trento, an informer lamented that in the Veneto 'the commemoration of 23 March was characterized this year...by the complete absenteeism of the crowd and of the fascists from the various ceremonies'. There had been only thirty people present at the ceremony in Trento, six at Rovereto; at Padua the *federale* himself spoke of 'complete absenteeism'. Exactly the same phrase was used to describe events in Venice itself, while, in the hinterland, the day had passed off 'almost unnoticed'. The province of Rovigo had distinguished itself for 'absolute indifference' to the anniversary. The informer ended his report by saying that 'the symptom

---

[70] ACS, PNF, SPEP, b. 20, Milan, 2 March 1940.   [71] ACS, Ibid., 15 May 1939.

[72] ACS, MI, DGPS, Polizia Politica, b. 219, 23 July 1940. It is revealing that this letter was sent to police chief Bocchini with the request that it be handed personally to Mussolini. The writer clearly felt he could not trust anyone in the PNF headquarters to deliver the letter.

is very serious and I leave it to you to draw conclusions'.[73] He was reluctant himself to state the logical conclusion of his description—that, in many areas, the fascist movement, at least in its provincial manifestation, was dead on its legs.

No lesser figure than Giuseppe Bottai picked up this mood during a visit to Florence at the end of March 1940. He found people depressed and lacking any sense of direction, with the local fascist leaders having no kind of answer to anything. Always critical of the way the party had evolved, he could not resist a certain sarcasm: 'The leaders, possessed by the demon of organization, organize. But what, and why? the political impotence of the Party, omnipotent everyone says, has never reached such levels'. Reflecting on the fact that 'the fascists no longer know where Fascism is', he wrote a letter to general secretary Muti in which he described what he had found, 'a kind of inertia in the party, by now incapable of penetrating, understanding, and directing public opinion'. The letter was read to Mussolini, who failed to take the point, commenting tersely that no people likes war.[74]

It was almost inevitable in the circumstances of uncertainty that prevailed in late 1939 and early 1940 that Mussolini's position would again be put in question. In September he had appealed to the people 'not to disturb the pilot' in his navigation, but the silence he had imposed took its toll. His reputation as the magician in foreign affairs had in any case already taken a serious knock in August 1939 with the signing of the Molotov–Ribbentrop pact. It was obvious to everyone that he had not been consulted by Hitler and had been taken by surprise, something that seriously dented his image as the man who determined and did not follow events. But it was the internal situation that was most damaging to him. In particular, nothing seemed to be being done to improve the economic conditions of the population, despite all the protests, and Muti had failed to curb the malpractices of the *gerarchi*.

There were suggestions in conversations overheard and reported that the battle between rich and poor was not really between plutocratic and proletarian nations, as fascist propaganda asserted, but between leaders and led within Italy. 'If the *duce* only knew' became much less credible as an excuse for the fascist leader and, it seems, many people had stopped making excuses for him. In November 1939 one informer wrote that it was now 'public opinion' that Mussolini knew about the newly enriched *gerarchi* and kept quiet about it, for fear of the damage revelations would generate: 'to ordinary people this keeping quiet is complicity'. People no longer blamed simply the lower officials: 'No, it goes to the top, to the Regime, to the Chief. . . These are the things people are saying in the workshops, in the *dopolavoro*, in the offices'.[75] Another report of the same time stated that 'they discuss. . . the responsibilities of Mussolini, who presides over the ruins of his system'.[76] Soon after, informers noted that people were beginning to use the conditional tense when talking about Mussolini's future. Again, his permanence was linked with calls for social justice. By March 1940 people were saying that 'if Mussolini

---

[73] ACS, Ibid., 1 April 1940.
[74] Bottai, *Vent'anni e un giorno* (2008 edition), entries for 25 and 30 March 1940.
[75] ACS, MI, DGPS, Polizia Politica, b. 219, 26 November 1939.
[76] ACS, Ibid., 24 November 1939.

wants to remain in his place (!!) he must give the Italians some satisfaction, treating them all in the same way'.[77]

People were looking towards a future in which Mussolini had no part; they were considering political alternatives, a serious sign of danger for a totalitarian regime. In Milan in March 1940, 'almost everywhere people are saying that Mussolini is about to go'.[78] The war in prospect was seen as a kind of catharsis. As one short *relazione* explained:

> There is a lot of discussion about the post-war [period] in the sense that, if there is not a radical change in the method of government (especially in the workings of Corporativism) it will be necessary to make a revolution in order to put Italy in order. They say that Italy has no need to enter the war and that there are no good reasons to do so, but that Fascism needs to do so in order to continue to exist.[79]

The impression of deep crisis found confirmation even among fascist leaders. Even Mussolini could not but sense popular resistance to the impending conflict. His rantings, in early 1940, about the Italians as 'a race of sheep', were evidence of this, as was his conclusion that '[e]ighteen years are not enough to transform them, you need a hundred and eighty or perhaps a hundred and eighty centuries'.[80] He did not see his own position as threatened, but others did. The ageing *quadrumvir*, Emilio De Bono, committed to his diary in January 1940 the conviction that Mussolini was finished because the people had turned against him: 'For me, he's already finished. He knows very well the extent of his mistakes but firmly believes that the Italians haven't noticed'. On the contrary, he continued, '[h]e is finished, reduced in prestige more in Italy than abroad'.[81] Again, the rumours began to circulate that the King was going to intervene, that he was going to ask Balbo to take over, that Ciano was the chosen successor, and so on.

It is illuminating that the many rumours that concerned the removal of Mussolini almost always made reference to the King. The King was to take command again, the King was to appoint Badoglio, the King was to abdicate in favour of his son, and so on. This is very suggestive of where legitimate authority lay in the eyes of those inventing the rumours and in those of the people who subsequently passed on the rumours from one to another. Despite almost fifteen years of full fascist dictatorship, ultimate and legitimate authority was still seen to lie with the monarchy. The same phenomenon can be seen later—during the war itself—in the diaries of ordinary soldiers, who often state their pride in fighting for the King but almost never refer either to Fascism or to Mussolini.[82] This constant reference to the King revealed a chink in the fascist armour—always present, of course, and at times discussed and debated irritably by the fascist leader himself, but for more

---

[77] ACS, Ibid., 6 March 1940. Exclamation marks in original.
[78] ACS, Ibid., 30 March 1940.
[79] ACS, Ibid., 7 June 1940.
[80] Quoted in De Felice, *Mussolini il duce*, vol. 2, 691.
[81] Ibid., 686, note 157.
[82] See the diaries edited by Massimo Borgogni in the series Parole di guerra, Siena, Cantagalli. 2003–9.

than a decade perfectly possible to ignore. It is worth reflecting, however, on the degree to which this ultimate lack of legitimacy for Fascism may have further conditioned attitudes towards the provincial *gerarchi*, seen not only for what many of them were—arrogant, corrupt, and inefficient—but also as usurpers of a legitimacy that, really, still lay elsewhere. Personal charisma permitted Mussolini to put this problem to one side for many years, even if not permanently, but it may be doubted that the same was true for many of his local lieutenants.

10.3. INTO THE WAR

The Italian declaration of war on 10 June 1940, at the moment when it seemed that Hitler was on the point of winning the war without Italian help, is open to various explanations. It was, of course, an obvious move of political opportunism, about which Mussolini himself made no secret. After months of humiliating neutrality, he needed 'a thousand Italian dead' in order to be able to exert his influence at the apparently imminent and inevitable peace conference and in order not to appear totally subordinate to the Germans. The presumption, on which fascist propaganda was based, was that the war would be short and—obviously—victorious. For the regime not to have moved in June, when it seemed that all was over bar the shouting, would have been a denial of all the values the movement had attempted to instil in the Italian people over the previous eighteen years. The fascist message had been that war was not only necessary on occasions but that it was actually good for you; it strengthened, purified, defined. To remain immobile in the face of what looked like certain military victory would have represented a failure to meet the test the fascist movement had set for itself, to say nothing of the loss of face in the eyes of the Nazis, with consequent denial of Italian pretensions to enlarge her borders.

Whether—as in 1914–15—the decision to go to war was also a response to a rapidly worsening internal situation is debatable, but certainly worth considering. As has already been sufficiently illustrated, the reports from the provinces were extremely depressing for government. 'Disastrous', 'catastrophic', were words that appeared with too great a frequency in the descriptions of popular opinion to permit any sense of complacency among the authorities. And Mussolini was never a man to underestimate or ignore public mood. The message so many of the informers were relaying—essentially 'don't push the people too far'—was difficult to ignore. In this context there is no question that a quick, and decisive, military victory followed by a successful peace conference would have been of enormous value to the regime on the home front, silencing doubts, complaints, and rumours of rebellion. Mussolini—'Munich man'—would have triumphed again on the European stage and his internal detractors would have no ground left to stand on. On this basis it would be possible to 'relaunch' Fascism within the country, utilizing victory to pull the party out of the mire and push further the drive towards a truly totalitarian state.

Such considerations may well have been on Mussolini's mind when he overcame his uncertainty, determined by an acknowledged lack of preparation, and decided to enter the war, although it is likely that the final decision to engage the French was provoked by the rapid French military collapse in May and early June 1940 and the fear of an exclusively German victory. The situation on the home front was undoubtedly worrying, but there were few suggestions that the regime did not have the weapons to deal with popular discontent and unrest; the many-faceted fascist repressive machine remained intact. It is likely that Mussolini, in respect of internal politics, was more concerned to outflank certain of his critics among the fascist leaders, some of whom remained obstinately opposed to the German alliance, than by any serious preoccupation with a clearly disoriented public opinion.

Many were profoundly shocked and perplexed by the course of events. According to reports immediately preceding the intervention, strong anti-German sentiment in many rural areas and in certain towns and cities (Milan in particular) was forced to come to terms with the reality of a probable German victory. People were 'resigned' to the idea of Italian participation in the conflict and, although ashamed of taking advantage of the defeat of the French, well aware of the fact that it was better to be on the winning side as co-belligerent than as passive ally. Informers noted a general lack of enthusiasm for the enterprise, however, even among the fascist middle and lower-middle classes. 'A fairly sizeable mass, composed especially of elements of the lower-middle class, does not make a mystery of the fact that it is against the war'. Only a minority made up of students and 'the most rabid fascists' (but not, evidently, the others) showed any eagerness for battle.[83] More generally the mood seems to have been that a short war might be worth fighting, given that victory was assured, if it were to mean an end to the long period of uncertainty and economic hardship: 'Everyone hopes that our entry hastens the end of the conflict and gives Europe a very lengthy period of peace'.[84]

This position represented no more than conditional support for the fascist war and, of course, the conditions were not realized. Inevitably the reality of war changed to some extent the context within which people reasoned, injecting considerations of patriotism into a situation that could not be analysed exclusively in terms of the fortunes of the fascist state. In respect of creating national cohesion, patriotism might well be able to do what Fascism had failed to do and many of those critical of the regime undoubtedly felt that patriotism required them to overcome their reservations. Even so, the nationalist mobilization that should have been consequent on intervention hardly seems to have been forthcoming; nor did intervention do anything to restore the fortunes of the fascist party.

Indications of an immediate sense of lack of confidence in the fascist party and in its capacity for local organization come from many of the informers' reports immediately following the announcement of belligerency on 10 June. Milan was kept awake on the night of 11 June by air-raid alarms and thrown into confusion by another alarm at midday on the 12th. The (false) alarms had two effects. There was general panic, because people did not know where to go to find shelters—hardly surprising because, as one informer observed (adjusting his language to the

---

[83] ACS, PNF, SPEP, b. 20, Milan, 17 May 1940.   [84] ACS, Ibid., 10 June 1940.

requirements of the regime), 'Milan lacks anti-air raid shelters in a totalitarian way' (i.e. there were none). Many had tried to leave the city with their families; 'at the station there were scenes unworthy of a well-organized state...everything [happening] with the glaring absence of any form of control or assistance'. All this, according to the same report, because of the 'lack of spiritual guidance or encouragement on the part of the fascist hierarchy...'[85] A similar situation was generated in Genoa, although with more cause, because British bombers did appear overhead on the nights of 11 and 12 June, hitting the Galliera hospital and other buildings and causing casualties.[86]

An immediate secondary effect of the alarms in Milan had been to confirm what people had known for a long time—namely, that fascist propaganda and information, communicated through the radio and the newspapers, was not in any way credible. The Italian war correspondents had been suggesting that the French and the British were down to their last handful of aircraft and yet they had, apparently, managed a raid on Milan. The unreliability of information had been a common cause of complaint for a long time, as we have seen, and spoke volumes about the trust people had in the authorities. Indeed, more than one informer had protested about the stupidity of always printing or relaying by radio an orthodox, exaggeratedly optimistic party line in order to convince readers and listeners, pointing out that the effect was usually exactly the opposite. It was because of the poor quality of information available that, in 1938, fascist agents had been forced to report widespread attention to republican Radio Barcelona, and would shortly be denouncing the same offence in relation to Radio London.

One of the most striking features of many of the reports of summer 1940 is the way in which informers comment on the population's lack of enthusiasm for the war effort. Fascist 'New Men' are strangely absent from the picture. On 15 June— less than a week after the declaration—a report from Florence described the mood of the citizens as 'very depressed', characterized by the conviction that Italian participation in the war had been unnecessary, and that 'win or lose—the consequences of the war are going to be catastrophic'.[87] Hoarding of essential foodstuffs was the order of the day. In the main, people were just waiting for the conflict to end and wanted it to end as soon as possible. The hopes of victory were secondary to the desire for the war to finish. In July one fascist agent wrote from Milan that, despite the importance of international events, people were talking mainly about shortages and rationing, demonstrating 'the spirit of incomprehension among the masses' of the war effort.[88] A further report observed that 'a war mentality is not working among the masses', while, among the shopkeepers, complaints of lack of business revealed 'a mentality from the past, which corporative discipline and the

---

[85] ACS, Ibid., 12 June 1940.

[86] Not all the bombs exploded. One is still exhibited in the Galliera hospital—as I discovered when (in a slightly disquieting moment) doctors took me to see 'the British bomb' while I was being treated there.

[87] Quoted in Renzo Martinelli (ed.), *Il fronte interno a Firenze 1940–1943*, Florence, Dipartimento di Storia, 1989, 74.

[88] ACS, PNF, SPEP, b. 20, Milan, 7 July 1940.

fascist idea have still not permeated and transformed totally'.[89] Already by September, after only three months of war, even a very optimistic informer in Milan could not avoid noticing that the population was showing signs of disappointment because the war was not yet over.[90] Later, in October, despite the invasion of Greece, the attitude seemed unchanged: 'Lack of any kind of enthusiasm for the war is matched by a very strong and ever-increasing desire for the war to finish as soon as possible'.[91] By November reports were speaking of 'a limit to endurance', as prices rose and food became scarcer, with there being 'very active and widespread discontent' among the population of Milan.[92]

In all these reports there is hardly a reference to activities of the local party organizations that attempted to restore public confidence or to control prices. The PNF is almost completely absent from the picture as an effective force for generating support for the war effort. Only the occasional, half-hearted, compulsory demonstration, organized through the usual convocations by postcard, is noted, and then only to remark that such demonstrations served only to increase the irritation and frustration of the population. Choosing his words carefully, the ex-*squadrista* prefect of Milan wrote in late September 1940 that the local party was 'a bit downhearted' but took consolation from the fact that 'Milanese Fascism suffers from the same problem that has afflicted Fascism in all provinces for years'. He was happy to be able to add that the population was increasingly turning for help towards the Prefectures in the Milan area 'for the rapid action that these are able to take'.[93] This was a backhanded reference to the crisis of the party. The implication was that what the party was incapable of doing, the organs of the state could do.

Even more revealing was an informer's letter from Florence some two months later, which attested to a situation of generalized, almost total despair with the war: 'From what I hear, it is possible to identify a fervid and ever-increasing discontent among all social classes'. Shortages of basic foodstuffs were common, imposed by rationing, and all hopes had disappeared: 'there are only a few fanatics and schoolboys who still retain their illusions'. Even so the facade of national solidarity had to be maintained, but on terms the informer had no reticence in describing in detail:

> There is the sensation ... that confidence in the *duce* is greatly diminished and tends to diminish even more, and, even if He is still greeted with applause and [shouts of] 'Long live ...' and the demonstrations for him are well attended, it is the general conviction that the applause and the demonstrations are not spontaneous and are not indications of the real feelings of the people ... [given that] nobody can refuse to go to the demonstrations and to applaud for fear of beatings and of reprisals of various types.

The purely formal and obligatory nature of the demonstrations was obvious to everybody: 'people say that approval and applause gained in this way has no value'.[94]

---

[89] ACS, Ibid., 20 July 1940.   [90] ACS, Ibid., 30 September 1940.
[91] ACS, Ibid., 30 October 1940.   [92] ACS, Ibid., 14 November 1940.
[93] ACS, Ibid., b. 6, Milan, 30 September 1940.
[94] Martinelli, *Fronte interno*, entry for 7 November 1940.

In reality, war changed little for the party. If anything it accentuated and made even more obvious the deficiencies of the PNF machine. The state of emergency represented by mobilization for war required an efficient state and party administration for its success and June 1940 highlighted the extent to which this was missing. Few documents recount the degree to which the fascist provincial organizations, party included, had failed than a letter to Mussolini, sent at the end of June 1940. The letter was anonymous—signed 'Veridicus' and claiming to be from a loyal doorman—because, although the writer was very flattering towards Mussolini himself, the rest of what he had to say clearly put him at risk. Victory was in sight, the letter began: 'The war can be considered won', thanks to the genius of the *duce*, but Italy's problems were not over. 'Your labours have been great...but Your labours at home are not equal to those realized outside our borders'. The targets of the writer's attack were the party, the press, and the bureaucracy. After denigrating various Ministries ('The Ministry of the Corporations...is the most anti-corporative organization that exists'), Veridicus turned his attention to the party and the *gerarchi*, these last characterized by their 'disgraceful appetites and extremely damaging mimicry of Mussolinian attitudes'.

The PNF, despite its undoubted dominant position in the country, was judged in almost every respect to be inadequate:

> The Party, with its high and low hierarchies, has not gained the respect of the Italians; on the contrary the demonstrable ineptitude of its leaders, the infiltration of numerous profiteers with no faith, has heaped discredit on the organism which ought to be the basis of the regime.

Certain problems had been confronted, but with little success: 'The famous accumulation of jobs is flourishing more than ever...', involving the highest and the lowest state employees, all 'dedicated to the research of monthly cheques extorted from the cowardice or the self-interest of leading businessmen. Everything is just an intense activity aimed at making money as fast as and as much as possible'. Italy under Fascism had become 'a field of plunder, not a Nation', where public money was being continuously stolen and wasted.

Attention was then turned to the bureaucracy which, as we have already seen, was a common target for a criticism often bordering on hatred. There was no mincing of words. The bureaucracy was accused of being 'a slow, lifeless, wordy, confused, and often corrupt organism, with the further characteristic of a certain and assured impunity. It dominates the country but does not serve it'. Laws, decrees, and circulars were often difficult to understand and required the assistance and interpretation of state employees, forthcoming only with 'the prior greasing of the palm of the person responsible'. According to Veridicus, the consequences were inevitable. Italians were honest, but 'the Italian citizen is hungry for justice' and, not finding justice, 'the average citizen...is easily led to judge the regime in the worst light'.[95] The remedy this letter invoked was a total reform of the party and

---

[95] ACS, MI, DGPS, Polizia Politica, b. 219, 'Veridicus', undated but with office stamp early in July 1940.

state structures, principally in terms of personnel, and, above all, a restoration of 'moral values'.

The subsequent history of the party during the years up to July 1943 suggests that the need for such a remedy was appreciated in many quarters, but that nothing effective was done to realize it. Nor could it have been otherwise. The very lack of success of the measures taken to try to revitalize the party are indicative of the weaknesses within the fascist construction. So many of the criticisms levelled at the regime—even by fascist believers like Veridicus—reflected the fact that Fascism had been the appropriation of public authority by a part of Italian society that had then used that authority for its own, often private, ends. This abuse of power had been especially evident in the provinces, where the 'local' component of the movement had never been adequately brought to heel. Indeed, many of the problems that came to a head in the late 1930s had been intrinsic in provincial Fascism almost from the start. The degree to which the movement could reform itself in the direction indicated by those who wanted change, without at the same time destroying itself, was highly questionable, therefore. A radical clean-up risked contradicting what many local fascists had always seen to be the meaning of Fascism, at least from the point of view of their personal position.

Party secretary Muti asked to return to his unit in the air force on the outbreak of war, and Mussolini agreed, possibly reasoning that he could do less harm there than he had as party secretary. Muti had made some attempts to meet the disastrous situation created by Starace, but results had been few—as the pages above tend to demonstrate—and by June 1940 some, with evident incredulity, were even beginning to feel nostalgia for the former secretary. The Milan syndicalist Pietro Capoferri, appointed in Muti's place as provisional party leader, showed in his speeches a good understanding of the failures of the party, recognizing that discipline and conviction were very different things. He faced the question openly: '*federali*, it is not enough for us to take pleasure in seeing our comrades more numerous every day and militarily regimented. It is not enough to concern ourselves with the external, aesthetic, order. We have to create consciousness, we have to work on the essence of the individual...'[96] Spot on in his analysis, he was unable to put this understanding into effective reforms. Purges, rotations, and the policy of 'streamlining' the party, begun by Muti, merely translated themselves into a slowing-down of the activities of the party and a deepening of the crisis.

It was Capoferri's successor—Adelchi Serena—appointed at the end of October 1940, who showed the keenest awareness of the need for radical transformation. Serena, who had been vice-secretary of the party under Starace, was above all an able administrator (but without the fanaticism of Starace for the ludicrous detail) and believed that moves towards a more efficient totalitarianism could be made through an increased attention to the capillary organizations, linking the various components of the fascist machine together more effectively and increasing levels of popular involvement with Fascism through the strengthening and 'moralizing'—the fascist word for a clean-up—of the party organizations. Particular attention was to

---

[96] Quoted in Gentile, *La via italiana*, 230.

be paid to the youth organizations, in part to prepare a new leadership but also in order to meet the more immediate problem of apathy and lack of interest in Fascism reported among the young people at the time.

Serena's vision of the party, and of the role of the party, was in many ways far more radical than that of Starace. It was a radicalism which had at its centre an idea implicit in some of the criticisms made of the party in the 1930s—that it had become too big, too unwieldy, and too much dominated by opportunists, and that it was necessary to return to a party of the ideologically motivated elite. The belief that there was an 'aristocracy' of Fascism that should be distinguished from the mass had been growing in the later part of the 1930s and represented dissatisfaction within the movement over the watering-down of the fascist message seen at provincial level during the decade, when so much seemed purely formal mass participation and blatant personal ambition. Both frustrated ex-*squadristi* and idealist youth could recognize themselves in this vision of a new elite, as, no doubt, could the man who had advised Mussolini in 1940 to set up his own version of Hitler's SS. Hard times stimulated hard thinking and the need for regeneration of both party and movement produced some radical positions that would not have seemed out of place in the intransigent Fascism of the first half of the 1920s.[97] The renewed calls for the constitution of a 'revolutionary totalitarian party' seemed once again to place the party, rather than the state, at centre stage.

But the task was really impossible. Serena's period as party secretary—he was removed in December 1941—is more interesting for the intentions expressed than for what it realized.[98] In the event, it was too late to turn the party round. The exigencies of war, the departure for the front of many of the more active and committed fascists in the provinces, the difficulties caused by shortages and rising prices, the fall in morale consequent on the first Italian defeats in Greece and North Africa—all determined that little regeneration of the party could be achieved. Both men and means were lacking, and renewed party activity served only to make people even more convinced that the party lay at the origin of their problems. Possibly the best measure of Serena's achievement lies in the fact that he was sacked by Mussolini. His ideas about the 'continuing revolution' clearly prefigured the creation of a politically active party which might have generated the same problems for the *duce* as did the intransigent party of 1924–5. Mussolini, holding firm to the state (and to *his* government), was not going to let that happen again. The irritation on Mussolini's part was presumably the sense of Bottai's remark (reproducing what Mussolini had said to him), 'Serena got on the wrong track, making the Party contest the organs of Government in continuation'.[99] It was an oblique way of saying what had been evident since 1925—that Mussolini and the party could coexist only if the party were subservient. As if to make the point even more firmly, Mussolini chose his next party secretary very carefully. Aldo Vidussoni was 27, had few

---

[97] Some of this renewed radicalism would find its way eventually into the positions expressed, at least formally, by the *Repubblica sociale italiana* after September 1943.

[98] For Serena's period as party secretary see Gentile, *La via italiana*, Chapter 7.

[99] Ibid., 290.

ideas, little experience, and was almost totally unknown. He was, according to Lupo, 'a notorious imbecile'.[100]

The efforts to give the PNF a new energy and a new direction in the post-Starace period found little reflection in the reports from the provinces. During 1941 popular opinion became even more critical of the war and of those who had supported Italy's participation in it. An informer writing in early 1941 claimed to reflect the opinions of 'every category of citizen' when he recounted the 'naked truth' about public discontent. 'The great mass of the population...curses the war and complains about sacrifices and restrictions, the consequence—some say—of twenty years of dictatorship...If a revolution has two moments—one in ascent and one in descent,' he wrote, 'we are now in the downward parabola'. Despite the authorities' efforts to pretend that everything was under control, below the *esteriorità* of Fascism there was a population that had two faces, 'one—outward—which is silent and passive (and you can understand why), and another—inward and authentic (which is shown at home, together with friends, and in meeting places)'. He warned that central to the 'kitchen table' talk were the women, who had now started to protest violently about shortages, 'and women, within the family, are propagandists who are believed'.

The same informer noted the chasm that now existed between the people and the regime. Summarizing opinion he had heard, he wrote that the army was thought to be doing its job in defending the fatherland, even if it did not quite know why, but that the population viewed the blackshirts in a different light; 'in the blackshirts they see an army created to defend the regime from the Italian citizens'. According to what people were saying, many of these blackshirts were 'draft-dodgers', kept at home in well-paid office jobs, 'only ready to wage war on the "internal enemy", which in fact is the great mass of Italians who do not sympathize with or approve the politics of the Regime'. The alliance with the Germans was seen to be dictated exclusively by 'party interests' and had been presented falsely to the Italians as something of national interest: 'they try to portray as collective support [for the war] what is nothing other than the work of a few leaders, who arrogate to themselves the right to speak for everyone'. The people seemed to go along with this, the informer observed, but 'most of them are either not involved, or keep quiet, or submit passively because they are afraid of possible vendettas'. The writer reminded his readers that 'a single word of complaint or criticism or irritation can irremediably ruin an individual or a family'. He called for a remedy that, in fact, reflected many of the problems of the past: 'Those old personal antagonisms, all the problems of the local *beghismi*, which have pushed so many away from Fascism, must cease...' (they were evidently still going on, despite the war). Italy, he believed, needed to find again the post-Caporetto spirit.

Mussolini no longer escaped criticism. In the same report the spy recounted that people were now convinced that it was 'impossible that Mussolini doesn't really know how things are'.[101] Already in November 1940 it had been noted that 'the

---

[100] Lupo, 'L'utopia totalitaria', 461.
[101] ACS, MI, DGPS, Polizia Politica, b. 219, undated, unsigned, but early 1941.

people, particularly the rural population, do nothing except speak badly of Mussolini'.[102] From Florence at the beginning of the same month an informer noted that 'I have the feeling—always according to what I hear—that confidence in the *duce* is much diminished and tends to diminish even more'.[103] Another report of November, again from Florence, spoke of 'feelings of hatred for the *duce* and the regime, hatred growing day by day'.[104] In December the phrase was 'everyone is opposed to what the *duce* and the regime have done'.[105] The impression that Hitler had taken over and that the fascist leader was no longer in control of things was now general: 'people are saying, generally, that "Mussolini has lost all his prestige"...';[106] 'very many no longer believe in Him'.[107] The message had finally got home that the *duce did* know—and did nothing: 'Bad feeling directed at the *duce*...is unanimous...in all categories of people. People no longer have confidence in Him and little respect...'[108] Moreover, people were now prepared to say this openly, in the street and in the tram. By February 1941, the cult of the invincible *duce* had disappeared totally from Florence: 'You can detect an absolute lack of confidence in victory on the part of the great majority of the population, among whom defeat is considered to be a liberation from the regime'.[109]

Rumours of palace revolutions developed once again in early 1941, with De Vecchi, Grandi, and Caviglia at their centre, while the difference between Mussolinism and Fascism was again recorded, but this time to reverse the usual argument: 'there can be a Fascism beyond a Mussolini dead or senile'.[110] Army officers in Vercelli were reported as prefacing their view of the future in the words 'with the fall of the *duce*...', as if this were a foregone conclusion. Some were looking towards a new, reformed Fascism, 'after the victory', but most were convinced that the war would see defeat and the end of the regime. Party activists, encouraged by Serena's revolutionary rhetoric, moved once again in several centres to relaunch the violence of the squads against so-called 'defeatists', but the mood of the public was such that, as in the previous September, they got a very frosty reception. 'It wouldn't have been possible to find a worse system for further exasperating public opinion', wrote one observer.[111] An informer said that people in Rome were talking of 'immediate reactions' to the new *squadristi*,[112] another reported that 'the public will not put up with their actions'.[113] Here, friction between the party and the people seemed on the point of exploding. The same mood was shown in the report from Rome of 25 April 1941—a moment when, with the spring offensive, the war seemed to be taking a turn for the better: 'they are saying that, with this victory, the fascists will raise their heads again, but that, with the return of the troops at the end of the war, they will have to lower them permanently because war will be followed by political change'.[114] The spectre of a returning army, strongly radicalized, began to appear.

[102] ACS, Ibid., 5 November 1940.   [103] Martinelli, *Fronte interno*, 108.
[104] Ibid., 112.   [105] Ibid., 115.
[106] ACS, MI, DGPS, Polizia Politica, b. 219, 6 January 1941.
[107] Martinelli, *Fronte interno*, 117.   [108] Ibid., 121.   [109] Ibid., 153.
[110] ACS, MI, DGPS, Polizia Politica, b. 219, 16 February 1941.
[111] ACS, Ibid., Rome, 14 December 1940.   [112] ACS, Ibid., Rome, 12 December 1940.
[113] ACS, Ibid., Rome, 25 April 1941.   [114] Ibid.

Food shortages, rationing, and the call-up increased the exasperation of the population with the regime. Perhaps the best account of what was happening on the ground in 1941, visionary projects of revitalization and regeneration of the party notwithstanding, can be found in the report of an informer in late August. It is, in some ways, an almost definitive verdict on the regime and on the part played by the party. The informer—one Roberto Rossi, number 557—was one of the most experienced spies of the regime; he had probably worked for the police even before the advent of Fascism and he had certainly been very much involved with the Milan *fascio* up until about 1930.[115] Even in its title—'Towards the disintegration of the fascist state?'—the report seemed to presage the worst. The opening lines did nothing to change the tone: 'No longer symptoms but serious, most serious, facts give the clear impression of finding oneself in a regime in rapid disintegration, with a central power uncoordinated, stultified, incoherent, devoid of any intelligent authority. These are not just my observations, but form the patrimony of the most advanced part of the Italian population...' The writer complained that the army high command despised the fascists, that the economy was in the hands of a 'plutocracy' which simply used Fascism for its own purposes, that the corporative state was considered 'nothing more than the pure utopia of woolly-headed doctrinaires of Fascism', and that the party was an accomplice to hoarding of produce and price speculation.

Passing to the state bureaucracy, he made many of the same criticisms as those we have outlined above, auguring that one day it would be possible to verify the 'dishonesty of functionaries' through checks on their standard of living, on those of their families and their lovers, and on the fortunes of their relations 'until recently, penniless'. He warned that the working class was 'exactly at the antipodes' in its relation to Fascism and that it would require little to produce a violent reaction to the regime. He drew attention to basics rather than to ideology. Even if an anti-fascist revolutionary mentality was not yet present, 'the Italian workers demand... the security of bread for themselves and for their families, and have no intention of putting up with privations of this kind'. Otherwise things might change. 'The lack of bread may signal the sporadic beginnings of revolutionary conflicts, and the day the Russians enter Berlin (dreadful hypothesis), the mass of the workers will fight in the streets and the squares of Italy for the affirmation of their principles. And many fascists will be in the front line with them...' With the victory of the Russians there would be the 'establishment of a levelling Bolshevism, hoped-for today even in some areas of Fascism'.

The strongest accusations were reserved for the PNF. 'The Party has the greatest responsibility for all the breakdown recounted in this report'. The attack was directed principally at Starace: 'of all the traitors who have blossomed around the *duce*, Achille Starace must have the place of honour'. Showing that he had little faith in Serena's reforms—we are already at the end of August 1941—the informer continued, 'he [Starace] has persecuted, humiliated, destroyed, all the ranks of the best men formed in the old guard of the revolution'. Stooges were put in the places

---

[115] See Canali, *Le Spie*, 200–201.

of able men: 'from top to bottom, from centre to periphery, all the vast and complex construction of Fascism has been filled with *gerarchi* who are inept, arrogant,
often dishonest, always cowards'. The consequences were inevitable and in front of
everybody's eyes: 'In this way we have arrived at the total destruction of the aristocracy of the revolution', creating instead 'a class of *gerarchi* without any revolutionary merits, chosen among elements who are servile, remissive, narcissistic and
superficial'. The result was that people had now lost all confidence in Fascism: 'At
this point the fascists, the others, those who think correctly, say "Fascism is finished, the nation is rotten, Mussolini cannot save himself because he is alone and
would not even know where to begin the job of purging"'.

An informer's job was to report accurately on the mood of the population and
the state of the party. Few *relazioni fiduciari* can have been quite as damning as this
one. The remedy prescribed was predictable—'[g]ive the Party men who are able,
who have demonstrated their faith, men of intelligent courage'. At that point it
would be possible to hope for the 'resurrection' and the 'salvation' of the regime.[116]
Instead, as we know, Mussolini gave the party Vidussoni.

[116] ACS, MI, DGPS, Polizia Politica, b. 219, 22 August 1941.

11

The Failure of the Party

The picture we have presented in the preceding chapters is that of a fascist party increasingly unable to come to terms with widespread popular discontent and, in many situations, itself one of the prime causes of that discontent. As fascist informers acknowledged repeatedly, by 1939 the party had lost all authority and a large part of the population had turned its back on it. In its task of generating 'totalitarian' support for the regime—the role assigned to the party—the PNF was a failure. The thesis of this book turns around this failure. Put simply, the thesis is that the fascist party was unsuccessful in its central task of producing a nation of convinced fascists and that this lack of success represented more than just the failure of the party; ultimately it represented the failure of Fascism. It was clear by the late 1930s that, without the effective operation of the party, there was to be no new sense of common, collective purpose among Italians, no lasting popular identification with the fascist state, no community of believers. Thus, the basic premises of national palingenesis had not been realized. Agostino Lanzillo's ambition of moulding history with his own hands, so passionately expressed in 1918, was not to be fulfilled.

Moreover, the failure of the fascist regime was already in evidence in 1939 and early 1940; it was not occasioned by the disasters of war, therefore. Entropy, as Robert Paxton has termed the final, stagnant, phase of totalitarian regimes, was apparent in Italy before a shot had been fired.[1] Again, it is worth repeating, this did not mean that the fall of Fascism was imminent—only the war would ensure that. What it did mean was that the mission the fascists had given themselves was not to be realized and that the goal of the *nazione totalitaria* was not be achieved.

This is in no way to underrate what the party had done during the 1920s and, more particularly, during the 1930s. The relationship between the centre and the periphery had changed considerably under the impact of the PNF. The activities of the party in the areas of welfare, youth work, and leisure did constitute a real novelty in the organization of provincial life and the extent of these activities was, by any standards, remarkable. What Mariuccia Salvati has called the 'nationalization of customs' seen under Fascism was in large part the work of the party.[2] Yet the paradox represented by the PNF is that, the more its power grew, the more it extended its responsibilities in such a way as to invade almost every aspect of the life of ordinary people, the more it worked to saturate the spaces in which people

---

[1] See Robert O. Paxton, *The Anatomy of Fascism*, New York, Knopf, 2004, Chapter 6.
[2] Salvati, *L'Inutile salotto*, Introduction. Nationalization of customs was very different from what is generally understood by nationalization of the masses.

lived, worked, played, and thought, the less it seems to have achieved the objectives set for it. Bottai's juxtaposing of the words 'omnipotence' and 'impotence' in relation to the party was very telling. If fascist Italy in some ways moved ever closer to being 'objectively' a totalitarian regime by the end of the 1930s, it seems to have been anything but that in subjective terms. Popular identification with the regime was, according to almost all accounts, in rapid decline, even if most people had no clear idea of what they hoped might follow it.

It is for this reason that this account ends with Italy's entry into the Second World War. The decision to go to war and to abandon Italy's non-belligerent status injected a new element into the picture. Mussolini's desire to be in at the death, to see—as he put it to Hitler—'at least a representative section of the Italian army fight together with your soldiers to seal, on the battlefield, the brotherhood of arms and the comradeship of our Revolutions',[3] produced an anguished crisis of conscience in many Italians.[4] In the circumstances, patriotism and fascist nationalism might easily be confused. Some of those who had previously been critical of the regime rallied to the flag: 'once war is declared, opinions disappear...' wrote one man to Mussolini, expressing his hopes of an Italian victory.[5] The patriotic card trumped many doubts and the prospect of an easy victory made the card all the more powerful.[6] But the war did little to change the problems the regime was facing.[7] Indeed, after the brief moment of enthusiasm for intervention, the conflict did nothing but accentuate those problems. Even the passing glance we have given in the previous chapter to the disastrous experiment with party secretary Muti, the brief and inconclusive 'totalitarian' adventure with his successor, Serena, and the plunge into the incompetence and anonymity of Vidussoni at the end of 1941, would seem to confirm that picture.

Clearly, with the war, the party had a different role to play. The war provided an opportunity to show the positive face of the party to a population confronted by a whole series of difficulties. Some, particularly young, fascists did see the war as a challenge with a 'revolutionary' potential. But there is little to suggest that, in the midst of chronic shortages and rationing, the party was able to exploit this opportunity and become in any real way an effective force for mobilizing the population in fascist terms. With able personnel called to the front, it is difficult to think that what the party had not done in the 1930s could be done in the much less favourable circumstances of an undesired and unpopular war for which the nation was unprepared. In Italy, the war—a war of aggression—never assumed the status of the 'great patriotic war' that was to be so useful to Stalin. If anything, what we see with the war is an accentuation of the divergent tendencies mentioned above—an increasing radicalization of the totalitarian thrust of the movement under the

---

[3] De Felice, *Mussolini il duce*, vol. 2, 838.   [4] Ibid.
[5] Ibid., 822.
[6] Compare with a similar situation in Germany on the occasion of the *Anschluss*. Peter Fritzsche cites the diary of an opponent of Nazism, who nonetheless writes '*not* to want it, just because it has been achieved by Hitler, would be folly': P. Fritzsche, *Life and Death in the Third Reich*, Cambridge (Mass.), Harvard University Press, 2008, 35.
[7] For the party during the war see Di Nucci, *Lo Stato-partito*, Chapter 10.

pressures of the conflict, accompanied at the same time by an ever-increasing distancing of the population from the regime.[8]

But why should the alleged failure of the party be considered so important? Was the PNF really so central to the success of the regime? After all, all the text books tell us that the PNF was subordinated to the state between 1925 and 1927 and, while we might want to qualify the terms of that subordination, there seems no reason to quarrel with the overall judgement. Subordination would imply that the PNF was never anything other than a secondary device, of limited significance after the defeat of Farinacci and the intransigent wing of Fascism, that its role involved no more than the regimentation of the masses and the maintenance of social control. To extend Bottai's supercilious metaphor, it would seem that the PNF simply passed from being the instrument of the 'cattle raisers' of the early and mid-1920s to being that of the 'cattle herders' of the 1930s, pushing an essentially passive and bovine population into its various pens. Was this all it was expected to do? If so, it would be an exaggeration to link the failure of the regime to the deficiencies of the PNF. If judged purely as 'cattle herders', the provincial party organizations had done their job rather well.

The risks of giving excessive attention to the party's role in the regime, and to the part it played in the failure of the regime, may also be suggested by a further consideration, very much related to what we saw in the final section of Chapter 6 about the expansion of state holding companies and the many institutions of the *parastato*. It is evident from this kind of administrative and bureaucratic development that, despite so much of what has been said so far, Italian Fascism was not just the party. The PNF was at the centre of the regime, but there was much more to the regime than the PNF. As is well known, the solution to the Matteotti crisis permitted Mussolini to work not only through the party but also, and perhaps prevalently, through the mechanisms of the state. The conflicts between prefect and *federale* in the provinces had provided a clear indication of these parallel jurisdictions, reproduced in Rome in the frequent confrontations between party and ministries. The fascist regime expressed itself in the provinces not only through the party, the unions, and the *Dopolavoro*, therefore. Side by side with these organizations, in which the party would play a role, there developed other networks and other institutions dependent directly on central government, independent of the local federations of the PNF.

The PNF has to be placed in this broader context of fascist government—and this, in a way, gives one answer to the question posed above about the importance of the party, which is that a great deal of what happened during the fascist *ventennio*

---

[8] Alessandra Staderini charts a high degree of fascist mobilization in Rome at the level of the city district (*rione*), particularly among young people of pre-military age eager to further the war effort and confident of a renewal of Fascism after the victory. See A. Staderini, 'La Federazione romana del Pnf (1940–43)' in (2003) 11(3) *Roma moderna e contemporanea* 431, 'Roma in guerra 1940–43', (special issue edited by Lidia Piccione). But, as Piccioni observes in her introduction to the issue (359), the reaction of the population to these initiatives remains in doubt, given that there was at the same time an increasing popular tendency to attribute to the party the responsibility for hardship and shortages.

did not depend on the successful functioning of the party at the provincial level. The territorial extension of the state administration to the whole country and the reorganization of the economy under the corporative thrust were achieved without particular reference to the party structures. A corrupt and inefficient party, heartily disliked by the population, might seem relatively unimportant, therefore. Certainly, Fascism was much more than just the PNF.

To see the failure of Fascism in terms of the failure of the party is not to deny that there were important developments that took place under Fascism and that represented real changes to public administration and economic organization, therefore. The regime did realize a great deal in these areas. The point made here is that these changes were not central to the job the fascists had set themselves; indeed, they often were not, per se, specifically fascist in nature. In Italy, an authoritarian *dirigisme* reproduced many features of restructuring of the state and the economy that can be found elsewhere. Banks were rescued and reorganized by the state in democracies as well as in Italy; between the wars local administrations were reinforced almost everywhere as social needs became a more pressing problem for the political agenda.[9] What was different about Italian Fascism, what marked it out from other non-totalitarian projects of the period, was its objective—nothing less than the transformation of the Italian people. If it were to survive across the decades, if it were to continue beyond the inevitable death of the *duce*, the New Italy required New Italians. And, the creation of the New Italian was, above all, the job of the party.

The regime had never, of course, been under the illusion that the entire Italian population would somehow acquire the characteristics of the *duce*. Such an objective would, after all, have been bordering on blasphemy. Fascist ideology was clear about the fact that there were leaders and there were led. The great mass of the population—what Mussolini, improvising the political theorist with Emil Ludwig, defined as the 'herd of sheep'—was considered incapable of autonomous political activity.[10] The task facing the fascist regime was precisely that of giving direction to this disorganized and inchoate mass through regimentation, education, and through example. If the nation were to become a cohesive whole, if private concerns were to be subordinated to, and subsumed in, the fascist state, the population had to be guided towards the realization of its integration with that state. And the population had to accept the legitimacy of the fascist regime in directing this *process* of integration; otherwise, clearly, the process could not work. The successful implementation of this process was a basic premise for the creation of the totalitarian community, in which the individual would have significance exclusively in terms of the all-encompassing relationship achieved with the fascist state. Failure to realize the premise would, inevitably, put the whole construct in jeopardy, because fascist claims to legitimacy were based on the affirmation of an identity of

---

[9] See Charles S. Maier, *Recasting Bourgeois Europe, Stabilization in France, Germany and Italy in the Decade after World War One*, Princeton, Princeton University Press, 1975.
[10] Emil Ludwig, *Colloqui con Mussolini*, Milan, Mondadori, 1950, 121.

interest between the individual and the fascist state and of the recognition by Italians of this identity of interest.

The direction of what many fascists recognized to be a long-term project was the function assigned more and more clearly over the years to the party, the pedagogic role of which was given ever-increasing emphasis. Deprived of any dynamic political function in terms of the formulation of political projects, the provincial parties were expected to organize, regiment, and propagandize the population, preaching the message by word and by example in such a way as to transform obligatory conformism into spontaneous commitment. From this operation, the New Italian would emerge—or rather, perhaps, the New Italians, because it was clear from the fascist vision of the totalitarian community that different kinds of New Italian were envisaged. There were the leaders, and here the emphasis on the training of young people looked to the formation of a new elite, and there were the led, who had, nonetheless, to be firmly convinced and committed to the cause in order to effectuate their integration with the national community. No less than the leaders, these were to undergo a transformation of modes of thought and behaviour such as to produce an active engagement with Fascism. No less than the leaders, these too were to become New Fascist Men.

The project was, of course, always unrealizable—at least in those terms. Fascist social engineering had considerable limits and, in any case, New Men, even New Fascist Men, are not of this world. Here it is obviously necessary to avoid the temptation to identify failure on the basis of what were impossible objectives (although in 1944 Bottai would half-admit, half-boast, that Fascism had consciously aimed to realize 'the impossible'). Certainly, men like Lanzillo had looked to Fascism to create a new order and a new civilization, establishing a new relationship with history; the illusion of a 'new beginning' had been widespread among the first fascists. But, shorn of its mystical rhetoric and translated into language more appropriate to the real world, the fascist project did include objectives that were eminently realizable. The project had aimed at the creation of a strong national identity, at the formation of a sense of the state among Italians, at the realization of a strong feeling of social cohesion, and at the achievement for Italy of 'a place in the sun'. These objectives required the creation of an effective governing elite, operating at both national and local levels, capable of commanding respect and reproducing itself over the years. They required the formation of a solid conviction among the population of the justice of the fascist cause and of the capacity of Fascism to resolve the many problems facing the Italian nation. They further required the disposition on the part of a large section of the population to work for national renewal and to support the fascist regime wholeheartedly in its attempts to realize this objective. The result was intended to express energy, direction, unity, and cohesion.

Instead, by the second half of the 1930s—and particularly in the two years immediately before the Second World War—we have reports from many sources emphasizing apathy, passivity, weariness, fragmentation, and resignation among the population—and some reports which, as we have seen in the preceding chapter, begin to utter dark warnings about popular discontent finding expression in serious public disorder. A further, and significant, aspect of this discontent, according to many of the informers, was that it was now being expressed by people from all classes, *and* by many fascists. Indeed, some of the informers suggested that the fascists were the most vocal. There was a sense of total loss of direction. As the writer of a letter from Varese lamented in 1939, 'I ask myself "where are we going and how did we get here?"... The spirit, the real spirit of the people is totally absent today... on our side there isn't anyone the people believe in'.[11] Invariably, in explaining this discontent and loss of motivation, the finger was pointed at the PNF, which was failing to do its job and—worse—generating disaffection. The unpopularity of the party was extremely damaging for the fascist project. It meant, in essence, that the essential link between movement and masses—the link that was to permit the constitution of the new fascist society—had not been formed in any adequate manner. The process of building a totalitarian society was thereby severely hampered.

This situation has been illustrated in later historiography. In a little-noted passage, Renzo De Felice—generally regarded as the prophet of the thesis of mass consensus for Fascism—picks up this mood of the late 1930s, accurately identifying the paradox concealed by frenetic fascist activity. 'Beneath the appearance of an extreme politicization of the masses, an ever more marked and real depoliticization of society [was taking place]... [which] led to an ever more accentuated separation from, and an ever-increasing disdain of the PNF and... to a general disgust for politics as such...'[12] Disdain of the PNF and disgust for politics as organized by the fascists were hardly the signs of a successful operation of totalitarian indoctrination. Here it is worth reminding ourselves that 'Mussolinism' was *not* Fascism; the cult of the *duce* could not by itself create a new Italian society.

Depoliticization among the population is, of course, a familiar feature of totalitarian regimes. It constitutes a rejection by the population of precisely this process of totalitarian 'politicization' by which, through the observation of rituals, the acceptance of myths, and the internalization of dominant precepts, the population is expected to become an active and convinced part of the process of symbiosis between the people, the state, and its leaders. Sometimes depoliticization reflects a never-ending ritual which provokes mental withdrawal. Often it is also the impotence felt by the population faced with abuse of power that persuades people to shun the 'politicizing' public sphere, such as it is, and to find refuge in private and family affairs. Fear of denunciation compounds this flight. The kitchen table rather than the public square becomes the *locus* of any political conversation. Numerous examples of this phenomenon can be found in the communist countries of Eastern Europe after 1945. Formal participation often masked real disaffection, but, in the absence of alternatives, the rituals had to be observed. In the same way, in fascist Italy presence at the mass demonstration was obligatory, the uniform could not be avoided on an increasing number of occasions, and participation in the activities of the 'fascist Saturday' had to be accepted. But, as so many informers wrote, this

---

[11] ACS, PNF, SPEP, b. 224, letter of 20 April 1939, forwarded from Milan to Rome by an informer, 8 June 1939.
[12] De Felice, *Mussolini il duce*, vol. 2, 221.

represented nothing more than '*esteriorità*'—the excessive attention to outward appearances. Regimentation and compulsory participation was very different from conviction for the cause.

This tension—essentially between consent and coercion—had always been present in the fascist movement. The requisites of continuing revolution on the one hand and social stability on the other were difficult to reconcile. In the final analysis, the fascist movement had always sought to make a revolutionary political omelette without breaking social and economic eggs. In this recipe, ideology was to be the magic ingredient. But one of the essential components of political ideologies that seek radical social transformation is confidence in the future, and all the evidence suggests that it was precisely this confidence that was disappearing during the course of the 1930s. By being drawn into the war it had always postulated as inevitable, but which a large part of the population had hoped to avoid, the fascist regime called its own bluff and was found wanting.

Many fascists recognized the weakness of their position in this respect. As long as expression of fascist 'faith' was compulsory, it was impossible to judge the degree of real belief among the population. As already seen in a large number of informers' reports, many observers suspected superficiality. Yet, in some ways, the regime seems to have had a very ambiguous position in respect of the question of inner conviction, preaching challenge, risk, and adventure—even, eventually, '*la bella morte*' ['beautiful death']—but often in fact settling for a very sedentary and passive conformism. Certainly, the mobilizing forces of the regime, together with all the propaganda devices—direct and indirect—sought to achieve conviction. '*Credere, obbedire, combattere*' ['believe, obey, fight'] were heady imperatives, designed to ensure unquestioning *belief* in the fascist mission (it was no accident that 'think' was not among them: the irrational supplanted the rational in fascist discourse). At the same time and despite the military language, so much about Fascism was anything but aggressively activist. Much support for the regime was based on the very staid, conservative conformism of the petty bourgeoisie, for whom fighting wars was the last item on the agenda. In their studies of the administration under the regime, both Guido Melis and Mariuccia Salvati have stressed the degree to which that new class, the employees of state and *parastato*, generally considered to be the backbone of the regime, was hardly the exemplification of youthful, dynamic Fascism. Even if identifying strongly with the fascist conception of order and hierarchy, the office workers seem to have shared little else with the ideology of the regime. The essentially conservative, defensive position of these workers is summed up by Salvati's observations on their attitudes to hierarchy, where defence of status and of minor privileges was one of the principal priorities. This much was demonstrated when, in 1934, badges indicating rank were introduced within the bureaucracy, provoking bedlam—the bureaucrats of level C protesting vociferously because the ushers were included in their level, those at level B complaining that they should be at level A, and those at level A defending their position against all comers.[13]

[13] Salvati, *Impiegati*, 203.

In much the same tone, Melis writes that the attempts of the administration to politicize the bureaucracy had the effect of realizing 'an obligatory but external fascistization of the dependents'—and that this was apparently enough to satisfy the administration.[14] And, through the pages of contemporary authors Carlo Emilio Gadda and Luisa Adorno, it is again Melis who offers us a picture of employees 'little involved with, in reality intimately hostile to, that grand picture which Fascism proclaimed in those years to be the objective and the destiny of the Italians', people for whom 'Fascism consisted in diligently wearing the fascist badge in their button-hole', and for whom one thing above all was clear: 'the total prevalence...of private, family, and domestic values over public values'.[15] Such behaviour was a long way from the 'sacrifice of blood' the children were vowing to make every morning in the schools of the nation.

The crisis of the fascist movement at the end of the 1930s was, in many ways, no more than was to be expected of a movement that had always had a relatively weak ideological base among the mass of the population. Despite the continued insistence on the importance of fascist 'faith', the regime had in fact imposed a formal catechism of slogans on Italians that required little to undermine it. Not being transcendental in nature, the 'political religion' of Fascism was subject to verification in this world, not the next. Unlike communism, Italian Fascism had no equivalent of historical inevitability to pull it through the hard times. Ordinary people knew that the prospect of a European war meant that a miserable present was likely to be replaced by an even more miserable future. Few informers' reports give any sense that Italians were confident of their capacity and their preparation to fight a European war. That 'dual reality' ascribed by historians to Soviet society of the 1930s—the belief that, despite difficulties, the system worked and that the unpleasant realities of the present would be superseded by the inevitable socialist paradise—could not be exploited in a fascist Italy that saw no promise in a future at best dominated by Hitler.[16]

Pervasive absence of fascist 'faith' suggests, in turn, that, by the late 1930s, the 'message' of Fascism, the 'myth' of the great fascist future that the regime attempted to communicate to the population through so many channels, was a 'weak' message, insufficient to overcome misgivings and fears about the direction events were taking. In this regard the Nazis had one powerful weapon that the fascists could never match—the bitter memory of defeat in 1918 and subsequent humiliation in Paris. These events were etched on every German's soul in a way in which 'mutilated victory' was not for the average Italian. Hitler's speeches made repeated reference to 1918, keeping resentment burning;[17] in Italy the regime was straddled between glorifying the victory and demanding revision of the results—a much less potent propaganda position.

But even the degree and intensity with which many Italians 'lived' the national message has itself to be questioned. Here again we need to return to the particular

---

[14] Melis, *Storia dell amministrazione*, 337.   [15] Ibid., 371.

[16] See, for a good example of dual reality at work, Stephen Kotkin, *Magnetic Mountain. Stalinism as a Civilization*, Berkeley and Los Angeles, University of California Press, 1995, 228–9.

[17] See Richard J. Evans, *The Third Reich at War*, London, Penguin, 2009.

characteristics of Italian political life. In the perfect fascist world, personal interest and national interest were to be as one; 'sense' and 'meaning' were to be provided by the nation and by national goals. This identity of interest was far from easy to engineer. It was not, perhaps, that the message of national renewal and revived national greatness was without significance; it was more that it was a message that had only limited significance for many Italians, who had other, more restricted, but—for them—more important, priorities. Those 'big ideas' relating to national affirmation which, according to Ian Kershaw, carried Hitler forward in the German popular imagination despite the numerous criticisms made of the Nazi regime, could and did exist in Italy as well. National greatness was, of course, acceptable as an objective, but only as long as that objective was compatible with and did not threaten other, more immediate, priorities. Family, Church, local society, local position continued to dominate the concerns of most Italians, not yet 'nationalized' to the same extent as the German population. Thus, it was possible, for example, to participate wholeheartedly in the 'battle for wheat', fully convinced that your contribution was helping to make Italy into a great nation, but less easy to accept expansionist foreign policies that clearly threatened to disrupt existing stabilities (and in this respect it is clear that Italians were well able to distinguish between an 'easy' colonial war and a possible European conflict). Battle was a powerful and useful metaphor for mobilization, but the reality was less attractive. Popular attachment to traditional (and local) values did mean that any potentially destabilizing factor—and war was clearly such a factor—could produce an immediate reaction against the regime.

Comparisons with certain aspects of Soviet society are instructive in this respect, just as are those with post-1945 Eastern Europe. For example, Thomas Lindenberger has argued that there was a 'tacit minimal consensus' for the communist regime of East Germany, despite the many repressive aspects of the GDR dictatorship.[18] According to his reading of the situation, the people were not, in the main, convinced communists and they had many complaints to make about the government of the ruling SED party, but they did accept some of the basic values that the regime claimed to represent and to defend—work, the family, individual security, and—above all—peace. In the context of an international situation in which any major war was likely to be fought on German soil, this last was a central consideration (dictated largely by the Keynesian rationale that 'in the short term we are still alive') and was reflected in the high value placed on stability. Such consensus—reluctant, begrudged, as it was—was nonetheless sufficient to guarantee the survival of the regime for several decades.

Even allowing for the very different circumstances, it is difficult to perceive a similar 'tacit minimal consensus' among the Italian population for the values represented by Italian Fascism—at least by the end of the 1930s.[19] As we have seen,

---

[18] See T. Lindenberger, 'Tacit Minimal Consensus: The Always Precarious East German Dictatorship', in Corner (ed.), *Popular Opinion in Totalitarian Regimes*, 208.

[19] The situation in Nazi Germany was significantly different. Even though some Germans resisted acceptance of Nazism, they did accept the general position of *revanche* and did envisage war as a possibly unavoidable means to achieve that end. With an extremely telling phrase, Peter Fritzsche writes

the workings of the PNF frequently invited ridicule and disgust. What people habitually referred to as the 'caste' continued to distinguish itself for its often shameless abuse of power. Even convinced fascists were reduced to screaming their desperation at what the PNF had become. Far from tacit consensus for basic values and positions, therefore, we have very vocal dissent. And, as we have seen, confidence in Mussolini was declining as those wider, underlying, themes of fascist rule that promised national greatness and international respect for Italy looked by the late 1930s to be more and more dangerous. The fascist regime had spent an enormous amount of time and energy in selling the future, but, by the end of the 1930s, it was obvious to all that that future was not going to happen. By 1939 the prospect was no longer that of a perhaps distant but nonetheless certain fascist paradise but of an imminent war of very uncertain outcome. The never-never land of fascist utopia disappeared behind the gathering clouds of war.[20]

The crisis of the late 1930s was a crisis of confidence in the capacity of the regime both to defend and to deliver. After almost twenty years in power it was almost inevitable that the regime, which had found its original legitimation in its relation to the by now rather distant First World War, came instead to be judged on its results. On the home front, shortages, increased taxes, and blatant corruption worked against the regime. These problems tested the regime's credibility in its claims to have found a 'third way' to the future, superior to either capitalism or communism. There was an all too obvious, and obviously increasing, gap between promises, declared objectives, and their realization. In foreign policy, mounting European instability after 1936 served to put Mussolini's supposed infallibility increasingly into question.

The negative reaction, at a popular level, to difficulty and threat was all the stronger because of the way in which the PNF had tried to put the fascist message over and because of the example it had so often given to onlookers. The continued references to *esteriorità* in informers' reports, letters, and subsequent memoirs is indicative of the way provincial Fascism worked, catering more to appearances than to content. The references are equally indicative of a fairly general awareness among fascist informers that much of the population was only superficially touched by fascist ideology, observing the outer forms required by regimentation and formal participation but without any really deeply rooted conviction. The *Dopolavoro* is perhaps the best example of this. It had a massive following in terms of numbers who frequented the sections, yet—as we have seen—it was judged to be falling down on its job of 'fascistizing' the masses because of a basic fear among organizers of any kind of meaningful political discussion. Political discussion, with the politics taken out, could only produce depoliticization.

of a diarist, 'while Erich hated the Nazis, he loved the Third Reich' because the Reich seemed, in many respects, to be the embodiment of a 'German-ness' with which all Germans could identify. It is difficult to think of Italians expressing the same sentiment in respect either of Fascism or, indeed, of Italy. The fact that many Italians hated the fascists but loved Mussolini hardly had the same enduring cohesive and mobilizing force. See Fritzsche, *Life and Death*, 35.

[20] Compare with Germany, according to Fritzsche, Ibid., 64; 'Germans increasingly identified their own future with the future of the Third Reich'.

It is possible that the decline of the regime in the late 1930s might have been less rapid if the PNF had itself been employed in a different way. The rather uncomfortable and ambiguous position of the party *vis-à-vis* the structures and institutions of the state did not encourage any positive and dynamic affirmation of the local federations. Clearly it was Mussolini who engineered this situation of division of competencies, partly from political necessity and partly in order to preserve his position as the fulcrum of diverse centres of power. Such an arrangement may have reinforced his position, but the effect on the party was devastating. As we have had ample occasion to note, the continued existence of parallel administrative structures throughout the *ventennio* produced persistent friction and tension and worked to the detriment of party efficiency.[21] In purely theoretical terms of party efficiency, Farinacci, with his uncompromising conception of the intransigent party that would control all, had probably seen more clearly, and it is not surprising that Hitler looked at him with interest as a possible successor to Mussolini after July 1943.

The failings of the PNF, and its unpopularity, are features that Fascism shares with other totalitarian regimes. In Nazi Germany and in many communist countries, local, non-elected (or not freely elected) officials, with arbitrary power controlled only feebly by central government, often behaved in much the same way as their Italian counterparts. Party activity could be characterized by a stagnant and largely meaningless ritual in just the same way as was that of the PNF under Starace, and frequently, as in Italy, the totalitarian party became identified with an immovable, impersonal, and elephantine bureaucracy.

Italian Fascism shared these general features, which can be related to the workings of mass dictatorships. But in Italy there was a further factor that gave a particular twist to the operation of the PNF. The basic problem with the functioning of the party in Italy was linked, not to dictatorship as such, but to a more fundamental issue that had its roots in the origins of the fascist movement itself. For all its nationalizing, modernizing, and centralizing efforts, for all its idolatry of the state, the fascist regime never really outgrew its origins, which were dominated in the first instance by local and provincial considerations. The initial centrifugal forces represented by the provincial fascist movements *vis-à-vis* the state, particularly in the North of Italy, flowed into the provincial party structures and were never fully checked by the centre. Despite all efforts, the reality of what fascist control meant in the provinces ensured that local and personal issues could never be prevented from coming to the fore. In administrative terms the national party directorate could seek to come to terms with provincial indiscipline and could do so with undoubted effect; disciplinary measures, rotations, expulsions, special commissars—all were ways in which the unruly provincial movements were brought to heel. Yet, even so, the centrifugal impulse of the provincial movements was never fully eradicated.

This impulse found its expression repeatedly in the conviction of provincial fascists that politics meant essentially local politics and that the fascist movement was a vehicle for the achievement of local power. As was to be expected, after the

---

[21] This is the central theme of Di Nucci, *Lo Stato-partito*, who describes the institutional conflict between the Ministry of the Interior and the PNF with the phrase 'systemic chaos' (610).

fascist victory most fascists saw their future in the province in which they had conducted their battles and counted on having their efforts rewarded in terms of their position within that province. At the provincial level, the clear message of the fascist triumph was that local fascists would assume local control; the old politics had been defeated, now the new men would take over. This was the local perception. Emphasis on the centrality of the fascist state was unable to change this perception, in large part because local people *were* inevitably required to run the provincial movements. The regime forced such people to make more reference to Rome than had been usual before 1922, but the primary importance attributed to local power did not change. Provincial fascists more often than not looked on Rome as a resource for reinforcing local domination and in many cases the new men reproduced the old methods of realizing that domination. The internal squabbles of the provincial movements—those *beghe* which had such disastrous effects on so many of the provincial federations over the course of the years—had their origins in this conception of political activity. It was the conception of those who paid lip-service to the nationalizing and centralizing project of the fascist movement, while keeping their eyes focused closely on the local situation.

There was a further, and important, consequence of the persistence of this local vision of the fascist movement. Provincial leaders, once they had achieved power, retained their restricted horizons and tended to see themselves as local potentates and to behave as such. The 'Napoleonic' uniforms they created for themselves were a fair indication of this; the figure they cut in local society was a key factor in their thinking. Not all *federali* were arrogant, corrupt, and self-seeking—the fascists 'in good faith' were no doubt many—but, at least to judge from the documentation of police and party, a fair number did display these characteristics. And, as in many dictatorial regimes, the absence of any firm and continuing controls over the activities of local politicians produced situations that could be exploited for personal and family advantage. Local party secretaries had considerable discretionary power and, providing they could avoid inspection, it was a discretionary power that could be used to great effect. Often, in the exercise of power, the public and the private became virtually fused, with public power being used for private gain and to favour family and friends. This practice was a long way from the fascist idea that private values should be subordinated to the public, represented by the highest expression of fascist politics, the fascist state.

The fusion of the public and the private (to the benefit of the private) represented one of the many ways in which actions and words failed to correspond under the regime. The initial impulse of political 'moralization' which had inspired the early fascists found little correspondence in later political activity. Rather paradoxically, but also very predictably, the political vices for which liberal Italy had been so roundly condemned by the fascists—parochialism, clientelism, corruption, factional divisiveness—were reproduced under Fascism, and all too often it was the local party that was guilty of reproducing them.[22] The *locus* of power was

---

[22] Massimo Rocca had been prophetic here, predicting in 1923 that a big risk for the fascist movement was 'to continue [its progress]...by substituting the old Giolittian provincial satrapies and the old political hacks with new satrapies and new hacks, given over to copying the methods and the systems of their predecessors...': *Critica fascista*, 1, 7, 23 September 1923.

perceived as local, the function of power prevalently private and personal. The 'moralization' of politics found little space in this conception—something which was to prove extremely damaging for the reputation of the PNF, as people struggled to discover what distinguished the much-vaunted 'new' from the much-deprecated 'old'. In fact, it was the reproduction of the old methods of local politics, more often than not around private interest rather than political belief, that ultimately produced instability, paralysis, and popular disaffection. As we saw in Chapters 7 and 8, the public perception of the party was heavily conditioned by abuse of power, the generalized assumption being that *federali* and other fascist officials were guilty (of almost everything) until proved innocent.

In conclusion, it will not escape notice that this analysis of the failure of the fascist movement makes frequent reference to several basic coordinates—centre and periphery, local and national, public and private. These are, of course, the same coordinates that occur in relation to the study of other periods in the history of united Italy. As a plethora of studies makes evident, the question of relating an extremely variegated periphery to a single political centre has presented persistent difficulties for government both before Fascism and after, just as the problems relating to the formation of a clear national identity in political terms have reflected a disjunction between state institutions and the society they administer, in turn reproduced in an often conflictual relationship between public and private spheres.

The fascist movement presented itself as a movement capable of resolving these problems. Like Massimo D'Azeglio many decades before him, Mussolini had wanted to 'make Italians', but on condition that those Italians were also fascists. That the movement was eventually defeated by its inability to do this—indeed, by the fact that the movement was itself, almost from the outset, permeated by the same problems it had set out to solve—lends credence to the idea that, unlike Nazism, Italian Fascism was always working *against* a deeply entrenched political grain.[23]

An analysis of this political grain goes beyond the scope of this study and is, in any case, more likely to involve the sociologist (in particular, the sociologist of the perception and uses of power in Italy) than the historian. Yet the fact that the fascist movement reproduced and accentuated many of the problems it had identified in liberal Italy suggests that its successes and, more particularly, its failures should be read in the light of deep-seated problems that faced the nation—problems that in no way began with Fascism and would in no way end with the collapse of the regime.[24] The fascist project faltered essentially on the unhappy relationship

---

[23] As John Davis has put it (summing up historiographical trends in relation to liberal Italy), 'the central thrust of Fascism—strengthening the power of the central state, elimination of the "private" sphere, the nationalization of culture and ideology—ran directly counter to the fundamental traits in Italy's social and political development that had been evident in the nineteenth century': J. A. Davis, 'Remapping Italy's Path to the Twentieth Century', in (1994) 66 *Journal of Modern History* 291, 319.

[24] The kind of corrupt political practice outlined above seems, in particular, to have been a legacy of Fascism. Guido Crainz, among many others, makes the point about elements of continuity between Fascism and the Republic, when he writes that 'those mental habits [developed under Fascism] could not just dissolve like snow' in 1945: Crainz, *Autobiografia di una repubblica. Le radici dell'Italia attuale*, Rome, Donzelli, 2010, 29.

between the party and the people. The dynamic totalitarian thrust foundered on popular weariness, apathy, and passivity, and, in the later years, on clear popular rejection, generated by the malfunctioning of the provincial party organizations. It was the failure of the party to assert itself as a truly national, unifying, institution, capable of giving cohesion and direction to Italian society, that was to prove fatal to fascist pretensions. The PNF was national in name, but provincial in expression, with all that this implied in terms of political organization and operation. Essentially, under Fascism, in the struggle between centre and periphery, the periphery won—with disastrous consequences for the regime.

Select Bibliography

Abse, T., *Sovversivi e fascisti a Livorno: Lotta politica e sociale (1918–1922)*, Milan, Franco Angeli, 1991

Achilli, F., 'Classe dirigente e dinamica interna nel fascismo piacentino degli anni venti', in Istituto mantovano di storia contemporanea (ed.), *Fascismo e antifascismo nella Valle Padana*, Bologna, Clueb, 2007

Albanese, G., *Alle origini del fascismo. La violenza politica a Venezia 1919–1922*, Padua, Il Poligrafo, 2001

——, 'Dire violenza, fare violenza. Espressione, minaccia, occultamento e pratica della violenza durante la Marcia su Roma', (2003) 13 *Memoria e ricerca* 51

Alberico, F., *Le origini e lo sviluppo del Fascismo a Genova*, Milan, Unicopli, 2009

Altamura, F., 'I sindacati fascisti nelle campagne baresi degli anni trenta', (2009) 50(4) *Studi storici* 1065

Anastasia, M., *Interessi di bottega. I piccoli commercianti italiani nella crisi dello Stato liberale 1919–1926*, Turin, Zamorani, 2007

Angeli, L., 'L'istituto podestarile. Il caso di Torino in prospettiva comparata (1926–1945)', (2001) 52 *Passato e presente* 19

Antonini, C., *Piacenza 1938–1945. Le leggi razziali*, Piacenza, ISREC, 2010

Apih, E., *Italia, fascismo, e antifascismo nella Venezia Giulia 1918–1943*, Bari, Laterza, 1966

Applegate, C., *A Nation of Provincials. The German Idea of* Heimat, Berkeley, University of California Press, 1990

Aquarone, A., *L'organizzazione dello stato totalitario*, Turin, Einaudi, 1965 (repr. 1995)

——, 'Violenza e consenso nel Fascismo italiano', (1979) 10(1) *Storia contemporanea* 147

Bajohr, F., 'La corruzione nel regime nazionalsocialista', (2004) 7(1) *Contemporanea* 69

Balbo, I., *Diario 1922*, Milan, Mondadori, 1932

Baldassini, C., 'Fascismo e memoria. L'autorappresentazione dello squadrismo', (2002) 3 *Contemporanea* 475

Baris, T., *Il fascismo in provincia. Politica e realtà a Frosinone (1919–1940)*, Rome & Bari, Laterza, 2001

Baù, A., 'Tra prefetti e federali. Note sul Fascismo padovano degli anni trenta', (2007) 46 *Storia e problemi contemporanei* 51

Benedusi, L., *Il nemico dell'uomo nuovo: l'omosessualità nell'esperimento totalitario fascista*, Milan, Feltrinelli, 2005

Berezin, M., 'The Festival State: Celebration and Commemoration in Fascist Italy', (2006) 4(1) *Journal of Modern European History* 62

Bevilacqua, P., *Le campagne del mezzogiorno tra Fascismo e dopoguerra. Il caso della Calabria*, Turin, Einaudi, 1980

Bianchi, R., *Pace, pane, terra. Il 1919 in Italia*, Rome, Odradek, 2006

Blinkhorn, M., 'Afterthoughts', (2004) 5(3) *Totalitarian Movements and Political Religions* 507

Borgogni, M., *Diario di prigionia del sergente maggiore Giuseppe Aldo Carmignani*, Siena, Cantagalli, 2005

Bosworth, R., *Mussolini*, Oxford, Oxford University Press, 2002

——, *Mussolini's Italy. Life under the Dictatorship 1915–1945*, London, Allen Lane, 2005

Bottai, G., *Vent'anni e un giorno*, Milan 1949 (new edition, Milan, Rizzoli, 2008)
——, *Diario 1935–1944*, Milan, Rizzoli, 1982
Buzzegoli, T., *La polemica antiborghese nel fascismo (1937–1939)*, Rome, Aracne, 2007
Canali, M., *Il delitto Matteotti*, Bologna, Il Mulino, 2004
——, *Le spie del regime*, Bologna, Il Mulino, 2004
——, 'Repressione e consenso nell'esperimento fascista', in E. Gentile (ed.), *Modernità totalitaria. Il Fascismo italiano*, Rome & Bari, Laterza, 2008
——, 'The Matteotti murder and the origins of Mussolini's totalitarian Fascist regime in Italy', (2009) 14(2) *Journal of Modern Italian Studies* 143
Canepa, A., *L'Organizzazione del PNF*, Palermo, Ciuni, 1939
Cannistraro, P.V., *La fabbrica del consenso: Fascismo e mass media*, Rome & Bari, Laterza, 1975
Cappelli, V., 'Politica e Politici', in P. Bevilacqua and A. Placanica (eds), *Storia d'Italia. Le Regioni dall'Unità a oggi. La Calabria*, Turin, Einaudi, 1985
——, *Il Fascismo in periferia. Il caso della Calabria*, Rome, Riuniti, 1992
——, 'Identità locali e Stato nazionale durante il fascismo', (1998) 32 *Meridiana* 53
Cardeti, B., *L'internamento civile fascista: il caso di 'Villa Oliveto' (1940–1944)*, Florence, Edizioni dell'Assemblea, 2010
Cardoza, A.L., *Agrarian Elites and Italian Fascism. The Province of Bologna 1901–1926*, Princeton, Princeton University Press, 1982
——, *Mussolini: The First Fascist*, London, Longman, 2005
Cassese, S., *Lo stato fascista*, Bologna, Il Mulino, 2010
Cavazza, S., 'Il palio e le tradizioni popolari senesi durante il fascismo', in A. Orlandini (ed.), *Fascismo e antifascismo nel Senese*, Florence, Olschki, 1994
——, *Piccole Patrie. Feste Popolari tra Regione e Nazione durante il Fascismo*, Bologna, Il Mulino, 1997
Ceci, L., ' "Il fascismo manda l'Italia in Rovina". Le note inedite di Monsignor Domenico Tardini (23 settembre–13 dicembre 1935)', (2008) 120(1) *Rivista storica italiana* 294
Cianetti, T., *Memorie dal carcere di Verona*, Milan, Rizzoli, 1983
Ciocca, P.L., *Ricchi per sempre?*, Turin, Bollati Boringhieri, 2009
Clark, M., *Mussolini: A Study in Power*, London, Pearson Longman, 2005
Colapietra, R., *Napoli fra dopoguerra e fascismo*, Milan, Feltrinelli, 1962
Colarizi, S., *Dopoguerra e fascismo in Puglia*, Bari, Laterza, 1971
——, *L'opinione degli italiani sotto il regime fascista 1929–43*, Rome & Bari, Laterza, 1991 (revised edition, 2009)
Collotti, E., *Il fascismo e gli ebrei*, Rome & Bari, Laterza, 2006
Confino, A., *The Nation as Local Metaphor. Württemberg, Imperial Germany, and National Memory, 1871–1918*, Chapel Hill, University of North Carolina Press, 1997
Cordova, F., *Le origini dei sindacati fascisti*, Bari, Laterza, 1974
——, *Uomini e volte del Fascismo*, Rome, Bulzoni, 1980
——, *Il fascismo nel Mezzogiorno: le Calabrie*, Soveria Mannelli, Rubbettino, 2003
——, *Verso lo stato totalitario*, Soveria Mannelli, Rubbettino, 2005
——, *Il consenso imperfetto*, Soveria Mannelli, Rubettino, 2010
Corner, P., *Fascism in Ferrara 1915–1925*, London, Oxford University Press, 1975
——, 'L'economia italiana fra le due guerre', in G. Sabbatucci and Vittorio Vidotto, *Storia d'Italia*, vol. IV, *Guerre e fascismo*, Rome & Bari, Laterza, 1997
——, 'Italian Fascism: Whatever happened to Dictatorship?', (2002) 74 *Journal of Modern History* 325
——, (ed.), *Popular Opinion in Totalitarian Regimes. Fascism, Nazism, Communism*, Oxford, Oxford University Press, 2009

——, 'The Plebiscites in fascist Italy: national unity and the importance of the appearance of unity', in R. Jessen and H. Richter (eds), *Elections in Twentieth Century Dictatorships*, Campus Verlag, Frankfurt, New York, 2011

Covino, R., 'Dall'Umbria verde all'Umbria rossa', in R. Covino and G. Gallo (eds), *Storia d'Italia. Le regioni dall'Unità a oggi, L'Umbria*, Turin, Einaudi, 1989

Crainz, G., *Autobiografia di una repubblica. Le radici dell'Italia attuale*, Rome, Donzelli, 2010

D'Attorre, P.P., 'Aspetti economici e territoriali del rapporto centro/periferia', (1991) 184 *Italia contemporanea* 405

Davis, J.A., 'Remapping Italy's Path to the Twentieth Century', (1994) 66 *Journal of Modern History* 291

De Begnac, Y., *Taccuini Mussoliniani*, Bologna, Il Mulino, 1990

De Felice, R., *Mussolini*, seven vols, Turin, Einaudi, 1966–97

——, *Intervista sul Fascismo* (ed. M. Ledeen), Rome & Bari, Laterza, 1975

De Grazia, V., *The Culture of Consent. Mass Organisation of Leisure in Fascist Italy*, Cambridge, Cambridge University Press, 1981

Demers, F., *Le origini del fascismo a Cremona*, Rome & Bari, Laterza, 1979

di Figlia, M., *Farinacci, il radicalismo al potere*, Rome, Donzelli, 2007

Di Nucci, L., *Nel cantiere dello stato fascista*, Rome, Carocci, 2008

——, *Lo Stato-partito del fascismo. Genesi, evoluzione e crisi 1919–1943*, Bologna, Il Mulino, 2009

Dogliani, P., *Storia dei giovani*, Milan, Bruno Mondadori, 2003

Dunnage, J. 'Surveillance and Denunciation in Fascist Siena, 1927–1943', (2008) 28(2) *European Historical Quarterly* 244

——, 'Ideology, clientelism and the "fascistisation" of the Italian state: fascists in the Interior Ministry Police', (2009) 14(3) *Journal of Modern Italian Studies* 267

Duranti, S., *Lo spirito gregario*, Rome, Donzelli, 2008

——, *Studiare nella crisi. Interviste a studenti universitari negli anni del fascismo*, Grosseto, Isgrec, 2011

Ebner, M. 'The political police and denunciation during Fascism: a review of recent historical literature', (2006) 11(2) *Journal of Modern Italian Studies* 209

——, *Ordinary Violence in Mussolini's Italy*, Cambridge, Cambridge University Press, 2011

Eksteins, M., *Rites of Spring. The Great War and the Birth of the Modern Age*, New York, Doubleday, 1989

Evans, R.J., *The Third Reich at War*, London, Penguin, 2009

Fabbri, F., *Le origini della guerra civile. L'Italia dalla Grande Guerra al Fascismo, 1918–1921*, Milan, Utet, 2010

Farinacci, R., *Un periodo aureo nel Partito Nazionale Fascista*, Foligno, Campitelli, 1927

——, *Andante mosso 1924–25*, Milan, Mondadori, 1929

Fimiani, E. (ed.), *Vox Popoli? Pratiche plebiscitarie in Francia, Italia, Germania (secoli XVIII–XX)*, Bologna, Clueb, 2010

Fitzpatrick, S., *Everyday Stalinism. Ordinary Life in Extraordinary times: Soviet Russia in the 1930s*, Oxford, Oxford University Press, 1999

——, 'Russia under pre-war Stalinism', in Corner (ed.), *Popular Opinion in Totalitarian Regimes*, 2009, 17

Focardi, F., 'La memoria della guerra e il mito del "bravo italiano". Origine e affermazione di un autoritratto collettivo', (2000) 220–21 *Italia contemporanea* 393

——, 'L'ombra del passato. I tedeschi e il nazismo nel giudizio italiano dal 1945 a oggi', (2000) 3 *Novecento* 67

Foderaro, S., *La Milizia Volontaria e le sue specialità*, Padua, Cedam, 1939

Forno, M., 'Aspetti dell'esperienza totalitaria fascista. Limiti e contraddizioni nella gestione del "quarto potere" ', (2006) 47(3) *Studi storici* 781

Franzinelli, M., *I tentacoli dell'OVRA: agenti,collaboratori e vittimi cella polizia politica fascista*, Turin, Bollati Boringhieri, 1999

——, *Delatori. Spie e confidenti anonimi: l'arma segreta del regime fascista*, Milan, Mondadori, 2001

——, *Squadristi! Protagonisti e tecniche della violenza fascista 1919–1922*, Milan, Mondadori, 2004

Frascani, P., 'Nitti, Beneduce e il problema della regolazione del capitalismo italiano', (2009) 31(123) *Società e storia* 97

Frei, N., 'Hitler's Popular Support', in H. Mommsen (ed.), *The Third Reich between Vision and Reality: New Perspectives on German History*, Oxford, Berg, 1991

Fritzsche, P., *Life and Death in the Third Reich*, Cambridge (Mass.), Harvard University Press, 2008

Gagliardi, A., 'I ministeri economici negli anni trenta', in Melis (ed.), *Lo Stato negli anni Trenta. Istituzioni e regimi faseisti in Europa*, Bologna, Il Mulino, 2008

——, *Il corporativismo fascista*, Rome & Bari, Laterza, 2010

Galimi, V., 'Le commissioni storiche', in M. Cattaruzza, M. Flores, S. Levis Sullam, E. Traverso (eds.), *Storia della Shoah. La crisi europea, lo sterminio degli ebrei e la memoria*, Milan, UTET, 2008

Gellately, R., *Backing Hitler. Consent and Coercion in Nazi Germany*, Oxford, Oxford University Press, 2001

Gentile, E., *Il mito dello Stato nuovo dall'anti-Giolittismo al Fascismo*, Rome & Bari, Laterza, 1982

——, *Storia del Partito Fascista 1919–1922. Movimento e Milizia*, Rome & Bari, Laterza, 1989

——, *Il culto del littorio. La sacralizzazione della politica nell'Italia fascista*, Rome & Bari, Laterza, 1993

——, *La via italiana al totalitarismo: il partito e lo Stato nel regime fascista*, Rome, NIS, 1995

——, *Le origini dell'ideologia fascista*, Bologna, Il Mulino, 1996 (first edn. Bari, Laterza, 1975)

——, 'New Idols: Catholicism in the face of fascist Totalitarianism', (2006) 11(2) *Journal of Modern Italian Studies* 143

Germinario, F., *Fascismo e antisemitismo: Progetto razziale e ideologia totalitaria*, Rome & Bari, Laterza, 2010

Germino, D., *The Italian Fascist Party in Power. A Study in Totalitarian Rule*, Minneapolis, University of Minnesota Press, 1959

Giorgi, C., *La previdenza del regime. Storia dell'Inps durante il fascismo*, Bologna, Il Mulino, 2004

Gribaudi, M., *Mondo operaio e mito operaio*, Turin, Einaudi, 1987

Griffin, R., *The Nature of Fascism*, London, Pinter, 1991

——(ed.), *Fascism*, Oxford, Oxford University Press, 1995

——, *Modernism and Fascism. The Sense of a Beginning under Mussolini and Hitler*, Basingstoke, Palgrave Macmillan, 2007

Halberstam, M., *Totalitarianism and the Modern Conception of Politics*, New Haven (Conn.), Yale University Press, 1999

Harper, J.L., *America and the Reconstruction of Italy, 1945–48*, Cambridge, Cambridge University Press, 2002

Havel, V., *Open Letters,* New York, Random House, 1992

Hellbeck, J., *Revolution on my mind. Writing a diary under Stalin,* Cambridge (Mass.), Harvard University Press, 2006

Imbriani, M.A., *Gli italiani e il duce; il mito e l'immagine di Mussolini negli ultimi anni del fascismo (1938–1943),* Naples, Liguori, 1992

Kelikian, A.A., *Town and Country under Fascism,* Oxford, Clarendon Press, 1986

Kershaw, I., *Popular Opinion and Political Dissent in the Third Reich. Bavaria 1933–1945,* Oxford, Clarendon Press, 1983

——, *The 'Hitler Myth'. Image and Reality in the Third Reich,* Oxford, Oxford University Press, 1987

——, *Hitler, 1889–1936: Hubris,* London, Penguin, 1998

——, *Hitler: 1836–1845: Nemesis,* London, Penguin, 2000

Knox, M., *To the Threshold of Power, 1922/33. Origins and Dynamics of the Fascist and National Socialist Dictatorships,* Cambridge, Cambridge University Press, 2007

Koon, T., *Believe, Obey, Fight. Political Socialization of Youth in Fascist Italy 1922–43,* Chapel Hill, University of North Carolina Press, 1985

Kotkin, S., *Magnetic Mountain. Stalinism as a Civilization,* Berkeley and Los Angeles, University of California Press, 1995

La Rovere, L., *Storia dei GUF,* Turin, Bollati Boringhieri, 2003

Labanca, N., *Una guerra per l'impero. Memorie della campagna d'Etiopia 1935–6,* Bologna, Il Mulino, 2005

Lanzillo, A., *La disfatta del socialismo. Critica della guerra e del socialismo,* Florence, Libreria della Voce, 1918

Lindenberger, T., 'Tacit Minimal Consensus. The Always Precarious East German Dictatorship', in Corner (ed.), *Popular Opinion in Totalitarian Regimes,* 2009

Lüdtke, A. (ed.), *The History of Everyday Life. Reconstructing Historical Experiences and Ways of Life,* Princeton, Princeton University Press, 1995

Ludwig, E., *Colloqui con Mussolini,* Milan, Mondadori, 1950

Lupo, S., 'L'utopia totalitaria del fascismo (1918–1942)', in M. Aymard and G. Giarrizzo, (eds) *Storia d'Italia. Le Regioni dall'Unità ad oggi. La Sicilia,* Turin, Einaudi, 1987

——, *Il fascismo: la politica di un regime totalitario,* Rome, Donzelli, 2000

Luzzatto, S., *Il corpo del duce,* Turin, Einaudi, 1998

Lyttelton, A. 'Fascism in Italy: the Second Wave', (1966) 1(1) *Journal of Contemporary Italian History* 75

—— (ed.), *Roots of the Right. Italian Fascisms from Pareto to Gentile,* London, Cape, 1973

——, *The Seizure of Power: Fascism in Italy, 1919–1929,* London, Weidenfeld and Nicolson, 1973 (3rd edn. 2004)

——, 'Cause e caratteristiche della violenza fascista. Fattori costanti e fattori congiunturali', in L. Casali (ed.), *Bologna 1920. Le origini del fascismo,* Bologna, Cappelli, 1982

——, 'Fascismo e violenza: conflitti sociale e azione politica in Italia del primo dopoguerra', (1982) 6 *Storia contemporanea* 965

Maier, C.S., *Recasting Bourgeois Europe, Stabilization in France, Germany and Italy in the Decade after World War One,* Princeton, Princeton University Press, 1975

Mangoni, L., *L'interventismo della cultura. Intellettuali e riviste del Fascismo,* Rome & Bari, Laterza, 1974

Mann, M., *Fascists,* Cambridge, Cambridge University Press, 2004

Marchesi, D., *La scuola dei gerarchi. Mistica fascista: storia, problemi, istituzioni,* Milan, Feltrinelli, 1976

Martin, S., *Football and Fascism*, Oxford, Berg, 2004

Martinelli, R., (ed.), *Il fronte interno a Firenze 1940–1943*, Florence, Dipartimento di Storia, 1989

Matsumura, T., 'L'Unità 731 e la guerra batteriologica dell'esercito giapponese', in G. Contini, F. Focardi, M. Petricioli (eds), *Memoria e rimozione. I crimini di guerra del Giappone e dell'Italia*, Rome, Viella, 2011

Mazzoni, M., *Livorno all'ombra del fascio*, Florence, Olschki, 2009

Melis, G., 'Società senza Stato? Per uno studio delle amministrazioni periferiche tra età liberale e periodo fascista', (1988) 4 *Meridiana* 91

——, *Storia dell'amministrazione italiana*, Bologna, Il Mulino, 1996

—— (ed.), *Lo Stato negli anni Trenta. Istituzioni e regimi fascisti in Europa*, Bologna, Il Mulino, 2008

Meneghello, L., *I piccoli maestri*, Milan, Rizzoli, 1976

Missori, M., *Gerarchie e statuti del PNF Gran Consiglio, Direttorio nazionale, Federazioni provinciali: quadri e biografie*, Rome, Bonacci, 1986

Morgan, P., 'I primi podestà fascisti: 1926–32', (1978) 3 *Storia contemporanea* 407

——, 'Augusto Turati', in Cordova (ed.), *Uomini e volte del Fascismo*, 1980, 475

——, 'The prefects and party–state relations in fascist Italy', (1998) 3(3) *Journal of Modern Italian Studies* 241

——, ' "The Party is Everywhere": The Italian fascist party in Economic life, 1926–40', (1999) 114(455) *English Historical Review* 85

Moro, R., 'Religione del transcendente e religioni politiche: il cattolicesimo italiano di fronte alla sacralizzazione fascista della politica', (2005) 1 *Mondo contemporaneo* 9

Morris, J., *The Political Economy of Shopkeeping in Milan, 1886–1922*, Cambridge, Cambridge University Press, 1993

Mosse, G., *The Nationalisation of the Masses: political symbolism and mass movements in Germany from the Napoleonic wars through the Third Reich*, New York, H. Fertig, 1975

Musiedlak, D., *Lo stato fascista e la sua classe politica 1922–1943*, Bologna, Il Mulino, 2003

Mussolini, B., *Opera omnia* (ed. E. and D. Susmel), Florence, La Fenice, 1951

Nelis, J., 'The Clerical Response to a Totalitarian Political Religion: la Civiltà Cattolica and Italian Fascism', (2011) 46(2) *Journal of Contemporary History* 245

Noakes J. and Pridham, G., *Nazism 1919–1945*, vol. 2, *State, Economy and Society*, Exeter, Exeter University Press, 1984

O'Brien, P., *Mussolini in the First World War*, Oxford, Berg, 2005

Orsi, P.L., 'Una fonte seriale: i rapporti prefettizi sull'antifascismo non militante', (1990) 2 *Rivista di storia contemporanea* 280

Overy, R., *The Dictators*, London, Allen Lane, 2004

Padullo, G., 'I finanziatori del Fascismo', (2010) *Le carte e la storia*, quaderno n.1, 2010

Palla, M., *Firenze nel regime fascista (1929–34)*, Florence, Olschki, 1978

——, 'Fascisti di professione: il caso toscano', in G. Turi (ed.), *Cultura e società negli anni del fascismo*, Milan, Cordero, 1987

——, 'I podestà di nomina regia nella provincia di Forlì', (1993) 1 *Memoria e ricerca* 69

Panunzio, V., *Il 'secondo Fascismo' 1936–1943. La reazione della giovane generazione alla crisi del movimento e del regime*, Milan, Mursia, 1988

Pardini, G., *Roberto Farinacci, ovvero della rivoluzione fascista*, Florence, Le Lettere, 2007

Parisini, R., *Dal regime corporativo alla Repubblica Sociale: Agricoltura e Fascismo a Ferrara 1928–1945*, Ferrara, Corbo, 2005

Parsons, G., *The Cult of Saint Catherine of Siena. A Study in Civil Religion*, Aldershot, Ashgate, 2008

Pasquinucci, D., 'Classe dirigente liberale e fascismo a Siena. Un caso di continuità', (1991) 184 *Italia contemporanea* 441

Passerini, L., *Mussolini immaginario*, Rome & Bari, Laterza, 1991

Paxton, R.O., *The Anatomy of Fascism*, New York, Knopf, 2004

Pelini F. and Pavan I., *La doppia epurazione. L'Università di Pisa e le leggi razziali tra guerra e dopoguerra*, Bologna, Il Mulino, 2009

Pellizzi, C., *Una rivoluzione mancata*, Milan, Longanesi, 1949 (new edition Bologna, Il Mulino, 2009)

Petacco, A., *L'uomo della provvidenza*, Milan, Mondadori, 2006

Petersen, J., 'Il problema della violenza nel Fascismo italiano', (1982) 6 *Storia contemporanea* 985

Peukert, D., *The Weimar Republic*, New York, Hill and Wang, 1989

Piazzesi, M., *Diario di uno squadrista toscano 1919–1922*, Rome, Bonacci, 1980

Piccioni, L., *San Lorenzo. Un quartiere romano durante il Fascismo*, Rome, Edizioni di Storia e Letteratura, 1982

Pintor, G., *Il sangue d'Europa* (ed.V. Gerratana), Turin, Einaudi, 1965

Ponziani, L., *Il Fascismo dei prefetti. Amministrazione e politica nell'Italia meridionale 1922–26*, Catanzaro, Meridiana libri, 1995

——, 'Fascismo e autonomie locali', in M. Palla (ed.), *Lo stato fascista*, Milan, La Nuova Italia, 2001

Procacci, Giovanna, 'Osservazioni sulla continuità della legislazione sull'ordine pubblico tra fine Ottocento, prima guerra mondiale e Fascismo', in P. Del Negro, N. Labanca, and A. Staderini (eds), *Militarizzazione e Nazionalizzazione nella Storia d'Italia*, Milan, Unicopli, 2005

——, 'La società come una caserma. La svolta repressiva nell'Italia della grande guerra', (2006) 3 *Contemporanea* 423

Rapone, N., 'L'Italia antifascista', in G. Sabbatucci and V. Vidotto (eds), *Storia d'Italia*, vol. 4, *Guerre e Fascismo*, Rome & Bari, Laterza, 1997, 519

Reichardt, S., *Faschistische Kampfbünde: Gewalt und Gemeinschaft im italienischen Squadrismus und der deutschen SA*, Böhlau, 2002 (Italian trans. *Camicie nere, camicie brune. Milizie fasciste in Italia e in Germania*, Bologna, Il Mulino, 2009)

Rochat, G., *Italo Balbo*, Turin, UTET, 1986

Romanelli, R., *Il commando impossibile*, Bologna, Il Mulino, 1995

—— (ed.), *Storia dello stato italiano dall'Unità ad oggi*, Rome, Donzelli, 1995

Rossi, F. (ed.), *Certaldo negli anni del fascismo; un comune toscano fra le due guerre (1919–1940)*, Milan, La Pietra, 1986

Rotelli, E., 'Le trasformazioni dell'ordinamento comunale e provinciale durante il regime fascista', in S. Fontana (ed.), *Il Fascismo e le autonomie locali*, Bologna, Il Mulino, 1973

Sabbatucci, Giovanni, *I combattenti nel primo dopoguerra*, Rome & Bari, Laterza, 1974

Sabrow, M., 'Consent in the Communist GDR or How to Interpret Lion Feuchtwanger's Blindness in *Moscow 1937*', in Corner (ed.), *Popular Opinion in Totalitarian Regimes*, 2009

Salustri, S., *La nuova guardia. Gli universitari bolognesi fra le due guerre (1919–1943)*, Bologna, Clueb, 2009

Salvati, M., *Il regime e gli impiegati. La nazionalizzazione piccola-borghese nel ventennio fascista*, Rome & Bari, Laterza, 1992

——, *L'Inutile salotto. L'abitazione piccolo-borghese nell'Italia fascista*, Turin, Bollati Boringhieri, 1993

——, 'The Long History of Corporativism in Italy: A Question of Culture or Economics?', (2006) 15(2) *Contemporary European History* 227

Santoro, L., *Roberto Farinacci e il partito nazionale fascista 1923–1926*, Soverio Mannelli, Rubbettino, 2008

Sarfatti, M., *Gli ebrei nell'Italia fascista; vicende, identità, persecuzione*, Turin, Einaudi, 2000 (trans. *The Jews in Mussolini's Italy: from Equality to Persecution*, Madison, University of Wisconsin Press, 2006)

Sechi, S., *Dopoguerra e fascismo in Sardegna*, Turin, Fondazione Luigi Einaudi, 1971

Setta, S., 'Achille Starace', in Cordova (ed.), *Uomini e volte del Fascismo*, 1980

Snowden, F., *Violence and Great Estates in the South of Italy: Apulia 1900–1922*, Cambridge, Cambridge University Press, 1986

——, *The Fascist Revolution in Tuscany 1919–1922*, London, Cambridge University Press, 1989

Sole, G., 'Lettere anonime e lotta tra le fazioni nel Cosentino 1926–43', (1986) 15(4) *Rivista di Storia Contemporanea* 586

Staderini, A., 'La Federazione romana del Pnf (1940–43)' in (2003) 11(3) *Roma moderna e contemporanea* 431, 'Roma in guerra 1940–43', (special issue edited by Lidia Piccione)

Stephenson, J., 'Popular Opinion in Nazi Germany: Mobilization, Experience, Perceptions: the View from the Württemberg Countryside', in Corner (ed.), *Popular Opinion in Totalitarian Regimes*, 2009

Suzzi Valli, R., 'The Myth of *Squadrismo* in the Fascist Regime', (2000) 35(2) *Journal of Contemporary History* 131

Sylos-Labini, P., *Saggio sulle classi sociali*, Rome & Bari, Laterza, 1974

Tabor, D., 'Operai in camicia nera? La composizione operaia del fascio di Torino, 1921–1931', (2004) 17(36) *Storia e problemi contemporanei* 39

Terhoeven, P., *Oro per la patria*, Bologna, Il Mulino, 2006

Toniolo, G., *L'economia dell'Italia fascista*, Rome & Bari, Laterza, 1980

Tosatti, G., 'Il Ministero dell'Interno e le Politiche Repressive del Regime', in Melis (ed.), *Lo Stato negli anni Trenta*

Turati, A., *Un popolo, un'idea, un uomo*, Milan, Istituto fascista di cultura, 1927

——, *Il partito e i suoi compiti*, Rome, Libreria della Littoria, 1928

Turi G. and S. Soldani (eds), *Fare gli italiani. Scuola e cultura nell'Italia contemporanea*, Bologna, Il Mulino, 1993

Varvaro, P., *Una città fascista: potere e società a Napoli*, Palermo, Sellerio, 1990

Venafro, F., 'Il partito fascista a Bologna. Dalle origini al regime', (2007) *Italia contemporanea* December, 249

Villeggia, N., *La scuola per la classe dirigente. Vita quotidiana e prassi educative nei licei durante il Fascismo*, Milan, Unicopli, 2007

Vinci, A.M., *Sentinelle della patria: il fascismo al confine orientale 1918–1941*, Rome & Bari, Laterza, 2011

Visani, A., 'Italian reactions to the racial laws of 1938 as seen through the classified files of the Ministry of Popular Culture', (2006) 11(2) *Journal of Modern Italian Studies* 170

——, 'The Jewish enemy. Fascism, the Vatican, and anti-Semitism on the seventieth anniversary of the 1938 race laws', (2009) 14(2) *Journal of Modern Italian Studies* 168

Vivarelli, R., *Storia delle origini del Fascismo. L'Italia dall grande guerra alla marcia su Roma*, Bologna, Il Mulino, 1991

Volpe, G., *L'Italia in cammino: l'ultimo cinquantennio*, Milan, Treves, 1928

——, *Storia del movimento fascista*, Rome, Ispe, 1943

Weber, E., *Peasants into Frenchmen. The Modernization of Rural France 1870–1914*, Stanford, (Cal.): Stanford University Press, 1976

Willson, P., *Peasant Women and Politics in Fascist Italy; the* Massaie rurali, London, Routledge, 2002

Zamagni, V., *Dalla perifieria al centro. La seconda rinascita economica dell'Italia*, Bologna, Il Mulino, 1993

Zangrandi, R., *Il lungo viaggio attraverso il Fascismo. Contributo alla storia di una generazione*, Milan, Feltrinelli, 1962

Index of Names